FIRST EDIT

COLLECTORS'

U.S. Auctions &Flea Markets

by Susan Wasserstein
with an Introduction to Auctions and Glossary
by Jerry E. Patterson
and an Introduction to Flea Markets and Checklist
by Linda Campbell Franklin

PENGUIN BOOKS

Penguin Books Ltd, Harmondsworth,
Middlesex, England
Penguin Books, 625 Madison Avenue,
New York, New York 10022, U.S.A.
Penguin Books Australia Ltd, Ringwood,
Victoria, Australia
Penguin Books Canada Limited, 2801 John Street,
Markham, Ontario, Canada 13R 1B4
Penguin Books (N.Z.) Ltd, 182-190 Wairau Road,
Auckland 10, New Zealand

First published 1981

Set in Century Expanded and Franklin Gothic.

Printed in the United States of America by
Hampshire Press, Inc.

We wish to give very special thanks to Andrea DiNoto and
Kathi Hushion for their help and advice during the
preparation of this book. We also want to acknowledge the
cooperation of Cynthia Carr, Pamela Green, Marilyn Jenkins
and consultants Joan W. Hess, Lar Hothem and Burton
Spiller. Further thanks go to Barbara Moynehan for the
guidance given on important antique shows in her article in
the January 1980 *Americana* magazine. Finally, we are
grateful to all the flea market owners and auctioneers who
are this book.

CONTENTS

PREFACE

The COLLECTORS' GUIDE TO U.S. AUCTIONS & FLEA MARKETS is organized according to the major geographical regions and is designed especially for the traveling collector who need only pack it into the glove compartment before setting off cross-country, or across town, in search of treasures.

For the traveler's convenience, we have organized entries alphabetically, by town or city, within each state. An introductory profile to each of the six regions in the country—Mid-Atlantic, New England, Southeast, Midwest, Southwest, and Northwest—cites specialties in particular areas, tells where the auctions and flea markets are concentrated, describes museums and restoration sites and antique shows, and lists trade papers that regularly give updates, calendar listings, and reviews of both auctions and flea markets.

Most established auction houses offer brochures or schedules of coming sales. Collectors should get on the mailing lists of those auctioneers who regularly sell items of particular interest to them. The collectors' magazines and newspapers listed at the end of each regional introduction and in the addenda starting on page 277 should be scanned for announcements of sales. Daily and weekly advertisements are especially important because auctioneers often have to sell quickly (to settle an estate, for example), and have little time to publicize sales.

This first edition of the COLLECTOR'S GUIDE was compiled from information supplied by auctioneers and flea market managers, and their representatives. It is inevitable that some new markets and auction houses will have been established (and that some will have gone out of business) by the time of publication. Hours and schedules will have been adapted to new demands; management and contacts in some cases will have changed. This is why it is always important to call ahead.

Happy Hunting!

SUSAN WASSERSTEIN

AN INTRODUCTION TO AUCTIONS

By Jerry E. Patterson

The American collector is a passionate auction-goer—both by choice and necessity. By choice, because auctions provide the most lively and entertaining way to build a collection; by necessity because only at an auction can the collector find such a quantity and variety of choice items at a single place and time.

The collecting boom of the 1970s saw the ranks of collectors swell from a traditional elite whose focus was essentially fine art and antiques, to a virtual democracy of zealous individuals searching for "collectibles" —the not-quite-antique artifacts of the 19th and 20th centuries—usually the products of mass production, often with little intrinsic value. Auctioneers accommodated this boom with enthusiasm. Not only did the auction industry itself expand with hundreds of new galleries opening nationwide, but the most conservative institutions began to establish specialized sales of collectibles in addition to their traditional sales of furniture, silver, glass and paintings.

Today it is not uncommon to find auctions devoted to dolls, guns, decoys, vintage automobiles, linens and lace, Oriental carpets, even Christmas tree ornaments, to name just a few. Indeed, it would take some ingenuity to collect something not sold at auction now.

WHAT IS AN AUCTION?

The nature of an auction is the rapid public sale of objects based on verbal competition between bidders. The technique lends itself especially well to the dispersal of collections, or accumulations of objects, too large for any one shop or antique dealer to conveniently handle. For centuries auctions have been one of the main sources for buyers adding to their collections, and for sellers who want to quickly dispose of property. Auctions of art and antiques have been held in many countries since they began on a regular basis in the Netherlands in the 16th century. In North America there were auctions in Boston as early as 1717. Books were the first collected objects to be sold regularly.

The form of the auction has changed little over the centuries. A sale is advertised; a crowd assembles before an auctioneer who stands or sits at a podium or table; the auctioneer announces an object or group of objects (a "lot") by number or name and asks for a bid; someone in the audience responds by speaking, raising a hand, or signalling with a paddle; the auctioneer calls for a larger sum, and finally, when responses to his calls cease, cries "sold!" to the highest bidder, brings down his gavel and announces the next lot. Each sale is a little drama, and the auctioneer, who needs a touch of the actor, is often a colorful character. People often go to auctions not only to buy but to have fun.

GOING TO AN AUCTION

Newcomers to auctions need more protection from themselves than they do against the wiles of the auctioneer, whose stock in trade is skillful cajoling. Random buying, failure to inspect lots beforehand, failing to stick to a pre-determined bidding limit— these are the dangers for inexperienced auction-goers, and they can be avoided. Not much help is forthcoming if a mistake is made by the buyer. Although a few auction firms today extend guarantees concerning authenticity of items they sell (for example, the attribution of paintings to certain artists), the essence of the business is, as it always has been, *buyer beware.* Generally speaking, buyers who know their fields and who inspect the lots before the sale have nothing to fear. Courage comes from knowing as much as possible about what you are buying. Auctions can teach a collector a great deal about prices, availability, and the current popularity, but they are not especially good places to learn about workmanship or quality of objects. The pace of the entire operation is fast, while the study of antique objects is by nature slow and involves observation, reading and talking with fellow collectors and dealers. You may often pick up exceedingly useful information at auctions, as much from the audience as from the objects. Mainly, however, auctions are places to buy, and the wise collector comes with homework done.

No part of the auction process should be confusing or intimidating to the first-time auction-goer who comes prepared. It is essential to learn the terminology used by auctioneers, both verbally and in their catalogs. To help the novice become familiar with the language of auctions, I have compiled a glossary of the most common terms, immediately following this introduction. Mastery of the basic auction vocabulary removes a great deal of the mystery.

The auction process actually begins with the pre-sale exhibition or viewing. This is the single most important step taken by a collector in preparation for buying. Custom and law require that objects sold at auction first be placed on exhibition for interested parties to inspect before the bidding begins. Any auction that does not allow inspection should be shunned. The pre-sale exhibition may last several days before the sale or just one day. In the case of some small country auctions, inspection may only be possible for an hour or so before the sale or, to the chagrin of those who don't call ahead, the day or night before.

Any lot or object of interest should be scrutinized as carefully as possible in the time allowed. Inspection consists of much more than deciding that an item is attractive. More importantly, it is the moment of truth when the buyer evaluates the item in terms of its suitability, rarity and condition, and decides on the price he is willing to pay. Each area of collecting has its own hazards. Damage, restoration, refinishing, substitutions, missing pieces, overcleaning and repainting are pitfalls common to many fields of antiques and collectibles. In dealing with aged objects you can expect to encounter a certain amount of noticeable wear and, usually, restoration. The point is not that you should avoid such objects entirely, but that you should not pay for them what you would pay for more valuable untouched or mint condition pieces.

While viewing, the best procedure—particularly if the sale is to be a long one—is to make notes on the condition of items of interest and your top bid, in the catalog or a notebook. If an item is to occupy a specific place, you should measure it and write down the dimensions. Veteran auction-goers always carry a tape measure. A portable black light is handy to inspect china for small cracks and skillful repairs otherwise invisible to the naked eye. A flashlight is invaluable for peering at the undersides of pieces of furniture, as is a magnifying glass for reading hallmarks on silver or signatures on pictures.

The auction house staff expects your scrutiny and is usually available during the exhibition to answer questions, to pull a piece of heavy furniture away from the wall so that the back can be inspected, to hold items while they are measured, to place a painting in the light for a better look. Most auctioneers prefer adequate presale inspection by customers because it prevents disputes after the sale.

SETTING YOUR BID

Well-prepared by having done homework at the pre-sale exhibition, you can then decide what each object of interest is worth to you and fix a price which should be adhered to regardless of the temper of the bidding. In many cases, the auctioneer will have published a list of pre-sale price estimates in the catalog. These are not appraisals but rather prices that similar objects have brought at recent auctions. They should not be taken as gospel, nor should they sway the prospective buyer from his considered judgment of what the item is worth. Items often bring far more or far less than estimated. One rule of thumb suggests that an auction price should be less than retail (what you would find at an antique dealer), and learning those retail prices is part of your pre-sale homework. By keeping to your bidding limit, you protect yourself against "auction fever," that phenomenon in which bidders vie in heated competition for an object until they bid it up far beyond its true market value.

IN THE SALE ROOM

Sometimes entry to a sale requires purchase of the catalog. Any serious bidder would have bought one well in advance, to study, and brings it to the sale as the ticket of entry, and as an aid in following the progress of the sale and for making detailed notes. The practice is often adopted for big sales, and it benefits the buyers by eliminating disinterested gawkers who might crowd and disrupt the saleroom.

As buyers enter the saleroom, they are usually asked to register by giving their name, address, and some form of credit. If the auction house does not accept the buyer's credit (perhaps a particular credit card is considered inadequate), a cash deposit may be required—even before the sale begins. Once the buyer's credit is established, he is issued a bidding number, often in the form of a paddle with the number printed on it.

Bidding is usually easy to follow. The auctioneer opens the bids by either asking for, or setting, a price— "Do I hear $50.00?" He then sets the increments with the second bid. These increases are regular—$5.00, $20.00 or $100.00—and the bidding proceeds thus: $25.00, $30.00, $35.00, or in multiples of the increment, in this case $5.00, but never less than that.

When the auctioneer calls a figure acceptable to the bidder, the bidder raises his hand or paddle or nods to the auctioneer. The bidding progresses until the item is either sold to the highest bidder or bought-in if it fails to meet its reserve (see Glossary). Occasionally a bidder gets confused as to which lot is being sold. If the bidder misunderstands or finds that he is bidding on the wrong lot, he should let the auctioneer know immediately by calling out "Not my bid." Sometimes the confusion comes from not knowing if a lot consisting of more than one item is being sold as a group or if each item is to be sold individually within the lot. The terms for such lots will be stated in the Conditions of Sale, as set forward in the catalog or explained by the auctioneer at the beginning of the sale.

Apocryphal stories of bidding blunders are rife in the auction world. Stories about the innocent who is scratching his nose and finds himself the buyer of a stuffed giraffe are standard, but wildly exaggerated. Few auctioneers, it is certain, want to knock down something to an unwilling buyer from whom it will be difficult if not impossible to collect. Stories circulate of the need for elaborate bidding signals, such as pushing eyeglasses to the forehead or raising one eyebrow discreetly, but in fact such subtle maneuvers would take place only in the big international salerooms where millions of dollars may be at stake. They have little if anything to do with the average auction.

GOSSIP

Auctions, especially those of specialized collections, or the property of a well-known collector, generate a social atmosphere that can be delightful. Competition adds zest to a gathering of collectors and dealers who exchange information, reminisce, gossip and boast. Buyers can be divided into two groups: those who brag about getting bargains, and those who boast about how much money they spend. It is often impossible not to overhear, but wise bidders listen with a certain skepticism. While chats with experienced collectors and dealers about items being sold and prices realized can be instructive, the seasoned bidder never lets himself be swayed from his pre-established bidding limit.

Collecting is a jealous affair and some collectors find it irresistible to plant suspicion about the origin and condition of lots about to be sold so as to discourage competition. Others praise property to be sold because they have a vested interest in it.

At one auction a viewer kept calling attention to "bargains" as lots were knocked down, speaking loudly enough that his neighbors could overhear. They gradually became convinced that they too should be bidding if such bargains were to be had, and the sale went better and better, to the immense satisfaction of the speaker who was, of course, the owner. In short, there may be motives for almost anything one hears at auctions.

PAYMENT AND PICKUP

The buyer who makes a successful bid must pay according to the Conditions of Sale, that are either published in the catalog or announced at the start of the auction. A glance at a number of entries in this GUIDE will reveal how widely schedules and methods of payment or credit can differ. On one hand, buyers may be asked for a cash deposit or the full amount immediately after the item is knocked down to them; while in another case, accounts may be settled at the end of the sale or even at a later date.

Transport of purchases can be a problem if you buy a large item or a great many lots. It is wise to know in advance how long you have to pick up purchases and if the auctioneer offers moving services.

SELLING AT AUCTION

When a collector changes the direction of his collecting interest, or when there is a move or a death, collections are often sold at auction. Many collectors like to sell through auctioneers from whom they have bought and who they know to be reliable. Auction firms either sell on consignment or purchase property outright for their own account. Consignment is often more to the seller's benefit because the pieces will then be auctioned for the seller's account to a large number of bidders. Chances of realizing a profit are thus increased. If the merchandise is bought outright, the seller receives only that purchase amount, while the auctioneer may resell the item for a much higher price.

If property is consigned, the owner receives a contract covering its sale, one copy of which is signed and returned to the auctioneer. Some contracts are very simple; others, covering very valuable lots, can be very complex. Contracts vary greatly from firm to firm as do charges for cataloguing, illustration, and insurance against theft and fire. Consignors receive a copy of the catalog listing their property, and payment is made about 30 to 45 days after the sale.

THE AUCTION MARKETPLACE

The most memorable headline-grabbing sales in any auction are the record highs. Unexpected lows also make the news, but are rarely splashed across the front page. The high and low prices represent extremes that bracket a more moderate and usually more reliable view of current market values. A close examination of prices realized at a sale of, say, art glass, would reveal that only a small percentage of items (those signed by top name artists such as Tiffany or Galle, for example) consistently fetch blockbuster prices. But no auction has a guaranteed outcome and no experienced auctioneer will ever presume to predict his results. Much depends on how merchandise is grouped for sale, whether the sale is specialized or general, how well it is advertised, whether it is a famous collection, what the prevailing mood is in the saleroom, and last, but by no means least, what the weather is like. Unlike postmen, auction-goers are often discouraged by rain, snow or sleet. The valiant few that drag themselves to a sale on a bad day often wind up with bargains, simply because nobody came.

Collectors argue the pros and cons of buying at the general versus the specialized sale. Many feel that they have a better chance of getting an item at a lower price if it is offered as part of a miscellany, the theory being that such a sale would attract less competition in the form of highly specialized collectors. But most collectors view specialized sales with a mixture of emotions: pleasure because so many objects in their field are being offered at once; and apprehension because these sales, which are usually well-publicized, bring out more competition and result, in the opinion of many auctioneers and collectors and dealers, in higher prices. This is not always true. Occasionally specialized sales overload a limited market to the extent that some items sell cheaply, and by no means is every consignor made happy.

Not even in the sale of a famous collection is the consignor guaranteed of receiving top dollar for every item. Naturally you expect to pay a premium for any items that come with a distinguished pedigree. But certainly collectors of modest means should not be discouraged from attending such sales because they think that no items could possibly fall into their range. The chances are that in any collection some items will not have increased greatly in value—especially if out of love they were bought high to begin with.

THAT DIAMOND IN THE ROUGH

Without question, the most successful buyers at auction are experts who are keenly aware of current trends and prices. Conventional wisdom states that it is getting more and more difficult to find unrecognized treasures, even at country auctions. Still every sale has at least one good story, and extraordinary finds and bargains, as well as disappointments over what got away, are almost routine.

A few years ago, a fine arts dealer was wandering through the presale exhibition at one of the smaller auction houses in New York City where, along with secondhand furniture and incomplete sets of flatware, there were a few paintings displayed. The dealer spotted a landscape hanging among the clutter. He recognized it as a work by a German 19th-century landscape painter, Heinrich Burkel, but he was afraid to show too much interest for fear someone else might look closely at it. The dealer also didn't want to be seen bidding on the picture at the sale because that might induce competition, so he sent his wife, who was unknown in the trade. Her instructions were to bid up to $15,000. She went to the sale and bought a few pieces of china to make it appear that she was an ordinary bidder. When the painting came up, no one else recognized it, and it was knocked down for $50.00. Cleaned, properly researched and catalogued, it was put up that same year at a major New York auction house, where it attracted great attention from European buyers and was finally sold, after vigorous competition, for $45,000 to a German dealer!

AUCTION GLOSSARY

The terms below are used in the Guide *entries to describe merchandise, services and terms of sales offered by auctioneers. Auction-goers who become familiar with these terms are better equipped to understand catalogs, advertisements and the auctioneer's patter during the course of a sale.*

ANTIQUES. According to a definition accepted by the United States Customs, objects made more than one hundred years ago are antiques. In 1981, therefore, objects made in the year 1881 or earlier are antiques. The term is, however, used very loosely. In practice it is applied to almost any object made before living memory, or to more recent objects of intrinsic value.

APPRAISAL. Many auctioneers offer to give appraisals or valuations of an object for a fee. Their figures are usually an estimate of what the object might bring if sold at auction, although in insurance appraisals the sum is usually what it would cost to replace the object. Appraisals can either be a verbal opinion or a written document. Only the latter is valid for legal purposes such as probate. Many appraisals are done on the auctioneer's premises. If the auctioneer has to travel to the property, expenses are charged in addition to the fee. The method of charging is indicated in the Guide entries.

ARTIFACT. Properly reserved for archeological objects such as Indian arrowheads, "artifact" is often used, especially by country auctioneers, to refer to almost any kind of antique.

BUYER'S PREMIUM. A percentage (usually 10% but varying) is added to the *hammer,* or *knock-down,* price by some auctioneers. The buyer's premium is the price paid by the buyer for services of the auctioneer.

BUY-BACK. See RESERVE

BOUGHT-IN. See RESERVE

CATALOG SALE. A sale for which a printed or mimeographed list of items to be sold is prepared in advance; at the sale, bids are taken on the numbered lots in the order in which they appear in the catalog list.

COLLECTIBLES. Nineteenth and 20th-century mass-produced objects that generally have not yet acquired status as antiques are known as collectibles. Examples are collectors' plates, Depression glass, Hummel figurines, beer cans, postcards, etc. Sometimes the objects are definitely old enough to be *antique,* but they are still called collectibles.

CONDITIONS OF SALE. Certain legal terms govern the proceeding at any auction. It is under these conditions of sale that bidding is accepted. They include details of payment and delivery, taxes, buyer's premium, etc. If there is a printed catalog, the Conditions of Sale appear in it; if there is no catalog, they are posted in the room. In addition, they are often read by the auctioneer before the sale begins to the assembled crowd.

CONSIGNMENT. An item, or group of items, turned over to an auctioneer by an individual, an estate, business or other owner for sale on a commission basis, is a consignment.

ESTATE SALE. Property belonging to a deceased person, put up at auction—either on site or at an auction gallery—constitutes an estate sale.

ESTIMATE. When a sale has a printed catalog, it is customary, though not invariable, that each item be given an estimate as to what it may bring at the sale, usually in the form of a range, such as $50.00 to $100.00. These estimates are based by the auctioneer on prices brought by similar objects at earlier auctions. They are not appraisal prices.

GENERAL SALE. See SPECIALIZED SALE

HAMMER PRICE. The final amount called by the auctioneer, which is the price at which the item is sold, is the hammer price. Also called the *knock-down* price.

HOUSEHOLD GOODS. Items of furniture and equipment, such as washing machines, that make no pretension to being collector items, are household goods. They are often sold along with art, antiques and collectibles at estate sales.

INSPECTION. See PRE-SALE EXHIBITION

KNOCK-DOWN PRICE. See HAMMER PRICE

LOT. The term used for an object or group of objects, assigned one number in a printed auction catalog or offered at one time at an uncatalogued sale, is "lot."

MAIL and TELEPHONE BIDS. Many firms accept bids from customers who cannot be present at the auction. The bid is the top limit to which the absentee bidder is willing to go. These bids are executed by the auctioneer or his clerk during the sale.

PADDLE. At many auctions prospective bidders are asked to sign a book with name and address before the sale begins, and then each is given a numbered paddle with which to bid by attracting the auctioneer's attention. The paddle number is called when the bidder is successful and the bills are made up under that number.

PRE-SALE EXHIBITIONS. All auctioneers give prospective bidders an opportunity to inspect, or view, items to be sold before a sale. At larger auction houses, this viewing may be the better part of a week; smaller firms a day or two; and often at country auctions only the night before or an hour or so before the sale begins.

PROPERTY PURCHASED FOR SALES. Many auctioneers buy items privately at a price agreed with the owner and then sell them at public auction for their own account.

RESERVE. The minimum price below which an object cannot be sold is the reserve, also known as a *buy-back*. It is set by the owner when he puts the item up for sale. An object that does not get a bid as high as its reserve is *bought-in*.

SPECIALIZED SALE. A sale devoted to one type of collected object, such as art glass, dolls or lighting devices, is a specialized sale, as opposed to a *general sale* containing objects from many fields of collecting.

Jerry E. Patterson, a former vice-president of both Sotheby Parke Bernet and Christie's, is the author of several books on antiques and collecting. Titles include *Porcelain*, which was done for the Smithsonian Institution, Cooper-Hewitt Museum; *The Collectors' Guide to Relics and Memorabilia;* and *Antiques of Sport*. He frequently writes articles on antiques and auctions for leading periodicals such as "Connoisseur" and "Maine Antique Digest," and financial publications such as "Institutional Investor."

AN INTRODUCTION TO FLEA MARKETS

By Linda Campbell Franklin

Even if you never thought of yourself as an archaeologist, a good flea market might be your Tutankhamen's tomb, a burial ground of treasures that—just possibly—nobody else will recognize.

At a flea market, the potential for surprise, entertainment and satisfaction is unlimited. Regular attendance at flea markets is one of the best ways to find what you want, although you may walk many miles in the search. Maybe you've got something in mind for the second shelf of your whatnot, the blank page in your Tuck's Views postcard album, or to fill a gap in any of your collections. You may be searching for something new to collect; or you may just want a day's fun. Anything is possible at a flea market.

The nature of flea markets is that there are many items for sale by a number of dealers. The nature of flea market buyers is that few of them are, fortunately, looking for exactly the same thing. Beyond that, and the fact they are all in some way bazaars and entertainments, markets cannot be characterized with a single description.

Some fleas are held outdoors in the summer, in a field, a drive-in theatre, a parking lot, a church yard or racetrack. Some are indoors, open year round, with permanent lock-up stalls, cafeterias and electricity. A flea may lose some of its charm when it retires safely inside, but on the other hand buyers and sellers don't have to worry about the vagaries of the weather. Some flea markets are small weekly affairs run by the owners of a roadside property. Others are large annual charity benefits held in rented space, with food offered by local churches or fraternal organizations. A number of flea markets are indistinguishable from antique shows. Some, at the other extreme, are primarily places to buy discount clothing, incense candles and assorted household wares.

Nearly a quarter of a century ago, a man named Russell Carrell introduced high-quality flea markets with loads of antiques to Americans. They more closely resembled the Paris Flea Market than rural produce markets. Mr. Carrell was already the respected manager/promoter of a prestigious antique show, held at the 67th Street Armory in New York City, so it was natural—if somewhat adventurous—for him to ask 80 antique dealers to set up their fine wares in the cow pasture next to his shop in Salisbury, Connecticut. They did, and the dealers and buyers at that 1958 flea market were so pleased with the whole affair that any doubts about this new kind of antique arena were dispelled. The next year, the late Gordon Reid of Brimfield, Massachusetts, opened his vast hay field to dealers, and the town now has several simultaneous fleas three times a year.

WHEN TO GO TO A FLEA MARKET

Antique dealers, experienced collectors and "pickers" who scout for stock for shop dealers, are all early arrivals at flea markets. The merchandise on any day is all there from the beginning. Some avid buyers stand by a likely dealer's truck as it is being unloaded, in order to get first choice. Pre-dawn hours, attended by cold, dew, the smell of Thermoses of coffee, shadowy signals of flashlights, the glare of headlamps, cheery or grumpy calls through the dark, are part of the adventure of flea markets, and they prove to be the best time for serious buyers.

During the daylight hours flea markets become less mysterious, a bit more egalitarian, but there are many finds still to be made. In fact, some items which may have looked perfect under flashlight are very often revealed as less than what they seemed.

At any time there are two distinct kinds of flea market-goers; those who do a lightning tour of the entire market, expecting any treasures to sing out, and those who believe that the treasures are more likely to be hidden in the bottom of a pile of tools or closed up in a drawer.

BUYING

Part of the excitement of flea markets is that so many things are happening at once. All around you, people are buying and selling, and dealers are calling out to prospective buyers, and jokes are flying back and forth. Unless it's a very sleepy crowd, the sense of competition is tough. You must evaluate every object you are attracted to, do it quickly, and try to avoid letting either the dealer or other buyers around the table know what it is you are interested in. Some frequent flea market buyers believe that it is best to be direct: pick up the item, decide on its condition, quality, and value to you, then ask the dealer "How much is this?" or "What's the best you can do on this?" Other buyers prefer to finger half the items on a table, perhaps casting disparaging glances on those things which they most desire, asking the prices of a number of things. This is guaranteed to annoy some sellers and to completely fool others. A poker face combined with questions about two or three objects, followed by a thoughtful pause which gives you time to consider your next step, seems to work best for most people.

Set a limit on spending by putting only so much cash in your pocket. Only the rarest and most spectacular find will get you to try to cash a check. It is tempting to buy anything which seems significantly underpriced, but remember that a bargain isn't a bargain if you don't really want it. The wise collector isn't talked into a purchase by anyone, least of all by a dealer.

If a seller holds up a yellow metal candlestick and tells you "It's real brass and a great bargain at $27.50" you don't have to buy it, especially if you don't know anything about candlesticks or hate brass. Leave it behind.

BARGAINING

One buyer's tip is found in the $27.50 price. The seller has either just marked it down from $30.00 or is willing to sell it for $25.00. Haggling over the price is common at almost all flea markets, although some sellers will price objects with the added note " ... firm." Haggling takes several forms. In the example of the brass candlestick, which you might decide you would like if it were cheaper, you could counter with "I'll give you $20.00." Whereupon the dealer will respond "Sold!" or "Are you kidding?" or "Give me $25.00." If he says "Sold" you will immediately wish you had offered $18.00, although there is no way of knowing what the dealer would have said to that. If the dealer says "Are you kidding?" he either wants you to raise your offer or pay the quoted price. If he says "Give me $25.00" you may now either say "I'll take it" or "How about $22.50?"

Whatever your technique, everyone agrees that there is one unwritten rule of flea market etiquette: don't get a price and then walk away without a word or without buying. The ritual words "Thanks. I'll think about it" are heard more often than any others at flea markets. They save face, are noncommittal, polite, and even possibly true.

PAYMENT AND PICKUP

At the finest flea markets, where everyone is an established antique dealer, personal checks are often accepted with proof of identification. Occasionally a dealer is able to offer credit card service—usually because he has a shop. Cash, however, is the medium of most exchanges. Carry a variety of bills and coins— don't expect dealers to change a fifty or hundred dollar bill for you.

If possible, take your purchase with you. There is often confusion at the end of the selling day, and your purchase may get packed up and driven away before you make it back to that corner of the market. Without a public address system, or a receipt with your name and address on it, there is little chance that the dealer can find you. If what you have bought is quite large or heavy, drive your car over to load it up, even if it means sacrificing a good parking spot. If the flea is an indoor permanent market with daily or weekly sales, it is possible that some arrangement can be made with management for storage or delivery.

SELLING AT A FLEA MARKET

Sellers at flea markets are sometimes weekend dealers who have other occupations. Or they may be collectors trying to unload duplicates, or collectors who tried it once and fell for the fun and excitement of buying (as if for a personal collection) and the profit of selling. Some dealers become so addicted to flea marketeering that they take it on full time, traveling the summer and winter circuits, living out of huge campers and setting up in a new location every week or month.

If you have had a successful yard or garage sale, or are a collector with surplus items or a collection you are tired of, or if you think you have the knack of buying cheap and selling at a profit, you may want to try flea market selling.

Start small and don't take everything for your first attempt, particularly not heavy furniture. Pick a flea market with inexpensive space rentals, one that you've been to as a buyer. Be sure it has a good cross-section of dealers and buyers. It's usually a bad idea to become the only dealer in, say, fine old timepieces in a market with 90% new and secondhand merchandise. The buyers you need just won't be there. Before you set up price everything in a notebook, in your head, or on the pieces, and fix a limit as to how low you'll go. Be openminded about bargaining—most buyers expect it. Find out the rules and regulations of setting up and taking down: some managers advertise their hours and the number of dealers, and in order not to disappoint customers they want dealers who remain at their posts during the market hours. Find out about collecting local sales tax and obtaining any necessary selling licenses.

Be prepared with a patter, something to say to the people who slow down in front of your space. One dealer at the sprawling Englishtown New Jersey market achieved some kind of fame as the man who would play his squawky violin and yell "How much will you give me...to stop playing?" Remember that a seller has to be something of a performer, because winning the attention of the buyers away from other sellers is of prime importance.

Take a mixture of wares and something in every price range. A small box of nickel items will often draw people who are willing to spend a lot more. If you fail the first time, try again, and apply everything you've learned by observing other sellers and from the remarks of buyers. Finally, learn the value of what you sell. There is nothing more infuriating to an experienced collector than finding something in his special field which has been grossly overpriced.

CHECKLIST FOR FLEA MARKET BUYERS

☐ Call ahead to check hours and dates.

☐ Go early and stay late—some of the best bargains come when dealers can't face packing up again.

☐ Don't go with someone who collects the same thing you do.

☐ If you plan to travel with your pet, ask if pets are allowed, or be prepared to keep the animal anywhere but locked up in your car.

☐ Wear comfortable shoes and be prepared for mud, sand, dust and gravel.

☐ Wear comfortable clothing, and expect to shed or add layers.

☐ Take a hat: under the sun, your notions of what's a bargain and what isn't can quickly become half-baked.

☐ Consider having a tee-shirt made telling what it is that you collect, even if you are shy. Successful collectors advertise.

☐ Carry as little as you can. A flea market rule is that every pound of excess baggage weighs five pounds after an hour and a ton after two hours. Some people use shopping carts, or pull little red wagons behind them. Try that, or consider a backpack or a shoulder-hung canvas tote.

☐ Don't be afraid to take something you'd like to sell or swap, if it's small and the value is unquestionable. Don't expect sellers to assay gold or weigh your grandmother's silver epergne.

☐ Take a small, lightweight flashlight, a strong magnifying glass and a small magnet to test for steel or iron. Some that glitters may be plated.

☐ Take a small notepad and pen to jot down addresses, or make notes on what you see.

☐ Make motel or hotel reservations ahead, particularly in the case of large annual shows which attract people from several states. Room at the inns may be in great demand—and booked by dealers well in advance.

□ Be prepared for primitive or nonexistent toilet facilities. Many of the flea markets listed in the GUIDE do have facilities—often portable toilets set up on the edge of field or lot—but others do not.

Linda Campbell Franklin, a lecturer and writer on the subject of collecting, is the author of several books including *From Hearth to Cookstove: Kitchen Collectibles from 1700 to 1930; Antiques and Collectibles: A Bibliography of Works in English;* and *Three Hundred Years of Kitchen Collectibles.*

UNITED STATES REGIONAL MAP

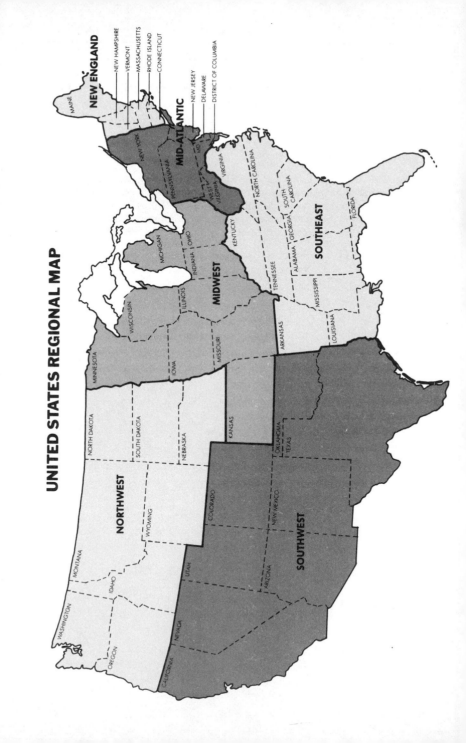

NEW ENGLAND
MAINE
NEW HAMPSHIRE
VERMONT
MASSACHUSETTS
RHODE ISLAND
CONNECTICUT

MID-ATLANTIC
NEW YORK
PENNSYLVANIA
NEW JERSEY
DELAWARE
MD
WEST VIRGINIA
VIRGINIA
DISTRICT OF COLUMBIA

MIDWEST
MICHIGAN
OHIO
INDIANA
ILLINOIS
WISCONSIN
IOWA
MISSOURI
MINNESOTA

SOUTHEAST
NORTH CAROLINA
SOUTH CAROLINA
GEORGIA
ALABAMA
FLORIDA
KENTUCKY
TENNESSEE
MISSISSIPPI
LOUISIANA
ARKANSAS

NORTHWEST
NORTH DAKOTA
SOUTH DAKOTA
NEBRASKA
WYOMING
MONTANA
IDAHO
WASHINGTON
OREGON

SOUTHWEST
KANSAS
OKLAHOMA
TEXAS
COLORADO
NEW MEXICO
UTAH
ARIZONA
NEVADA
CALIFORNIA

NEW ENGLAND

Connecticut, Maine, Massachusetts, New Hampshire, Rhode Island, Vermont

Antiquing is a time-honored custom in New England, where every town seems to have a white-spired church, at least one historic landmark dating back to colonial times, and something really old in every house. All six states in the region have auction houses offering a wide variety of collectibles, and many that feature specialties at regularly-scheduled sales. In addition, tours of flea markets in the region always yield something fine or unusual in practically any collecting field.

Not surprisingly, sales in New England often reflect the area's history. Generally speaking, the region is good for early furniture, rare books and historical documents, silver and pewter, plus many English antiques. Long recognized as a center for glassmaking, New England is also a primary source for antique glassware. A broad range—from paperweights to carnival glass—appears regularly at auctions and fleas. Robert W. Skinner Galleries in Boston and Bolton, Massachusetts, offers specialized sales of rare bottles, historical flasks and early glass, while Globe Antiques of Pembroke holds sales of Sandwich Glass.

Connecticut has been the clockmaking center of the country since Eli Terry peddled his own wooden-geared clocks from farmhouse to farmhouse. And clocks are still found in Connecticut; special sales of them are held at the Robert H. Glass auction galleries in Central Village.

In New Hampshire and Vermont several auction houses hold specialized sales of old tools. Among them are Brookline Gallery in Brookline, New Hampshire, and Your Country Auctioneer in Hillsboro, New Hampshire, and J. P. Bittner in Putney, Vermont. One added benefit for collectors who buy in New Hampshire: there is no sales tax!

Southern Maine is the home of several long-established auctioneers who feature fine Americana and Victoriana (both American and English in origin)—including the F. O. Bailey and Baridoff galleries in Portland; James D. Julia's Auction in Fairfield; and Richard Oliver's Auction in Kennebunk.

The greatest concentration, by far, of auctions and fleas is found in Massachusetts. Auction specialties range from military collectibles in Woburn to antique smoking pipes in Newburyport. Along Cape Cod, both Robert C. Eldred and Richard A. Bourne hold auctions of marine art and antiques—another reflection of the seafaring background of the area. A drive along Highway 6A, the road which is close to the Bay shore of the Cape, should be taken cautiously, with a "We Stop for Antiques" bumper sticker, because there are so many antiquing opportunities. One large flea market is found on the Cape, at Wellfleet—three-quarters of the way to Provincetown. Many flea markets are off the Massachusetts Turnpike between Springfield and Boston, and one is truly spectacular. It is really several markets held simultaneously in the same town. Several times a year, Brimfield, Massachusetts, on Route 20 off the Turnpike, is transmogrified from a small expectant town into the biggest antiques and collectibles market in the country, with thousands of dealers and buyers filling every available pasture and meadow with the sound of tramping feet, parked cars, or multifarious merchandise.

Connecticut has a good share of New England's flea market activity too. It is so easy to reach from surrounding states that many antiquers from New York or Massachusetts spend the day or weekend at one of the big fleas—particularly in Fairfield and New Haven Counties. Most are easily reached off I-95, which goes along the southern shore of Connecticut. Woodbury and Southbury are sites of big flea markets, and an outdoor antique *show* which could pass for a top-notch flea, and which fills half a fairground, is held bi-annually at Danbury. The bargains are overseen by some wonderful painted lifesize animals stationed above the midway.

As in other regions, New England has many attractions for the collector who is traveling. Natural beauties compete with a number of museums and restorations. Connecticut has several: in Bristol is the American Clock and Watch Museum, where the prototype of Eli Terry's clock is to be seen. There are early farm implements at the Stanley-Whitman House in Farmington, and Mystic Seaport has a huge maritime collection in several buildings in Mystic. Also noteworthy is the Winchester Gun Museum in New Haven.

In Maine are found the Boothbay Railway Museum in Boothbay Harbor, and the Shaker Museum at Poland Spring. In Massachusetts you can combine a trip to Old Sturbridge Village, a huge restoration in Sturbridge, with Brimfield, which is only about seven miles away! Also in Massachusetts are several museums in Boston; historic Deerfield, where there are a number of restored houses; a Pilgrim village called Plimoth Plantation in Plymouth; Hancock Shaker Village in Pittsfield; the Merrimack Valley Textile Museum in North Andover; many different restorations in Essex; and whaling museums in Sharon, Nantucket and New Bedford.

In New Hampshire are the Strawbery Banke restored houses in Portsmouth. In Rhode Island are found Belcourt Castle in Newport—one of the loveliest towns in the country, and a sight for Victoriana eyes—and Old Slater Mill in Pawtucket, where there are exhibits on early American textiles and milling. Finally, Vermont has a number of wonderful museums and restorations. The Bennington Museum in Bennington has a huge collection of the famous Bennington pottery, in all its marbled beauty; the Vermont Country Store restorations in Rockingham and Weston; and Shelburne Museum village in Shelburne, are where some of the most interesting 18th and 19th century examples of everyday objects are to be found.

Some of the big antique shows are the Stamford Antiques Show in Connecticut; the Annual Salisbury Antiques Fair in Connecticut; the Connecticut Antiques Show in Hartford; the Ellis Memorial Antiques Show in Boston; the New Hampshire Antique Dealers Show in Concord; the Hyannis Antiques Show on Cape Cod; and the Ellsworth Antiques Show in Maine.

For listings and reviews of auctions, flea markets and antique shows check *Antiques and the Arts Weekly, Maine Antiques Digest, Antique Trader, Collectors News, Joel Sater's Antiques and Auction News, Antique Monthly, Spinning Wheel, The Magazine ANTIQUES*, and local newspapers.

Key to Flea Market Symbols

The following letters and symbols are a quick guide to what each flea market offers collectors—in terms of size, frequency, and whether auctions are held. The obvious deduction is that a market with over 200 dealers, open daily, and offering an auction of antiques and collectibles is your best bet. This is not always true; as luck would have it, the tiny annual market might be the one where you find the greatest treasure.

★ Auction at the flea market

D Daily, 4-7 days a week

W Weekly or Weekends

M Monthly or 2 times a month

A Annually or up to 4 times a year

X Up to 50 dealers

XX 51-100 dealers

XXX 101-200 dealers

XXXX 201 or more dealers

CONNECTICUT

Canton Barn Auction
Richard E. Wacht, Auctioneer
79 Old Canton Road
Canton, Connecticut 06019
(203) 693-4901 or (203) 379-0500
(Take Routes 44 and 202 to Canton; turn on Old Canton Road at Amoco service station; barn located one-tenth mile down on left)

Doors open every Saturday night at 5:00 p.m. for a general sale beginning at 7:30 p.m.; estate sales; no consignments; all merchandise purchased for sales.

No buyer's premium; telephone bids accepted; traveler's checks, certified checks, or personal checks with two forms of ID accepted; no credit cards. Payment in full same day; pickups within one week.

Oral and written appraisals offered for fee dependent on value of item.

Robert H. Glass Auction Gallery
Robert H. Glass and family, Auctioneers
Box 237, Route 12
Central Village, Connecticut 06332
(203) 564-7318
(Exit 89 off Connecticut Turnpike, one-half mile on right)

A family-run business; antiques, collectibles and home furnishings featured in Thursday evening sales, held 6:00 to 11:00 p.m., and on Saturdays from 10:30 to 4:30 p.m.; specialized sales featuring clocks, coins, books held three times a year; estate sales; consignments; property purchased for sales.

No buyer's premium; mail and telephone bids accepted; checks accepted with established credit through bank reference; no credit cards. Full payment day of purchase; pickups as soon as possible.

Sale announcements mailed; written appraisals, in accord with IRS and insurance requirements, offered for fee of $75.00 per hour.

Sage Auction Gallery
Paul Sage, Auctioneer
Route 9-A
Chester, Connecticut 06412
(203) 526-3036
(Interstate 95 to 9 North, Exit 6 onto Route 148, east to 9-A North)

Year-round auctions of antiques, collectibles, and home furnishings, held every other week on Friday at 6:00 p.m.; all-day inspection every Thursday before sale from 10:00 to 5:00 p.m.; estate sales; consignments; property purchased for sales.

No buyer's premium; mail and telephone bids accepted; traveler's checks or personal checks with proper ID accepted; no credit cards. Full payment day of sale; pickups within three days.

Written appraisals offered for fee of $60.00 per hour.

Country Auction Gallery
Steven Smith, Auctioneer
1140 Main Street (Route 31)
Coventry, Connecticut 06238
(203) 742-9698

Set in an old church; auctions twice a month on Fridays at 7:00 p.m.; featuring antiques and collectibles, early American furniture and furnishings, some period furniture; consignments; property purchased for sales.

No buyer's premium; telephone bids accepted; in-state checks, Master Charge or Visa accepted; full payment same day; pickups within four days.

Oral and written appraisals offered free of charge for single items at gallery; other items for negotiable fee.

Ralston Antique Toy Auction Service
Lloyd W. Ralston, Auctioneer
447 Stratfield Road
Fairfield, Connecticut 06432
(203) 335-4054 or (203) 366-3399
(Sales held in hotel ballrooms—check mailings)

Specializing in the sale and appraisal of antique toys; at least two antique and collectible toy sales held each year; some mail auctions; consignments; property purchased for sales.

No buyer's premium; mail bids accepted; no telephone bids; checks accepted from established customers or with verified ID; no credit cards. Purchases held with a 10% deposit; full payment and pickups within 30 days.

Sale announcements and catalogs mailed; purchase of catalog required for entrance; oral or written appraisals offered for variable fee.

Note: Listings are alphabetical by town.

Joseph Pari Gallery
Joseph Pari, Auctioneer
3846 Whitney Avenue, Mt. Carmel
Hamden, Connecticut 06518
(203) 248-4951
(Off College Highway, Route 10)

General monthly sales usually on Monday evenings, sometimes on Saturdays; specialized sales feature antiques, collectibles, fine arts, and fine household furnishings; estate sales; consignments; no property purchased for sales.

No buyer's premium; telephone bids accepted; Connecticut checks accepted; out-of-state checks require bank reference; no credit cards. Purchases held with 10% deposit; payment in full and pickups within one week.

Sale announcements mailed; written appraisals offered for minimum fee of $100.00.

Harbor Auction Gallery
William Peterson, Auctioneer
238 Bank Street
New London, Connecticut 06320
(203) 443-0868 or (203) 536-9664
(Access from Interstate 95 North or South)

Holds general sales monthly; specialized sales feature advertising and paper products; consignments; property purchased for sales.

No buyer's premium; telephone bids accepted; local checks with proper ID accepted; Visa or Master Charge accepted; purchases held with a 25% deposit; full payment and pickups within one week.

Sale announcements mailed; written and oral appraisals offered for negotiable fee.

Helen Winter Associates
Mark Polon, Regina Madigan, Linda Slamm, Helen Winter, Auctioneers
355 Farmington Avenue (Route 10)
Plainville, Connecticut 06062
(203) 747-0714
(North of junction with Route 72 and south of junction with Route 6)

General twice-monthly sales featuring many privately-owned pieces; held Monday evenings at 7:00 p.m.; previews at 6:00 p.m.; specialized sales of jewelry and dolls; estate sales; consignments; merchandise purchased for sales.

Ten percent buyer's premium; telephone bids accepted; in-state checks accepted; out-of-state checks from established customers; Master Charge and Visa accepted. Variable deposit necessary to hold purchases; full payment within one month; pickups within one week.

Sale announcements mailed; catalogs for all sales; written appraisals offered for an hourly fee of $50.00.

Auction by Cameron
R. J. Cameron, Auctioneer
1488 Sullivan Avenue, PO Box 468
South Windsor, Connecticut 06074
(203) 644-8962
(Sales held on site or at rented halls—check mailings)

Monthly auctions include specialized sales of dolls, steins, and paper ephemera; estate sales; consignments; merchandise purchased for sales.

No buyer's premium; mail and telephone bids accepted; out-of-state checks accepted only if previously approved through bank reference; no credit cards. Purchases held with a 25% deposit; full payment and pickups within 24 hours.

Sale announcements and some catalogs mailed; written appraisals offered for minimum charge of $40.00.

Alvin S. Josephson, Auction Sales and Appraisals
PO Box 240
Trumbull, Connecticut 06611
(203) 261-8872 or (203) 268-3495
(Sales held at Congregation B'Nai Torah Hall, Merritt Parkway, Exit 48, then north on Route 25 (for two and one-half miles)

Specializing in antique and estate sales; sales held irregularly; merchandise consigned or purchased for sale.

No buyer's premium; mail bids accepted with 25% deposit; checks accepted from established customers; payment in full and pickups day of sale only.

Sale announcements mailed; written appraisals offered for time-based fee; oral appraisals for $10.00 per item.

Maison Auction Company, Inc.
William Ulbrich, Auctioneer
128 East Street
Wallingford, Connecticut 06492
(203) 269-8007 or (203) 272-3844
(Off U S Route 5 between 191, Exit 13, and Wilbur Cross, Exit 64)

General sales, including 50% antiques and collectibles such as furniture and china, generally held every other week; specialized sales feature prints and paintings, toys, Hummels, Victorian costumes; estate sales; consignments; property purchased for sales.

No buyer's premium; mail and telephone bids not accepted; certified checks, traveler's checks, or in-state checks accepted; out-of-state checks must be accompanied by bank letter of credit. Full payment day of sale; pickups within seven days.

Written appraisals offered for negotiable hourly fee.

Villa's Auction Gallery
Richard Villa, Auctioneer
Office: 106 Layton Street
West Hartford, Connecticut 06110
Gallery: Route 44
Norfolk, Connecticut 06058
Weekends: (203) 542-5626; weekdays: (203) 232-3580
(West of Winsted, just over Norfolk town line—eight miles out of Winsted on Route 44)

Weekly auctions held Saturdays at 7:00 p.m., generally from May to September; general and antique merchandise, including oak and Victorian furniture; estate sales; consignments only; no property purchased for sales.

No buyer's premium; telephone bids accepted; checks with proper ID accepted; Visa and Master Charge accepted. Payment in full night of auction; pickups until noon the following day.

Some sale announcements; written appraisals offered for negotiable fee.

Enfield Flea Market ★ W XX
35 Pearl Street
Enfield, Connecticut 06082
(203) 745-8981
Contact: Richard Fortin
(Exit 48 off I-91)

Indoor market; 83 dealers; began in 1977; open Sunday, 9:00 a.m. to 4:00 p.m., year round except June, July and August; 50¢ admission; space rental; $15.00 for 8' x 12'; reservations needed.

All antiques, collectibles, or secondhand merchandise; restaurant; restrooms; parking; nearby motels; antiques and collectibles auction usually held every other week.

Litchfield Flea Market A XXX
White Memorial Grounds, Route 202
Litchfield, Connecticut
Contact: Russell Carrell, Salisbury, Connecticut 06068, (203) 435-9301

Outdoor market; 150 dealers; began in 1971; held annually last Saturday in June, 10:00 a.m. to 5:00 p.m.; $1.50 admission; space rental: $25.00 for 16' x 24'; reservations needed one year in advance.

All antique merchandise; food; restrooms; parking; nearby motels.

Milford Swap N' Shop W XXXX
230 Cherry Street
Milford, Connecticut 06460
(203) 878-5600
Contact: Lee Peterson, Milford Drive-In Theatre, (203) 878-5300
(I-95 to Exit 39A, go left at fork to Milford Drive-In Theatre)

Outdoor market; 225 to 300 dealers; began in 1917; open every Sunday, 7:00 a.m. to 4:00 p.m., March to November; admission 99¢ per carload, 50¢ walk in; space rental: $8.00 for 18' x 10'; no reservations, but seller permits required.

Mostly new and secondhand merchandise, some produce, few antiques and collectibles; food; restrooms; parking for 550; four motels nearby.

Peddler's Market   W   XX
Route 63
Naugatuck, Connecticut 06770
(203) 729-1791
Contact: Alice Slade or Mary Schildgen, 1106 New Haven Road, Naugatuck, Connecticut 06770, (203) 729-7397

Outdoor market; 50 to 70 dealers; began in 1972; open every Sunday from May to December; free admission; space rental: $8.00 for 20' x 30'; no reservations needed.

Variety of antiques, new and used merchandise, arts and crafts, produce; food; restrooms; parking; nearby motels.

New London Trader   ★   W   X
238 Bank Street
New London, Connecticut 06320
(203) 443-0868 or (203) 443-3559
Contact: Philip Hendel or Karen Wenc
(New London Exit off I-95, to downtown New London; near Mystic Seaport)

Indoor market; 15 to 20 dealers; began in 1977; open Saturdays and Sundays, 10:00 a.m. to 5:00 p.m., year round; free admission; space rental: $12.50 for 9' x 12', $20.00 for weekend; reservations needed.

Mostly antiques, collectibles, some secondhand items; food stands; restrooms; parking; monthly auctions.

The Elephant's Trunk Bazaar   W   XX
Route 7
New Milford, Connecticut 06810
(203) 355-1448
Contact: Greg Baecker
(I-84 to Exit 7, north for seven miles)

Outdoor market; 100 dealers; began in 1976; open Sundays, May to October; free admission; space rental: $10.00 for 20' x 20'; no reservations needed.

Variety of antiques, collectibles, new merchandise and secondhand items; food; restrooms; parking; five nearby motels.

St. Rose Flea Market   W   XXX
Church Hill Road
Newtown, Connecticut 06470
(203) 426-2051
Contact: Robert Green, 8 Blakslee Drive, Newtown, Connecticut 06470
(Exit 10 off I-84)

Outdoor market; 150 to 200 dealers; began in 1975; open Saturday, 9:00 a.m. to 5:00 p.m.; free admission; space rental: $20.00 for 16'; reservations needed.

Variety of used and new merchandise, antiques, collectibles, crafts, art objects; food; restrooms; parking.

Barn Shoppes Antique Center   W X
41 West Main Street, Route 156
Niantic, Connecticut 06357
(203) 739-7315
Contact: Maureen F. Wirth (203) 739-5044
(I-95 to Exit 72, two miles east to Route 156)

Indoor market; nine dealers; began in 1972; open every Saturday and Sunday; free admission; space rental; $35.00 per month and up for areas 12' x 12' to 24' x 33' area; reservations needed.

Mostly antiques and collectibles, some other merchandise; food available locally; restrooms; parking; nearby motels and beaches.

Old Mystic Antique and Flea Market   W X
Route 27 at I-95
Old Mystic, Connecticut 06372
(203) 536-9665
Contact: Sonny Hendel
(Exit 80 off I-95, go south)

Just north of Mystic Seaport; 35 dealers; began in 1975; open Sundays April 1 to November 1; free admission; space rental: $16.00 for 20' x 20'; reservations needed.

Mostly quality antiques, some collectibles, fewer secondhand items; food; restrooms; parking; nearby motels.

County Fair Flea Market   A   XXX
Midsex Avenue
Portland, Connecticut 06480
Contact: Judy Lane, Rosehill Road, Portland, Connecticut, (203) 342-2581
(Twenty minutes from Hartford Highway, 17A)

Outdoor market; 150 dealers; began in 1975; held annually on last Saturday in April, 10:00 a.m. to 4:00 p.m.; free admission; space rental: $15.00 for 20' x 20'; no reservations needed.

Variety of new and used merchandise, antiques, collectibles, crafts; food; restrooms; parking.

Ridgefield Flea Market   A ★★★★
Veterans Park Playing Field
Off Main Street, Routes 33 & 35
Ridgefield, Connecticut
Contact: Russell Carrell, Salisbury, Connecticut 06068, (203) 435-9301

Outdoor market; 200 dealers; began in 1960; held annually first Saturday in June, 10:00 a.m. to 5:00 p.m.; $2.00 admission; space rental: $25.00 for 16' x 24'; reservations needed one year in advance.

All antique merchandise; food; restrooms; parking; nearby motels.

Salisbury Flea Market   A ★★★
Route 44 north of Salisbury Village
Salisbury, Connecticut
Contact: Russell Carrell, Salisbury, Connecticut 06068,
(203) 435-9301

Outdoor market; 200 dealers; began in 1956; held Saturday after Labor Day, 10:00 a.m. to 5:00 p.m.; $2.00 admission; space rental: $25.00 for 16' x 24' ; reservations needed year in advance.

All antiques; food; parking; restrooms; nearby motels.

Southbury Training School Flea Market   A ★★★
Southbury Training School
Southbury, Connecticut 06488
(203) 264-7148
Contact: Jane Miller
(Exit 14 off I-84)

Outdoor market; 125 dealers; began in 1970; held third Sunday in May, 10:00 a.m. to 5:00 p.m.; free admission; space rental: $10.00 for 20' x 20'; reservations needed.

Mostly secondhand merchandise, antiques, collectibles, crafts and art objects; food; restrooms; parking; nearby motels.

TAC Antique Show and Flea Market   A XX
24 Hyde Avenue
Vernon, Connecticut 06066
Contact: Anne Fluckiger, 58 Grandview Circle, Storrs, Connecticut 06268,
(203) 429-4429
(I-86 to Exit 98, west on Route 31 to Route 30, turn right)

Indoor/outdoor market; 100 dealers; began in 1975; held last weekend in May and August; $1.00 admission; space rental: indoors $30.00 per weekend for 10' x 10', outdoors $10.00 per day for 20' x 24'; reservations needed.

Mostly antiques and collectibles, some secondhand items; food, including a chicken barbecue event; restrooms; parking; nearby motels.

Redwood Country Flea Market   W XX
Hartford Turnpike
Wallingford, Connecticut 06492
(203) 269-5947 or (203) 269-3500
Contact: Walter and Roberta Dubar, 4 East Street, Wallingford, Connecticut 06492, (203) 269-5947
(Exit 64 off Merritt Parkway (Wilbur Cross), Exit 13 I-91, left then quick right over tracks)

Note: Listings are alphabetical by town.

Outdoor market; 85 sellers; began in 1972; open every Saturday, Sunday and some holidays, year round; free admission; space rental: $5.00 Saturday, $7.00 Sunday, $10.00 weekend; no reservations needed.

Mostly collectibles and antiques, lots of secondhand and household items; food; restrooms; parking.

Eastern Connecticut Flea Market   W XX

Mansfield Drive-In Theater
Junction Routes 31 and 32
Willimantic, Connecticut 06226
(203) 423-9890
Contact: Don Berg, 78 Bellevue Drive, Coventry, Connecticut 06238,
(203) 742-5477
(Route 32 Exit from I-86)

Indoor/outdoor market; 100 dealers; began in 1974; open Sundays, 8:00 a.m. to 3:00 p.m., April through November; free parking; space rental: $7.00 per day for 15' x 15' outdoor space; no reservations needed.

Mostly secondhand items, antiques and collectibles; food; restrooms; ample parking; nearby motels.

Tique Mart   W XXX

Route 6
Woodbury, Connecticut
Contact: R. H. Sprano, Middlebury Road, Middlebury, Connecticut 06762,
(203) 758-1571
(Exit 15 off I-84, almost five miles to show)

Outdoor market; 125 dealers; began in 1967; open every Saturday from third Saturday in April through third Saturday in November; free admission; space rental: $10.00 for 18' x 40'; reservations advisable.

Mostly antiques, some collectibles; food; restrooms; parking; nearby motels.

The Cob-Web   W XX

Route 44
Canton, Connecticut 06019
(203) 693-2658
Contact: Dolly Rudder, P O Box 354, Canton, Connecticut 06019,
(203) 693-4230
(West of Hartford at the junction of Routes 44, 202, 179)

Outdoor market; up to 55 dealers; began in 1970; open Sundays, May through September; free admission; space rental: $9.00 per day for 20' x 20'; reservations advisable.

Variety of antiques, collectibles, secondhand and new merchandise; food wagon, fried pizza special; no restrooms; parking; nearby motels.

MAINE

Jim Heckman

Jim Heckman, Auctioneer
Route 100-139, Bangor Road
Benton, Maine 04901
(207) 453-6870
(Just out of Waterville)

General goods, antiques and collectibles sold approximately once monthly, usually on Sunday at 7:00 p.m.; estate sales throughout Maine; consignments; property purchased for sales.

No buyer's premium; mail and telephone bids not accepted; in-state checks accepted with proper ID, out-of-state checks with bank letter of credit; no credit cards; full payment day of sale; pickups within five days.

Sale announcements mailed; written appraisals offered for fee of $25.00 or 1.5% value of merchandise.

C. E. Guarino

C. E. Guarino, Auctioneer
Berry Road, Box 49
Denmark, Maine 04022
(207) 452-2123

Mail and phone auctions exclusively, held bi-monthly by illustrated catalogs; sales feature Americana, maps, graphics, documents, and paintings; consignments; merchandise purchased for sales.

No buyer's premium; only mail and telephone bids accepted; checks accepted from customers on catalog subscription list—apply by mail, giving name and address; Visa and Master Charge accepted; full payment within three days; merchandise shipped to customer after payment received.

Sale announcements and catalogs mailed; oral and written appraisals offered.

Morgan's Gallery

Morgan Willis, Auctioneer
Route 236
Eliot, Maine 03903
(207) 439-4515
(Five miles from Portsmouth, New Hampshire; three miles off I-95 from Kittery, Maine, Route 236 North)

Two to four general antiques sales held monthly, usually on Thursdays at 6:00 p.m.; estate sales; consignments; property purchased for sales.

No buyer's premium; checks accepted with valid ID, though merchandise for large purchases may be held until check clears; no credit cards. Purchases held with a 25% deposit; full payment in three days; pickups within two days.

Sale announcements mailed; written appraisal services offered for fee of $100.00.

Mayo Auctioneers & Appraisers, Inc.

Leonard and Wayne A. Mayo, Auctioneers
RFD 1, Box 285
Ellsworth, Maine 04605
(207) 667-8062, or (207) 667-2664
(Route 3—in downtown Trenton, on the coast midway between Bangor and
Bar Harbor)

Antiques sale held at least once monthly; specialized sales of advertising,
country store, Americana, and Victorian collectibles held annually; estate sales;
consignments; merchandise purchased for sales.

No buyer's premium; mail bids accepted; telephone bids from established
customers accepted; certified checks, traveler's checks, or personal checks with
two forms of ID accepted; Visa and Master Charge accepted. Full payment day
of sale; pickups generally within two days.

Sale announcements and some catalogs mailed; written appraisals offered for
an hourly fee of $25.00.

Julia's Auction Service

James D. Julia, Auctioneer
Route 201
Fairfield, Maine 04937
(207) 453-9725
(Fairfield-Skowhegan Exit, 1 mile north of Interstate 95)

Approximately 25 sales held yearly, featuring Americana, particularly country
furniture and accessories; specialized sale of rare books held each fall; estate
sales; consignments; merchandise purchased for sales.

No buyer's premium; mail and telephone bids accepted; checks accepted with
previously established credit through bank reference; no credit cards. Full
payment day of sale; pickups generally same day.

Sale announcements and book auction catalogs mailed; written or oral
appraisals offered for negotiable fee, generally 1.5% of value.

Richard Oliver's Auction and Art Gallery

Plaza 1
Route 1, PO Box 337
Kennebunk, Maine 04043
(207) 985-3600

Specializing in the sale of fine art and antiques; annual antiques sale held on the
third and fourth of July; specialized sales held approximately two to four times
monthly featuring jewelry, Victoriana, Americana, guns, books, coins, paintings; estate sales; consignments; merchandise purchased for sales.

No buyer's premium; mail and telephone bids accepted; checks accepted from
established customers; establish credit in advance through bank reference; no
credit cards. Purchases held with a 30% deposit; full payment in seven days;
pickups within 30 days.

Sale announcements and some catalogs mailed; oral and written appraisals
offered for a negotiable fee.

F.O. Bailey Company, Inc. Auction Gallery
Franklin Allen, Auctioneer
141 Middle Street
Portland, Maine 04111
(207) 774-1479

Specializing in estate sales, antiques, and collectibles; sales held approximately twice monthly; specialized sales of jewelry, books, Victoriana, Americana; winter estate sales held at gallery; summer estate sales held on site throughout Maine; consigned merchandise only.

No buyer's premium; mail and telephone bids accepted from established customers only; checks accepted with bank letter of credit; no credit cards. Full payment and pickups at time of sale.

Sale announcements and some catalogs mailed; oral and written appraisals offered for negotiable fee.

Barridoff Galleries
William Edward O'Reilly, Auctioneer
242 Middle Street
Portland, Maine 04101
(207) 772-7396

Three major sales held each year, featuring 19th and early 20th century American and European paintings; consignments only; no property purchased for sale.

Ten percent buyer's premium; mail and telephone bids accepted; checks accepted with previously established credit; no credit cards. Full payment night of auction, or within 1 week if bidder is absent; pickups as soon as possible.

Sale announcements and catalogs available; written and oral appraisals offered for hourly fee of $50.00.

Foster's Antique Mall and Flea Market   ★ W XX
Route 1
Newcastle, Maine 04553
(207) 563-8150
(Fifty miles north of Portland)

Indoor market; 50+ dealers; began in 1974; open Saturday and Sunday, 8:00 a.m. to 5:00 p.m., May to October; free admission; space rental: $5.00 for 8' x 4' table with space; reservations needed for Sundays.

Mostly antiques and collectibles, some secondhand merchandise; lunch wagon; restrooms; parking; nearby motels; occasional auctions.

Bo-Mar Hall Flea Market and Antique Gallery   ★ D XX
Route 1
PO Box 308
Wells, Maine 04090
(207) 646-8843
Contact: Robert or Marlene Blair, Blair House Realty, (207) 646-7475
(I-95 to Exit 2, left to Route 1, one block left)

Indoor/outdoor market; 100 dealers; began in 1975; open daily 9:00 a.m. to 5:00 p.m., year round, closed Christmas Eve to February 1; free admission; space rental: $3.00 to $50.00 for showcase to 16' area; reservations needed inside.

Mostly antiques and collectibles, some secondhand merchandise; restaurants nearby; restrooms; parking; motels and campgrounds nearby; occasional auctions.

Montsweag Flea Market   W   XX
Route 1 and Mountain Road
Woolwich, Maine 04579
(207) 443-2809
Contact: Norma Thompson, PO Box 252, Woolwich, Maine 04579
(Six miles east of Bath)

Outdoor market; 60 to 70 dealers; began in 1976; open Saturday, Sunday and holidays, May, June, September, October, Friday, Saturday, Sunday in July and August; free parking; space rental: $5.00 for 3' x 8' table with lots of space; reservations needed.

Variety of used and new merchandise, collectibles, antiques and crafts; refreshment stand; restrooms for sellers only; parking; nearby motels.

MASSACHUSETTS

Collectibles Unlimited Auction Gallery
Tom Driscoll, Auctioneer
65 Agawam Shopping Court
Agawam, Massachusetts 01101
(413) 786-9884
(Five minutes from Springfield)

Weekly auctions Wednesday evenings include specialized sales of fine art, dolls, Hummels, American Victoriana, gambling machines, coins, jewelry, Oriental rugs, glass, and occasional cars; estate sales; consignments; merchandise purchased for sales.

Ten percent buyer's premium; mail and telephone bids accepted; traveler's checks or personal checks with established credit through bank reference accepted; Master Charge, Visa, and Bay Bank Merchant Express accepted; full payment within two days, pickups within one week.

Oral appraisals offered free of charge for items brought into gallery.

Robert W. Skinner, Inc.
Robert W. Skinner, Jr., Stephen L. Fletcher, Robert E. Cleaves, Auctioneers
Route 117
Bolton, Massachusetts 01740
(617) 779-5528
585 Boylston Street

Boston, Massachusetts 02116
(617) 236-1700
(Bolton gallery on Route 117, half mile east of Interstate 495; Boston gallery in Copley Square)

Specializes in early American and Victorian antiques; rare bottles, historical flasks and early glass. Year-round antique sales held in Bolton, usually three or four a month, on Friday mornings, sometimes evenings or weekends; generally one sale a month held in Boston, usually on Tuesday afternoons; specialized sales of military objects, Indian artifacts, paintings, books, photographica, dolls and toys, bottles and flasks, jewelry; estate sales; consignments; merchandise seldom purchased for sales.

Ten percent buyer's premium; mail and telephone bids accepted on limited basis; checks accepted with previously established credit, or merchandise held until check clears. Payment in full day of sale; pickups same day, unless other arrangements made.

Sale announcements mailed; catalogs for all sales; written appraisals offered for fee of $500.00 per hour, including travel time, at $500.00 minimum per day.

Carl R. Nordblom

Carl R. Nordblom, Auctioneer
PO Box 167
Harvard Square
Cambridge, Massachusetts 02138
(617) 491-0465 or (617) 491-1196
(Sales held at various rental halls or on site; check mailings for directions)

Sales held approximately every four weeks, featuring American antique furniture, Oriental porcelain and rugs; estate sales; consignments; property purchased for sales.

Ten percent buyer's premium; mail and telephone bids accepted from established customers only; in-state checks accepted with proper ID; out-of-state checks accepted with established credit from bank letter or credit or reference; no credit cards. Full payment day of sale; pickups within one week.

Sale announcements mailed; written appraisals offered.

Robert C. Eldred Company, Inc.

Robert C. Eldred, Jr. and Sr., Auctioneers
Route 6A
East Dennis, Massachusetts 02641
(617) 385-3116, (617) 385-3377
(Mid Cape Highway, Route 6, to Exit 9, Route 134, to Route 6A)

Specializing in estates and collections, featuring Oriental art, as well as American and European art and antiques; general antiques sale held every week in July and August, usually twice a month throughout rest of the year; specialized sales include Americana, marine art, weapons, paperweights, paintings, and guns; estate sales; consignments only—no property purchased for sales.

No buyer's premium; mail and telephone bids accepted with established

Note: Listings are alphabetical by town.

credit; checks accepted with ID, but merchandise may be held by auction house until check clears; no credit cards. Full payment at time of sale; pickups within three days.

Sale announcements mailed; some catalogs; oral appraisal offered free of charge; written appraisals, at office; for minimum of $35.00 or .75% of total value of merchandise; written appraisals, on location, for minimum of $100.00 or 1.5% of total value.

L. A. Landry Antiques
Robert Landry, Jack Donahue, Auctioneers
164 Main Street
Essex, Massachusetts 01929
(617) 768-6233
(Sales held at various locations—check mailings for directions)

Sales held twice monthly; specialized sales of dolls, glassware; also retail from gallery; estate sales; consignments; property purchased for sales.

No buyer's premium; telephone bids accepted; checks accepted with previously established credit through bank letter; no credit cards. Purchases held with a 50% deposit; full payment in 10 days; pickups within three days.

Sale announcements and some catalogs mailed; purchase of catalog required to enter some sales; written appraisals offered for negotiable fee.

Collector's Americana Mail Auction
Ben Corning, Auctioneer
10 Lilian Road Extended
Framingham, Massachusetts 01701
(617) 872-2229
(Second left off Prospect Street from Route 9, Framingham)

A mail auction house holding two major antique sales yearly; issues sales lists for specialized sales periodically, featuring a broad range of memorabilia (political, military, advertising, circus, fire and police, world's fairs, railroadiana) and paper ephemera (tradecards, postcards, playing cards, Currier & Ives, commics, posters, premiums); also, toys, early auto and aviation, Coca-Cola, and Indian and Western collectibles; consignments; property purchased for sales.

No buyer's premium; telephone as well as mail bids accepted; checks accepted, but merchandise may be held until check clears; no credit cards. No deposit necessary to hold purchase; full payment within 10 days after notification, unless three-month budget plan is arranged.

Sale announcements and catalogs for bidding mailed; oral and written appraisals offered for variable fee.

Mark Polon, Inc.
Mark Polon, Auctioneer
54 Hope Street
Greenfield, Massachusetts 01301
(413) 774-3631
(Exit 26 off Interstate 91 to the center of town)

Antiques sales held on Friday nights—monthly from October to March, every other month from April to September; specialized sales include fine art, metals, jewelry; estate sales; consignments; property also purchased.

Ten percent buyer's premium; mail and telephone bids accepted; checks accepted with ID or reference; Visa and Master Charge accepted; 20% deposit necessary to hold purchase; full payment and pickups within 30 days.

Sale announcements mailed; some sale catalogs; written appraisal services offered locally for $25.00 per hour.

The Auction Gallery of Paul J. Dias, Inc.

Paul J. Dias, Auctioneer
30 East Washington Street
Route 58
Hanson, Massachusetts 02341
(617) 447-9057
(Sales also held at various locations)

Specializing in antiques and collectibles; sales approximately once monthly; annual sales of antique automobiles in June; advertising and country store items in early May; specialized sales feature guns, toys and dolls; estate sales; consignments; property purchased for sales.

Ten percent buyer's premium; mail and telephone bids accepted; checks accepted with proper ID and bank letter of credit; Master Charge and Visa accepted. Full payment day of sale; pickups within one week.

Sale announcements mailed; purchase of catalog required to enter automobile sale; catalogs for all specialized sales; oral or written appraisals offered for negotiable fee.

Richard A. Bourne Company, Inc.

Richard, Thomas and William Bourne, Auctioneers
PO Box 141
Hyannis Port, Massachusetts 02647
Gallery:
Corporation Street
Hyannis, Massachusetts 02647
(617) 775-0797, (617) 775-0897

Three monthly sales feature Americana, Oriental rugs and paintings, and Continental fine art and antiques; specialized sales include decoys in July, dolls and toys in March, guns in May, and marine antiques in August; estate sales; consignments only; no property purchased for sales.

No buyer's premium; mail and telephone bids accepted; checks accepted with established credit, bank letter of credit, or reference; no credit cards. Full payment day of sale; pickups within one week or by agreement.

Sale announcements mailed monthly; illustrated catalogs for all major sales; oral appraisals offered free; written appraisals offered to banks, estates and private consignees considering merchandise for gallery's auction.

John Rosselle Company
John Rosselle, Auctioneer
Commercial Street
Lakeville, Massachusetts
(617) 947-4751
(Just off Route 105)

Handling mostly estate sales; featuring variety of antiques; 15 to 20 sales held yearly; consignments; property purchased for sales.

Ten percent buyer's premium; mail and telephone bids accepted; checks accepted with proper ID if in-state; out-of-state checks require bank letter of credit. Purchases held with a 25% deposit; full payment and pickups within seven days.

Sale announcements mailed; some catalogs; oral or written appraisals offered for negotiable fee.

Louis E. Caropreso Auctions
PO Box 1791
Lenox, Massachusetts 01240
(413) 243-2446
(Sales held on site or at Holiday Inn Hotels—check mailings)

Sales generally held monthly; featuring early American, Victorian, and turn-of-the-century antiques; estate sales; consignments only; no property purchased for sales.

Ten percent buyer's premium; mail and telephone bids not accepted; checks accepted from established customers through bank reference; no credit cards. Full payment and pickups day of sale.

Sale announcements mailed; some catalogs; written appraisals offered for negotiable fee.

Christopher L. Snow
Christopher L. Snow, Auctioneer
PO Box 914
Newburyport, Massachusetts 01950
(617) 465-8872
(On-site sales, see directions in ads and on mailings)

Handling estates, antiques, and collectibles; sales held every six to eight weeks; specialized sales include antique pipes, guns, and rugs; consignments; property purchased for sales.

No buyer's premium; mail and telephone bids accepted only after personal inspection of merchandise by bidder; checks accepted from established customers, or with bank letter of credit; no credit cards.

Full payment and pickups day of sale. Sale announcements mailed; written appraisals offered for an hourly negotiable fee.

Hubbard's Amherst Auction Gallery
William L. Hubbard, Auctioneer
Route 116
North Amherst, Massachusetts 01002
(413) 665-3811 of (413) 253-9914

Weekly sales of general household goods and some antiques on Saturdays at 10:00 a.m.; major sale, of more significant items, held monthly; book sales held twice a month on Sundays; several specialized sales, held throughout the year, feature paintings, silver, Oriental rugs, antique furniture; estate sales; consignments; property seldom purchased.

No buyer's premium; mail and telephone bids accepted; checks accepted with previously established credit; no credit cards. Full payment at sale; pickups when convenient.

Book sales announcements mailed; written appraisals offered for 1% of value of item.

Ken Miller's Auction Barn
Ken Miller and Son, Auctioneers
Warwick Avenue
Northfield, Massachusetts 01360
(413) 498-2749
(On borders of Massachusetts, New Hampshire and Vermont)

Specializes in estate merchandise from New England and New York homes; sales generally held three times a month, from April to November, on Mondays at 6:30 p.m., and approximately every three weeks from December to March, on Saturdays; inspection for Monday sales held on preceding Sunday, along with flea market; sales feature Victorian, oak and early American furniture and furnishings; and collectibles, including Hummels, postcards, art pottery, guns, decorated stoneware, specialized collections such as carnival glass; consignments; property purchased for sales.

No buyer's premium; mail and telephone bids accepted after in-person inspection of merchandise; cash or traveler's checks preferred; local checks generally accepted with proper ID; out-of-state checks accepted with bank letter of credit. Full payment day of sale; pickups within three days.

Sale announcements mailed; written appraisals offered for negotiable fee, with minimum charge of $50.00.

Merlyn Auctions
Marvin J. Rich, Auctioneer
Ryder's Galleries
204 Main Street
North Harwich, Massachusetts 02645
(617) 432-5863
(Mid-Cape Highway, Route 6, Exit 10, Route 124; first right Queen Anne Road, two and one-quarter miles to end, turn right a hundred yards)

Approximately 300 lots sold at weekly antiques sale, every Saturday from 7:00 to 10:30 p.m., January to December 15; specialized sales of Americana, militaria, steins and decoys; estate sales; consignments; little property purchased for sales.

No buyer's premium; mail and telephone bids not accepted; absentee bids allowed only after personal inspection of merchandise in person; checks accepted with proper ID; no credit cards. Full payment time of sale; pickups within two days.

Announcements and catalogs mailed for special sales only; oral appraisals offered for fee dependent on value of item.

Philip C. Shute, Inc.

Philip C. Shute, Auctioneer
70 Accord Park Drive
Norwell, Massachusetts 02061
(617) 871-3414 or (617) 878-7060
(Twenty minutes south of Boston at intersection of Routes 3 and 228; take Exit 30 off Route 3, left at bottom of exit and immediate right at Sunoco Station)

Antiques sale, featuring Victoriana and works of art, held approximately every two weeks throughout the year, generally on Monday evenings; specialized sales include Hummels, coins, stamps; estate sales; consignments; property purchased for sales.

Ten percent buyer's premium; mail and telephone bids accepted; certified and traveler's checks accepted; personal checks accepted with established credit, otherwise goods held until check clears; Visa and Master Charge accepted. Full payment on day of sale; pickups within seven days or by arrangement.

Sale announcements mailed; catalogs for all sales; oral appraisals free of charge at the gallery; off premises or written appraisals by arrangement.

Chaffee Auction Gallery

Robert E. Chaffee, Auctioneer
One Auction Place, PO Box 468
Palmer, Massachusetts 01057
(413) 267-9737 or (413) 283-3841
(Exit 8 on Massachusetts Turnpike to Main Street and turn left, over railroad bridge and turn right by supermarket; US Routes 20 & 32)

General sales of estate, antique, farm, and commercial merchandise, held, as availability of material permits, on Wednesdays at 6:00 p.m. during July and August; Saturdays at 10:00 a.m. from September through June; specialized sales of antiques only on first Saturday of May, July and September; consignments; merchandise purchased for sales.

No buyer's premium; no mail and telephone bids accepted; certified or traveler's checks, but no personal checks, accepted; Master Charge and Visa accepted. Full payment and pickups at time of sale.

Written appraisals offered for an hourly fee of $20.00, $50.00 minimum.

Globe Antique Galleries, Inc.

Charles (Bud) Bartlett, Auctioneer
221 Mattakeeset Street (Route 14)
Pembroke, Massachusetts 02359
(617) 294-0987
(From Route 3 south, take Route 53 south, to Route 14 west; right on 14 at
Pembroke Center for about two miles)

Full-time staff includes numismatic specialist; general antiques sale, as well as
rare coin auction, held once a month; specialized sales of coins, Sandwich glass,
Oriental rugs; estate sales; consignments; property purchased for sales.

Ten percent buyer's premium; mail and telephone bids accepted; checks
accepted if credit is established prior to sale; Master Charge and Visa accepted;
purchases held with a 10% deposit; full payment within 30 days; pickups within
10 days.

Sale announcements and catalogs available; written appraisal services
offered for fee of $25.00 an hour.

Ruggi's Relics

Andy Ruggiano, Auctioneer
Shop: 373 Granite Street
Quincy, Massachusetts 02169
(617) 472-3608, (617) 471-9817
Auctions: Woodward School for Girls
1102 Hancock Street
Quincy, Massachusetts 02169

General antiques and collectibles sale held every month or two; specialized sales
of advertising collectibles and paper ephemera; estate sales consignments only;
no property purchased for sales.

No buyer's premium; mail and telephone bids not accepted; certified checks
and traveler's checks accepted; personal checks accepted from established
customers; otherwise, bank verification necessary; no credit cards. Purchases
held with a 50% deposit; full payment and pickups within seven days.

Sale announcements mailed.

Bob's Auction House

Bob Filippone, Auctioneer
295 Hartford Turnpike
Shrewsbury, Massachusetts 01545
(617) 791-6824
(Gallery located on Route 20, near intersection of Route 140. Sales at Knights
of Columbus Hall, two miles east on Route 20—434 South Street, every eight
weeks)

General antiques sale, including furniture, glass, china every Wednesday night
at 6:00 or 6:30 p.m. throughout the year; specialized coin sales held every other
month; estate sales; consignments; property purchased for sales.

Note: Listings are alphabetical by town.

No buyer's premium; mail and telephone bids generally accepted; in-state checks accepted from established customers; out-of-state checks not accepted; no credit cards. Full payment day after sale; pickups within three days.

Sale announcements mailed; written appraisals offered for negotiable fee.

Douglas Galleries
Douglas P. Bilodeau, Auctioneer
Route 5
South Deerfield, Massachusetts 01373
(413) 665-2877
(Exit 24 on Interstate 91, two miles north Route 5)

All types of antique, household, commercial and real estate auctions; headquarters for International Auction School, which trains auctioneers; weekly general sales; specialized sales feature fine art, steins, jewelry; estate sales; consignments; property purchased for sales.

No buyer's premium; mail and telephone bids accepted; checks accepted from established customers only; no credit cards. Full payment day of sale; pickups within three days.

Sale announcements mailed; some catalogs; written and oral appraisals offered for negotiable fee.

Kelley's
Harold Kelley, Auctioneer
North East Trade Center
100 Sylvan Road, Room 618
Woburn, Massachusetts 01801
(617) 935-8090, extension 488
Warehouse: 553 Main Street
Woburn, Massachusetts 01801
(617) 935-3389

Specializing in military collectibles and gun auctions; specialized military sales held at the North East Trade Center or the Sons of Italy Club in Woburn; estate sales, including household merchandise and antiques, held monthly; consignments; property purchased for sales.

No buyer's premium; telephone and mail bids accepted; checks accepted from established customers; no credit cards. Full payment day of sale; pickups as arranged.

Sale announcements and catalogs mailed; written appraisals offered for fee of $100.00.

Auburn Antique and Flea Market   W   XXX
773 Southbridge Street, Route 12
Auburn, Massachusetts 01501
(617-832-5458 or (617) 832-2763
Contact: Harry Kotseas
(Exit 10 off Massachusetts Turnpike or Exit 8 from I-290 or Exit 7 from Route 52, then take Route 12 South about half mile, close to Old Sturbridge Village)

Indoor/outdoor market; 125 sellers indoors, 50 outdoors; began in 1975; open every Sunday, 9:00 a.m. to 5:00 p.m., year round; admission free in summer, 50¢ all other times; space rental: 9' x 9' indoor space with table, chairs and electricity is $12.00 summer, $15.00 winter, $5.00 outdoors; reservations recommended in winter.

Variety of antiques, collectibles and secondhand items, stamps and coins, very little new merchandise or crafts; food; restrooms, parking; nearby motels.

Neponset Drive-In Flea Market   W   XXXX
775 Gallivan Boulevard
Boston, Massachusetts 02122
(617) 282-3501
Contact: Morty Bornstein
(Off Southeast Expressway at Neponset Circle, five minutes south of downtown Boston)

Outdoor market; 400 dealers; began in 1970; open Sunday and Monday holidays, 7:00 a.m. to 5:00 p.m., March through December; admission 50¢ per person, $1.00 per car; reservations recommended.

Variety of antiques, collectibles, secondhand and new merchandise, produce and crafts; food; restrooms; parking; nearby motels.

May's Antique Market   A   XXXX
US Route 20
Brimfield, Massachusetts 01010
(413) 245-9271
Contact: Richard May
(Seven miles east of Old Sturbridge Village)

Outdoor market; 350 dealers; began in 1976; held three times a year, Wednesday noon through Saturday, in May, July and September, call ahead for exact dates; free admission; space rental: $60.00 for a 20' x 24' space for three-and-a-half days; reservations essential.

Only antiques and collectibles; food concessions; restrooms; parking; motels in nearby Sturbridge and Springfield.

Gordon Reid's Famous Antique Flea Market   D   XXX
Auction Acres, Route 20
Brimfield, Massachusetts 01010
(413) 245-3333
Contact: The Gordon Reid Company, 138 Kispert Court, Swansea, Massachusetts 02777, (617) 379-0828
(On Route 20 halfway between Exits 8 and 9 off I-90), near Old Sturbridge Village)

Outdoor market; 750 dealers; began in 1959; held 10:00 p.m. Wednesday through 5:00 p.m. Saturday in May, July and September—call for exact dates; $1.00 admission; space rental: $65.00 for 20' x 24'; reservations essential.

Only antiques and collectibles; food concessions; restrooms; parking; nearby motels.

The Reid Girls Famous Flea Market

A XXXX

Route 20
Brimfield, Massachusetts 01010
(413) 245-3436
Contact: J & J Promotions
(Route 20 Exit off I-95 or I-86, near Old Sturbridge Village)

Outdoor market; 700 dealers; began in 1975; held three times a year, daybreak Friday to 4:00 p.m. Sunday, in May, July and September—call for exact dates; $1.00 admission; space rental: $60.00 and up for 20' x 24' up to 30' x 30'; reservations essential.

Only antiques and collectibles; food concessions; restrooms and washrooms; parking; motels.

Harvard Square Market Place

★ W X

30 Church Street
Cambridge, Massachusetts 02138
(617) 661-7894
Contact: Peter Bennett, 122 Mt. Auburn Street, Cambridge, Massachusetts 02138
(Take Larz Anderson Bridge off Storrow Drive)

Indoor/outdoor market; 50 dealers; began in 1976; open Saturday, March through December, plus six days a week for two weeks before Christmas; free admission; space rental: $10.00, $20.00 or $30.00 for 3' x 3', 3' x 6' or 3' x 8' table; reservations needed.

Equal variety of antiques, collectibles, new and used merchandise, crafts and art; food vendors; restrooms; local parking; nearby motels; auctions once or twice a year.

Bev's Flea Market

W XX

Route 20
Charlton, Massachusetts 01507
(617) 248-7031
Contact: Beverly Cooper-Daoust, PO Box 73, Charlton, Massachusetts 01507
(Twelve miles east of Sturbridge, twenty-three miles east of Brimfield)

Outdoor market; 50 to 75 dealers; began in 1969; open Saturdays, Sundays and holidays, dawn to dusk, mid-April through mid-November; free admission; space rental: $5.00 for 15 square feet; no reservations needed.

Mostly antiques and collectibles, some new and used merchandise and crafts; food; restrooms; parking; nearby motels.

Florence Civic Association Flea Market

A X

North Main and Park Streets
Florence, Massachusetts 01060
(413) 584-7891
Contact: Marian Conant, 139 North Main Street, Florence, Massachusetts 01060, (413) 584-7048
(Take I-91 to Route 9, three miles west of downtown Northhampton)

Outdoor market; 50 sellers; began in 1968; held first Sunday after Memorial Day and last Sunday in September, every year; free admission; space rental: $8 for 18' x 18', reservations needed.

Mostly antiques and collectibles, some secondhand and household items, little new merchandise; home-style luncheons and snacks; on-street parking; restrooms; nearby motels.

Grafton Flea Market ★ W XXX

299 Upton Street
Grafton, Massachusetts 01519
(617) 839-2217
Contact: Harry Peters, Box 206, Grafton, Massachusetts 01519
(I-90 to Route 495 Milford Exit, take 495 to Upton Exit to Route 140)

Outdoor market under trees and indoors; 65 indoor sellers, 100 outdoors; began in 1969; open every Sunday and holiday, year round; 50¢ admission; space rental: $10.00 for 10' x 8' indoors, $5.00 for 20' x 20' outdoors; indoor reservations needed.

Variety of collectibles, antiques, new and used merchandise, and crafts; food concession; restrooms; parking; nearby motels; horse and antique carriage auction held every April.

Ken Miller's Flea Market ★ W XX

Warwick Avenue
Northfield, Massachusetts 01360
(413) 498-2749
Contact: Rosemary Miller, 158 Main, East Northfield, Massachusetts
(Exit 28A off I-91 to Route 2)

Indoor/outdoor market; 100 dealers; began in 1962; open Sundays, 6:00 a.m. to 5:00 p.m.; free admission; space rental: $8.00 outside for 20' x 50'; $10.00 inside for 8' x 8'; reservations needed inside only.

Mostly tools, secondhand merchandise, antiques, collectibles such as coins and postcards, art objects, few crafts; snackbar and food stands; restrooms; parking; antique auctions held.

Mac Sonny's Antique Flea Market W XXX

Main Street, Route 28
North Reading, Massachusetts 01864
(617) 664-8623
Contact: Marilyn C. Paul, 4 Longstreet Road, Peabody, Massachusetts 01960, (617) 532-0606
(Route 28 North from Route 128, or Route 62 East from Route 93 or Route 62 West from Route 1)

Indoor/outdoor market; 150 dealers; began in 1972; open Sunday, 9:00 a.m. to 5:00 p.m., year round; 50¢ admission; space rental: $15.00 for 12' x 12'; reservations needed.

Variety of antiques and collectibles, new and secondhand merchandise, arts and crafts; snack bar; restrooms; parking; nearby motels.

Norton Flea Market Antique Sale W XXX
Route 140
Norton, Massachusetts 02766
(617) 339-8554
Contact: Richard Pino, Smith Street, Norton, Massachusetts 02766, (617) 235-6640
(Mansfield Exit or 7S Exit off I-95)

Outdoor market; 100+ dealers; began in 1970; open Sunday and Monday holidays from third Sunday in April through October; 50¢ admission; space rental: $10.00 for 20' x 20'; no reservations needed.
    Antiques, collectibles and crafts; food; restrooms; parking; nearby motels.

The Red Geranium A X
Route 20, Park Street
Palmer, Massachusetts 01069
(413) 596-6578
Contact: Tess Cambo, 3 Brookmont Drive, Wilbraham, Massachusetts 01095

Outdoor market; 40 to 45 sellers; began in 1975; held in May, July and September, call for exact dates; free admission; space rental: 20' x 20' area for five days is $50.00; reservations needed.
    Mostly antiques and collectibles, some secondhand items and art; food; restrooms; parking; nearby motels.

Antiques Flea Market W XX
Cordage Park
Plymouth, Massachusetts 02360
(617) 837-6665
Contact: Paul Reynolds, 374 Webster Street, Marshfield, Massachusetts, (617) 834-6709
(Route 3 south to North Plymouth Exit 9, turn right on Route 3A)

Indoor market; 75 dealers; began in 1972; open every Sunday, year round; 50¢ admission; space rental: $13.00 for 10' x 13'; reservations needed.
    Only antiques and collectibles; food; restrooms; free parking; nearby motels.

Country Place Antique Flea Market W XXXX
South Shopping Center
South Street
Raynham, Massachusetts 02767
(617) 823-8923
Contact: J.L. Mason, Box 75, West Bridgewater, Massachusetts 02379, (617) 584-4432.
(At Routes 24 and 44)

Indoor market; 325 dealers; began in 1973; open Sundays, September through June; 50¢ admission; space rental: $15.00 per day for 10' x 8'; reservations needed.
    Variety of merchandise including new and used items, produce, antiques, collectibles, art and crafts; food; restrooms; parking; nearby motels.

Revere Drive-In Flea Market   W XXXX
Squire Road
Revere, Massachusetts 02151
(617) 482-5401
Contact: Charles Johnson
(Five minutes from Boston on Route 1 at Route 60)

Outdoor market; 500 dealers; began in 1970; open Sunday and holidays,
7:00 a.m. to 5:00 p.m., March to December; admission 50¢ per person, $1.00 per
car; no reservations needed.

Variety of new merchandise, secondhand items, antiques, collectibles; food;
restrooms; parking; nearby motels.

Historic Todd Farm Flea Market   D X
Route 1A
Rowley, Massachusetts 01969
Contact: F. Payson Todd, 166 Main Street, Rowley, Massachusetts 01969,
(617) 948-3300
(From Route 1 or I-95 to Route 133 to Route 1A)

Indoor market; 50 dealers; began in 1972; open daily, year round; free admission;
space rental: $75.00 to $140.00 per month for 12' x 14'; reservations needed.

Mostly antiques, collectibles and secondhand merchandise; food; restroom;
parking; nearby motels.

Antique Marketplace   W XX
Shetland Industrial Park
29 Congress Street
Salem, Massachusetts 01970
(617) 745-9393
Contact: Edison G. Forbes, 16 Vista Drive, Danvers, Massachusetts 01923,
(617) 774-6677
(Route 1A into Salem to corner of Derby and Congress Streets, turn right to
water's edge, Pickering Wharf)

Indoor market; 65 sellers; began in 1976; open every Sunday, 9:00 a.m. to
5:00 p.m., year round; 25¢ admission; space rental: $12.00 for 100 square feet;
reservations needed.

Mostly antiques and collectibles, some arts and crafts; food; restrooms; free
parking; motel; lots of historic sites to explore.

Sheffield Historical Society Outdoor Antique Market   A XXX
Route 7A
Sheffield, Massachusetts 01257
(413) 229-8388
Contact: Henry Coger, 4503 Rawlins, Dallas, Texas 75219, (214) 559-0677
(One block off Route 7)

Outdoor market; 150 to 200 dealers; began in 1976; held last Saturday in May,
10:00 a.m. to 5:00 p.m.; $2.00 admission; space rental: $30.00 for 16' x 24' in large
field; reservations preferred.

Note: Listings are alphabetical by town.

Only antiques and some collectibles; food; restrooms; free parking; nearby motels.

Wellfleet Drive-In Flea Market   W   XXX
Route 6, Box 811
Wellfleet, Massachusetts 02667
(617) 349-2520
Contact: Eleanor Hazen, Box 811, Wellfleet, Massachusetts 02667
(Route 6 to Wellfleet-Eastham line on Cape Cod)

Outdoor market; 100 to 200 sellers; began in 1975; open Sundays mid-April to October, Wednesdays mid-June to mid-September; admission $1.00 per car; space rental: $5.00 for 18' x 21' area; no reservations needed.

Mostly antiques and new merchandise, some collectibles and secondhand items; food; restrooms; parking; motels and campground nearby.

Saconesset Homestead Flea Market   D   XX
Route 28-A
West Falmouth, Massachusetts 02574
(617) 548-5850
Contact: Dorothea Gifford
(On Route 28 from Bournbridge, take Sippewissett Exit)

Indoor/outdoor market; 60 dealers; began in 1968; open every day from Memorial Day to Columbus Day, 10:00 a.m. to 5:00 p.m.; 50¢ admission per car; reservations needed for space rental.

Mostly antiques, collectibles, variety of secondhand merchandise, produce, crafts, art objects; food; restrooms; parking; nearby motels.

Golden Ball Antiques Flea Market   A   XX
Golden Ball Tavern
662 Boston Post Road
Weston, Massachusetts 02193
(617) 894-1751
Contact: Russell Carrell, Salisbury, Connecticut 06068, (203) 435-9301
(I-90 to Route 128 North, Exit 49 West to Weston)

Outdoor market; 100 sellers; began in 1965; held annually last Saturday in September, 10:00 a.m. to 50:00 p.m.; $2.00 admission; space rental: call for information; reservations needed.

Antiques and collectibles only; food; restrooms; parking lot with free shuttle bus; local hotels.

Weston Flea Market   A   XX
Golden Ball Tavern grounds
Old Boston Post Road, Main Street
Weston, Massachusetts
Contact: Russell Carrell, Salisbury, Connecticut 06068, (203) 435-9301

Outdoor market; 100 dealers; began in 1970; held last Saturday in September; 9:00 a.m. to 5:00 p.m.; $2.00 admission; space rental: $25.00 for 16' x 24'; reservations needed year in advance.

All antiques; food; restrooms; parking; nearby motels.

NEW HAMPSHIRE

Brookline Auction Gallery
Ronald P. Pelletier, William J. Pelletier, Auctioneers
Proctor Hill Road (Route 130)
Brookline, New Hampshire 03033
(603) 673-4474, or (603) 673-4153
(Ten miles from Route 3 in Nashua, New Hampshire)

One or two family-run auctions each month; specialized sales include antique tools, stamps and coins, toys and model trains, Victorian and oak furniture; gallery and grounds rented to other auctioneers in the summer for weekly outdoor tent and evening sales; estate sales; consignments; property purchased for sales.

No buyer's premium; mail and telephone bids accepted with a 25% deposit; cash payment preferred; checks accepted with previously established credit through bank reference or credit check; no credit cards. Full payment day of sale; pickups within three days.

Sale announcements mailed; oral and written appraisals offered for negotiable fee.

Paul McInnis, Inc.
Paul McInnis, Auctioneer
Route 1, Box 97
Hampton Falls, New Hampshire 03844
(603) 926-3982
(Sales held on site or at specified locations—check mailings)

Specializing in the sale of Americana approximately three times a year; estate sales; consignments; property purchased for sales.

No buyer's premium; mail and telephone bids accepted; checks accepted with established credit through bank letter; no credit cards. Full payment and pickups day of sale.

Sale announcements mailed; written appraisals offered for negotiable fee.

Ronald J. Rosenbleeth, Inc.
Ronald J. Rosenbleeth, Auctioneer
Box 296
Henniker, New Hampshire 03247
(603) 428-7686 or (603) 428-7639
(Auctions held in rented ballrooms or hotels during winter; outdoor tent during summer)

Specializing in antiques and decorative arts from the 18th and 19th centuries; sales held throughout New England; monthly sales from November through April held in rented halls; weekly tent sales from May through October; specialized sales feature books, Oriental rugs; estate sales; consignments; merchandise purchased for sales.

No buyer's premium; mail and telephone bids not accepted; checks accepted with two proper forms of ID; no credit cards. Full payment same day of sale; pickups as arranged.

Sale announcements and some catalogs mailed; written appraisals offered for an hourly negotiable fee.

Richard W. Withington, Inc.
Richard W. Withington, Auctioneer
Hillsboro, New Hampshire 03244
(603) 464-3232

Weekly sales held mid-May to beginning of November; monthly sales held on the first of January, February and March at the Sheraton Rolling Green Motor Inn, Andover, Massachusetts; specialized sales of early American furniture and furnishings, Victoriana, dolls, coins; estate sales; consignments; property purchased for sales.

No buyer's premium; mail and telephone bids not accepted; checks accepted from established customers or with approved credit; no credit cards. Full payment and pickups at time of sale.

Sale announcements mailed; oral and written appraisals offered for negotiable fee.

Your Country Auctioneer, Inc.
Richard A. Crane, James Sweet, Auctioneers
RD 2, Box 339
Hillsboro, New Hampshire 03244
(603) 478-5723 or (603) 478-5579
(Sales held on site or at specified locations—check mailings for directions)

Specializes in antique tools; several major auctions held each year throughout the Northeast area; estate, business and farm liquidation sales held Wednesdays and Saturdays during summer; twice a month on Saturdays in winter; consignments; property purchased for sales.

No buyer's premium; mail bids accepted; telephone bids (tool sales only) must be verified in writing before auction; checks accepted with established credit through bank letter and two proper forms of ID; no credit cards. Full payment day of sale; pickups generally day of sale.

Sale announcements mailed; oral and written appraisals offered for negotiable fee.

Hooksett Trading Post & Auction Gallery

Philip Fitanides, Auctioneer
1407 Hooksett Road
Hooksett, New Hampshire 03106
(603) 627-4969
(Interstate 93 North to Exit 9 North—Route 3 North, three miles)

Weekly sales held Saturdays at 6:00 p.m., featuring variety of antiques and collectibles, including furniture, glass, porcelain, Civil War and military collectibles; specialized sales, feature stamps, dolls, toys and trains, and paper collectibles, including rare postcards, tobacco and baseball cards; estate sales; consignments; property purchased for sales.

No buyer's premium; mail and telephone bids accepted; checks accepted with proper ID; Visa and Master Charge accepted; full payment at time of sale; pickups within three days.

Sale announcements and catalogs of specialized sales mailed; written appraisals offered for an hourly fee of $25.00.

George H. LaBarre Galleries

PO Box 27
Hudson, New Hampshire 03051
(603) 882-2411

Mail auctions only—specializing in Americana collectibles; featuring political campaign items, advertising collectibles, World's Fair memorabilia, radio premiums, medals, early photography, and paper ephemera, including old stocks and bonds, financial documents, Revolutionary War and military or historical documents, autographs; approximately two sales—of 2,000 to 3,000 lots—held annually; some merchandise from estates; almost all property purchased outright; small number of consignments.

No buyer's premium; mail bids only; no telephone bids accepted; checks accepted, though merchandise may be held until check clears; no credit cards accepted. Full payment within 10 days upon receipt of invoice; merchandise sent immediately upon receipt of payment.

Catalogs for three sales available for fee of $3.00; specialized price catalog of old stocks and bonds and financial documents sent free of charge upon request; oral or written appraisals offered for negotiable fee.

Voice of Antiquity (V.O.A. Auctions)

Bruce T. Amadon, Auctioneer
111 North Street
Keene, New Hampshire 03431
(603) 352-0362
(At Gilbo Mountain Auction Barn—Route 12, in East Westmoreland, New Hampshire, north of Keene)

General antiques sale, featuring Victorian goods, held every three weeks in East Westmoreland; specialized sales include country store and advertising collectibles; estate sales; consignments; merchandise purchased for sales.

No buyer's premium; telephone bids accepted; checks accepted at the discretion of the company; credit cards not accepted. Full payment day of sale; pickups within three days.

Sale announcements mailed; written appraisals offered for negotiable fee.

Young Fine Arts Gallery

George M. Young, Jr., Auctioneer
56 Market Street
Portsmouth, New Hampshire 03801
(603) 436-8773
(From Interstate Route 95, take Exit 7 to Market Street, downtown
Portsmouth; municipal parking at rear)

Monthly auctions held featuring antique paintings and prints; specialized sales include books, autographs, historical documents; some mail auctions; consignments; merchandise purchased for sales.

Ten percent buyer's premium; mail and telephone bids accepted; checks accepted if buyer establishes credit one week before sale through bank reference; American Express, Visa, Master Charge accepted. Full payment day of auction; pickups within five days.

Sale announcements and catalogs mailed; written appraisals offered for minimum fee of $40.00.

Ed's Country Auction House

Edward G. Stevens, Auctioneer
Main Street
RR #1, Box 20
Rindge, New Hampshire 03461
(603) 899-6654
(Off Routes 119 and 202)

Primarily estate sales, held every Saturday, year-long, except December, at auction house or on site; featuring household and business goods, antiques and collectibles; specialized sales of stamps, coins, antique tools, jewelry; consignments; merchandise purchased for sales.

No buyer's premium; mail and telephone bids not accepted; checks accepted only after credit check; make application for courtesy card; no credit cards; purchases held with a 20% deposit; full payment within seven days; pickups generally within seven days.

Sale announcements mailed; written appraisals offered for negotiable fee.

Wayne Mock, Inc.

Wayne Mock, Auctioneer
Route 16, Box 37
Tamworth, New Hampshire 03886
(603) 323-8057
(Between West Ossipee and Chocorua, New Hampshire)

Specializing in antique and estate sales; nationally advertised sales held approximately every two to three weeks, April through November; specialized sales feature advertising and country store collectibles, rare books, ephemera, art glass, antique tools; estate sales; predominantly consigned merchandise; property seldom purchased for sales.

No buyer's premium; mail and telephone bids accepted with check sent in advance; traveler's checks or cashier's checks accepted; personal checks accepted with previously established credit or bank letter of credit; no credit cards. Full payment day of sale; pickups as arranged.

Sale announcements and some catalogs mailed; written appraisals offered for an hourly fee of $20.00 to $40.00.

Outdoor Antique Market   W XXXX
Route 122
Amherst, New Hampshire 03031
(617) 641-0600
Contact: Carlson Management, 51R Dudley Street, Arlington, Massachusetts 02174, (617) 641-0600
(Highway 101 West from Route 3, to Route 122)

Outdoor market; 200+ dealers; began in 1960; open Sundays, mid-April to November, 6:00 a.m. to 3:00 p.m.; 75¢ admission; space rental: $10.00 per day; no reservations needed.

Antiques only; food; restrooms; parking; nearby motels.

Cornett's Farm Flea Market   W XX
RFD 1
Contoocook, New Hampshire 03229
(603) 746-3960
Contact: Bertha Cornett
(Penacook Road, off I-89, west of Concord)

Outdoor market; 70 dealers; began in 1972; open Sundays, May 1 to October 15; free admission; space rental: $5.00; no reservations needed.

Mostly collectibles and antiques, some secondhand merchandise; lunch wagon; restroom; parking; nearby motels.

Grand View Farm Antique and Flea Market   W XXX
Junction of Route 28 and 28 By-Pass
Derry, New Hampshire 03038
(603) 432-2326
Contact: Albert Gidley, PO Box 443, Salem, New Hampshire 03079
(Take Derry Exit off I-93, go about three miles)

Indoor/outdoor market; 75 to 180 dealers; began in 1968; open Sunday, 7:00 a.m. to 4:00 p.m., year round; 50¢ admission; space rental: summer $6.00 outside, $8.00 inside, winter, $12.00; reservations needed.

Variety of antiques, collectibles, new and used merchandise, art and crafts; food; restrooms; parking; nearby motels.

Note: Listings are alphabetical by town.

Hollis Flea Market   W XXX
Route 122, Silver Lake Road
Hollis, New Hampshire 03049
(603) 882-6134
Contact: Gilbert and Alice Prieto, Hollis Country Store, RFD 3, Milford,
New Hampshire 03055
(Exit 6 off Route 3, left to Route 130, right onto 122)

Outdoor market; 150 to 175 dealers; began in 1974; open Sundays and holidays,
7:00 a.m. to dusk, April through October; free admission; space rental: $7.00 for
16' x 22'; reservations recommended.

   Mostly antiques, collectibles and secondhand merchandise, some crafts and
produce; food; restrooms; parking; nearby motels.

Don Holt's Antique Show and Sale   W XX
14 Melendy Road
Hudson, New Hampshire 03051
(603) 434-7398
Contact: Don Holt, PO Box 115, Derry, New Hampshire 03038
(I-93 to Route 111 to Hudson)

Indoor market; 100 dealers; began in 1966; open Sundays, 8:00 a.m. to 3:00 p.m.,
October to April; 50¢ admission; space rental: $20.00 for 3' x 8' table;
reservations needed.

   Only antiques and collectibles; food; restrooms; parking; nearby motels.

VOA Flea Market   ★ d X
Route 12 South
Keene, New Hampshire 03431
Contact: Debbie Devurger, Marboro Street, Keene, New Hampshire,
(603) 352-7286

Indoor market; 26 dealers; began in 1978; open six days a week, 10:00 a.m. to
5:00 p.m., closed Monday; free admission; space rental: $15.00 a week for 8'; no
reservations needed.

   Mostly antiques, secondhand merchandise, collectibles, some crafts and
produce; nearby restaurants and motels; no restrooms; parking; auctions every
Friday night and Saturday.

Burlwood Antique Market   W X
US Route 3
Meredith, New Hampshire 03253
(603) 279-6387
Contact: Tom and Nan Lindsey, RFD 2, Meredith, New Hampshire 03253
(From I-93 take Exit 23 to Route 104, east to Route 3)

Indoor/outdoor market; 35 dealers; began in 1964; open Friday, Saturday and
Sunday, June to Labor Day, Saturday and Sunday, Labor Day to October 15,
10:00 a.m. to 5:00 p.m.; free admission; space rental: $6.00 per day to $14.00 for
three days for 12' x 20' covered space; reservations needed.

Only antiques and collectibles; food available nearby; restrooms; parking; nearby motels and rooms in main building.

Colonial Plaza Flea Market   D   XX
Route 12A
West Lebanon, New Hampshire 03784
(603) 298-8132
Contact: Norman and Linda Patch
(Exit 20 off I-89)

Indoor/outdoor market; 80 to 90 dealers; began in 1976; open indoors, 9:00 a.m. to 5:00 p.m. daily, outdoors, last Sunday in April to last Sunday in October; free admission; space rental: $13.50 per week for 8' x 10'; reservations advised.

Mostly antiques and collectibles, some secondhand and new merchandise; food and nearby restaurant; restrooms; parking; nearby motels.

Knotty Pine Flea Market   D   XXX
Route 10
West Swanzey, New Hampshire 03469
(603) 352-5252
Contact: Joan Pappas
(Five miles south of Keene, New Hampshire)

Indoor market; 108 dealers; began in 1977; open seven days a week, 9:00 a.m. to 5:00 p.m.; free admission; space rental: $70.00 per month for 4' x 8'; reservations needed.

Mostly antiques and collectibles, some secondhand merchandise; restrooms; parking; nearby motels.

RHODE ISLAND

Jack Martone
Jack Martone, Auctioneer
290 Pulaski Street
Coventry, Rhode Island 02816
(401) 826-1564
(95 North from Connecticut or 95 South from Massachusetts to Route 117 West; then four and three-tenths miles to auction)

General antiques sale held twice monthly; estate sales; consignments; property purchased for sales.

No buyer's premium; mail and telephone bids accepted; checks from established customers accepted; no credit cards. Purchases held with a 10% deposit; full payment and pickups within two days.

Sale announcements and catalogs mailed.

Henry W. Kunz

Henry Kunz, Auctioneer
PO Box 561
Newport, Rhode Island 02840
(401) 846-4951
(Sales held at Hotel Viking Convention Center in Newport)

Yearly sales from private consignments held in the spring and fall; featuring antique furniture, Oriental rugs, paintings, jewelry, and averaging about 400 lots; estate sales; predominantly consignments; limited amount of property purchased for sales.

No buyer's premium; telephone bids accepted; checks under $500.00, local checks, or checks from established customers, accepted; no credit cards. Full payment at time of sale; pickups generally same day.

Sale announcements mailed; catalogs for all sales; oral appraisals offered free of charge.

Old World Auction Galleries

Broderick Macari, Auctioneer
725 Branch Avenue
Providence, Rhode Island 02903
(401) 272-5491 or (401) 274-4729
(Intersection of Route 146 and Branch Avenue)

General antiques sale held twice a month, including furniture, glassware, silver, and collectibles; specialized sales, held approximately three times a year, feature Oriental rugs, paintings, jewelry; estate sales; consignments; property purchased for sales.

Ten percent buyer's premium; mail and telephone bids accepted with references; checks accepted with two proper forms of ID; no credit cards at present. Full payment at time of sale; pickups as arranged.

Sale announcements and catalogs mailed; written appraisals offered for fee of $25.00 or 2% value of item; oral appraisals offered free of charge.

Fortunate Finds Book Store & William D. Longo Associates

William D. Longo, Mildred E. Longo, Auctioneers
14 West Natick Road
Warwick, Rhode Island 02886
(401) 737-8160
(Off Route 195)

Ten to 12 auctions held yearly by mail; specialized book auctions yearly; estate sales; consignments; merchandise purchased for sales.

No buyer's premium; mail and telephone bids accepted; checks with proper ID accepted; no credit cards; full payment upon receipt of bill; pickups for estate auctions within 24 hours.

Sale announcements mailed; catalogs for book sales only; written appraisals offered for negotiable fee, at $25.00 minimum.

Ashaway Flea Market ★ W X
Route 3
Ashaway, Rhode Island 02804
Contact: John Marley, 2 Juniper Drive, Ashaway, Rhode Island 02804, (401) 377-4947
(Exit 1 off I-95 to Route 3 S, near Mystic Seaport)

Indoor/outdoor market; five dealers; began in 1968; open every Saturday and Sunday, 9:00 a.m. to 5:00 p.m., year round; free admission; space rental: $6.00 daily, $10.00 weekend for 12' x 12'; no reservations needed.

Lots of secondhand merchandise, antiques and collectibles; stamps and coins; restaurant; restrooms; free parking; motels nearby; annual auction.

General Stanton Inn W XX
Routes 1 and 1A
Charlestown, Rhode Island
(401) 364-8888
Contact: Angelo Falcone
(From New York take I-95 to Exit 76 to Route 1, or continue on I-95 to Highway 78 twelve miles north on Highway 1)

Outdoor market; 100 dealers; began in 1963; open Sunday and holidays; May to October; free admission; space rental: $10.00 per car space; no reservations needed.

All antiques and collectibles; food; restrooms; parking; nearby motels.

Americana Flea Market ★ W XXXX
Rocky Hill Fairgrounds
East Greenwich, Rhode Island 62852
(401) 884-6020
Contact: Christie Mercurio, Box 175, North Kingstown, Rhode Island 62852
(Exit 7 off I-95, take Route 2 for five hundred yards)

Indoor/outdoor market; 400 to 500 dealers; began in 1958; open Sunday, April 15 to December 15, 5:00 a.m. to 5:00 p.m.; free admission space rental: $8.00 per car; no reservations needed.

Mostly collectibles and new merchandise, plus antiques, some produce and secondhand items; six food vendors; restrooms; free parking; nearby motels; eight antique auctions per year on Friday evenings.

American Flea Market W XXXX
Narragansett Race Track
Pawtucket, Rhode Island
(401) 726-0081
Contact: Carmen Carcerri, 300 Twin River Road, Lincoln, Rhode Island 02865
(Call for directions)

Indoor/outdoor market; 400 dealers; began in 1978; open Saturday, Sunday and holidays, 8:00 a.m. to 5:00 p.m., year round; 50¢ admission; space rental: varying prices for 8' x 10' spaces, booths and rooms; reservations advisable.

Variety of antiques, collectibles, new and used merchandise, produce, arts and crafts; food; restrooms; parking; nearby motels.

Big Top Flea Market   W   XXX
120 Manton Avenue
Providence, Rhode Island 02909
(401) 274-0060
(Exit 16 off I-95, then take Route 10 North to Olneyville Exit, three blocks to former Atlantic Mills)

Indoor market; 100+ dealers; began in 1976; open Saturday 9:00 a.m. to 4:00 p.m., Sunday 9:00 a.m. to 5:00 p.m., September through April; 50¢ admission; space rental: $8.00 per day, $15.00 per weekend for 10' x 8'; reservations needed.

Mostly secondhand and household items, some new merchandise, antiques and collectibles; snack bar; restrooms; parking; nearby motels.

Route 177 Flea Market   W   XX
1560 Bulgarmarsh Road (Route 177)
Tiverton, Rhode Island 02878
(401) 624-9354
Contact: Tom Ouellette, 8 Campion Avenue, Tiverton, Rhode Island 02878, (401) 624-9354
(About fifteen miles north of Newport, nine miles south of Fall River, Massachusetts)

Indoor/outdoor market; 75 to 100 sellers depending on season; began in 1967; open every Saturday, Sunday and holiday, all day, year round; free admission; space rental: $8.00 for 12' x 12'; reservations recommended for inside space.

Mostly new and secondhand merchandise, few antiques or collectibles; food; restrooms; free parking; motels nearby.

VERMONT

Paul W. Lawton & Son
PO Box 551
Brattleboro, Vermont 05301
(802) 254-8969
Sales: Rollerdome
Putney Road
Brattleboro, Vermont 05301

Sales featuring both general merchandise and antiques held every Wednesday at 6:30 p.m.; antiques (approximately 50% furniture) and collectibles featured at sale held once each month; estate sales; consignments; property purchased for sales.

No buyer's premium; mail and telephone bids accepted; traveler's checks accepted; personal checks accepted with proper ID and bank letter of credit; no credit cards. Full payment at time of sale; pickups within one week.

Antiques sales; announcements mailed; written appraisals offered for an hourly fee of $30.00; oral appraisals offered free of charge for item brought into gallery.

J. P. Bittner

J. P. Bittner, Auctioneer
RFD 3
Putney, Vermont 05346
(802) 387-4234
(On site or in rented halls in Brattleboro area)

Specializing in antique tool collections; four to six annual sales including a regularly-scheduled antique tool auction the first Saturday after Easter; estate sales; consignments; property purchased for sales.

No buyer's premium; mail and telephone bids not accepted; checks from established customers accepted; no credit cards. Full payment and pickups day of sale.

Sale announcements and illustrated catalogs of tool sales mailed.

Outdoor Flea Market   W   XX

Route 7
Charlotte, Vermont 05445
Contact: Larry Lavalette, c/o Bostwick Farm, Shelburne, Vermont 05482,
(802) 985-3702
(Half mile south of Junction F5)

Outdoor market; 65 to 85 dealers; began in 1971; open Saturdays, Sundays and holidays, May through October or November (depending on weather), 7:30 a.m. to 5:30 or 6:00 p.m.; free admission; space rental: $2.00 on Saturday, $3.00 on holiday, $5.00 on Sunday; no reservations needed.

Mostly secondhand or household items, some new merchandise, antiques, collectibles, crafts, little produce, art; food; restrooms; parking; nearby motels.

Manchester Flea Market   W   X

Route 11 and 30
Manchester Center, Vermont 05255
(802) 362-1631
Contact: John Wessner
(East three miles on Route 11 and 30 from the junction of Route 7)

Outdoor market; 40 dealers; began in 1970; open Saturdays, May through October; free admission; space rental; $5.00 for car length; reservations needed.

Mostly antiques and collectibles, very little new merchandise, produce in season; food; restrooms; parking; nearby motels.

Note: Listings are alphabetical by town.

MID-ATLANTIC

The six Mid-Atlantic states, plus Washington, DC, have more antique auctions and flea markets than any other region of the country. Much of the activity centers around New York City or within a two-hours' drive from the city; in Lancaster, Bucks, Delaware and Philadelphia Counties in Pennsylvania; and in Hunterdon, Somerset and Mercer Counties in New Jersey— along the border of Pennsylvania. The only state in the Mid-Atlantic region which does not rate high in antiquing activity is West Virginia, although this is changing. It is understandable because of the relatively sparse population and the absence of any large urban centers.

Manhattan is not only the indisputable art auction center of the United States; with recent record sales of antiques and fine arts, it is conceivably the auction capital of the world. Many prestigious houses are located in the heart of the city's museum and gallery district on the upper East Side. Sotheby Parke Bernet was founded in London in 1744 and is probably the leading auction firm in the world, with a massive network of 40 offices in 19 countries, staffed by over 200 experts in many fields. Christie, Manson & Wood International, founded in London in 1766, and Phillips Auctioneers, founded in London in 1796, are also international houses specializing in antiques and fine arts. New York also has the broadest range of *specialized* auction sales—including rare books and photographica at Swann Galleries, Japanese netsuke at Sotheby's, pre-Columbian artifacts at Manhattan Galleries, paintings by the old masters at William Doyle, Turkish carpets at Edelmann Galleries and porcelains at Lubin Galleries.

While New York City dominates the international auction market, attracting bidders and making headlines throughout the world, it is not so strongly represented by flea markets, although a few offer buys to collectors who can't or don't want to leave the city on weekends. New York State, however, is studded with country auctions and flea markets. A great number of these attractions are located within a relatively short distance of Manhattan, in nearby Westchester and Rockland Counties, and further north in Dutchess County and the Catskill region.

Southeastern Pennsylvania, and the adjacent western section of New Jersey, has an astonishing number of flea markets and auctions, and the count grows each year. I cannot imagine an antiquing trip there lasting less than a week—preferably with a weekend at *each* end. Lancaster and Bucks Counties are undoubtedly among the richest sources in the whole country for interesting Americana and folk art (19th and 20th century). Both counties have been centers for crafts since colonial days, and artisans of English or German heritage produced ironwares, copper and tin wares, pewter, grandfather clocks, country furniture and vast quantities of quilts and coverlets right up to the beginning of the 20th century. Especially noteworthy are *frakturs* (illustrated documents of the Pennsylvania Germans), decorated boxes, embroidered samplers, painted furniture, and carved three-dimensional objects in the form of every living and imaginary being. It constantly amazes me and other travelers to Pennsylvania how the lode of so-called country or "primitive" antiques seems to be inexhaustible. Several Pennsylvania auction houses, notably Pennypacker's in Reading, hold regular sales of folk art, where lots attract avid collectors from all over the country.

Most of the flea markets in Pennsylvania are also in the southeastern part of the state. Just one small area, reached via Exit 21 off the Pennsylvania Turnpike, has more than a weekend's worth of fleas. This is Adamstown/Denver. Renninger's, an indoor-outdoor market, is one of the largest in the country. Like most big flea markets, it is almost overwhelming on the first visit—but that can be the greatest thrill for the collector. Hummer's and the market at the Black Angus are also along the main drag in Adamstown, and Shupp's Grove—one of the most charming places to find yourself at 5:30 on a summer morning, if it doesn't rain—is another large flea market about two miles from Renninger's, on 897.

The Mid-Atlantic region enjoys the distinction of being the home of two of the oldest auction houses in the country—Samuel T. Freeman of Philadephia, which has been under direct father-to-son ownership for over 175 years, and C. G. Sloan & Company in Washington, DC, which was established in 1853. It would be interesting to speculate, when attending a sale at such an old house, what item on the block might have been there before—perhaps a hundred years ago.

Baltimore is an excellent area for auctions and flea markets. Early 19th-century furniture, some of it crafted in the Baltimore area, fine silver and rare books are all specialties of the area. Several flea markets are found off the Beltway which encircles Baltimore. Baltimore itself has become a pioneer among cities—leading the way in urban restoration and preservation—and it is perhaps this dedication to the past which has given the impetus to new auctions and flea markets.

What draws many collectors to any area are the extra attractions—the scenery, the regional food specialties, the weather, or the opportunities for viewing collections of interesting old things in museums and restorations. The Mid-Atlantic is rich in such attractions. New York City has many specialized museums with permanent and temporary exhibitions of everything from Judaica to African masks, from weathervanes to comic book art. An excellent restored village, just a ferry boat ride away, is Richmondtown on Staten Island, near the site of two flea markets.

Pennsylvania has a score of intriguing museums and sites—including Old Economy Village in Ambridge, the Hershey Museum in Hershey, Hopewell Village National Historic Site, the fabulous Pennsylvania Farm Museum of Landis Valley in Lancaster, the Mercer Museum in Doylestown, and many many museums in Philadelphia itself.

In Delaware, the most famous museum of decorative arts in the whole country is found: the Henry Francis Du Pont Winterthur Museum near Wilmington. Here over 100 rooms of furniture and decorative arts give the visitor a glimpse of American life from 1640 to about 1840. Washington, DC is worth extra visiting time because of the vast holdings at the Smithsonian, where everything from coffee roasters to First Ladies' gowns are exhibited in various divisions and buildings of the institution. In Wheaton, Maryland, is the National Capital

Trolley Museum, where you can see antique streetcars. An 18th-century millhouse is open to the public in Westminster, Maryland, and in Lutherville is the Fire Museum of Maryland.

For traveling collectors, some of the highspots in New Jersey include the imaginative display of soup bowls, ladles and tureens at the Campbell Museum near Camden; Edison State Park at Menlo Park; and the excellent collection of decorative arts and Oriental objects at the Newark Museum. One of the biggest draws in West Virginia is the Appalachian Arts & Crafts Festival at Beckley, held every fall. The Master Armorer's House in historic Harpers Ferry is a restoration of interest to collectors of guns. Huntington, the site of a large flea market, has a display of interest to collectors at the Cabell-Wayne Historical Society. The glass industry has been very important in West Virginia for a long time, and glassmaking displays and tours are found in Milton, at Blenko Glass Company, Viking Glass Company in Huntington and New Martinsville; Fenton Art Glass Company in Williamstown, Erskine Glass & Manufacturing Company in Wellsburg and West Virginia Glass Specialty in Weston.

A final bonus is given collectors by the quality antique shows held in a region. The Mid-Atlantic region has several of national importance: the "Annapolis Heritage Antiques Show" in Annapolis, Maryland; the "Winter Antiques Show" in New York City; the "Bucks County Conservancy Show" in Jamison, Pennsylvania; the "Hunt Valley Antiques Show and Sale" in Hunt Valley, Maryland; the "York Antiques Show and Sale" in York, Pennsylvania; the "Lancaster Antiques Show and Sale" in Lancaster; Philadelphia's "University Hospital Show", and the twice-a-year "Eastern States Antiques Fair" at White Plains, New York.

For listings and reviews of auctions, flea markets, and for dates of the big shows, check *The New York-Pennsylvania Collector, Antique Trader, Joel Sater's Antique and Auction News, Antique Monthly, Collectors News, Spinning Wheel, The Magazine ANTIQUES*, and local newspapers.

DELAWARE

Wilson's Auction Sales, Inc.
Dave Wilson, Auctioneer
Route 113, PO Box 84
Lincoln, Delaware 19960
(302) 422-3454
(Two miles south of Milford, Delaware)

Sales held every Saturday at 1:00 p.m., featuring variety of antique merchandise, particularly early 20th century oak furniture and general merchandise, including glassware, used furniture and appliances; specialized sales of coins, Delaware books and items; estate sales; consignments only; no property purchased for sales.

No buyer's premium; mail and telephone bids accepted after personal inspection of merchandise; checks accepted with bank letter of credit; traveler's checks accepted; no credit cards. Full payment day of sale; pickups within five days.

Sale announcements mailed; written appraisals offered for negotiable fee.

Iron Hill Auction
Joe and Larry Baines
1115 Elkton Road
Newark, Delaware 19711
(302) 453-9138
(On Route 279 one mile north of Elkton Road Exit off Interstate 95)

General auction, including antiques and collectibles, and general merchandise—held every Friday evening at 6:30 p.m.specialized sales feature glass, coins, and guns; estate sales; consignments; property purchased for sales.

No buyer's premium; mail and telephone bids accepted; Delaware and Maryland checks only, accepted with two forms of ID; no credit cards. Full payment day of sale; pickups within two days.

Sale announcements mailed; written appraisals offered for fee dependent on value of item.

Sebul's Antiques and Auction Galleries
Walter Sebul and Associates, Auctioneers
775 South DuPont Highway
New Castle, Delaware 19720
(302) 834-0500

Specializing in estate liquidations; weekly sales on Monday at 4:00 p.m. featuring household goods, antiques and collectibles, Victorian furniture, Depression glass, pottery, china, brass, Russian icons and figurines, lamps, pens, clocks; consignments; property purchased for sales.

No buyer's premium; mail and telephone bids accepted; checks accepted with bank letter of credit; Master Charge and Visa accepted. Full payment at time of sale; pickups within 48 hours.

Sale announcements mailed; some catalogs; oral and written appraisals offered for negotiable fee.

Spence's Bazaar ★ XX
South and New Streets
Dover, Delaware 19901
(302) 734-3441
Contact: Gregory Spence, PO Box 338, Dover, Delaware 19901
(Two blocks west of Kent General Hospital)

Indoor/outdoor market; 100 dealers; began in 1933; open Tuesdays and Fridays, 8:00 a.m. to 9:00 p.m., year round; free admission; space rental: outside $7.00 per table with 65 square feet; no reservations needed.

Mostly secondhand and household items, some antiques and collectibles; food; restrooms; parking; nearby motels; auctions Tuesday and Friday at 5:30.

Shore's Largest Flea Market W XX
US-13 Dual at Route 9E
Laurel, Delaware 19956
(302) 875-2478
Contact: George Purnell, RD 1, Box 19B, Laurel, Delaware 19956
(Fifteen miles north of Salisbury, Maryland, thirty miles south of Dover)

Outdoor market with shade trees; 60 dealers; began in 1977; open Saturday and Sunday, year round; free admission; space rental: $5.00 for 10' x 10', larger trailer spaces $7.50 to $10.00; no reservations needed.

Mostly collectibles and secondhand items, some antiques; food; restrooms; parking; nearby motels.

Sebul's Antiques and Galleries ★ W XX
775 South DuPont Highway
New Castle, Delaware 19720
(302) 834-0500
Contact: Walter Sebul
(On US 13 four miles south of Greater Wilmington)

Indoor/outdoor market; 75 dealers; began in 1977; open Saturday, Sunday and Monday, year round; free admission; space rental: $12.00 per day for 15' x 30'; reservations needed.

Variety of antiques and collectibles, arts and crafts; food; restrooms; parking; nearby motels; tailgate auctions Mondays, 4:00 p.m. to midnight.

DISTRICT OF COLUMBIA

Adam A. Weschler & Son, Inc.
905-9 E Street NW
Washington, DC 20004
(202) 628-1281

A fourth generation family-owned business. General household merchandise sales held each Tuesday year-round; three-day estate sales held each December, February, May and September; consignments only; no property purchased for sales.

Note: Listings are alphabetical by town.

Ten percent buyer's premium; mail and telephone bids accepted (telephone bids require written confirmation prior to sale); local checks with proper ID accepted; out-of-town checks with letter of credit from bank. Deposit necessary to hold purchases; full payment within three days; most pickups within three days.

Sale announcements mailed; catalogs available for estate sales; written appraisals offered for fee of $75.00 per hour with $100.00 minimum; $500.00 per diem.

C. C. Sloan & Co.

Russell E. Burke, III, John P. Gallogly, Stephanie A. Kenyon, Auctioneers
715 Thirteenth Street NW
Washington, DC 20005
(202) 628-1468 or (800) 424-5122

(A few blocks from the White House)

Founded in 1853; five major auctions held every other month from September through June, lasting four days, (generally Thursday through Sunday) near the end of the month; pre-sale exhibitions held one week before sale for five days, from Thursday to Monday; major sales feature American and European paintings and furniture from 17th through 19th centuries, silver, porcelain, jewelry, and glassware; regular sales, featuring less valuable items, held approximately every two weeks on weekends throughout the year, including summer months; representative office in Baltimore handles appraisals and consignments; estate sales; consignments only; no property purchased for sales.

Ten percent buyer's premium; mail and telephone bids accepted; checks accepted with driver's license; Visa and Master Charge accepted. Full payment and pickups within five working days (same day preferred).

Sale announcements and catalogs for five major sales mailed; catalog required to enter sales; dollar charge to enter pre-sale exhibition goes to non-profit organization; written appraisals at gallery for $50.00 for first piece, $15.00 for each piece after up to four written appraisals at home for $100.00 per hour plus $50.00 per hour travel expenses; oral appraisals at gallery free of charge if considering consignment; at-home oral appraisals for negotiable fee.

Georgetown Flea Market   W X

Wisconsin Avenue & S Street
Washington, DC
(202) 333-0289
Contact: Michael Vezo, 2700 Q Street, NW, Suite 231, Washington DC 20007
(Take Wisconsin Avenue Exit off Capital Beltway, Route 495)

Outdoor market; 30 dealers; began in 1972; open Sunday, 9:00 a.m. to 6:00 p.m., March to November; free admission; space rental: $15.00 for 8' x 15', $20.00 for 8' x 22'; no reservations needed.

Mostly furniture, variety of secondhand merchandise, antiques, collectibles and art objects; food; restrooms; parking; nearby motels.

MARYLAND

Alex Cooper's Auctioneers, Inc.

Joseph Cooper, Bruce Levinson, Auctioneers
345 North Charles Street
Baltimore, Maryland 21201
(301) 752-4868

Estate and antique sales held approximately every four to five weeks throughout the year—finer quality items, such as period furniture, Chinese works of art, jewelry, coins, silver, featured on one floor of gallery; consignments; property purchased for sales.

No buyer's premium; mail and telephone bids accepted with certified check; certified checks or checks with bank letter of credit accepted; no credit cards. Full payment at time of sale; pickups within five days; pickups for on-site estate sales merchandise must be made immediately.

Mailing list for sale announcements; written appraisals offered for negotiable fee; oral appraisals free of charge for items auctioned by gallery.

Harris Auction Galleries, Inc.

Barr Harris, Auctioneer
875 North Howard Street
Baltimore, Maryland 21201
(301) 728-7040

Sale of estates, antiques and household goods, held every other Wednesday at 10:30 p.m.; specialized catalog sales, featuring books and autographs, paper Americana, photographica, and graphics, held 10 times a year; consignments; limited amount of property purchased for sales.

Ten percent buyer's premium; mail and telephone bids accepted; checks accepted with proper ID; Master Charge and Visa accepted. Purchases held with a 10% deposit; full payment within 48 hours; pickups within one week.

Catalogs of specialized sales available individually or by subscription; written appraisals offered for an hourly fee of $50.00 minimum of two hours.

Sam W. Pattison & Company, Inc.

Sam W. Pattison Rea, Auctioneer
407 North Howard Street
Baltimore, Maryland 21201
(301) 685-1320

Founded in 1893; weekly sales held Thursdays at 10:30 a.m.; featuring estates, household goods, antiques and collectibles, (including furniture, glassware, paintings); consignments only; no property purchased for sales.

No buyer's premium; mail and telephone bids accepted from known customers; traveler's checks, certified checks or local checks with proper ID accepted; no out-of-state checks or credit cards accepted. Full payment and pickups at time of sale.

Oral or written appraisals offered for an hourly fee of $50.00.

Bel Air Auction Gallery, Inc.
William H. Amoss, Auctioneer
13 Ellendale Street
Bel Air, Maryland 21014
(301) 838-3000
(Thirty-five miles north of Baltimore)

Sales of household items and antiques held every Friday at 6:30 p.m.; monthly antiques sale, including oak furniture, silverware, jewelry, and collectibles, held on a Saturday at 6:30 p.m.; specialized sales of coins; estate sales; consignments; property seldom purchased for sales.

No buyer's premium; mail and telephone bids not accepted; checks accepted with proper ID; no credit cards. Full payment night of sale; pickups within one week.

Oral or written appraisals offered for negotiable fee.

American Auction Gallery
C.P. Jacobs, Jr., Auctioneer
Route 70 East
Frederick, Maryland 21701
(301) 662-3530
(Three miles east of Frederick)

Specializing in antiques and collectibles; 12 sales yearly on the last Sunday of every month at 11:00 a.m., including early oak, walnut, mahogany and country furniture, glass, clocks; estate sales; consignments; property purchased for sales.

No buyer's premium; mail and telephone bids accepted; checks accepted with proper ID or bank letter of reference; American Express, Master Charge, and Visa accepted. Full payment day of sale; pickups within one week.

Sale announcements and catalogs mailed; oral or written appraisals offered for negotiable fee.

Mary L. Martin
7915 Putney Terrace
Glen Burnie, Maryland 21061
(301) 768-0412
(Just off Route 301)

A mail auction house specializing in rare postcards; six mail auctions held each year featuring antique postcards; annual rarity auction held in December; estate sales; consignments; property purchased for sales.

No buyer's premium; mail and telephone bids accepted; checks accepted; no credit cards. No deposit necessary to hold purchase; full payment within five days.

Sale announcements and catalogs mailed; oral and written appraisals offered for fee of 10% of total value of item.

Town & Country Auctions
Houck Avenue
Hampstead, Maryland 21074
(301) 239-7776

Sales held first and third Friday of each month, with general estate merchandise, household goods, farm produce, antiques and collectibles; consignments only; no property purchased for sales.

No buyer's premium; mail and telephone bids accepted from known customers; traveler's checks, certified checks, or local checks with proper ID accepted; no out-of-state checks or credit cards. Payment at time of sale; pickups when convenient.

Oral or written appraisals offered for negotiable fee.

Col. James Auction Galleries
9160 B Bursa Road
Laurel, Maryland 20810
(301) 490-2828 or (301) 953-9492

Sales held every Friday at 7:00 p.m., featuring household goods, used furniture, collectibles, particularly glassware; estate sales; consignments; property purchased for sales.

No buyer's premium; mail and telephone bids accepted; checks accepted with proper ID; Master Charge and Visa accepted. Full payment day of sale; pickups within two days.

Oral and written appraisals offered for negotiable fee.

R. C. Burkheimer & Associates; North East Auction Gallerie
R. C. Burkheimer, Auctioneer
US Route 40
North East, Maryland 21901
(301) 287-5588; (302) 575-1881
(One mile east of Route 272 and US Route 40)

Sales held every Tuesday at 6:30 p.m. year-round, and the first Saturday of every month except January; specialized sales feature fine art, Oriental rugs, stamps, coins, and glass; estate sales; consignments only; no property purchased for sales.

No buyer's premium; mail and telephone bids accepted; checks accepted with two forms of ID; no credit cards. Purchases held with 25% deposit; full payment in 24 hours; pickups within two days.

Sale announcements mailed; some catalogs; written appraisal services offered for fee of $35.00.

Rogers Auction Gallery
Barry and Jay Rogers, Auctioneers
12101 Nebel Street
Rockville, Maryland 20852
(301) 881-5544
(Off Randolph Road, one traffic light from Rockville Pike; seventeen miles from Washington, DC)

Sales feature antiques; some close-outs and bankruptcy sales; general sales held every Friday at 7:30 p.m.; four specialized sales held yearly, featuring Oriental art, antique and estate jewelry, fine art, and period furniture; estate sales; consignments; merchandise purchased for sales.

No buyer's premium; in-state checks accepted with proper ID; no out-of-state checks accepted; Master Charge and Visa accepted. Purchased held with 25% deposit; full payment within 48 hours; pickups within one week.

Catalogs for the four specialized collectors sales only; oral and written appraisals offered for fee of $50.00 and up.

Edmondson Drive-In Flea Market   W   XXXX
6000 Baltimore National Pike
Baltimore, Maryland 21228
(301) 747-5425
Contact: George Brehm
(Baltimore Beltway—695—to Route 40 west)

Outdoor market; 300 to 350 dealers; began in 1968; open every Saturday and Sunday, 9:00 a.m. to 4:00 p.m., March till mid November; 25¢ admission; space rental; $4.00 for 20' x 20'; no reservations needed.

Variety of collectibles, crafts, antiques, new and secondhand merchandise; food; restrooms; parking; nearby motels.

Farmers Market Flea Market   W   XXXX
9919 Pulaski Highway (Highway 40)
Baltimore, Maryland 21220
(301) 687-5505
Contact: Ken Hill
(Exit 35 off Baltimore Beltway—695—on US Route 40 East)

Indoor/outdoor market; 200+ dealers; began in 1967; open every Saturday and Sunday, 7:00 a.m. to 5:00 p.m., April through November; free admission; space rental: $6.00 for 10' x 20'; no reservations needed.

Lots of antiques and collectibles, some crafts, secondhand and new merchandise; food; restrooms; parking; nearby motels.

North Point Drive-In Flea Market   W   XXX
4001 North Point Boulevard
Baltimore, Maryland 21234
(301) 477-5084
Contact: Frank Durkee, 5436 Harford Road, Baltimore, Maryland 21214,
(301) 426-4410
(Exit 41 off Baltimore Beltway—695—to Cove Road)

Outdoor market; 100 to 200 dealers; began in 1970; open every Saturday and Sunday, 8:00 a.m. to 4:00 p.m., April to October; 25¢ admission; space rental: $6.00 a day; no reservations needed.

Mostly secondhand and household items, some antiques, collectibles and new merchandise; food; restrooms; parking; nearby motels.

Farmer's Flea Market   W   XX
7155 Wisconsin Avenue
Bethesda, Maryland 20015
(202) 966-3303
Contact: Jim Bonfils, 4539 Alton Place NW, Washington DC 20016
(Washington Beltway—495—to Wisconsin Avenue Exit)

Outdoor market; 50 to 75 dealers; began in 1974; open every Sunday, 9:00 a.m. to 6:00 p.m., March through October; free admission; space rental; $13.00 for 10' x 6', $23.00 for 20' x 20'; no reservations needed.

Mostly antiques and collectibles; food; restrooms; nearby motels.

Bill Bentley's Antiques Show Mart   D   X
10854 York Road
Cockeysville, Maryland 21030
(301) 667-9184
Contact: Bill Bentley
(Exit 17 off I-83, turn left at York Road)

Indoor market; 48 dealers; began in 1970; open Wednesday through Saturday, 10:00 a.m. to 5:00 p.m., Sunday 12:00 to 6:00 p.m.; free admission; space rental: call for information; no reservations needed.

Mostly antiques and collectibles, some secondhand merchandise; food; restrooms; parking; nearby motels.

The New Columbia Flea Market   W   XX
The Mall, Inc.
Columbia, Maryland 21044
(301) 995-0118
Contact: Bellman Promotions, Inc., PO Box 1113, Columbia, Maryland 21044
(Route 29 between Baltimore and Washington, DC)

Outdoor market under cover; 100 dealers; open every Sunday, 10:00 a.m. to 5:00 p.m.; April through October; free admission; space rental: $25.00 for two parking stalls; reservations helpful.

Mostly antiques, some collectibles; food; restrooms; parking; nearby motels.

Bonnie Brae Flea Market   W   XX
1301 Pulaski Highway
Edgewood, Maryland 21040
(301) 676-9812
Contact: L.M. Merritt, 1003 Magnolia Road, Joppa, Maryland 21085,
(301) 679-2210
(Route 40, twenty miles northeast of Baltimore)

Note: Listings are alphabetical by town.

Indoor/outdoor market; 50 to 60 dealers; began in 1974; open every Saturday and Sunday, 9:00 a.m. to 5:00 p.m.; free admission; space rental: $5.00 for 12' x 10'; no reservations needed.

Mostly antiques and collectibles, some secondhand and new merchandise; food; restrooms; parking; nearby motels.

Odd & Ends Shops
Carroll & South Streets
Frederick, Maryland 21701
(301) 662-5388
Contact: Dennis Dugan

Indoor market; 23 dealers; began in 1970; open Friday, Saturday, Sunday, from 9:00 a.m. to 6:00 p.m.; free admission; space rental: $45.00 to $55.00 a month for 8' x 8' to 12' x 20' booth; reservations needed.

Mostly books and magazines, antiques and collectibles, some secondhand merchandise and art objects; no food available; restrooms; parking; nearby motels.

Rhodside Flea Market   ★ W XX
Route 15 and Biggs Ford Road
Frederick, Maryland 21701
(301) 898-7502
Contact: James L. Bryan, 10905 Harney Road, Emmitsburg, Maryland 21727
(Four miles north of Frederick)

Indoor/outdoor market; 40 to 60 dealers; began in 1974; open Friday, Saturday and Sunday, April through November; free admission; space rental: $6.00 Saturday, $8.00 Sunday, 12' x 25'; no reservations needed.

Variety of antiques, collectibles and secondhand merchandise; food; restrooms; parking; nearby motels; monthly auctions.

Collectors East Coast Paradise   ★ W X
13350 Baltimore Boulevard
Laurel, Maryland 20810
(301) 953-3842
Contact: Maletta Humphrey, 8510 Spruce Hill Drive, Laurel, Maryland 20810, (301) 776-6704
(On Route 1 just south of Laurel)

Outdoor market; 25 dealers; began in 1980; open Saturday and Sunday, 8:00 a.m. to 5:00 p.m., April 1 through October; free admission; space rental: $10 for unlimited outdoor space, or 10' x 10' under cover; no reservations needed.

Mostly antiques and collectibles, some secondhand items; food; restrooms; parking; nearby motels; occasional auctions.

The Golden Door Shows Flea Market   D   XX

Convention Hall
4001 Philadelphia
Ocean City, Maryland 21842
Contact: The Golden Door Shows, 214 East Market Street, Laurel, Delaware
19956, (302) 875-5084
(Route 13 to Route 113 to Route 90, turn right at Ocean Highway)

Outdoor market (under cover in rain); 40 to 60 dealers; began in 1970; open
Easter Saturday to mid October; free admission; space rental: $10.00 for about
three car spaces; reservations taken.

Mostly antiques and collectibles, some new and secondhand merchandise;
restaurants nearby; restrooms; parking; nearby motels.

Hunter's Sale Barn, Inc.   ★ W XX

Box 427, Route 276
Rising Sun, Maryland 21917
(301) 658-6400
Contact: Norman Hunter
(Exit 7 off I-95, north on 275, turn right on 276)

Indoor/outdoor market; 70 dealers; began in 1974; open Monday, 3:00 p.m. to
9:30 p.m., year round; free admission; space rental: $10.00 for 8' x 16' with two
tables; reservations recommended.

Lots of new and used merchandise, few antiques or collectibles, some
produce; food; restrooms; parking; nearby motels; livestock, produce and
household auctions.

Carroll County Farm Museum Flea Market   A XXX

500 South Center Street
Westminster, Maryland 21157
(301) 848-7775
Contact: Cindy Hofferberth

Outdoor market; 90 to 120 dealers; began in 1968; open first Sunday in June,
second Saturday in August; free admission; space rental: $10.00 for 12' x 12';
reservations needed.

Mostly secondhand and household items, some crafts, collectibles and
antiques; food; restrooms; free parking; nearby motels.

NEW JERSEY

Asbury Galleries
700 Main Street
Asbury Park, New Jersey 07712
(201) 776-7373 or (201) 775-9423

Specializing in sale of estates and antiques; sales held once or twice each month—usually on Sunday at 12:30 p.m.—featuring large or unusual decorative items, jewelry, fine art, general antiques and collectibles; specialized sales include clocks, stamps and coins, bric-a-brac, early American furniture; estate sales; consignments; property purchased for sales.

Ten percent buyer's premium; mail and telephone bids accepted; checks accepted from established customers; otherwise, merchandise held until check clears; no credit cards. Purchases held with a 25% deposit; full payment in seven days; most pickups within 10 days.

Sale announcements and some catalogs mailed; written appraisals offered for negotiable fee, at $500.00 minimum charge; free oral appraisal of items brought to gallery; items sold by the gallery appraised free.

Farrant Associates, Auctioneers
Colonel Donn Fagans, Auctioneer
PO Box 1815
Cherry Hill, New Jersey 08034
(609) 983-8841 or (609) 983-8809
(Sales held on site or in rented halls—check mailings for directions)

Specializing in estate and antique sales as merchandise becomes available; all sales held on Saturdays, but no fixed schedule; specialized sales of Hummels and firearms; consignments only; no property purchased for sales.

No buyer's premium; mail and telephone bids accepted; checks accepted with previously established credit through bank reference and three forms of ID; no credit cards. Purchases held with a 10% deposit; full payment and pickups within five days.

Sale announcements mailed; written appraisals offered for an hourly fee of $30.00.

Berman's Auction and Appraisal Service
(also known as Berman's Barn)
Edward Berman, Auctioneer
75 Bassett Highway
Dover, New Jersey 07801
(201) 361-3110
(Five minutes off Route 80)

A family business; sales held three times a month on middle Wednesday at 6:00 p.m. and second and fourth Saturdays at 7:30 p.m.; specialized sales of American cut glass, art glass, art pottery, steins and Orientalia; estate sales; consignments; property purchased for sale.

No buyer's premium; mail and telephone bids accepted; checks accepted if credit has been established five days before sale; otherwise, merchandise held until check clears; no credit cards. Full payment same day; pickups by arrangement.

Sale announcements mailed; catalogs for all Saturday sales; oral and written appraisals offered for variable fee.

Elmer Auction
Bob Brooks, Auctioneer
Broad Street
Elmer, New Jersey 08318
(609) 358-3222
(Route 40 twenty miles east of Delaware Memorial Bridge)

Specializing in farm, business, personal property and estate liquidations; general sales held every Friday; antique sales held monthly; estate sales; consignments; merchandise purchased for sales.

No buyer's premium; mail and telephone bids accepted; checks accepted only with bank letter of credit; no credit cards. Full payment due at sale; pickups within two days.

Sale announcements mailed; both written and oral appraisals offered for hourly fee ranging from $10.00 to $20.00.

Jerry Krawitz
Jerry Krawitz, Auctioneer
11 Paterson Avenue
Midland Park, New Jersey 07432
(201) 652-6424 or (914) 469-2359
(From George Washington Bridge, take Route 4 to Route 208 to Goffle Road, one and three-tenths miles north to gallery)

Sales held approximately twice monthly, featuring antiques, china, bric-a-brac, collectibles; specialized sales include books, old tools; estate sales; consignments; property purchased for sales.

No buyer's premium; mail and telephone bids not accepted; checks accepted with proper ID; no credit cards. Full payment day of sale; pickups as arranged.

Written appraisals offered for negotiable fee; oral opinions free of charge.

Lincoln Galleries
(Division of Lincoln Mayflower Storage Warehouse)
Reg. T. Blauvelt, Jr., Reg. T. Blauvelt, III, F. J. Schramm, Auctioneers
225 Scotland Road
Orange, New Jersey 07050
(201) 677-2000
(Off Route 280, between Main Street and Central Avenue)

Specializing in estate sales; sales held the middle of each month; exhibition and inspection on Monday; furniture, paintings and rugs on Tuesday; silver, porcelain and jewelry on Wednesday; mainly consignments; merchandise seldom purchased for sales.

Ten percent buyer's premium; telephone bids accepted; local checks accepted with proper ID; no credit cards. Purchases held with a 25% deposit; full payment and pickups by Friday, the week of the sale.

Sale announcements mailed; written appraisals offered for hourly fee.

Sterling Auction Gallery

Gerald and Celia Sterling, Auctioneers
62 North Second Avenue
Raritan, New Jersey
(201) 685-9565, (201) 464-4047
(From Somerville Traffic Circle, Route 202 South to second light—Raritan Exit—follow "Auction" signs)

General antiques sale held once a month, featuring silver and jewelry, as well as works of art and collectibles; specialized sales include photography and dolls; merchandise purchased outright or on consignment basis; estate sales.

No buyer's premium; telephone bids accepted; checks accepted with ID, or merchandise held until check clears; Visa and Master Charge accepted. Purchases held with a 50% deposit; full payment in two days; pickups within one week.

Sale announcements mailed; comprehensive catalog for all sales; written appraisal services offered for hourly fee of $70.00.

S & S Auction

Stephen Shivers III, Auctioneer
Repaupo Road
Repaupo, New Jersey 08085
(609) 467-3778
(Interstate 295—Exit 14)

Primarily a wholesale furniture house, features antiques to the trade; private collectors welcome; general sales held year-round, every other Tuesday from 10:00 a.m. to 9:00 p.m.; all merchandise handled on consignment basis; estate sales; consignments.

No buyer's premium; mail and telephone bids not accepted; traveler's or certified checks accepted; personal checks accepted only after several months purchasing with firm establishes credit; no credit cards. Payment in full due day of sale; pickups within two days.

Appraisals, both written and oral, available for hourly rate of $50.00 plus expenses, $200.00 minimum.

The Village Commons ★ W X

1490 Rahway Avenue
Avenel, New Jersey 07001
(201) 574-8599
Contact: Bernadette or Linda Pirone, 678 Sheridan Avenue, Plainfield, New Jersey 07060, (201) 754-8132
(Exit 12 off New Jersey Turnpike, follow West Carteret signs to Roosevelt Avenue [becomes Randolph], turn left at end)

Outdoor market; 35 to 40 dealers; began in 1968; open Saturday and Sunday, April to November; indoor shops open Wednesday, Saturday and Sunday, year round; free admission; space rental: $4.00 per table; no reservations needed.

Lots of secondhand merchandise, antiques and collectibles, some new merchandise, crafts and produce; food; restrooms; parking; nearby Holiday Inn; occasional auctions.

Bayonne Moose Lodge #2   W   X

21 West Twenty-fifth Street
Bayonne, New Jersey 07002
(201) 858-8403
Contact: Shirley Stiles, 70 Evergreen, Bayonne, New Jersey 07002
(Near Jersey City)

Indoor market; 25 to 30 dealers; began in 1980; open Thursday, 6:00 p.m. to 11:00 p.m.; free admission; space rental: $7.00 for 6' table; reservations needed.

Variety of new and used merchandise, antiques, collectibles, art objects, and produce; snack bar; restrooms; parking; nearby motels.

Five Acres Flea Market   ★   W   X

Route 46, RD
Belvidere, New Jersey 07823
(201) 475-2572
Contact: Totsy Phillips, PO Box 295, Belvidere, New Jersey 07823
(Route 80 to Exit 12, turn left and go south seven miles to Route 46, left at light, market on right)

Outdoor market; 50 dealers; began in 1970; open Saturday and Sunday, April through November; free admission; space rental: $5.00 for 15' x 15' space; no reservations needed.

Largely household and secondhand items, some antiques and collectibles, and new merchandise; lunch counter with restrooms in auction gallery next door; parking; nearby motels; auctions every other Sunday in July and August, every Sunday September through June, tailgate auctions every Wednesday evening.

Flea Market at Berlin Farmers Market   W   XXXX

41 Clementon Road
Berlin, New Jersey 08009
(609) 767-1284
Contact: Stanley Giberson
(Right off Route 30 [White Horse Pike] behind Lucien's Old Tavern)

Outdoor market; 400 dealers; began in 1960; flea market open Saturday and Sunday, 8:00 a.m. to 5:00 p.m., (entire market open later) year round when weather permits; free admission; space rental: $10.00 and up for 12' x 20'; reservations needed.

Lots of produce, secondhand and household merchandise; food; restrooms; parking; nearby motels.   *Note: Listings are alphabetical by town.*

Peddler's Market   W XXX
835 Roosevelt Avenue
Carteret, New Jersey 07008
(201) 541-1877
(Adjacent to Exit 12 of New Jersey Turnpike)

Indoor/outdoor market; 140 dealers; began in 1979; open Friday noon to 9:00
p.m.; Saturday 10:00 a.m. to 9:00 p.m., Sunday 11:00 a.m. to 7:00 p.m.; free
admission; space rental: $220.00 to $290.00 a month for paneled booth, 10' x 10'
to 12' x 12'; reservations needed.

   Mostly new merchandise, some collectibles, arts, crafts and antiques, lots of
produce outside; food concession; restrooms; free parking; nearby motel.

Route 130 Flea Mart and Antiques   W X
Cinnaminson Mall
Cinnaminson, New Jersey 08177
(609) 786-8730
Contact: Frank Cottrell, 120 Cornell Road, Audubon, New Jersey 08106,
(609) 546-6624
(Call for directions)

Indoor market; 12 dealers (room for 100); began in 1980; open Thursday and
Friday, 5:00 p.m. to 10:00 p.m., Saturday 3:00 p.m. to 10:00 p.m.; free admission;
space rental: $25.00 to $35.00 per week for 120 square feet; reservations
recommended.

   Arts, crafts, new merchandise, some antiques and collectibles; pizza and ice
cream; restrooms; parking; nearby motels.

Boys' Club Flea Market   M XX
802 Clifton Avenue
Clifton, New Jersey 07013
(201) 773-2697
Contact: Mary Oakley
(Call for directions)

Indoor market; 85 to 110 dealers; began in 1972; open third Sunday of each
month, September through May except big holidays; admission 25¢; space
rental: $10.00 for 8' table; reservations needed.

   Mostly new merchandise, lots of antiques, collectibles and secondhand items;
food concession; restrooms; parking; nearby motels.

Columbus Farmer's Market   W XXXX
Route 206
Columbus, New Jersey 08022
(609) 267-0400
Contact: Elwood Hammitt, Route 206, Columbus, New Jersey 08022, (609)
267-0051
(Take Exit 7 off New Jersey Turnpike to Route 206)

Outdoor market; 1,500 dealers; began in 1915; open Thursday, 7:30 a.m. to 3:00 p.m., year round, Sundays, April to December; free admission; space rental: $7.00 for 11' x 30'; no reservations needed.

Mostly new and secondhand merchandise, some antiques; food; restrooms; parking; nearby motels.

Bailey Terminal Enterprises Inc.   W XXX
Route 47 and Mauricetown Road
Dorchester, New Jersey 08316
(609) 825-0277
Contact: Mr. or Mrs. Bailey
(Route 47 south from Millville)

Outdoor market; 120 dealers; began in 1970; open every Saturday, Sunday and holiday; free admission; space rental: $4.00, $5.00 and $6.00 for various sized tables; no reservations needed.

Lots of secondhand and new merchandise, antiques and collectibles; food; restrooms; parking; nearby motels.

Dover Market Place   ★ W XX
67 Bassett Highway
Dover, New Jersey 07801
(201) 361-1350 or (201) 328-9207
Contact: John D. Stefano
(Exit 34A off Route 80, right at second traffic light, first right)

Indoor/outdoor market; 100 dealers; began in 1979; open Saturday and Sunday, 10:00 a.m. to 6:00 p.m., year round; free admission; space rental: $3.00 to $5.00 per day outdoors, $10.00 to $15.00 indoors; no reservations needed.

Mostly new and secondhand merchandise, some antiques and collectibles; food; restrooms; parking; nearby motels; auctions Wednesdays and Saturdays.

Methodist Church Antique and Flea Market   X
150 Dunellen Avenue
Dunellen, New Jersey 08812
(201) 968-4347
Contact: Jean Bush, 14 Blue Hills Terrace, Green Brook, New Jersey 08812, (201) 968-2794
(Route 22 to Washington Avenue, left onto Dunellen)

Indoor market; 50 dealers; began in 1968; held second Saturday in January, February and March, 10:00 a.m. to 4:30 p.m.; free admission; space rental: $8.00 for 3' x 6' table; reservations needed.

Mostly antiques, collectibles, and secondhand merchandise items; food; restrooms; on street parking; nearby motels.

Route 18 International Indoor Market ★ W XXXX
290 Route 18
East Brunswick, New Jersey 08816
Contact: Joanne or Hannah, 290 Route 18, East Brunswick, New Jersey, (201) 254-5080
(Take New Jersey Turnpike, Exit 9, then Route 18 east a quarter mile)

Indoor market; 500 dealers; began in 1977; open Friday, 12:00 p.m. to 9:00 p.m., Saturday, 10:00 a.m. to 9:00 p.m., and Sunday, 10:00 a.m. to 7:00 p.m.; free admission; space rental: $200.00 a month for 10' x 12'; reservations needed.

Mostly clothing, variety of secondhand merchandise, produce, antiques, collectibles, art objects; food; restrooms; parking; nearby motels; general auction held monthly.

Brick Church Flea Market W XX
540 Main Street
East Orange, New Jersey 07018
(201) 674-2226
Contact: John or Tony
(I-280, near Parkway)

Indoor market; 80 to 100 dealers; began in 1975; open Thursday, Friday and Saturday, 10:30 a.m. to 6:00 p.m.; free admission; space rental: $30.00 for table, $40.00 for booth, for all three days; reservations needed.

Variety of secondhand merchandise, antiques, collectibles, crafts, art objects; snack bar; restrooms; parking; nearby motels.

New Dover United Methodist Church Flea Market W XX
690 New Dover Road
Edison, New Jersey 08817
(201) 381-9478
Contact: Church Office
(Garden State Parkway to Exit 131, turn right onto Wood Avenue, two lights to New Dover Road)

Indoor/outdoor market; 75 dealers; began in 1971; open Tuesdays, 7:00 a.m. to 2:00 p.m., year round; free admission; space rental: $6.00 for 4' x 12' table; no reservations needed.

Mostly secondhand and household items, some new merchandise, few antiques or collectibles; lunch counter; restrooms; parking; nearby motels.

Englishtown Auction Sales W XXXX
90 Wilson Avenue
Englishtown, New Jersey 07726
(201) 446-6431
Contact: Steve Sobechko
(Exit 9 off New Jersey Turnpike, take Route 18 East and follow signs)

Indoor/outdoor market; 500+ dealers; began in 1929; open Saturday, dawn to 5:00 p.m., Sunday, 9:00 a.m. to 5:00 p.m., year round; free admission; space rental: $4.00 and up for area starting at 3' x 8'; no reservations needed.

Variety of antiques, collectibles, new and secondhand items, produce, arts and crafts; food; restrooms; parking; nearby motels.

Collingwood Park Auction Market ★ W XXXX
Junction of State Highways 33 & 34
Farmingdale, New Jersey 07727
(201) 938-7941
Contact: Ernest or Roland Schneider, RFD 2, Box 154, Farmingdale, New Jersey 07727
(New Jersey Turnpike, south on Garden State Parkway at Woodbridge South Exit, Freehold Exit West on 33)

Indoor/outdoor market; 300 to 500 dealers; began in 1957; open Friday noon to 10:00 p.m., Saturday 10:00 a.m. to 10:00 p.m., Sunday 10:00 a.m. to 7:00 p.m.; free admission; space rental: varies; no reservations needed.

Variety of new and secondhand merchandise, antiques, collectibles, lots of produce, crafts; food stands; restrooms; parking; nearby motels; year round auctions inside, auction off truck outside in spring and fall.

Flemington Fair Flea Market ★ W XX
Highway 31
Flemington, New Jersey 08822
(201) 782-7326
Contact: Melissa Kuhl, RD 1, Box 486, Flemington, New Jersey 08822
(Between Trenton and Somerville)

Indoor/outdoor market; 75 dealers; began in 1979; open Wednesdays 9:00 a.m. to 3:00 p.m., Sundays, 7:00 a.m. to 4:00 p.m., April through November; free admission; space rental: $3.00 to $6.00 for 10' x 10', $1.00 for 3' x 8' table; no reservations needed.

Mostly new and secondhand merchandise, a lot of antiques and collectibles; food; restrooms; parking; nearby motels; auctions every Sunday.

Haledon P.A.L. Flea Market M XX
Roe Street
Haledon, New Jersey 07508
Contact: Fleamarketeers, Glenn and Joan Hasbrouck, 3 Al-Lyn Court, Haledon, New Jersey 07508, (201) 595-5041
(Garden State Parkway to Route 3 West to Route 46 West to Union Avenue to end. Follow signs for market)

Indoor market; 85 dealers; began in 1969; open second Sunday of each month October to April; 10:00 a.m. to 5:00 p.m.; admission 25¢; space rental: $10.00 for table and 8' x 6' area; reservations needed.

Mostly new merchandise, lots of antiques and collectibles, some secondhand items or crafts; food; restrooms; parking.

Howell Antique Village and Flea Market   W   XXXX
2215 Highway 9, PO Box 564
Howell, New Jersey 07731
(201) 367-1105
Contact: Bobbi Horowitz
(Exit 11 off New Jersey Turnpike, go south on Highway 9 about thirty miles)

Indoor/outdoor market; 350 dealers; began in 1972; open Saturday and Sunday,
8:00 a.m. to 3:00 p.m., year round; free admission; space rental: $5.00 for first
table, $2.00 for each additional; no reservations needed.
   Mostly new and secondhand merchandise, some antiques, collectibles, crafts
and produce; two snack bars; restrooms; parking; nearby motels.

Rova Farm Flea Market   W   XXX
Route 571
Jackson, New Jersey 08527
(201) 254-5080
Contact: Ted Leonard or Helen Zill, RD3 Box 17, Jackson, New Jersey 08527
(Four and one-quarter miles from Great Adventure Sapphire Park)

Indoor/outdoor market; 150 dealers; began in 1980; open Tuesdays, 7:15 a.m. to
3:00 or 4:00 p.m.; free admission; space rental: $5.00 for 20'; no reservations
needed.
   Variety of new and used merchandise; produce, antiques, collectibles, crafts
and art objects; snack bar and restaurant; restrooms; parking.

Lafayette Antiques Festival   A   XXX
Route 15, Village Green
Lafayette, New Jersey
Contact: Irene Stella, Box 482, Paramus, New Jersey 07652, (201) 262-3063
(I-80 to Route 15, ten miles north)

Outdoor market; 125 dealers; began in 1976; held first Saturday and Sunday of
August, 10:00 a.m. to 6:00 p.m.; admission $1.25; reservations needed.
   Lots of antiques and collectibles, some crafts and new merchandise; food,
including the firemen's "Beef and Beer Bust"; street parking; nearby motels.

Golden Nugget Antique Flea Market   W   XXXX
Route 29
Lambertville, New Jersey 08560
(609) 397-0811
Contact: Daniel Brenna, 340 Hamilton Avenue, Trenton, New Jersey 08609,
(609) 393-2857
(Six miles north of Exit 1 off I-95)

Indoor/outdoor market; 240 dealers; began in 1965; open Saturday 8:00 a.m. to
5:00 p.m., Sunday 6:30 a.m. to 6:00 p.m., year round; free admission; space
rental: $3.00 Saturday, $7.00 Sunday per table; reservations needed.
   Mostly antiques and collectibles, especially period furniture, some new and
used merchandise; food; restrooms; free parking; nearby motels.

Governor's Antique Market ★ W XX
Route 179 North
Lambertville, New Jersey 08530
(609) 397-2010
Contact: E.M. Cad, PO Box 242, Lambertville, New Jersey 08530
(One and one-half miles north of Lambertville on Route 179)

Indoor/outdoor market; 75 to 100 dealers; began in 1976; open every Saturday and Sunday, 8:00 a.m. to 5:00 p.m.; free admission; space rental: $25.00 per week for a 12' x 14' booth; reservations needed.

Mostly antiques and collectibles, some jewelry, and arts and crafts; food; restrooms; parking; eight motels nearby; occasional auctions.

Lambertville Antique Flea Market W XXX
Route 29
Lambertville, New Jersey 08530
(609) 397-0456
Contact: Beverly C. Errhalt, RD 2, Box 199, Lambertville, New Jersey 08530
(From Somerville, New Jersey, take Route 202 South to Flemington, then pick up Route 179 to Lambertville)

Indoor/outdoor market; 135 dealers; began in 1965; open every Saturday and Sunday, year round; free admission; space rental; outside is $4.00 Saturday, $10.00 Sunday, inside is $17.00 to $80.00; reservations needed for Sundays.

Only quality antiques and collectibles; snack bar; restrooms; parking; nearby motels.

Manville Fire Company #2 M X
Washington Avenue & Thirteenth Avenue
Manville, New Jersey 08835
Contact: Gary Jeremiah, 123 South Eighth Avenue, Manville, New Jersey
(201) 526-2519
(Near New Brunswick and Somerville)

Indoor/outdoor market; 20 to 25 dealers; began in 1979; open first Sunday of the month, 9:00 a.m. to 5:00 p.m., year round; free admission; space rental: $5.00 outside, $7.00 inside for 3' x 8'; no reservations needed.

Mostly hardware and toys, variety of new and used merchandise, crafts, some antiques and collectibles; food; restrooms; parking; nearby motels.

Meyersville Grange Flea Market W X
Meyersville Road
Meyersville, New Jersey
(201) 647-97271
Contact: Larry Lindberg, Middle Valley Road, RD 3, Long Valley, New Jersey 07853, (201) 832-7422)
(Between Chatham and New Providence)

Note: Listings are alphabetical by town.

Indoor market; 30 dealers; began in 1977; open Sunday, 9:00 a.m. to 5:00 p.m., October to May; free admission; space rental: $7.00 to $15.00 for 8'; reservations needed.

Variety of furniture, house plants, antiques, collectibles; food; restroom; parking.

Neshanic Flea Market   W   XX
Neshanic Station
Neshanic, New Jersey 08853
(201) 369-3634
Contact: Mary Stone, Elm Street, Neshanic, New Jersey 08853

Outdoor market; 100 dealers; began in 1970; open Saturday, 8:00 a.m. to 6:00 p.m., and Sunday 6:00 a.m. to 6:00 p.m.; free admission; space rental: $7.00 for table, $6.00 for 4' x 7' space; reservations needed.

Variety of new and used merchandise, antiques, collectibles, crafts, art objects, and produce; restrooms; parking, nearby motels.

US No. 1 Flea & Antiques   W   XXXX
Routes 1 and 18
New Brunswick, New Jersey
(201) 846-0900
Contact: Ray Travis
(Quarter mile off New Jersey Turnpike, Exit 9)

Indoor/outdoor market; 500 dealers; began in 1975; open Friday, 12:00 p.m. to 9:00 p.m., Saturday, 10:00 a.m. to 9:00 p.m., and Sunday, 10:00 a.m. to 7:30 p.m.; free admission Friday and Saturday, $1.00 a carload admission Sunday; space rental: $20.00 daily, $65.00 weekly; no reservations needed.

Mostly new and used merchandise, produce, collectibles, crafts, few antiques; food stands; restrooms; parking; nearby motels.

New Egypt Auction and Farmers Market   ★ W   XXXX
Route 537
New Egypt, New Jersey 08533
(609) 758-2082
Contact: Esler G. Heller
(Six miles west of Great Adventure Amusement Park)

Indoor/outdoor market; 150 to 250 dealers; began in 1959; open Wednesday, Saturday and Sunday, 8:00 a.m. to 4:00 p.m., year round; free admission; space rental: $3.00 Wednesday, $4.00 Sunday, free Saturday; reservations needed for Sundays.

Equal amounts of secondhand items, antiques, collectibles and new merchandise; snack bar; restrooms; parking; nearby motels; tailgate auctions on Saturday, Antiques and Collectibles auction on Sunday.

Pennsauken Flea Market ★ W XXXX
Routes 73 and 130 Intersection
Pennsauken, New Jersey 08110
(609) 662-9838
Contact: Larry Sternberg, (609) 662-7800

Indoor/outdoor market; 500 to 600 dealers; began in 1965; open Friday, Saturday and Sunday, 8:00 a.m. to 5:00 p.m.; free admission; space rental; outside $3.00 to $7.50, inside $25.00 weekly; reservations needed.

Mostly new merchandise, some secondhand, antiques and collectibles; food; restrooms; parking; nearby motels; auctions of new merchandise only.

Friday Flea Market W XX
Italian American Club
Rahway, New Jersey
(201) 634-3936
Contact: Mary Lima, 138 Demorest Avenue, Avenel, New Jersey 07001
(Off St. George Avenue; near New Brunswick, New Jersey)

Indoor/outdoor market; 70 dealers; began in 1975; open Friday, 8:00 a.m. to 3:00 p.m.; free admission; space rental: $5.50 for 8'; no reservations needed.

Variety of secondhand merchandise, antiques, collectibles, few crafts; food; restrooms; parking.

William Spencer's Flea Market M XX
Creek Road
Rancocas Woods, New Jersey 08073
(609) 235-1830
Contact: Mr. Houser
(Off I-295 or Mount Holly Exit off New Jersey Turnpike, about fifteen miles east of Camden/Philadelphia)

Outdoor market; 100 dealers; began about 1960; open second Sunday of each month, May through November; free admission; space rental: varies; reservations needed.

Antiques and collectibles only; food; restrooms; parking; nearby motels.

Rodia's Flea Market W X
Bayview and Route 9
Rio Grande, New Jersey 08242
(609) 465-9767
Contact: Vincent Rodia, Steel Road, Cape May Court House, New Jersey 08210, (609) 465-5662
(On Route 9 between North Wildwood and Wildwood Boulevards)

Indoor/outdoor market; 25 to 30 dealers; began in 1968; open Saturday and Sunday, 9:00 a.m. to 6:00 p.m., year round; free admission; space rental; $6.00 per day outside, $15.00 per weekend for 8' x 20' inside; reservations needed for inside space.

Mostly antiques, collectibles and secondhand items, some new merchandise; food; restrooms; parking; nearby motels.

Rockaway Indoor Market ★ W XX
350 Route 46
Rockaway, New Jersey 07866
(201) 627-1030
Contact: A. S. Ferraiuolo or E. Ginsberg
(Call for directions)

Indoor market; 54 dealers; began in 1979; open Friday 11:00 a.m. to 9:00 p.m., Saturday 9:30 a.m. to 9:00 p.m., Sunday 10:00 a.m. to 6:00 p.m.; free admission; space rental: $2.50 a month; no reservations needed.

Variety of new merchandise, antiques, collectibles, crafts and produce; food; restrooms; parking; nearby motels; occasional auctions.

Route 3 Super Flea Market W XXXX
Route 3
Rutherford, New Jersey 07070
(201) 933-4388
Contact: Phillip LaPorta, 454 Park Avenue, Rutherford, New Jersey, (201) 933-4388
(Across from Meadowlands Sports Complex)

Outdoor market; 210 dealers; began in 1977; open every Saturday and Sunday, 9:00 a.m. to 5:00 p.m.; 75¢ admission per car; space rental: $15.00 daily, $25.00 per weekend for 18' x 10'; reservations on monthly basis only.

Variety of secondhand merchandise, antiques, collectibles, crafts, art objects, and produce; food; restrooms; parking; nearby motels.

Rutherford Street Fair A XXX
Park Avenue
Rutherford, New Jersey 07652
Contact: Irene Stella, Box 482, Paramus, New Jersey 07652, (201) 262-3063
(Route 3 to Park Avenue Exit, ten minutes from midtown Manhattan)

Outdoor market; 150 dealers; began in 1975; held annually on Labor Day; free admission; space rental: $45.00 per car space; reservations needed.

Mostly antiques and collectibles, some new merchandise, arts and crafts; lots of homemade food; restrooms; street parking; local Holiday Inn; entertainment.

Cowtown Auctioneers Flea Market ★ W XXXX
Box 32
Sharptown, New Jersey 08098
(609) 769-3000
Contact: Jessica Pariszewski, RD 3, Salem, New Jersey 08079, (609) 935-5555
(New Jersey Turnpike to Exit 1, take Route 40 east five miles to the "big cowboy")

Indoor/outdoor market; 425 dealers; began in 1941; open Tuesdays, year round; free admission; space rental: $12.00 to $15.00 per day for 10' x 10' and 12' x 12'; no reservations needed.

Mostly new merchandise, some antiques, collectibles, secondhand items and produce; food; restrooms; nearby motel; produce and livestock auctions.

Packard's Farm and Flea Market ★ XX
Route 206 South
Somerville, New Jersey 08876
(201) 369-3100
Contact: Thomas J. McDonald, 2 Ski Drive, Neshanic, New Jersey 08853
(Fifteen minutes north of Princeton)

Indoor market; 100 dealers; began in 1948; open Wednesday and Friday, 12:00 noon to 10:00 p.m., year round; free admission; space rental: $125.00 per month for 16' x 16' booth; no reservations needed.

Mostly new merchandise, produce, some antiques and collectibles; food concession; restrooms; parking; nearby motels; occasional auctions.

Stone Harbor Sea Market A XXX
Eighty-first Street and the Beach
Stone Harbor, New Jersey 08247
Contact: Hurley House, 905 Bay Avenue, Somers Point, New Jersey 08244
(Garden State Parkway to Stone Harbor Exit)

Outdoor market; 130 to 150 dealers; began in 1965; open first Sunday in August; free admission; space rental: $15.00 outside, $25.00 under tent; reservations needed.

Antiques, collectibles and crafts; food; restrooms; parking; nearby motels.

The Union Market W XXXX
2445 Springfield Avenue
Vauxhall, New Jersey 07088
(201) 688-6161
Contact: Howie Mann
(Take New Jersey Turnpike Exit 14 to Highway 24 West, exit 50B to Springfield Avenue)

Indoor market; 300 dealers; began in 1979; open Friday noon to 9:30 p.m., Saturday 11:00 a.m. to 9:30 p.m., Sunday 11:00 a.m. to 6:00 p.m.; free admission; space rental: $400.00 a month for 10' x 10'; no reservations needed.

No antiques, only collectibles, arts, crafts, new merchandise and produce; food; restrooms; parking.

De Paul High School Flea Market M XXX
1512 Alps Road
Wayne, New Jersey 07470
Contact: The Fleamarketeers, Glenn and Joan Hasbrouck, 3 Al-lyn Court, Haledon, New Jersey 07508, (201) 595-5041
(I-80 to 23 North approximately one and one-quarter miles to Alps Road)

Indoor market; 120 dealers; began in 1977; open third Sunday of each month October to April, 10:00 a.m. to 5:00 p.m.; admission 25¢; space rental: $12.00 for 8' table, 8' x 6' space; reservations required.

Mostly antiques, collectibles and secondhand items, some new merchandise and crafts; food; restrooms; parking; nearby motels.

Wayne PAL Flea Market   **M XXX**
PAL Drive
Wayne, New Jersey 07470
Contact: The Fleamarketeers, Glenn and Joan Hasbrouck, 3 Al-lyn Court,
Haledon, New Jersey 07508, (201) 595-5041
(I-80 to 23 North one mile, then follow signs)

Indoor market; 145 dealers; began in 1976; open first Sunday of each month
October to April, 10:00 a.m. to 5:00 p.m.; admission 25¢; space rental: $12.00 for
6' x 8' area with table; reservations required.
    Mostly antiques and collectibles, some secondhand items; food; restrooms;
parking; nearby motels.

NEW YORK

Colonel K. R. French & Co., Inc.
Kenneth French, Auctioneer
166 Bedford Road
Armonk, New York 10504
(914) 273-3674
(Near Exit 3, Route 684, Armonk)

Sales ranging from general household items to antiques and collectibles;
auctions held every other Friday, Saturday or Sunday; estate sales; bankruptcy
and liquidation sales at any time; specialized collectors' sales (clocks, trains,
etc.) when sufficient items accumulate; consignments; property purchased for
sales.
    No buyer's premium; mail and telephone bids accepted; personal checks
accepted with credit established through bank reference; traveler's and cashier's
checks accepted; Master Charge and Visa accepted. No deposit necessary to
hold purchase; full payment and pickups within one week.
    Sale announcements mailed; catalogs for all sales; oral and written appraisals
for negotiable fee, $25.00 minimum charge.

Avon Auction Gallery
Chuck Cottone, David Fleming, Auctioneers
239 Rochester Street
Avon, New York 14414
(716) 226-3140
(South of Rochester, half mile north of Routes 5 & 20)

Antiques sales held once monthly; specialized sales include art glass, paintings,
furniture; estate sales; consignments; merchandise purchased for sales.
    No buyer's premium; mail and telephone bids not accepted; checks with two
forms of ID accepted; no credit cards. Purchases held with 20% deposit; full
payment within one day; pickups within 20 days.
    Sale announcements and some catalogs mailed; written appraisals offered for
an hourly fee of $50.00.

The Bedford Gallery
John Clifton, Auctioneer
307 Railroad Avenue
Bedford Hills, New York 10507
(914) 241-2262
(Off Routes 117, 684 and the Saw Mill Parkway)

Gallery open seven days a week with general antiques auction and flea market on weekends; specialized sales of clocks, dolls and toys; estate sales; consignments; property purchased for sales.

No buyer's premium; telephone bids accepted; checks accepted with proper ID; no credit cards; full payment day of sale; pickups within three days.

Catalogs for all sales.

David W. Mapes, Inc.
David W. Mapes, Auctioneer
82 Front Street
Binghamton, New York 13905
(607) 724-6741
Gallery: Vestal Parkway
Vestal, New York

Specializing in fine art and antiques; approximately two sales held monthly; specialized sales feature clocks, postcards, art glass, and Americana; estate sales; consignments; some merchandise purchased for sales.

No buyer's premium; telephone bids accepted; checks accepted from established customers or with accompanying letter of credit; no credit cards. Purchases held with a 10% deposit; full payment and pickups as arranged.

Sale announcements mailed; written appraisals offered for an hourly fee of $35.00.

Dorothy Knapp and Associates
Dorothy Knapp and Ken Steffens, Auctioneers
Mayo's Hotel
Rockland Avenue
Congers, New York 10920
(914) 623-5710
(Located opposite railroad station; west of Routes 9 West and 303, between Tappanzee and Bear Mountain Bridges)

General sales held weekly throughout the year, on Tuesdays at 7:00 p.m.; 60% of merchandise is antique; specialized sales include coins and silver; estate sales; some consignments; property purchased for sale.

No buyer's premium; mail and telephone bids accepted; checks accepted with proper ID; no credit cards. Full payment day of sale; pickups within one week.

Sale announcements mailed; written appraisals offered for fee dependent on number of items and hours involved.

Note: Listings are alphabetical by town.

Cooper Barn Auctions
Karl Baeurle, Auctioneer
Cooper Lane
Cooperstown, New York 13326
(607) 547-2332

Weekly antiques and collectibles sale Friday evenings from May to October, featuring historic artifacts from New York State, furniture, china and glass; household goods; estate sales; consignments; property purchased for sales.

No buyer's premium; mail and telephone bids accepted; traveler's, certified checks or personal checks with ID accepted; no credit cards; full payment day of sale; pickups same day unless other arrangements made.

Sale announcements mailed; written and oral appraisals offered for fee dependent on nature of appraisal.

Mid Hudson Galleries
Martin Smith, Auctioneer
One Idlewild Avenue
Cornwall on Hudson, New York 12520
(914) 534-7827
(Exit 16 off New York Thruway, then Route 32 to Route 307; or from Connecticut: Interstate 84 to first Newburgh Exit—Route 9 West South to Route 218, left at blinker light)

Chiefly handles estate dispersals; sales held every five to six weeks; specialized sales include Oriental art, Victoriana, silver and paintings; consignments; merchandise purchased for sales.

Ten percent buyer's premium; mail and telephone bids accepted at gallery's discretion; checks may be accepted, or merchandise held until check clears; Master Charge and Visa accepted. Generally payment in full due day of sale, pickups within 30 days.

Sale announcements and catalogs mailed; complete appraisal service—for businesses as well as individuals—offered for 1% of total inventory or flat fee based on contents to be appraised.

C-Wright Auctions
Carolyn E. Wright, Auctioneer
Route 9 West
Coxsackie, New York 12051
(518) 767-2781 or (518) 731-9020
(One and one-half miles south of New York Thruway, Exit 21B)

Auctions every other week, Fridays at 7:00 p.m.; previews at 6:00 p.m.; merchandise includes antiques, used furniture, livestock and produce; estate sales; consignments; merchandise purchased for sales.

No buyer's premium; mail and telephone bids accepted; checks accepted with proper ID; no credit cards. Full payment at time of sale usually; pickups within three days.

Sale announcements mailed; written appraisals offered for flat fee.

The Durham Auction Barn
Chip Myers, Danny Young, Al Cardamone, Jr., Auctioneers
Route 145, Box 44
Durham, New York 12422
(518) 239-8475
(About twenty-nine miles southwest of Albany)

General antiques sale every Saturday at 7:00 p.m., April through November, and every Thursday at 7:00 p.m. in July and August; winter sales held every other Saturday at noon; estate sales; consignments; property purchased for sales.

No buyer's premium; mail and telephone bids accepted from known customers; checks accepted with proper ID; no credit cards, payment in full day of sale; pickup when convenient.

Sale announcements mailed; written appraisal services offered for fee dependent on nature of appraisal.

Bower's Auction Sales
Roger Bower, Auctioneer
Route 80
Fort Plain, New York 13339
(518) 993-2444

General sales, usually 50% antiques and collectibles, held as merchandise becomes available, or approximately every two to three weeks; estate sales; consignments; property purchased for sales.

No buyer's premium; mail and telephone bids not accepted; checks with proper ID accepted; no credit cards. Purchases held with a 15% deposit; full payment before pickups.

Sale announcements mailed; oral and written appraisals offered for negotiable fee.

Fox Creek Auction Sales
Douglas A. Cater, Douglas A. Cornwell, Auctioneers
Box 46
Gallupville, New York 12073
(518) 872-2510 or (518) 295-7228
(Route 443 to West Berne, New York)

Primarily estate sales including many antiques, held nearly every Sunday at the auction barn or on site; consignments; merchandise purchased for sales.

No buyer's premium; mail bids accepted; New York State checks accepted with proper ID; no out-of-state checks or credit cards accepted. Full payment same day; pickups within one week.

Sale announcements mailed—$3.00 yearly fee; written appraisals offered for hourly fee.

Gilbert Auctions
Richards C. Gilbert, Auctioneer
Alldone
Garrison, New York 10524
(914) 424-3635
(Sales held on site—check mailings for directions)

Holds estate sales in the East; specialized sales of jewelry, coins, art glass; consignments only; no property purchased for sales.

No buyer's premium; mail and telephone bids accepted; checks accepted if approved prior to sale through bank references; no credit cards. Purchases held with a $50.00 deposit; full payment and pickups as arranged.

Sale announcements and catalogs mailed; written appraisals offered for per diem fee of $450.00.

Pioneer Auction Gallery
William J. Barry, Michael G. Barry, Auctioneers
440 Exchange Street
Geneva, New York 14456
(315) 789-9817

Sales generally held every other Monday at 7:00 p.m.; featuring antiques and collectibles, some household goods; specialized sales of Oriental rugs, toys, carnival glass; estate sales; consignments; merchandise purchased for sales.

No buyer's premium; mail and telephone bids accepted; in-state checks accepted with proper ID; out-of-state checks accepted from established customers only; no credit cards. Full payment evening of sale; pickups within 10 days.

Sale announcements and some catalogs mailed; refundable purchase of catalog required to enter sale; oral or written appraisals offered for negotiable fee.

H. R. Tyrer Galleries
Bob Tyrer, Auctioneer
707 Upper Glen Street
Glens Falls, New York 12801
(518) 793-2244
(Northway to Exit 19—one block south to Route 9, forty-five minutes north of Albany)

Monthly sales held on Sunday of second or third week at noon; featuring estate merchandise, collectibles and antiques, including slot machines, jukeboxes, early autographs, silver, wicker, Americana, 18th and 19th century furniture, Oriental rugs; estate sales; consignments; property purchased for sales.

No buyer's premium; mail and telephone bids accepted; checks accepted with proper ID; Master Charge and Visa accepted. Purchases held with a 25% deposit; full payment and pickups within one week.

Illustrated brochure mailed; written appraisals offered for negotiable fee.

Plandome Book Auctions
113 Glen Head Road, PO Box 395
Glen Head, New York 11545
(516) 671-3209

Specializing in literary property, rare books, autographs, maps, graphics; 10 sales held each year, generally once monthly from September to June (closed July and August); estate merchandise; consignments; property purchased for sales.

No buyer's premium; mail and telephone bids accepted with $20.00 deposit, unless from known dealers and libraries; cash only accepted; no checks or credit cards. Full payment day of sale; pickups within three days.

Catalogs issued for each sale by subscription only ($25.00, first class mail, or $20.00, third class mail).

Glenn H. Munson & Son
Glenn H. and Glenn P. Munson, Auctioneers
448 Locke Road
Groton, New York 13073
(607) 898-3739, (607) 898-3323, or (315) 497-1331
(One mile north of Groton, on Route 38)

A family-run business; weekly general sales, including specialized sales of guns, carnival glass, and coins; estate sales; consignments; property purchased for sales.

No buyer's premium; telephone bids accepted; checks accepted with proper ID; no credit cards. Full payment day of sale; pickups within one week.

Sale announcements mailed; written appraisals offered for variable fee.

George Cole Auctioneers & Appraisers
George Cole, Auctioneer
14 Green Street
Kingston, New York 12401
(914) 338-2367
(Sales held at Ramada Inn, Route 28 West Kingston; New York Thruway, Exit 19)

Monthly sales feature antiques and collectibles, some general household merchandise; estate sales; consignments; property purchased for sales.

No buyer's premium; mail and telephone bids not accepted; checks accepted with established credit; no credit cards. Full payment and pickups day of sale.

Written appraisals generally offered for an hourly fee of $15.00, and $25.00 for first hour.

Dave & Fran DePuy's Bonded Auction Service
David A. DePuy, Auctioneer
Box 8
Madison, New York 13402
(315) 893-1883 or (315) 684-9512
(On South Street, just south of Route 20)

Antiques and collectibles, estate and household merchandise, featured in sales held approximately every two to three weeks at the gallery; estate sales; consignments; property purchased for sales.

No buyer's premium; mail and telephone bids accepted; New York State checks accepted; Master Charge and Visa accepted. Full payment day of sale, except mail and phone bids—five days; pickups generally within one week.

Sale announcements mailed; catalogs for all sales; oral and written appraisals offered for variable fee, ranging from $50.00 to $150.00.

Wyss Auction Service, Inc.
Bruce Wyss, Auctioneer
Office: Box 10
Madison, New York 13402
(315) 893-7945
Gallery: White Street
Waterville, New York 13480
(Gallery eighty miles west of Albany, Route 20)

Specializing in Early American country furniture and various period furniture and furnishings; sale held every five weeks; estate sales; consignments; property purchased for sales.

No buyer's premium; mail and telephone bids accepted; out-of-state checks with ID and local checks accepted; Visa and Master Charge accepted. No deposit necessary to hold purchase; payment in full within three days; pickups within two weeks.

Sale announcements and catalogs mailed; oral and written appraisals offered for fee dependent on nature of appraisal.

Montgomery Auction Exchange
Ralph Losinno, Auctioneer
151 Ward Street (Route 17K)
Montgomery, New York 12549
(914) 457-9549 or (914) 457-5364

Sales held monthly, featuring general merchandise, antiques and collectibles; specialized sales include wicker and oak furniture, clocks, jewelry; estate sales; consignments; property purchased for sales.

No buyer's premium; telephone bids accepted; mail bids accepted with 20% deposit paid by certified check; checks accepted with established credit through bank reference; no credit cards. Full payment at sale; pickups within seven days.

Sale announcements mailed; oral and written appraisals offered for fee of $50.00 per hour.

Jerry Schuster Auction Gallery
Jerry Schuster, Auctioneer
RD 4, Lyndon Lane, Box 127
New Windsor, New York 12550
(914) 562-0638

(Just south of Newburgh on Route 94)

Antiques sale held every five weeks on Saturday at 6:00 p.m.; exhibition same day; feature Tiffany lamps, bronzes, silver jewelry, coins, oil paintings; estate sales; consignments; property purchased for sales.

No buyer's premium; mail and telephone bids accepted; checks accepted, though merchandise may be held until check clears; no credit cards. Full payment within five days; pickups within three weeks.

Sale announcements mailed; catalogs for all sales; oral and written appraisals offered for negotiable fee.

Astor Galleries
Joseph Liebson, Ralph Levy, Auctioneers
1 West Thirty-ninth Street
New York, New York 10018
(212) 473-1658 or (212) 921-8861

Family owned and operated for almost 50 years; specializing in the purchase of estates; merchandise consists primarily of general antiques—furniture porcelain, silver, Oriental rugs and tapestries; sale every three weeks; specialized sales include firehouse memorabilia, paintings, and clocks; consignments; merchandise purchased for sales.

Ten percent buyer's premium; mail and telephone bids accepted; checks accepted with proper ID; no credit cards accepted. Purchases held with a 25% deposit; full payment and pickups within three days.

Sale announcements mailed; catalogs for all sales; oral and written appraisals offered for negotiable fee.

Christie, Manson & Wood International, Inc.
502 Park Avenue
New York, New York 10022
(212) 826-2888
and
Christie's East
219 East Sixty-seventh Street
New York, New York 10021
(212) 570-4141

Handles decorative and fine arts from all over the world; full facilities located in New York, London, Geneva, Amsterdam, Rome, Sidney, Glasgow; sales held twice a year in Tokyo; merchandise can be consigned for New York sales in Boston, Philadelphia, Palm Beach, Beverly Hills, Chicago and Vancouver; specialized sales (in conjunction with London sales) held one to three times weekly at Park Avenue gallery feature Americana, Art Nouveau and Art Deco, Oriental art, American, European and Continental furniture, Russian works of art, books and manuscripts, musical instruments, rugs, tribal art and antiquities, porcelain, paintings and prints; Christie's East features three weekly sales of similar merchandise of lower quality, as well as specialized sales of photography, dolls and toys, and clothes; mixed antiques sale held monthly; sales September through June; Christie's East holds some sales in July; neither gallery holds sales in August, though open for consignments only; estate sales; consignments only; no property purchased for sales.

Note: Listings are alphabetical by town.

Ten percent buyer's premium; mail and telephone bids accepted; checks accepted with established credit through bank reference; no credit cards. Full payment and pickups usually within seven days.

Catalogs available singly or by subscription; illustrated catalogs available for all but Christie's East general antiques sales; purchases of catalog required to enter on-site house sales only; oral appraisals and informal written appraisals offered free—either take material in or send photograph; written appraisals offered for $1,000.00 per diem fee, pro-rated, plus expenses.

William Doyle Galleries

175 East Eighty-seventh Street
New York, New York 10028
(212) 427-2730

General antiques sale held every other Wednesday; specialized sales feature art glass, clocks, and art works by the Old Masters; estate sales; consignments; merchandise purchased for sales.

Ten percent buyer's premium; mail and telephone bids accepted; checks accepted with bank reference; no credit cards. Purchase held with a 25% deposit; full payment and pickups within three days.

Sale announcements mailed; catalogs for all sales; written appraisals offered for negotiable fee.

John C. Edelmann Galleries

John C. Edelmann, Auctioneer
123 East Seventy-seventh Street
New York, New York 10021
(212) 628-1700

Specializing in Oriental rugs, textiles and tapestries; sales held at least once a month; consignments; merchandise occasionally purchased for sales.

Ten percent buyer's premium; mail and telephone bids accepted; checks accepted, but merchandise may be held until check clears; no credit cards; no deposit necessary to hold purchase; full payment and pickups within six days.

Sale announcements and catalogs, both illustrated and non-illustrated mailed; oral appraisals offered free for items auctioned at the gallery; written appraisals for $100.00 or more, depending on number of items.

Stanley Gibbons Auction Galleries

Louis Grunin, Seymour Kaplan, Auctioneers
Olympic Tower
645 Fifth Avenue
New York, New York 10022
(212) 582-0165

Specializing in sale of rare stamps, maps, banknotes, stock certificates; sales held monthly; estate sales; consignments; merchandise purchased for sales.

Ten percent buyer's premium; mail and telephone bids accepted; checks accepted with previously established credit; no credit cards. Full payment at sale; pickups within three days.

Sale announcements and catalogs for all sales mailed; oral or written appraisals offered for 1% to 2.5% of estimated value of property, with a minimum charge of $25.00.

The Greenwich Auction Room, Ltd.

Jesse Bien, Auctioneer
58 East Thirteenth Street
New York, New York 10003
(212) 533-5550

Estate sales and business liquidations, generally 50% antiques and collectibles, held every other week on Saturdays from September through May and every other week on Thursdays in June, July and August; four specialized yearly sales featuring paintings; consignments; property purchased for sales.

Ten percent buyer's premium; mail and telephone bids accepted; checks accepted with bank or other auction room reference; no credit cards. Purchases held with a 25% deposit; full payment within two days; most pickups within two days.

Sale announcements mailed; catalogs for all sales; written appraisals offered for negotiable fee.

Charles Hamilton Galleries, Inc.

Gregory Mozian, Auctioneer
25 East Seventy-seventh Street
New York, New York 10021
(212) 628-1666

All sales held at the Waldorf Astoria Hotel in New York City on Thursdays at 7:30 p.m., approximately every six weeks; specializing in autographs, documents and letters of famous people; consignments only; no property purchased for sales.

Ten percent buyer's premium; mail and telephone bids accepted; checks accepted; no credit cards; no deposit necessary to hold purchase; full payment within 10 days; pickups within 30 days.

Catalogs mailed; oral appraisals free; written appraisals for fee of $100.00.

Lubin Galleries, Inc.

30 West Twenty-sixth Street
New York, New York 10001
(212) 254-1080

Predominantly estate and liquidation sales. featuring furniture, furnishings, antiques and collectibles, reproductions, and general merchandise; sales held every other Saturday throughout the year; specialized sales of rugs, silver, porcelain, jewelry, fine art prints; consignments; property purchased for sales.

No buyer's premium; mail and telephone bids accepted; checks accepted only with established credit reference; no credit cards. Purchases held with a 25% deposit; full payment and pickup within three days.

Sale announcements mailed; catalogs for all sales; written appraisals offered for negotiable fee.

Manhattan Galleries, Inc.

201 East Eightieth Street
New York, New York 10021
(212) 744-2844

Antiques sale every other week, generally on Sundays at 11:00 a.m.; exhibition for Sunday sales on Thursdays, Fridays, and Saturdays; summer sales held Wednesdays; specialized sales of 18th century French, Continental, English furniture and decorations, Orientalia, pre-Columbian art, antique silver; estate sales; consignments; property purchased for sales.

Ten percent buyer's premium; mail and telephone bids accepted; checks accepted, though merchandise may be held until check clears; no credit cards. Purchases held with 20% deposit; full payment and pickups within two days, or as arranged.

Catalogs for all sales; oral and written appraisals offered for negotiable fee.

Phillips Auctioneers

C. J. Weston, R. G. Gowland, P. Fairbanks, T. A. Finley, Auctioneers
867 Madison Avenue
New York, New York 10021
(212) 570-4842
and
525 East Seventy-second Street
New York, New York 10021
(212) 570-4830

Specialized antiques and collectibles sales held at both galleries two to three times weekly, featuring fine furniture and decorations, American and European paintings and prints, books, autographs and manuscripts, Lalique, Royal Doulton, silver, lead soldiers, Oriental rugs, Art Nouveau and Art Deco, primitive art and jewelry, etc.; estate sales; consignments only; no property purchased for sales.

Ten percent buyer's premium; mail and telephone bids accepted; checks accepted with bank credit check; no credit cards. Full payment usually at time of sale; pickups within one week.

Sale announcements and catalogs mailed; oral and written appraisals offered for variable fee, $150.00 minimum.

Plaza Art Galleries, Inc.

Barry Hookway, Kenneth Leabman, James Lyons, Auctioneers
406 East Seventy-ninth Street
New York, New York 10021
(212) 472-1000

Established in 1916; weekly sales featuring furniture, decorations and paintings, held every Thursday; monthly sale featuring jewelry on Wednesdays; specialized sales of Art Nouveau and Art Deco, toys, banks and dolls, Japanese art and antiques; sales conducted also for the Provident Loan Society (a large pawn-broking firm), predominantly of jewelry, approximately six times a year; estate sales; consignments; some property purchased for sales.

Ten percent buyer's premium; mail and telephone bids accepted; checks accepted with previously established credit through bank reference; Visa and Master Charge accepted. Purchases held with a 25% deposit; full payment and pickups within three days.

Sale announcements and catalogs mailed; oral appraisals offered free of charge; written appraisals for a minimum fee of $250.00, or a percentage of value of item.

Sotheby Parke Bernet, Inc.

980 Madison Avenue
New York, New York 10021
(212) 472-3400
and
1334 York Avenue
New York, New York 10021
(212) 794-3000

Founded in London in 1744, Sotheby Parke Bernet's North American headquarters are based at 980 Madison Avenue, in the heart of New York's museum and gallery district; full-service facilities are also available in Los Angeles and Toronto, and representative offices are located in Boston, Philadelphia, Washington, Palm Beach, Chicago, Houston, San Francisco, Honolulu (especially noted for netsuke sales), and Vancouver; four to eight specialized sales weekly, including European and American furniture, decorations, paintings, prints, porcelain, silver, pewter, rugs, glass, books and manuscripts, Chinese, Japanese, Russian, Islamic, African and Oceanic, and Pre-Columbian works of art, Art Deco and Art Nouveau, Victoriana, Americana; all property exhibited for at least three days prior to sale; estate sales; consignments only; no property purchased for sales.

Ten percent buyer's premium; mail and telephone bids accepted; checks from established customers accepted; checks under $500.00 accepted from first-time purchasers with established credit; otherwise, merchandise held for check clearance or bank authorization; no credit cards accepted. Full payment and pickups usually by 5:00 p.m. day following sale.

Illustrated catalogs available three or four weeks prior to each sale, available singly or by subscription; newsletter listing sales held in New York, London, Los Angeles, and elsewhere, available for $3.00 per year; free informal appraisals and advice from 10:00 a.m. to 5:00 p.m., Monday through Friday (send photographs if pieces are too large to carry); on-site appraisals offered for variable fee.

Swann Galleries, Inc.

G. S. Lowry, E.V. Halbmeier, G.G.M. Kyles, Auctioneers
104 East Twenty-fifth Street
New York, New York 10010
(212) 254-4710

Specialized sales held every Thursday, featuring rare and antiquarian books; maps and atlases; autographs and manuscripts; prints and graphics; photographica; consignments only; no property purchased for sales.

No buyer's premium; mail and telephone bids accepted; cash only; no checks or credit cards accepted. Deposits necessary to hold purchases; full payment and pickups within seven days.

Catalogs for all sales; oral and written appraisals offered for negotiable per diem fee.

Tepper Galleries, Inc.
I. Hutter, R. Rosner, M. Drazen, S. Drazen, Auctioneers
110 East Twenty-fifth Street
New York, New York 10010
(212) 677-5300

General sale—of antiques and collectibles, used furniture and general merchandise—held every other Saturday; specialized sales feature paintings and jewelry; estate sales; consignments; property purchased for sale.

Ten percent buyer's premium; mail and telephone bids accepted; checks accepted with proper ID and bank verification; no credit cards. Purchases held with a 25% deposit; full payment and pickup within two days.

Sale announcements mailed; catalogs for all sales; both oral and written appraisals for negotiable fee.

Victoria Galleries
Larry Berler, Auctioneer
106 Greenwich Avenue
New York, New York 10011
(212) 929-5909

Sales held every other Saturday at noon; merchandise on exhibit the day before; specialized sales feature Orientalia, jewelry, glass, silver, enamels, Oceanic art, and bronzes; estate sales; consignments; merchandise purchased for sales.

No buyer's premium; mail and telephone bids accepted; checks accepted with established credit, or merchandise held until check clears; no credit cards. Purchases held with a 25% deposit; full payment and pickups usually within four days.

Catalogs for all sales; written appraisals offered for fee of generally $5.00 to $10.00.

York Antiques Ltd.
Manuel Reteguiz, Victor Spaghesi, Auctioneers
12 East Twelfth Street
New York, New York 10003
(212) 260-4449

Four major antiques sales held yearly in September, November, April and May; featuring English, French, and American furniture and furnishings, bronzes, porcelains; estate sales; no consignments; all property purchased for sales.

No buyer's premium; mail and telephone bids accepted; checks accepted, though merchandise may be held until check clears; no credit cards. Full payment within three days; pickups within four days.

Sale announcements and catalogs mailed; oral or written appraisals offered for negotiable fee.

Country Squires Auctions
Chuck Squires, Auctioneer
Route 414
North Rose, New York 14516
(315) 587-2689 or (315) 483-9872
(Fifteen miles north of New York State Thruway, Exit 41 at Waterloo)

At least one general sale of household goods each week; specialized sales feature Indian artifacts, dolls and toys, stoneware; flea market, antique show on premises; estate sales; consignments; merchandise purchased for sales.

No buyer's premium; mail and telephone bids accepted; checks accepted with proper ID and bank letter of credit. Full payment day of sale; pickups within seven days.

Written and oral appraisals offered for negotiable fee.

D.A.K. Auctions
Arlene Feinberg, Auctioneer
173 Main Street
Nyack, New York 10960
(914) 358-5459
(New York Thruway to Exit 11)

General antiques and bric-a-brac—anything from music boxes, to Tiffany glass or even a Bentley automobile—sold at monthly auctions held on Saturday night; specialized sales feature oak and walnut furniture; estate sales; consignments; merchandise bought for sales.

No buyer's premium; mail and telephone bids accepted; checks accepted with proper ID; no credit cards. Full payment day of auction; pickups within two weeks.

Sale announcements mailed.

Pearl River Auction
Peter Catanese, Auctioneer
35 West Central Avenue
Pearl River, New York 10965
(914) 735-4535 or (914) 735-6535

General antiques sales held twice a month on Friday evenings, sometimes Saturday, throughout the year (except on certain holidays); specialized sales feature 18th and 19th century paintings and decorative arts; estate sales; consignments; property bought for sales.

No buyer's premium; mail and telephone bids accepted with 15% deposit, credit card clearance or bank reference; traveler's or certified checks accepted; personal checks accepted only with established credit through bank reference; Visa and Master Charge accepted. Purchases held with a 15% deposit.

Sale announcements mailed.

Note: Listings are alphabetical by town.

Brzostek's Auction Service Inc.

Bernard Brzostek, Auctioneer
2052 Lamson Road
Phoenix, New York 13135
(315) 678-2542
(Five miles north of Baldwinsville, New York; one block west of Route 48; or,
New York State Thruway Exit 39—north on Route 690, then ten miles to
Route 48)

General antiques auction held every three to four weeks throughout the year;
closed July and August; specialized sales of dolls, toys, coins; estate sales;
consignments; property purchased for sales.

No buyer's premium; mail and telephone bids accepted; traveler's checks and
in-state checks accepted; out-of-state checks require bank verification; no credit
cards. Absentee bids held with a 25% deposit; full payment day of sale; pickups
preferred same day or within one week.

Sale announcements mailed; catalogs for all sales; written appraisals for
minimum fee of $25.00 per hour, depending on number of items and distance
traveled.

Pine Bush Trade Market

Lou Roberson, Auctioneer
Route 52
Pine Bush, New York 12566
(914) 361-4735 or (914) 744-9934
(A quarter mile west of Pine Bush)

Sales generally held twice a month on Saturdays at 7:00 p.m.; featuring antique
furniture ranging from early American to Victorian walnut and turn-of-the-
century oak; also glassware, lamps, and collectibles; specialized sales of pipes
and Americana; estate sales; consignments; merchandise purchased for sales.

No buyer's premium; telephone bids accepted; checks accepted with established credit or bank letter of credit; no credit cards; for first time payment by
check, merchandise held until check clears. Full payment night of sale; pickups
within one week.

Sale announcements and some catalogs mailed; written appraisals usually
offered for fee of $35.00.

Pleasant Valley Auction Hall

Calvin Smith, Bob Smith, Auctioneers
South Avenue
Pleasant Valley, New York 12569
(914) 635-3169
(Three and one-half miles west of Taconic State Parkway, just off Route 44;
five miles east of Poughkeepsie)

Specializing in estate sales in the Hudson Valley and surrounding areas; sales
held every other week on Saturdays, day or night; specialized sales of paintings,
dolls, guns, coins, Americana held Friday nights; consignments; merchandise
purchased for sales.

No buyer's premium; mail and telephone bids accepted; certified checks or personal checks with proper ID and bank letter of credit accepted; no credit cards. Full payment day of sale; pickups as arranged.

Sale announcements mailed; written appraisals offered for an hourly fee of $50.00.

Bill Rinaldi Auctions
Bill Rinaldi, Mike Fallon, Auctioneers
Box 85
Pleasant Valley, New York 12589
Auctions: Bedell Road
Poughkeepsie, New York
(914) 454-9613 or (914) 635-3156
(Bedell Road is a wide crossroad between Salt Point Turnpike and Vanwagner Road)

Antiques and general merchandise, including paintings, furniture, clocks, featured in sales held every three weeks; specialized sales feature Early American and Shaker furniture; estate sales; consignments; merchandise purchased for sales.

No buyer's premium; mail and telephone bids accepted; checks accepted with proper ID and letter of credit; no credit cards. Full payment and pickups within one day.

Sale announcements mailed; oral or written appraisals offered for negotiable fee.

Newman's Livestock Exchange Inc.
Harry Newman, Auctioneer
Box 3
Poland, New York 13431
(315) 845-8434 or (315) 826-3433
(Route 23-Newport, New York; thirteen miles north of Herkimer; fifteen miles east of Utica)

Cattle sales held every Tuesday, but antiques sales, featuring furniture, glass and collectibles, held as announced; estate and general merchandise sales on Saturdays; consignments; property purchased for sales.

No buyer's premium; mail and telephone bids not accepted; in-state checks with two forms of ID accepted; traveler's checks accepted; no credit cards. Full payment by 5:00 p.m. day of sale; pickups within two days.

Sale announcements mailed; oral and written appraisals offered for $5.00 per item, if appraised at the auction barn.

Iroquois Auctions
Gerald A. Petro. Auctioneer
Broad Street
Port Henry, New York 12974
(518) 942-3355
(New York Route 87 south from Albany to exit 29 and follow signs; forty-five minutes from Lake Placid; sixty miles from Burlington, Vermont)

Three to four major antique sales held yearly, featuring Tiffany lamps, clocks, American Victorian, oak, walnut and Early American furniture and furnishings, over 450 lots per sale; specialized items include clocks, Hummels, gold and silver; five to ten summer estate sales; consignments; property purchased for sales.

No buyer's premium; mail bids accepted; telephone bids accepted at discretion of the house; checks accepted through previously established credit through bank reference; no credit cards. Full payment day of sale; pickups as arranged.

Sale announcements and catalogs mailed; written appraisals offered for an hourly fee of $50.00.

F. E. S. Auctions, Inc.
Frank E. Seipp, Auctioneer
9 Park Lane
Rockville Centre, New York 11570
(516) RO-4-7459
(Sales held at various locations or on site—check mailings)

Pharmaceutical collectibles featured in sales held approximately twice yearly; estate sales; consignments; property purchased for sales.
No buyer's premium; mail and telephone bids not accepted; cash preferred; no checks or credit cards accepted. Full payment and pickups at time of sale.
Sale announcements mailed; written appraisals offered for variable fee, $50.00 minimum.

NASCA—Numismatic & Antiquarian Service Corporation of America
Herbert Melnick, Auctioneer
265 Sunrise, County Federal Building, Suite 53
Rockville Centre, New York 11570
(516) 764-6677
(Sales held at hotels—check mailings for directions)

Eight to ten sales held a year, lasting two to four days, generally midweek; specializing in coins and banknotes, but also featuring antiquities, Wedgwood, pocket watches, Chinese porcelain; estate sales; consignments; property purchased for sales; some mail-bid sales.

Five percent buyer's premium; mail and telephone bids accepted; checks accepted with proper ID, though merchandise may be held until check clears. Full payment generally due within five days; pickups as arranged.

Catalogs for all sales, annual subscription available for $15.00; oral or written appraisals offered for negotiable fee.

Mesko Auction House
Roy L. Martin, Auctioneer
North Main Street
Sherburne, New York 13460
(607) 674-9680

General sales held the first Sunday of every month; specialized sales include Hummels, dolls and toys; estate sales; consignments; property purchased for sales.

No buyer's premium; mail and telephone bids accepted; checks accepted with bank reference; Visa accepted. Full payment at sale; pickups within 30 days.

Sale announcements and catalogs mailed; written and oral appraisals offered for fee of 5% of value.

Willowcreek Auction Barn

Col. Bill Kenny
5353 Ridge Road West
Spencerport, New York 14559
(Route 104 West, about fifteen miles west of Rochester)

General sales third Thursday of every month; some unscheduled Thursday and Saturday sales; specialized sales of coins, silver, antiques and collectibles; estate sales; consignments; merchandise purchased for sales.

No buyer's premium; mail bids accepted; certified checks, personal checks from established customers or with letter of credit accepted; no credit cards. Full payment day of sale; pickups within five days.

Sale announcements mailed; oral or written appraisals offered for variable fee.

Richmond Galleries

Clare H. Brown, Bentley L. Brown, Gerard McGee, Auctioneers
947 Castleton Avenue
Staten Island, New York 10310
(212) 273-1120

Estate and warehouse sales, featuring 1,000 lots of antiques, used furniture, and new merchandise, held every six to eight weeks; no specialized sales; consignments only; no property purchased for sales.

No buyer's premium; mail bids accepted; local checks accepted, or out-of-state checks with established credit; no credit cards. Purchases held with a 25% deposit; full payment and pickups within five days.

Sale announcements mailed; written appraisals offered for fee of $50.00 to $200.00.

Staten Island Auction Gallery Ltd.

Brian Windsor, Leon Sanna, Auctioneers
3599 Richmond Road
Staten Island, New York 10306
(212) 979-4805
Auction:
397 Clarke Avenue
Staten Island, New York 10306
(Located in historic Richmondtown)

Situated in a scenic village composed of 17th to 19th century historic buildings; monthly sales feature 18th and 19th century American and English antiques; specialized sales of Americana, Victoriana, Tiffany, art glass, Art Deco, paintings and Continental furniture; general sales of household goods and collectibles held weekly; estate sales; consignments; property purchased for sales.

No buyer's premium; mail and telephone bids accepted; checks accepted with proper ID and previously established credit; no credit cards. Purchases held with a 25% deposit; full payment and pickup usually one day after sale.

Sale announcements and catalogs for all monthly sales mailed; oral and written appraisals offered for negotiable fee.

Rockland Auction Services Inc.
Col. Sy Cohen, Auctioneer
72 Pomona Road
Suffern, New York 10901
(914) 354-3914
(Sales at Holiday Inn Holidome, Suffern—Airmont Road, Exit 14B off New York Thruway)

Offers a variety of collectibles, including art glass, cameo glass, art pottery, Art Deco, Art Nouveau, lamps, clocks, porcelain, jewelry, and Oriental ivories and netsuke; estate sales; consignments; property purchased for sales.

No buyer's premium; mail and telephone bids accepted; checks accepted, though goods may be held until check clears; Visa and Master Charge accepted. Full payment and pickups within three days.

Sale announcements mailed; catalogs for all sales; written appraisals offered for negotiable fee.

Campbell's Auctions
Bill Campbell, Auctioneer
Box 80, RD 2
Valley Falls, New York 12185
(518) 663-8379 or (518) 663-5551
(Two blocks off Route 7, Pittstown, New York)

A family-run auction; antique and collectibles sale held year round, on Fridays at 7:00 p.m.; estate sales; consignments; no property purchased for sales.

No buyer's premium; no mail or telephone bids accepted; checks accepted with bank letter of credit and personal ID; Master Charge and Visa accepted. Full payment at time of sale; pickups within two days.

Sale announcements mailed; oral and written appraisals offered for fee dependent on evaluation and travel expenses.

Ben's Auction House
Ben Nowakowski, Auctioneer
Route 233
Westmoreland, New York 13490
(315) 853-2891
(One mile south of Thruway Interchange)

General merchandise (ranging from carpet tacks to locomotives) and antiques sale held every other Sunday; estate sales; consignments; property purchased for sales.

No buyer's premium; mail and telephone bids accepted; checks with proper ID accepted; no credit cards. Purchases held with a 20% deposit; full payment within seven days; pickups within 10 days.

Sale announcements mailed; oral appraisals offered for variable fee.

White Plains Auction Rooms
Stephen B. Liebson, Thomas K. Salese, Gary P. Guarno, Auctioneers
572 North Broadway
White Plains, New York 10603
(914) 428-2255
(Route 287 [Cross Westchester Expressway] Exit 6 to Route 22; one and one-half miles north on Route 22)

Monthly sales of furnishings and accessories of all periods; also, bronzes, jewelry, Orientalia; specialized sales feature Early American furniture, paintings, coins; estate sales; consignments; property purchased for sales.

Ten percent buyer's premium; telephone bids accepted; checks accepted with proper ID or with credit check; no credit cards. Full payment at sale; pickups within three days.

Sale announcements mailed; catalogs for all sales; written appraisals offered for minimum fee of $50.00.

Ole Country Auction
Joseph DeLango, Auctioneer
Route 55 East
Winedale, New York 12594
(914) 832-6123 or (914) 832-9943
(On Connecticut border)

Features antiques, collectibles, and memorabilia; sales held every two weeks on Saturday at 7:00 p.m.; specialized sales include dolls, tools, and paintings; estate sales; consignments; property purchased for sales.

No buyer's premium; telephone bids accepted; checks accepted with proper ID and bank reference; no credit cards. Purchases held with a 50% deposit; full payment within one week; pickups before next sale.

Sale announcements mailed; written appraisals offered for time-based fee.

Hickey's Flea Market   W   XX
11,822 Main Road
Akron, New York 14001
(716) 542-4538
Contact: M. Hickey
(State Route 5 between Batavia and Buffalo)

Indoor/outdoor market; 100 dealers; began in 1963; open every Sunday, May through October; 5:00 a.m. to 5:00 p.m.; free admission; space rental: $7.00 for a car space; reservations advisable.

Mostly antiques and collectibles, very little new or secondhand merchandise; food; restrooms; parking; nearby motels.

Kiwanis Flea Market   ★ W   X
Genesee County Fairgrounds
Batavia, New York 14020
Contact: Bernard Kowalski, 24 Richmond Avenue, Batavia, New York 14020,
(716) 343-1594
(Route 5, quarter mile east of Batavia)

Note: Listings are alphabetical by town.

Indoor market; 25 sellers; began in 1973; open every Sunday, May to October, 8:00 a.m. to 5:00 p.m.; free admission; space rental: $6.00 per day; no reservations needed.

Variety of secondhand merchandise, antiques, collectibles, crafts and produce; refreshment stand; parking; restrooms; nearby motels; annual auction usually in June.

UA Bay Shore Drive-In Trade and Sell   W   XXX
1881 Sunrise Highway
Bay Shore, New York 11706
(516) 665-1111
Contact: U.A. Theatres, Inc., 185 Middleneck Road, Great Neck, New York 11021
(Southern State Parkway to Exit 42 South, make right on Fifth Avenue, go one mile to Sunrise Highway, then go east two miles)

Outdoor drive-in market; 100 to 125 sellers; open every Sunday, April to December, 8:00 a.m. to 4:00 p.m.; $1.50 per car admission; space rental: $5.00 per car length; no reservations needed.

Mostly secondhand and new merchandise, few antiques; food; parking; restrooms.

Barterama   ★ W XXXX
Belmont Racetrack
Belmont, New York 11003
Contact: Sheldon Hills, Barterama Corporation, 257 Hempstead Turnpike, Belmont, New York 11003 (516) 775-8774
(Cross Island Parkway to Exit 26B, Hampstead Turnpike East)

Outdoor market; 1,500 dealers; began in 1974; open every Saturday from third Saturday in October to third Saturday in December, 8:00 a.m. to 5:00 p.m., every Sunday from third Sunday of October to third Sunday in December from 7:00 a.m. to 5:00 p.m.; admission $1.50 per car, 50¢ for walk-in;space rental: $15.00 and up for about 12' x 25'; reservations needed.

Half new merchandise, plus antiques, collectibles, secondhand items and crafts; food; restrooms, parking; occasional auctions.

Castile Flea Market   W   XX
Routes 19A and 39
Castile, New York 14427
(716) 493-2697
Contact: Phil or Pat Walczak, 3341 Wethersfield Road, Gainesville, New York 14066, (716) 786-3495 or (716) 786-2274
(Call for directions)

Outdoor market; 50 to 90 dealers; began in 1974; open every Sunday, Memorial Day through October; free admission; space rental: $5.00 per week; reservations advisable.

Lots of secondhand items, antiques and collectibles, some new merchandise and crafts; food; restrooms; parking; motels nearby.

Super Flea Market ★ W XXXX

2500 Walden Avenue
Cheektonaga, New York 14225
(716) 685-2902
Contact: Joseph Sceusa or Tony Battista, 2500 Walden Avenue, Cheektowaga,
New York 14225

Indoor/outdoor market; 300 to 500 dealers; began in 1974; open every Saturday
and Sunday, 7:30 a.m. to 6:00 p.m.; free admission; space rental: $9.00 per day
inside, $7.00 outside; no reservations needed.

Mostly secondhand and household items, some antiques, collectibles and new
merchandise; food; restrooms; parking; nearby motels; occasional auctions.

The Great Chautauqua Antique Market A XXXX

Chautauqua County Fairgrounds
1089 Central Avenue
Dunkirk, New York 14048
(716) 366-4752
Contact: Dick and Roma Taylor, 135 Salan Road, Chagrin Falls, Ohio 44022,
(216) 247-8319
(I-90 to Exit 59)

Indoor/outdoor market; 225 sellers; began in 1980; held the last weekend in
June; admission $1.00; space rental: inside $20.00 per day, outside $15.00 on
Saturday, $20.00 on Sunday; reservations needed.

Antiques and collectibles only; food; restrooms; parking; nearby motels.

East Avon Downs Flea Market W XXX

Route 15
East Avon, New York 14414
(716) 226-8593
Contact: Doug Stephenson, 1520 Rochester Road, Avon, New York 14414
(Half mile north of Routes 5 and 20, nine miles south of New York Thruway,
Exit 46)

Outdoor market; 200 dealers; began in 1968; open every Sunday, May 15 to
October 15; free admission; space rental: $5.00 for 15' x 30'; no reservations
needed.

Antiques, collectibles and new merchandise, some secondhand items and
produce; refreshment stand; parking; restrooms; five motels nearby.

Route 110 Flea Market W XXX

1815 Broadhollow Road
East Farmingdale, New York 11741
(516) 454-0405
Contact: John Marin
(Route 495 to Exit 49 South, two miles to market)

Indoor market; 300 sellers; began in 1978; open every Friday 10:00 a.m. to 9:00 p.m., Saturday and Sunday 10:00 a.m. to 6:00 p.m.; year round; free admission; space rental: $10.00 Friday, $25.00 Saturday and Sunday; reservations recommended.

Variety of new and secondhand items, arts and crafts, collectibles, produce, some antiques; food; restrooms; parking; nearby motels.

East Greenbush Flea Market   W   XX
Greenbush Fair Shopping Center
Junction of Routes 4, 9 and 20
East Greenbush, New York 12061
(518) 477-5897
Contact: Jean Goldman, Gilligan Road, East Greenbush, New York 12061,
(518) 477-5897
(Four miles east of Albany, or Exit 9 of I-90 then east three miles)

Indoor market; 65 dealers; began in 1977; open every Saturday and Sunday, 9:00 a.m. to 5:00 p.m., year round; free admission; space rental: $20.00 to $22.00 per weekend for 12' x 12' with table; reservations advisable.

Mostly quality antiques and collectibles, little new and secondhand merchandise; snack bar with home-cooked food; restrooms; parking lot; nearby motels.

The Foreman Center Flea Market   W   X
41 O'Connor Road
Fairport, New York 14450
Contact: Gordon Hounslea
(Near Fairport Village)

Indoor market; 50 dealers; began in 1977; open Sundays, October to first week in May; 8:00 a.m. to 5:00 p.m.; free admission; space rental: $10.00 per day for 6' x 12'; reservations needed.

Variety of secondhand merchandise, antiques, collectibles, crafts, and art; food; restrooms; parking; nearby motels.

Flushing Flea Market   W   XX
31-35 Downing Street
Flushing, New York 11354
(212) 358-1332
Contact: Joe Molloy, 16-70 Bell Boulevard, Bayside, New York 11360, (212) 423-0764
(Van Wyck Expressway to Linden Place exit)

Indoor market; 90 dealers; began in 1972; open Friday 5:00 p.m. to 10:00 p.m., Saturday 11:00 a.m. to 9:00 p.m., Sunday 11:00 a.m. to 6:00 p.m.; free admission; space rental: $50.00 per week for 8' x 8' booth; no reservations needed.

Variety of antiques, collectibles, new merchandise, secondhand items and produce; snack bar; restrooms; parking; nearby motels.

Lowman Flea Market   W   XX
Route 17
Lowman, New York 14861
(717) 596-2508
Contact: James Stage, RD 2, Gillett, Pennsylvania 16925, (717) 596-2508
(Five miles east of Elmira, fifty miles west of Binghamton)

Outdoor market; 90 sellers; began in 1970; open Saturday, Sunday and holidays
from April to November; free admission; space rental: $3.00 Saturday, $9.00
Sunday for 16'; no reservations needed.

Mostly secondhand and household items, a lot of antiques and collectibles,
some new merchandise; food; restrooms; parking; nearby motels.

Middletown Drive-In Flea Market   W   X
Bradley Corners, Route 6 and 17
Middletown, New York 10940
(914) 343-5551
Contact: Otto Eime, RD 3, Box 2, Port Jervis, New York 12771,
(914) 856-8017
(Exit 3E off I-84, at corner of Route 6 and 17)

Outdoor market; 40 dealers; began in 1974; open Sunday, April to October, close
about 2:00 p.m. in hot summer; admission 25¢ per car; space rental: $3.50 per car
space; no reservations needed.

Mostly collectibles, antiques and secondhand merchandise, some new merchandise, arts and crafts; food; restrooms; parking; nearby motels.

Mid Valley Mall Flea Market (Tri-State Flea Market, Inc.)   ★   W   XX
Route 32 off Route 9W
Newburgh, New York 12550
Contact: Aaron A. Alt, 131 Sunset Drive, Balmville, New York 12550,
(914) 561-4515
(Junction of I-84 and Route 9W, Exit 17 off New York Thruway)

Indoor market; 100 dealers; began in 1980; open Saturday, Sunday, and holidays,
10:00 a.m. to 6:00 p.m., year round; free admission; space rental: $12.50 per day,
$150.00 per month for booth; no reservations needed.

Mostly new merchandise, lots of antiques and collectibles; some secondhand
and household items; gourmet and ethnic food; restrooms; parking; eight local
motels; antiques and auto auctions every other week.

The Canal Street Flea Market   W   XX
335 Canal Street
New York, New York 10013
Contact: Joel Kaufmann, 8 Greene Street, New York, New York 10013,
(212) 226-7541
(Lower Manhattan)

Outdoor market; 40 to 70 dealers; began in 1973; open Saturdays and Sundays,
April through November; free admission; space rental: $25.00 per day for 8' x 8';
no reservations needed.

Mostly secondhand and household items, a lot of antiques and collectibles; food; restrooms; street parking.

Essex Street Flea Market   W XXX
140 Essex Street
New York, New York 10002
(212) 673-5934
Contact: Debbie Greenberg
(Near Houston Street in Lower Manhattan)

Indoor/outdoor market; 100+ dealers; began in 1979; open every Saturday and Sunday, 10:00 a.m. to 6:00 p.m., year round; free admission; space rental: $100.00 and up per month for 8' x 8' to 8' x 12'; reservations needed.
   Mostly new merchandise, some antiques and collectibles; food; restrooms; parking.

SoHo Canal Flea Market   D X
369 Canal Street
New York, New York 10013
(212) 226-8724
Contact: Joel Mathieson
(Lower Manhattan)

Indoor market; 40 to 50 dealers; began in 1972; open daily except Tuesday, 11:00 a.m. to 6:00 p.m., year round; free admission; space rental: $40.00 to $50.00 per week for 8' x 12' to 15'; reservations needed.
   Mostly antiques and collectibles; local restaurants; restrooms; street parking.

Walter's World Famous Le Fleamarket   ★ D XX
252 Bleecker Street
New York, New York 10014
(212) 255-0175
Contact: Walter or Warren
(In Greenwich Village between Sixth and Seventh Avenues)

Indoor/outdoor market; 52 dealers; began about 1976; open Thursday through Sunday, noon to 8:00 p.m., year round; free admission; space rental: $25.00 per day for a booth; reservations advised.
   Mostly collectibles and antiques, especially jewelry, some new and used merchandise; food; restrooms; street parking; auctions on Friday and Saturday.

5th Annual Norwich, New York Antique & Collectible Show   A XXX
County Fairgrounds
Norwich, New York 13815
(607) 334-4184
Contact: A. Miller

Indoor/outdoor market; 200 dealers; began in 1975; held annually on Sunday of Labor Day weekend, 8:00 a.m. to 5:00 p.m.; $1.00 admission; no reservations needed.

Variety of antiques, collectibles, secondhand merchandise, and art objects; food; restrooms; parking; nearby motels.

Fantastic Flea Market   XXX

Monroe County Fair Grounds
Calkins Road and Henrietta Road
Rochester, New York 14620
(716) 334-4000
Contact: Glenn Nichols, PO Box 22848, Rochester, New York 14692
(Exit 46 off New York State Thruway)

Indoor market; 150 dealers; began in 1980; open second Saturday and Sunday of every month, 10:00 a.m. to 5:00 p.m.; free admission; space rental: $15.00 for 10' x 8' booth, both days; reservation necessary.

Variety of collectibles, secondhand merchandise, antiques, crafts; some art objects, produce; food; restrooms; parking; nearby motels.

Acreage Antiques   A   X

Box 1203
Savona, New York 14879
(607) 583-2517
Contact: Lorrie Teske
(Exit 40 off Route 17, one mile north on #415, near Corning)

Outdoor market; 15 sellers; began in 1977; open Labor Day, Fourth of July and Memorial Day weekends; free admission; space rental: $3.00 per day, $5.00 a weekend; no reservations needed.

Mostly collectibles and secondhand merchandise, some antiques; light lunch available; restrooms; parking; nearby motels.

Dutch Mill Antique and Flea Market   ★ W XXX

3633 Carman Road
Schenectady, New York 12303
(518) 355-3420
Contact: Jeannette Mastrianni
(One mile from Route 20 on Route 146)

Indoor/outdoor market; 200 dealers; began in 1974; open every Saturday and Sunday, 10:00 a.m. to 5:00 p.m., year round; free admission; space rental: inside $10.00 per day with table, shelves and pegboard, outside $5.00 for 20' x 30' lawn space; reservations needed for inside.

Mostly antiques and collectibles, some secondhand and new merchandise; snack bars; restrooms; parking; nearby motels; occasional auctions.

Aqueduct Racetrack Flea Market   ★ W XXXX

Aqueduct Racetrack
South Ozone Park, New York 11416
Contact: Sheldon Hills, Barterama Corporation, 257 Hempstead Turnpike, Elmont, New York 11003, (516) 775-8774
(Cross Island Parkway to Belt Parkway to Lefferts Boulevard Exit)

Note: Listings are alphabetical by town.

Outdoor market; 1,500 dealers; began in 1974; open every Saturday from May to second Saturday in October, 8:00 a.m. to 5:00 p.m., every Sunday from May to second Sunday in October, 7:00 a.m. to 5:00 p.m., every Tuesday from March to third Tuesday in December, 8:00 a.m. to 5:00 p.m.; admission $1.50 per car, 50¢ for walk-in; rental space: $15.00 and up for 12' x 25' area; reservations needed.

Mostly new merchandise plus antiques, collectibles and secondhand items; food; restrooms; parking; occasional auctions.

Willowcreek Auction Barn Flea Market ★ W X
5353 Ridge Road West
Spencerport, New York 14559
(716) 352-6450
Contact: Bill and Dot Kenny
(Call for directions)

Outdoor market; 10 to 20 dealers; began in 1974; open every Sunday, May to October; free admission; space rental: $5.00 for 26' x 22'; no reservations needed.

Variety of collectibles, antiques, new merchandise, secondhand items and produce; food; restrooms; parking; nearby motels; auctions on third Thursday of each month.

Antique, Arts and Crafts Flea Market A XXX
Richmondtown Restoration
441 Clarke Avenue
Staten Island, New York 10306
(212) 351-1611
Contact: Mable MacDonald
(From bridges follow signs for Richmondtown Restoration)

Outdoor market; 125 dealers; began in 1980; open second Sunday in June, 9:00 a.m. to 5:00 p.m.; admission 50¢ adults, 25¢ children; space rental: $20.00 for parking space; reservations needed.

Variety of antiques, collectibles, crafts and secondhand merchandise; food; restrooms; parking in Richmondtown restoration; nearby motel.

Yankee Peddlar Flea Market A XXX
Staten Island Historical Society
441 Clarke Avenue
Staten Island, New York 10306
(212) 351-1611
Contact: Mrs. Canille Zampina
(From various bridges follow signs for Richmondtown, from Manhattan
Ferry, Bay Street to Vanderbilt Avenue to Richmond Road and follow signs)

Outdoor market; 125 sellers; open first Sunday in May, 9:00 a.m. to 5:00 p.m.; admission 50¢ adults, 25¢ children; space rental: $20.00 for parking space; reservations needed.

Variety of antiques, collectibles, crafts and secondhand merchandise; food; restrooms; parking in Richmondtown restoration; nearby motel.

Stormville Antique Show and Flea Market   A XXXX
Airport
Route 216
Stormville, New York 12582
(914) 226-6561
Contact: Pat Carnalan, Box 85, Stormville, New York 12582
(Exit Route 52 off Taconic Parkway to Route 216)

Outdoor market; 600 + dealers; began in 1970; open Memorial Day, Labor Day
and Fourth of July weekends; free admission; space rental: $25.00 for 20' x 20';
reservations needed.

Variety of new merchandise, secondhand items, antiques, collectibles,
produce, arts and crafts; food concession; portable toilets; parking; nearby
motels.

Bet-Mar Flea Market   ★ W XXX
2100 Park Street
Syracuse, New York 13206
(315) 471-3655
Contact: Bob Mangin, (315) 488-0361
(Accessible from Routes I-690, I-81, State Route 11 and New York Thruway)

Indoor/outdoor market; 150 to 200 dealers; began in 1973; open every Sunday
April through October, 7:00 a.m. to 4:00 p.m.; free admission; space rental: $6.00
to $10.00 for 9' x 27'; reservations recommended inside.

Mostly antiques, collectibles and secondhand items, some new merchandise
and crafts; food; restrooms; parking; nearby motels; tailgate auctions every
Sunday at 10:30 a.m.

Tarrytown Flea Market   A XXX
635 South Broadway
Tarrytown, New York
Contact: Russell Carrell, Salisbury, Connecticut 06068, (203) 435-9301

Outdoor market; 160 dealers; began in 1971; held annually first Saturday in May,
10:00 a.m. to 5:00 p.m.; $2.00 admission; space rental: $25.00 for 16' x 24';
reservations needed year in advance.

All antiques; food; restrooms; parking; nearby motels.

Busy Flea Market and Antiques Center   W X
55-11 Queens Boulevard
Woodside, New York 11377
(212) 779-0500
Contact: Robert V. Hauff
(Queens Boulevard Exit off Long Island Expressway to Fifty-fifth Street and
Queens Boulevard)

Indoor market; 30 dealers; began in 1976; open Friday, 5:00 p.m. to 10:00 p.m.,
Saturday and Sunday, 10:00 a.m. to 8:00 p.m., year round; free admission; space
rental: $60.00 to $100.00 per week for 8' x 16' or 7' x 22'; reservations sometimes
needed.

Mostly antiques and collectibles, some arts and crafts; snack bar; restrooms; parking; nearby motels.

PENNSYLVANIA

Americana Mail Auction
George M. Rinsland, Auctioneer
4015 Kilmer Avenue
Allentown, Pennsylvania 18104
(215) 395-3939

A mail auction house featuring a range of historical and collectible memorabilia; four or more sales held by catalog yearly; consignments only; no property purchased for sales.

No buyer's premium; telephone as well as mail bids accepted; checks accepted with proper references; no credit cards. No deposit necessary to hold purchase; full payment within 10 days of receiving notice or as arranged; pickups when convenient.

Catalogs for all sales; free copy upon request; oral or written appraisals offered free of charge.

J. J. Mathias
J. J. Mathias, Auctioneer
Office: 863 Bristol Pike
Andalusia, Pennsylvania 19020
Gallery: 1065 Bristol Pike
Andalusia, Pennsylvania 19020
(215) 639-5111
(Near northeast Philadelphia; close to Liberty Bell Harness Track)

An auction service for all types of merchandise, specializing in antiques and collectibles, coins, tools and machinery; sales held on Wednesday evenings—dates determined after merchandise is acquired; estate sales; consignments; property purchased for sales.

No buyer's premium; mail and telephone bids not accepted; local checks accepted with bank letter of credit; no credit cards. Full payment at sale; pickups within three days unless special arrangements are made.

Sale announcements and catalogs mailed; written appraisals offered for fee of 2% of total value of item plus auctioneer's travel expenses, minimum $25.00; appraisal fee refunded if merchandise is liquidated or purchased by J.J. Mathias.

Hartzell's Auction Gallery, Inc.
Raymond M. and Raymond D. Hartzell, Auctioneers
RD 2, Bangor-Richmond Road
Bangor, Pennsylvania 18013
(215) 588-5831 or (215) 588-4614
(Between Routes 191 & 611, just north of Easton, Pennsylvania)

A family business for three generations; sales conducted every Friday at 7:00 p.m. and include from antiques, general merchandise, to machinery and cattle; specialized collectors sales have included Hummels, guns, dolls, and Indian artifacts; estate sales; consignments; property purchased for sales.

No buyer's premium; telephone bids accepted; checks accepted with bank reference; no credit cards. Purchases held with a 20% deposit; full payment and pickups within 10 days.

Sale announcements and catalogs mailed; oral and written appraisals offered for variable fee.

Lee Wamsher Auction Service

527 Monocacy Creek Road
Birdsboro, Pennsylvania 19508
(Most sales held at Monarch Fire Company, Monocacy, just off Route 422, ten miles east of Reading)

Located in Pennsylvania Dutch Country, general consignment sales and estate sales are held at the Monarch Fire Company, and often include Early American and country furniture with general household furnishings; estate sales; consignments; property purchased for sales.

No buyer's premium; mail and telephone bids not accepted; certified or traveler's checks accepted; local checks with proper ID accepted; no credit cards. Full payment and pickups day of sale.

Written appraisals offered for an hourly fee of $10.00.

Bob, Chuck & Rich Roan, Inc.

Rich, Chuck and Don Roan, Auctioneers
Box 118, RD 3
Cogan Station, Pennsylvania 17701
(717) 494-0170
(On Route 15, twenty miles from Interstate 80, Exit 30 North)

A family-run business for 65 years; monthly general antiques and collectibles sales and annual Memorial Day and pre-Christmas sales; specialized sales include pattern glass goblets, miniature lamps, Indian artifacts, and guns; estate sales; consignments; property purchased for sales.

Ten percent buyer's premium on gallery sales only; telephone bids accepted; checks accepted from established customers only; no credit cards. Purchases held with a 25% deposit; full payment within 30 days; pickups as arranged.

Sale announcements and some catalogs mailed; written appraisals offered for a minimum hourly fee of $50.00.

McMenamin's Auction

Jim McMenamin, Auctioneer
Macdade Boulevard & Chester Pike
Collingdale, Pennsylvania 19023
(215) 586-72923
(Route 13, two miles from southwest Philadephia)

General merchandise sold at weekly auction every Monday night; antiques sale held every six weeks, featuring glass, china, antique furniture; estate sales; consignments; property purchased for sales.

No buyer's premium; mail and telephone bids accepted; cash only accepted; no checks or credit cards. Full payment same day; pickups within four days.

Sale announcements mailed; oral or written appraisals offered for fee of 5% of total value of item.

Liberty Valley Auction
Joe Kinn, Auctioneer
RD 1, Box 33
Danville, Pennsylvania 17821
(717) 275-0635
(Four miles west of Danville at Route 642 West)

Two major antique auctions held each month throughout the year, including specialized sales, such as postcard or antique firearms; on-site estate sales; consignments; property purchased for sales.

No buyer's premium; mail and telephone bids accepted; cashier's check or personal check with proper ID accepted; no credit cards. Full payment day of sale; pickups within five days.

Sale announcements mailed; written appraisal offered—fee dependent on value of item.

Patton's Auction Centre
1504 Third Avenue
Duncansville, Pennsylvania 16635
(814) 695-0812
(Sales at Marietta's Laurel Room—three miles west of Duncansville, on old Route 22)

General antiques and fine art sale generally every two months, April through December; specialized sales include dolls, glass and china, early furniture; estate sales; consignments; merchandise purchased for sales.

No buyer's premium; mail and telephone bids accepted; certified checks or checks with bank reference, accepted; no credit cards. Full payment same day; pickups as arranged.

Sale announcements and some catalogs mailed; written appraisals offered for negotiable fee, ranging from $50.00 to $250.00.

Barr's Auction & Exchange
Route 322
Ephrata, Pennsylvania 17522
(717) 733-9694
(Quarter mile east of Route 222)

General sale, of household goods, antiques, collectibles and new building supplies, held every Wednesday evening at 5:30 p.m.; specialized sales of antiques held at flea market just up the road; estate sales on Wednesdays or Saturdays; consignments; property purchased for sales.

No buyer's premium; mail and telephone bids accepted; cashier's checks or certified check preferred, though personal checks accepted with bank letter of credit; Visa accepted. Purchases held with a deposit; merchandise held until full payment is received; pickups within one week.

Oral and written appraisals offered for negotiable fee.

Farmersville Auction House
John J. Rutt, Auctioneer
RD 4
Ephrata, Pennsylvania 17522
(717) 354-5095

Mixed sale of household goods and some antiques, usually held every other week on Tuesday at 5:30 p.m.; annual antiques and collectibles sales on July Fourth and New Year's, including furniture, quilts, dolls; estate sales; consignments; merchandise purchased for sales.

No buyer's premium; mail and telephone bids not accepted; traveler's checks or in-state checks with proper ID accepted; no out-of-state checks or credit cards. Full payment and pickups day of sale.

Sale announcements mailed.

J. Omar Landis Auction Service
J. Omar Landis, Jay M. Witman, Auctioneers
Box 501
Apple and Robert Streets
Ephrata, Pennsylvania 17522
(717) 733-7917 or (717) 665-5735
(Sales held on site at various locations—check mailings)

Specializing in estate and antique sales, real estate and machinery liquidations; specialized sales of antique automobiles, Hummels, Norman Rockwells; consignments only; no property purchased for sales.

No buyer's premium; mail and telephone bids not accepted; checks accepted if approved prior to auction; no credit cards. Full payment and pickups day of sale.

Sale announcements and some catalogs mailed; oral and written appraisals offered for negotiable fee.

Ralph W. Zettlemoyer Auction Co.
Ralph and Sherwood Zettlemoyer, Auctioneers
Route 100 and Claussville Road
PO Box 215
Fogelsville, Pennsylvania 18051
(215) 395-8084
(Sales held on site or in rented social halls—check mailings)

Three sales held weekly from May through September; primarily early country furniture and furnishings from old Pennsylvania German homes in Eastern Pennsylvania area; consignments only; no property purchased for sales.

No buyer's premium; mail and telephone bids not accepted; local checks

Note: Listings are alphabetical by town.

accepted; out-of-state checks accepted only with bank letter of credit or credit established by phone two or three days prior to sale; no credit cards. Full payment at sale; pickups at time of sale or as arranged.

Sale announcements mailed; written appraisals offered for an hourly fee of $35.00.

Jim's Country Auction
James Sizemore, Auctioneer
RD 6
Gettysburg, Pennsylvania 17325
(717) 334-6354
(Four miles north of Gettysburg)

Sales of general merchandise and some antiques held weekly on Saturdays at 6:00 p.m.; antiques and collectibles sale held last Saturday of every month at 6:00 p.m.; estate sales; consignments; property purchased for sales.

No buyer's premium; mail and telephone bids not accepted; checks accepted with proper ID; no credit cards. Full payment day of sale; pickups within one week.

Written appraisals offered for negotiable fee.

Sanford A. Alderfer, Inc.
Sanford A. Alderfer, Auctioneer
665 Harleysville Pike, PO Box 1
Harleysville, Pennsylvania 19438
(215) 723-1171 or (215) 256-8892
(Sales held on site—check mailings for directions)

Weekly sales, including liquidation of antiques, machinery, furnishings and businesses; specialized sales of Hummels, firearms, pottery, coins; consignments only; no property purchased for sales.

No buyer's premium; mail and telephone bids accepted with deposit; checks accepted; no credit cards. Full payment and pickups at time of sale.

Announcements for specialized sales mailed; written appraisals offered for variable fee.

Hatfield Gallery Auctions, Inc.
Paul C. Derstein, Christian Hubscher, Auctioneers
501 Fairground Road
Hatfield, Pennsylvania 19440
(215) 368-6646, (215) 368-6647
(Take Exit 31 Lansdale Interchange, Pennsylvania Turnpike, left off turnpike and left at first traffic light; two miles past blinking light take first left, then follow signs)

General sale, including household goods, held every Tuesday evening; specialized sales of antiques and collectibles held once a month on Friday evening; special coins sale held once a month on Saturday; estate sales; consignments; property purchased for sales.

No buyer's premium; mail and telephone bids accepted; certified, traveler's, or local personal checks with two forms of ID accepted; no credit cards. Payment in full same day; pickups within two days.

Sale announcements mailed; written appraisals offered for fee of $100.00.

Martin Auctioneers, Inc.

Box 71
Blueball, Pennsylvania 17506
(717) 354-7006
Martins' Sales Pavilion
Route 340 and New Holland Road
Intercourse, Pennsylvania 17534
(Fifteen miles east of Lancaster)

Specializing in the sale of carriages, sleighs, coaching and driving equipment, anything related to equestrian field; three major sales held each year, in May, August and October; other sales include antique tools, country furniture, china and glassware, some quilts; specialized sales include private collections of carriages or driving equipment; estate sales; consignments; property purchased for sales.

No buyer's premium; mail and telephone bids accepted; checks accepted with bank letter of credit; no credit cards. Full payment day of sale; pickups within two weeks.

Sale announcements and May and October catolog sales mailed; oral or written appraisals offered for negotiable fee.

Kennett Auction Inc.

Kenneth Grist, Frank McCraghan, Auctioneers
Cedar Croft Road
Kennett Square, Pennsylvania 19348
(215) 444-5940 or (215) 444-9981
(Along Route 1)

Sales held every other Sunday at 6:30 p.m., featuring antiques, collectibles, oak and modern furniture; estate sales; consignments; limited amount of property purchased for sales.

No buyer's premium; mail and telephone bids not accepted; checks accepted with proper ID or bank letter of credit approved prior to auction; no credit cards. Full payment day of sale; pickups within one week.

Written appraisals offered for negotiable fee.

Fulton Market Auction

William R. Wood, Auctioneer
607 North Plum Street
Lancaster, Pennsylvania 17602
(717) 393-8604

General auctions held every Friday night; sales include antiques, tools, machinery, household furnishings; estate sales; consignments; property purchased for sales.

No buyer's premium; mail and telephone bids accepted; cash only; no personal checks or credit cards accepted. No deposit necessary to hold purchase; full payment and pickups within seven days.

Sale announcements, for special antiques sales, mailed.

C. Hinden, Jr. Auction Service
2475 Lincoln Highway East (Route 30)
Lancaster, Pennsylvania 17602
(717) 392-0943
(Six miles east of Lancaster)

Third generation in auction business; sales of antiques held as merchandise becomes available; estate sales; consignments only; no property purchased for sales.

No buyer's premium; mail and telephone bids not accepted; certified or traveler's checks accepted; personal checks accepted only from established customers; no credit cards. Full payment day of sale; pickups within two days.

Sale announcements mailed; written appraisals offered for variable fee.

Claude F. Smith
Claude F. Smith, Auctioneer
1776 Lincoln Highway East
Lancaster, Pennsylvania 17602
(717) 392-7492

Approximately 50 sales conducted yearly, including estates and antiques; consignments only; no property purchased for sales.

No buyer's premium; mail and telephone bids not accepted; in-state checks with proper ID accepted; no out-of-state checks or credit cards. Full payment at time of sale; pickups within two days.

Sale announcements mailed; written appraisals offered for fee ranging from $50.00 to $200.00, dependent on time required.

Clements & Sons
Joe Clements, Auctioneer
11 South Lansdowne Avenue
Lansdowne, Pennsylvania 19050
(215) 622-9825
(Five miles south of Philadelphia off Old Route 1)

Sales of general and antique merchandise every Tuesday at 6:30 p.m.; monthly specialized sales feature antique furniture, automobiles, guns, fine art, Americana; estate sales; consignments; property purchased for sales.

No buyer's premium; mail and telephone bids accepted from known customers only; cash or certified checks accepted; no personal checks or credit cards. Purchases held with a 20% deposit; full payment and pickups within three days.

Sale announcements mailed; oral or written appraisals offered for negotiable fee.

Conestoga Auction Company, Inc.
PO Box 1, Graystone Road
Manheim, Pennsylvania 17545
(717) 898-7284
(Seven miles north of Lancaster off Route 72)

General household sale held weekly on Tuesday at 6:00 p.m.; antiques sale held monthly on the last Monday at 6:00 p.m. and Tuesday at 10:00 a.m., featuring furniture, cut glass, china, silver, paper collectibles, quilts; estate sales; consignments; property purchased for sales.

Ten percent buyer's premium; mail and telephone bids accepted; checks accepted with proper ID; no credit cards. Full payment day of sale; pickups within one day.

Sale announcements mailed.

The Fine Arts Company of Philadelphia
John H. Frisk, Auctioneer
Mailing address: 1611 Walnut
Philadelphia, Pennsylvania 19103
Sales held at: Historical Society of Pennsylvania
1300 Locust
Philadelphia, Pennsylvania
(215) 564-3644
(In center of city)

Four to five major two-day antiques sales a year, usually held on Wednesdays and Thursdays, pre-sale exhibition on Mondays and Tuesdays; featuring fine arts, period furniture and furnishings; decorative arts including silver and porcelain, jewelry; estate sales; consigned merchandise only; no property purchased for sales.

Ten percent buyer's premium; mail and telephone bids accepted; checks accepted with two to three forms of ID; no credit cards. Purchases held with a 25% deposit; full payment and pickups within three days (or by Friday, week of sale).

Sale announcements mailed; catalogs for all major sales; oral appraisals offered free of charge; written appraisals for negotiable fee.

Samuel T. Freeman & Company
1808-10 Chestnut Street
Philadelphia, Pennsylvania 19103
(215) 563-9275

Under direct father-to-son ownership for 175 years; handles both general furniture and furnishings as well as fine art and antiques; general sales held three times a week on all floors; nine specialized sales a year feature art, antiques and collectibles including railroadiana, jewelry, Oriental rugs; estate sales; consignments only; no property purchased for sales.

No buyer's premium; mail and telephone bids accepted with a 25% deposit; checks with proper ID accepted; no credit cards. Purchases held with a 25%

deposit; full payment and pickups from weekly sales within 24 hours; payment and pickups of merchandise from nine specialized sales within seven days.

Sale announcements mailed; some catalogs; written appraisals offered for fee of $250.00 per day plus travel expenses.

Ted Maurer, Auctioneer
1931 North Charlotte Street
Pottstown, Pennsylvania 19464
(215) 323-1573
(Most major sales held at Firehall in Lionville, Pennsylvania)

Specializing in sale of toy electric trains and antique toys for boys; estate sales; consignments; property purchased for sales.

No buyer's premium; mail and telephone bids not accepted; cash only; checks and credit cards not accepted. Full payment and pickups day of sale.

Sale announcements and some catalogs mailed; oral or written appraisals offered for fee of $100.00 per diem plus expenses.

Pennypacker Auction Centre
Mr. C. Pennypacker, J. Pennypacker, Sr., S. Ferraro, Mrs. C. Pennypacker Andrews, Auctioneers
1540 New Holland Road
Kenhorst
Reading, Pennsylvania 19607
(215) 777-5890, (215) 777-6121
(On Route 625, just outside of Reading)

General sales held every Wednesday; antique sales held twice a month in spring and fall; specialized sales include blue historical china, folk art; estate sales; consignments only; no property purchased for sales.

No buyer's premium; telephone bids accepted; checks accepted with bank certification; no credit cards. Purchases held with a 25% deposit. Full payment within 10 days; pickups within 30 days.

Printed catalogs for antique sales only, at $15.00 per year; written appraisals offered for fee dependent on items and time involved.

Collectors' Cove, Ltd.
Nelson Weidenbaugh, Auctioneer
Route 33, Box 333
Sciota, Pennsylvania 18354
(717) 421-7439 weekdays, (717) 992-9161 Sundays
(Eight miles south of Stroudsburg)

A combination auction service and antique mall, housing over 100 dealers in individual shops; antique auction held second Sunday of every month; higher quality antiques sale held fourth Sunday of the month; specialized sales include toys, coin-operated machines, children's books, guns, German steins, clocks, lamps; estate sales; consignments; property purchased for sales.

Ten percent buyer's premium; telephone bids accepted; checks accepted with proper ID and bank letter of credit; no credit cards. Purchases held with a 25% deposit; full payment and pickups within 30 days.

Sale announcements mailed; oral appraisals offered free.

Bonnie Brae Auction
Richard J. Mayer, Auctioneer
2 Bonnie Brae Road, PO Box 187
Spring City, Pennsylvania 19475
(215) 948-8050
(On Route 724, eight miles west of Valley Forge; midway between Spring City and Phoenixville)

Antiques and general household goods featured in frequent sales; specialized sales include jewelry and Hummels; estate sales; consignments; property purchased for sales.

No buyer's premium; mail and telephone bids accepted; checks accepted with bank reference; no credit cards. Purchases held with a 25% deposit; full payment and pickups within seven days.

Sale announcements and some catalogs mailed; written appraisals offered for variable fee.

Auctions by Theriault
George Theriault, Auctioneer
PO Box 174
Waverly, Pennsylvania 18471
(717) 945-3041
(Sales held in hotels throughout the country)

Dealing solely in antique and collectible dolls; sales held monthly in various hotels in the following locations: January: Scottsdale; February: West Palm Beach; March: Dallas; April: Los Angeles; May: Chicago; June: Washington, DC; September: San Francisco; October: Denver; November: Washington, DC; two-day auctions may feature antique dolls the first day, specialized Madame Alexander dolls on the second; no sales conducted in December, July and August; consignments only; no property purchased for sales.

No buyer's premium; mail and telephone bids accepted; cashier's checks preferred; otherwise, personal checks with two forms of ID accepted; Master Charge and Visa accepted. Full payment and pickups at time of sale.

Sale announcements and catalogs mailed; oral and written appraisals offered free of charge.

Waverly Books O.P.
PO Box 222
Waverly, Pennsylvania 18471
(717) 586-8242
(Auctions held at various locations in Washington, DC area—check mailings for directions.)

A book auction firm holding at least four yearly sales; specialized sales include modern first editions and illustrated books; estate sales of books only; consignments; books purchased for sales.

No buyer's premium; mail and telephone bids accepted; checks accepted with proper ID; no credit cards. Full payment and pickups day of sale.

Sale announcements and catalogs; written appraisals offered for fee dependent on value, or variable hourly fee of $20.00 to $30.00; oral appraisals offered free.

Note: Listings are alphabetical by town.

Chuck's Auction Center

James E. Lewis, Charles E. Tedrow, Auctioneers
J. C. Townend & Son Hardware Building
248 Wyoming Avenue
Wyoming, Pennsylvania 18644
(717) 693-1161, (717) 693-0372
Sales: Independent Hose House
South Sprague Avenue
Kingston, Pennsylvania
(One block off Route 11 at Kingston Corners)

A family-operated business; sales held, as announced, at two and three week intervals; some specialized antique sales; some mail auctions; estate sales; consignments; property purchased for sales.

No buyer's premium; mail and telephone bids accepted; purchase of catalog required to enter catalog sales; cash or traveler's checks preferred; otherwise, Pennsylvania checks accepted, or out-of-state checks from established customers; no credit cards. Full payment usually immediately after sale; pickups as arranged.

Sale announcements and some catalogs mailed; oral and written appraisals offered for negotiable fee.

Hake's Americana & Collectibles

Theodore L. Hake, Auctioneer
PO Box 1444
York, Pennsylvania 17405
(717) 843-3731

Exclusively mail auctions featuring such collectibles as "character collectibles" (The Yellow Kid, Elvis, the Beatles, Shirley Temple), comic characters, cowboy heroes, space heroes, toys, movie, political and advertising memorabilia, automobilia, Boy Scout, aviation, baseball, and paper doll collectibles; specialized sales of Disneyana, political Americana, radio premiums, or any of above categories; consignments; property purchased for sales.

No buyer's premium; telephone as well as mail bids accepted; checks from established customers accepted, or shipment held until check clears; Master Charge and Visa accepted. Purchases held with a 33.3% deposit; full payment within two weeks, unless 60-day lay-a-way plan is arranged; shipment made upon full payment.

Quarterly catalogs mailed; written appraisals offered for negotiable fee.

Cly Country Auction

W. L. Kohr, Sr., Philip L. Erb, Auctioneers
RD 1, Box 190
York Haven, Pennsylvania 17370
(717) 266-2048 and (717) 266-2444
(Between York and Harrisburg, Pennsylvania, off Interstate 83 at Exit 13, Newberrytown, south to Cly auction barn)

General goods, antiques, and collectibles sales held as merchandise becomes available; estate sales; consignments; property purchased for sales.

No buyer's premium; telephone bids accepted; certified checks, traveler's checks, or personal checks with proper ID accepted; no credit cards. Purchases held with a 10% deposit; full payment and pickups within two days.

Sale announcements mailed; oral and written appraisals offered for negotiable fee.

Shupp's Grove Antique Market   W XXX
Route 897
Adamstown, Pennsylvania 19501
(215) 484-4115
Contact: Frank Heilinger, PO Box 384, Adamstown, Pennsylvania 19501,
(717) 949-3656 or (215) 484-9314
(Two miles north of Pennsylvania Turnpike Exit 21 off Route 222, near
Denver)

Outdoor market in shady grove; 200 dealers; began in 1962; open Saturday and Sunday, 8:00 a.m. to 5:00 p.m., third weekend in April to the end of October; free admission; space rental: varies, call for information; reservations accepted.

Antiques and collectibles only; food; restrooms; parking; nearby motels.

Lakeside Flea Market   W X
Lakeside Park, Route 54
Barnesville, Pennsylvania 18214
(717) 467-2411
Contact: Ed McGrath, PO Box 376, Mahanoy City, Pennsylvania 17948
(Exit 37E off I-81)

Indoor/outdoor market; 50 dealers; began in 1969; open Sundays, 9:00 a.m. to 5:00 p.m., year round; free admission; space rental: call for rate for 9' x 2½' tables; reservations needed.

Variety of secondhand items, antiques and collectibles, some new merchandise and crafts; food; restrooms; parking; nearby motels.

Boalsburg Flea Market   A XX
Hess Memorial Field
Boalsburg, Pennsylvania 16827
Contact: Betty Gates or Margaret Tennis, RD 1, Box 151, Boalsburg,
Pennsylvania 16827, (814) 466-6311
(One mile off Routes 322 and 45 West)

Outdoor market; 50 to 100 dealers; held annually, usually in August; 50¢ admission; space rental: $17.50 for 30' x 24'; reservations needed.

Antiques and collectibles only; food, bake sale; restrooms; parking; nearby motels.

Up-Country Flea Market   M   XXX
Cedars Country Store
Route 73
Cedars, Pennsylvania 19423
(215) 584-4238
Contact: Jon Kirkbride, Route 73, Cedars, Pennsylvania 19423, (215) 584-4238
(Schulkill Expy to 363 North to Route 73 West, one mile; or Lansdale Exit
off North Eastern Extension of Pennsylvania Turnpike, south on Bustard
to 73)

Outdoor market; 128 dealers; began in 1964; open third Saturday of each month,
May to October; free admission; space rental: $22.00 for 20' x 20', $14.50 for
10' x 12'; reservations needed.
     Mostly antiques and collectibles, some crafts; food stands; restroom; parking; nearby motels.

Power House Flea Market   W   X
Route 29 North
Collegeville, Pennsylvania 19426
(215) 489-7388
Contact: Erv Shainline
(Near intersection of Routes 422 and 29)

Indoor/outdoor market; 25 dealers; began in 1970; open Sundays, 9:00 a.m. to
6:00 p.m., year round; free admission; space rental: $10.00 to $12.00 for 9' x 12'
with two tables; reservations needed.
     Variety of collectibles, antiques, new and secondhand merchandise; food;
restrooms; parking; nearby motels.

Hummer's Antiques and Collectibles   W   XX
Route 222
Denver, Pennsylvania 17517
(215) 267-3240
Contact: T.M. Carlock or Howard B. Katz, RD 3, Denver, Pennsylvania 17517
(Quarter mile from Exit 21 on Pennsylvania Turnpike, near Adamstown)

Indoor/outdoor market; 65 dealers; began in 1973; open every Sunday 7:00 a.m.
to 5:00 p.m.; free admission; space rental: $16.00 per week for 10' x 12' booth; no
reservations outside.
     Antiques and collectibles only; food; restrooms; parking; nearby motels.

Lancaster County Antiques and Collectibles Market   D   X
Route 272
Denver, Pennsylvania 17517
(215) 267-9943
Contact: Roger Faut, Box 23, Stevens, Pennsylvania 17578, (213) 267-2064

Indoor market, some outdoor spots; began in 1977; 20 dealers; open daily except
Tuesday, 9:00 a.m. to 9:00 p.m., year round; free admission; space rental: $20.00
per 8' x 9' booth; reservations needed.
     Only antiques and collectibles; nearby restaurants; restrooms; parking;
nearby motels.

Renninger's Antique Market   W   XXXX

Route 222
Denver, Pennsylvania 17517
(215) 267-2177
Contact: Terry Heilman, RD 1, Denver, Pennsylvania 17517
(Pennsylvania Turnpike Exit 21, near Adamstown)

Indoor/outdoor market; 700 dealers; began in 1967; open Sundays, 7:00 a.m. to 5:00 p.m.; free admission; space rental: $24.00 for 18' x 25'; reservations needed.
    Only antiques and collectibles; food; restrooms; parking; nearby motels.

The Trading Post Center   W   XXX

451 West High Street
Elizabethtown, Pennsylvania 17022
(717) 367-2321
Contact: Anthony Szafranic, 623 West Pine Street, Palmyra, Pennsylvania 17078, (717) 838-5278
(On Route 241 S, half mile west of Center Square)

Indoor/outdoor market, 150 dealers; began about 10/81 open Saturday and Sunday, 9:00 a.m. to 5:00 p.m., year round; free admission; space rental: varies for 8' x 12' and up; reservations needed inside.
    Mostly antiques and collectibles, some new and used merchandise, produce, art and crafts; food; restrooms; parking; nearby motels.

Green Dragon Farmers Market and Auction   W   XXXX

RD 4, North State Street
Ephrata, Pennsylvania 17522
(717) 733-2334
Contact: Larry Loose or William Rohrback
(Exit 21 off Pennsylvania Turnpike, go four miles south to Route 272)

Indoor/outdoor market; 250 dealers; began in 1932; open Friday, 10:00 a.m. to 10:00 p.m., year round; free admission; space rental: $10.00 for 10' x 8'; reservations needed.
    Mostly new merchandise and produce, very few antiques, collectibles or secondhand items; four restaurants; restrooms; free parking; nearby motels.

Fayetteville Flea & Farmers Market   D   X

225 Lincoln Way West
Fayetteville, Pennsylvania 17222
(717) 352-9915
Contact: Mr. Dymond
(Near Chambersburg and Gettysburg, Pennsylvania, off Route 30 on Lincoln Highway)

Indoor market; 30 to 35 dealers; began in 1980; open every day except Tuesday, 9:00 a.m. to 9:00 p.m.; free admission; inquire about space rental.
    Variety of secondhand merchandise, antiques, collectibles, and art objects, some crafts and produce; food; restrooms; parking; nearby hotels.

Frazer Flea Market   W X
351 Lancaster Avenue
Frazer, Pennsylvania 19355
(215) 644-9894
Contact: Edward Holst, 302 East Marshall Street, West Chester,
Pennsylvania 19380, (215) 436-4925
(From Downington, Pennsylvania, go east on Route 30)

Indoor market; eight dealers; began in 1978; open Friday, noon to 9:00 p.m.,
Saturday and Sunday, 9:30 a.m. to 5:00 p.m.; free admission; space rental: $80.00
to $100.00 monthly; no reservations needed.

Mostly secondhand merchandise and a mixture of antiques, collectibles; no
food; restrooms; parking; nearby motels.

Zern's Farmer's Market   ★ W XXXX
Route 73
Gilbertsville, Pennsylvania 19525
(215) 367-2461
Contact: John Speca or Jake Rhoads
(New Jersey Turnpike to Pennsylvania Turnpike, get off at Downington Exit,
take Route 100 North to Route 73)

Indoor/outdoor market; 350 dealers; began in 1922; open Friday, 2:00 p.m. to
10:00 p.m., Saturday, 11:00 a.m. to 10:00 p.m., year round; free admission; space
rental: $10.00 per weekend for 10' x 10' outside, 10' x 10' to 8' x 30' inside;
reservations needed.

Mostly new and secondhand merchandise, few antiques or collectibles; a
little produce; food; restrooms; parking; nearby motels; antiques auction Friday
and Saturday.

Harrisburg Drive-In Flea Market   W XXXX
6001 Allentown Boulevard
Harrisburg, Pennsylvania 17112
(717) 545-6441
Contact: Charles Lenker, 11 South Arlene Street, Harrisburg, Pennsylvania
17112, (717) 545-3476
(Exit 26 East off I-81)

Outdoor market; 100 to 350 dealers; began in 1968; open Saturdays and Sundays,
8:30 a.m. to 5:00 p.m., April through November; free admission; space rental:
$9.00 per day for 10' x 20' plus vehicle space; no reservations needed.

Variety of antiques, collectibles, new merchandise, secondhand items,
produce and crafts; food; restrooms; parking; nearby motels.

Olde Mill Flea Market   D X
Intersection of Bellvue, Hulmeville and Trenton
Hulmeville, Pennsylvania 19047
(215) 757-1777
Contact: Kathy Loeffler, PO Box 69, Penndel, Pennsylvania 19047
(I-95 to US 1, south to Highway 513, turn left for two miles; Exit 28 off
Pennsylvania Turnpike, US 1 to 513)

Indoor market located in old grist mill; 10 to 20 dealers; began in 1971; open Thursday and Friday 6:00 p.m. to 10:00 p.m., Saturday noon to 10:00 p.m., Sunday noon to 6:00 p.m.; free admission; space rental: $50.00 monthly for 8' x 12', larger space available; reservations needed.

Mostly antiques and collectibles, some used furniture; no food; restrooms; on-street parking; nearby motels.

The Kutztown Antique and Collectors Extravaganza   A   XXXX
Nobles Street
Kutztown, Pennsylvania 19530
(215) 683-6848, (215) 267-2177
(On Nobles Street, one and one-half miles out of Kutztown, which is located between Reading and Allantown)

Indoor/outdoor market; 1,300 to 1,400 dealers; held three times per year, in April, June, and September, call for specific dates; hours 8:00 a.m. to 5:00 p.m.; admission $1.00; space rental $40.00 for two days; reservations needed.

Mostly antiques and collectibles, some art; cafeteria; restrooms; parking; motels.

Rice's Sale and Country Market   ★   XXXX
Green Hill Road
Lahaska, Pennsylvania 18931
(215) 297-5808
Contact: Sherri Jamison, Street Road, Lahaska, Pennsylvania 18931, (215) 794-8185
(263 North to Green Hill Road)

Indoor/outdoor market; 400 dealers; began in 1880; open Tuesdays 7:00 a.m. to 1:00 p.m., year round, Fridays 3:00 p.m. to 9:00 p.m., part of year; free admission; space rental: $5.00 for 8' table; no reservations needed.

Variety of collectibles, new merchandise, antiques, some secondhand items and produce; food; restrooms; parking; nearby motels; auctions on Friday evenings.

Fruitville Pike Flea Market   W   X
1357 Fruitville Pike
Lancaster, Pennsylvania 17601
(717) 569-1832 or (717) 397-5411
Contact: Mile Vasile, 760 Bluegrass Road, Lancaster, Pennsylvania 17601
(Fruitville Pike Exit off Route 30, south for three-quarters mile)

Indoor/outdoor market; 22 dealers; began in 1977; open Saturday and Sunday, 10:00 a.m. to 4:00 p.m., year round; free admission; space rental: 8' x 10' in summer is $11.25, winter $15.00; 8' x 12': summer $15.00, winter $20.00; reservations needed.

Mostly antiques and collectibles, some secondhand and little new merchandise; food; restrooms; parking; nearby motels.

Note: Listings are alphabetical by town.

Meadowbrook Farmers Market and Antique Center W XXX
345 West Main Street
Leola, Pennsylvania 17540
(717) 656-2226
Contact: Wayne Stauffer
(Four miles east of Lancaster on Route 23)

Indoor market; 120 dealers; began in 1970; open Friday 9:00 a.m. to 8:00 p.m., Saturday 8:00 a.m. to 4:00 p.m.; free admission; space rental: $1.50 per foot; reservations needed.

Lots of collectibles and antiques, new merchandise, secondhand items, produce, arts and crafts; food; restrooms; parking; nearby motels.

Meadows Antique Flea Market M XXXX
Meadows Race Track, Racetrack Road
Meadowland, Pennsylvania 15347
Contact: Jewel Kirwan, Box 367, Meadowland, Pennsylvania, (412) 228-3045
(Exit 8 off I-79, twenty-five miles south of Pittsburgh)

Indoor/outdoor market; 350 to 400 dealers; began 1978; held monthly, on Sundays, 8:00 a.m. to 3:00 p.m.; $1.00 admission; space rental: $20.00 inside for 15' x 6', $15.00 outside; reservations needed inside.

Mostly antique furniture, collectibles, little used merchandise, crafts, art objects; snack bar; restrooms; parking; nearby motels.

Antique Village X
RD 6, Box 6657
Mercer, Pennsylvania 16137
(418) 748-3062
Contact: Edward Kudlac, 287 Morrisey Street, Pittsburgh, Pennsylvania 15214, (412) 231-4971
(Route 78 to 208 West, go one mile to blinking light)

Indoor/outdoor market; five dealers; began in 1980; open 9:00 a.m. to 5:00 p.m., May to October; free admission; space rental: $5.00; reservations needed.

Mostly antiques and collectibles, some secondhand items; food; restrooms; parking; nearby motels.

Twin Slope Market and Flea Market ★ W XX
Route 23
Morgantown, Pennsylvania 19543
(215) 286-9800
Contact: Ken Hertzler, Morgantown, Pennsylvania 19543, (215) 286-9164
(One mile west of Morgantown)

Indoor/outdoor market; 100 dealers; began in 1969; open Friday 11:00 a.m. to 9:00 p.m., Saturday 9:00 a.m. to 3:00 p.m., year round; free admission; space rental: $1.25 per foot, 10' x 8' to 20'; reservations needed.

Variety of new merchandise, some antiques, collectibles and produce; food; restrooms; parking; three motels nearby: Friday night auctions.

The Village Mall   D X
1 Morton Avenue
Morton, Pennsylvania 19070
(215) 543-5566
Contact: Albert Yannelli
(From I-95 take Route 420 North three miles)

Indoor market; 40 dealers; began in 1973; open Wednesday and Thursday 10:00 a.m. to 5:00 p.m., Friday 10:00 a.m. to 9:00 p.m., Saturday and Sunday noon to 6:00 p.m.; free admission; space rental: $125.00 and up per month; no reservations needed.

Mostly antiques and collectibles, some art; food; restrooms; parking; nearby motels.

Antique Emporium   D X
Routes 191 and 248
Nazareth, Pennsylvania 18064
(215) 759-8141
Contact: Bill Sadalia

Indoor/outdoor market; 50 dealers; began in 1977; open daily noon to 5:00 p.m., Sunday 9:00 a.m. to 5:00 p.m.; free admission; space rental: $10.00 and $15.00 for 10' x 8' and 20' x 8' spaces; no reservations needed.

Mostly antiques and collectibles, some arts and crafts; diner nearby; restrooms; parking; nearby motel.

Country Host Flea Market   W XX
Route 202
New Hope, Pennsylvania
Contact: Dorothy Kohler, 7311 Woodcrest Avenue, Philadelphia, Pennsylvania 19151, (215) 477-4541
(On border between Pennsylvania and New Jersey, fifteen miles north of Philadelphia)

Outdoor market; 60 dealers; began in 1968; open every Saturday, Sunday and holiday, April through November; free admission; space rental: $5.00 per table; reservations needed for Sundays.

Mostly antiques and collectibles, some crafts; restaurant; restrooms; parking; nearby motels.

Gateway Drive-In Flea Market   W X
133 Logan's Ferry Road
New Kensington, Pennsylvania 15068
(412) 335-1111
Contact: Alice LaPorte, 512 Murray Avenue, Arnold, Pennsylvania 15068, (412) 335-4356

Outdoor market; 50 dealers; began in 1978; open Sundays, 9:00 a.m. to 4:00 p.m., June to October; 50¢ admission; space rental: 50¢ for 20' x 20'; no reservations needed.

Mostly new merchandise, secondhand items and collectibles, some antiques and crafts; food concession; restrooms; parking; nearby motels.

The New Oxford Antique Market   A XXX
Center Square
New Oxford, Pennsylvania 17350
Contact: Mrs. Henry Stock, 2 Berlin Road, New Oxford, Pennsylvania 17350,
(717) 624-2342
(Located on US Route 30, between York and Gettysburg)

Outdoor market; 130 dealers; began in 1956; held annually, usually the third
Saturday in June; admission free; space rental $25.00; reservations needed.
    Mostly antiques and collectibles, also crafts and art objects; food stands
sponsored by local community service groups; restrooms; parking; motels
nearby.

Black Horse Flea Market   W XX
Route 30
Parkesburg, Pennsylvania 19365
Contact: Joe McCoy, RD 2, Box 345, Parkesburg, Pennsylvania 19365
(One mile west of Route 10)

Indoor/outdoor market; 50+ dealers; began in 1970; open Saturday, Sunday,
Monday and holidays, year round; free admission; space rental: $5.00 per day; no
reservations needed.
    Mostly antiques and collectibles, very little new merchandise; no food;
restrooms; parking; local motels.

Roosevelt Mall   W XXX
2329 Cottman Avenue
Philadelphia, Pennsylvania 19149
(215) 331-2000
Contact: Sy Goldberg
(US Highway 1 and 73)

Outdoor market; 115 dealers; began in 1976; open every Sunday, April till
October; free admission; space rental: $10.00 for 15' parking space; no reserva-
tions needed.
    Mostly secondhand and household items; food; no restrooms; parking;
nearby motels.

Quaker City Flea Market
Tacony and Comly Streets
Philadelphia, Pennsylvania 19135
(215) 744-2022
Contact: Kay Williams or Joe Breish
(I-95 between Bridge and Cottman Streets Exits)

Indoor/outdoor market; 150 dealers; began in 1974; open every Saturday and
Sunday, 10:00 a.m. to 5:00 p.m., year round; free admission; space rental: $25.00
inside, $8.00 outside; reservations needed.
    Mostly antiques and collectibles, some new and secondhand merchandise;
food; restrooms; parking; nearby motels.

Stadium Swap Meet   A   XXXX
Philadelphia Veteran's Stadium
Highways 76 and 95
Philadelphia, Pennsylvania 19145
Contact: David Groverman, PO Box 28711, Philadelphia, Pennsylvania 19151,
(215) 356-SWAP

Outdoor market; 500 dealers; began in 1977; held three times a year, call ahead
for dates; $2.00 admission; space rental: varies for 25' x 20' open and covered;
reservations needed for covered spaces.

Mostly antiques and collectibles, some new merchandise; food; restrooms;
parking; nearby motels.

Keystone State Grand Flea Market   W   XXXX
1500 Pennsylvania Avenue
Pittsburgh, Pennsylvania 15233
(412) 232-3338
Contact: Herbert Walker

Indoor/outdoor market, 900 dealers, began in 1979; open Saturday and Sunday,
9:00 a.m. to 5:00 p.m.; 25¢ admission; space rental: $50.00 for weekend; no
reservations needed.

Variety of books, produce, antiques, collectibles, crafts, secondhand merchandise, also artist gallery; snack bars; restrooms; parking; nearby motels.

Flea Market   M   X
Pleasant Gap Fire Company
East College Avenue
Pleasant Gap, Pennsylvania 16823
(814) 359-2102
Contact: Lyle M. Beal, 128 White Rock Avenue, Pleasant Gap, Pennsylvania,
(814) 359-2893
(At the Pleasant Gap Fire Hall, on Routes 26 and 144)

Indoor market; 29 dealers; began in 1965; held third Sunday of every month, 8:00
a.m. to 5:00 p.m.; free admission; space rental: $7.50 per 32" x 72" table;
reservations needed.

Mostly antiques and collectibles; some secondhand items, new merchandise,
crafts, and art objects; food; restrooms; parking; nearby motels.

Quakertown Flea and Farmers Market   ★ W   XXX
201 Station Road
Quakertown, Pennsylvania 18951
(215) 536-4115
Contact: Richard Seibert
(Half mile south of town)

Indoor/outdoor market; 120 dealers; began in 1972; open every Friday, Saturday
10:00 a.m. to 10:00 p.m., Sunday 11:00 a.m. to 5:00 p.m.; free admission; space
rental: $18.00 for 6' x 12' indoors, $4.00 for 8' x 12' outdoors; reservations needed
for indoor space.

Mostly antiques, collectibles and secondhand merchandise, some arts, crafts and produce; food; restrooms; parking; nearby motels; household and collectibles auctions on Friday nights.

King's Antique and Flea Market   W   XX

710 East King Street
Shippensburg, Pennsylvania 17257
(717) 243-6337
Contact: Norman Swidler, 849 Hamilton Street, Carlisle, Pennsylvania 17013
(Exit 10 off I-81)

Indoor market; 75 dealers; began in 1974; open Sundays, 8:00 a.m. to 5:00 p.m., year round; free admission; space rental: $6.00 for 10' x 10'; reservations needed.

Mostly antiques and collectibles, very little secondhand merchandise; food; restrooms; parking; motel next door.

Shippensburg Fairgrounds Flea Market   W   XX

Possum Hollow Road
Shippensburg, Pennsylvania 17257
(717) 532-8911
Contact: Richard Wright, RR 2, Chambersburg, Pennsylvania 17201
(Exit 9 off I-81)

Indoor/outdoor market; 25 dealers inside, limitless number outside; began in 1974; open Sundays 8:00 a.m. to 5:00 p.m., September to May; free admission; space rental: $5.00 for 10' area; no reservations needed.

Variety of antiques, collectibles, secondhand items and new merchandise; restrooms; parking; nearby motels.

Peddlers Cove   W   XXX

Routes 191 and 507
South Sterling, Pennsylvania 18460
Contact: Beatrice Delania
(Take Exit 5 off Route 84, five miles south on Route 507)

Indoor/outdoor market; 160 dealers; began in 1976; open Saturday and Sunday, 10:00 a.m. to 6:00 p.m.; free admission; space rental: $8.00 to $17.00 inside, $4.00 outside; reservations needed inside only.

Mostly oak furniture, antiques, collectibles, and art objects inside, secondhand merchandise, few crafts outside; food; restrooms; parking; nearby motels.

Waynesboro Antique Flea Market   A   XXX

323 East Main. Street
Waynesboro, Pennsylvania 17268
(717) 762-6512
Contact: Francis H. Miller
(On State Route 16 in downtown Waynesboro)

Outdoor market; 100 to 150 dealers; began in 1970; held second Saturday in June, third Saturday in September; free admission; space rental: $17.00 for a parking space; reservations needed.

Mostly antiques and collectibles, some crafts; food; restrooms; parking; nearby motels.

Mentzer's Antique Market   W XX
Route 18
West Middlesex, Pennsylvania 16159
(412) 528-2300
Contact: Fred Mentzer, Box 584, West Middlesex, Pennsylvania 16159, (412) 528-2300
(Exit 1-North on I-80)

Indoor/outdoor market; 80 to 100 dealers; began in 1974; open Wednesday, Saturday and Sunday, 9:00 a.m. to 5:00 p.m., year round; free admission; space rental: $16.00 for 10' x 12'; no reservations needed.

All antiques and collectibles; food; restrooms; parking; nearby motels.

Springetts Fire Company Flea Market   ★ M X
3013 East Market Street
York, Pennsylvania 17402
(717) 755-8769
(Route 462, east of York)

Indoor market; 15 dealers; began in 1976; open second Sunday of each month; free admission; space rental: $10.00 for two 8' tables; reservations needed.

Mostly antiques and secondhand items, some crafts; food; restrooms; parking; nearby motels; occasional auctions.

WEST VIRGINIA

Sun Valley Flea   W XX
Pipe Stem Drive-In Theatre
Athens Hinton State Route
Athens, West Virginia 24712
(304) 384-7382
Contact: Steve Luther, Athens Hinton State Route, Box 175 A, Athens, West Virginia 24712
(Route 20, four miles north of Athens)

Outdoor market; 100 dealers; began in 1972; open Saturday and Sunday; free admission; space rental: $3.00 for 22' x 30'; no reservations needed.

Variety of new merchandise, secondhand items, produce, crafts, antiques and collectibles; food; restrooms; parking; nearby motels.

Note: Listings are alphabetical by town.

Huntington Civic Center Flea Market   M   XX
Eighth Street and Third Avenue
Huntington, West Virginia 25727
(204) 696-5990
Contact: Loretta Covington, PO Box 2767, Huntington, West Virginia 25727

Indoor market; 100 dealers; began in 1977; open one weekend per month, call
ahead for dates; 50¢ admission; space rental: $20.00 for 10' x 10' enclosed booth;
no reservations needed.

Mostly antiques and secondhand items, some collectibles and new merchandise; food; restrooms; parking; nearby motels.

Baychar Farm Flea Market   W   XXX
Route 3, Box 322
Hurricane, West Virginia 25526
(304) 727-9939
Contact: Dorothy Cyrus or Mary Maynard, 314 Kentucky Avenue, Saint
Albans, West Virginia 25177
(Off I-64 at Hurricane, take State Route 34 South to Route 60, east one-half
mile)

Outdoor market; 100 to 125 dealers; began in 1973; open Sundays, 8:00 a.m. to
6:00 p.m., March to December; free admission; space rental: $3.00 per day for
18'; no reservations needed.

Secondhand and household items, new merchandise, crafts. produce, some
antiques and collectibles; food; restrooms; parking; nearby motels.

Fairplain Flea Market   A   XXX
Cedar Lakes Drive
Ripley, West Virginia 25271
(304) 372-3507
Contact: Hershel Reed
(Off I-77 near Highway 33)

Indoor/outdoor market; 150 to 200 dealers; began in 1974; held annually for five
days, usually starting second or third of July; free admission; space rental: price
varies for 12' x 12' to 12' x 24' area; reservations needed for inside space.

Variety of antiques, collectibles, new and used merchandise, art, crafts and
produce; restaurant; horse shows; country and western entertainment; restrooms; parking; nearby motels.

SOUTHEAST

Alabama, Arkansas, Florida, Georgia, Kentucky, Louisiana, Mississippi, North Carolina, South Carolina, Tennessee, Virginia.

The diversity of Southern antiques reflects the variety of cultural and ethnic influences in the eleven-state region. Everything from redware pottery made by the Moravians in North Carolina to decorative wrought iron architectural ornaments from New Orleans is found at auctions and flea markets in the Southeast. Elegant furniture—such as marble-topped sideboards and heavily-carved settees—and silver and porcelains embody the long-standing Southern tradition of hospitality and gracious entertaining. The South's rural past, much of it tied closely to slavery, is another influence.

Several auction houses in the Southeast cater to the strong regional pride in things Southern. Native yellow pine, cherry and walnut furniture are much in evidence. Other specialties include guns, Civil War and other military paraphernalia, cut glass, bird decoys from the southern flyways, an array of American and English Victoriana, and a disparate group of collectibles loosely termed "Black Americana"—some of it actually made by slaves or freedmen, some of it grossly caricatured, a lot of it in the form of paper ephemera. Not surprisingly in an area in which tobacco has long been a major industry, tobacco tins, tags and signs are a collector's specialty in North Carolina and Virginia.

The three largest Southern auction houses are in major cities: Morton's Auction Exchange in New Orleans; Trosby's Auction Galleries in Miami, West Palm Beach and Atlanta; and The Northgate Gallery of Clement's Antiques in Chattanooga. Popular tourist spots are often sites for auctions too—such as the Russakoff Auction in Nags Head, North Carolina, where the pirate Blackbeard was killed and near where the Wright brothers piloted the first manned and powered airplane.

Four of the largest flea markets in the Southeast are all located in the long skinny state of Tennessee, and buyers (and dealers) from Kentucky, Mississippi and Arkansas as well as Tennesseans attend. The Knoxville Fairgrounds Antique Flea Market has 250 dealers; the Memphis Flea Market has 250; the

Mid-South Flea Market, also in Memphis at the Fairgrounds, has TK; and the Nashville Flea Market, at the Fairgrounds there, has 350 dealers.

It is in Florida, however, where we found the greatest number of flea markets. They exist wherever there are tourists—and that is everywhere! Because so many people retire to Florida, often taking more with them than they eventually decide to keep, there is a constant supply of interesting small collectibles from the turn-of-the-century and later. Clearwater has two fleas with a total of nearly 500 dealers. In Ft. Lauderdale is an indoor-outdoor market called the Thunderbird Swap Shop where an astounding 2,000 dealers offer everything from new tee-shirts to Victorian porcelain vases. St. Augustine, the oldest city in the United States, is home of Ye Olde Flea Market, small by Florida standards, with only 25 dealers.

Among the museums and restoration sites which draw collector/travelers to the Southeast are the Sturdivant Hall Museum in Selma, Alabama; the Ante-Belleum Plantation in Atlanta, and the Owens-Thomas House in Savannah, Georgia; and Shakertown, a restored village in Pleasant Hill, Kentucky. The Natchez Pilgrimage, an annual spring tour, opens many fine ante-bellum homes to tourists in Natchez, Mississippi. More points of interest are 'the Tryon Palace Restoration in New Bern, and Old Salem, a restoration of a Moravian town, in Winston-Salem, North Carolina; and the whole city of Charleston, South Carolina. The Frank H. McClung Museum in Knoxville, and Andrew Jackson's home—The Hermitage—in Nashville have good collections of 18th- and 19th-century antiques. Virginia has everything from Colonial Williamsburg, not far from Richmond in the eastern part of the state, to Monticello—Thomas Jefferson's imaginatively-designed home—in Charlottesville, where there's a spectacular view of the Blue Ridge Mountains. And for those interested in the history of America's sea trade, the Mariners Museum and Library at Newport News offers a wonderful collection of prints, models, figureheads and nautical instruments.

Three large antique shows in the Southeast are the Annual Antiques Show and Sale in Natchez; the Dade Heritage Trust Antique Show in Miami; and the Southern States Antiques Show in New Orleans. There are, of course, many others.

For listings and reviews of auctions and flea markets, check *Southern Antiques, Southeast Trader, The Antiques Press, Antique Monthly, Collectors News, Antique Trader, The Magazine ANTIQUES, Spinning Wheel* and local papers.

ALABAMA

Hudson's Auction Gallery
Frank Hudson, Auctioneer
Route 1, Box 102
Decatur, Alabama 35671
(205) 355-7773

Eight antiques sales yearly; featuring Victorian and Belter furniture, accessories, art glass, silver; specialized sales of carnival glass, bric-a-brac, Limoges china, Pairpoint and Tiffany lamps; estate sales; consignments; property purchased for sales.

No buyer's premium; mail and telephone bids accepted with 25% deposit; checks accepted with bank letter of credit and proper ID; no credit cards. Full payment day of sale; pickups within one day.

Sale announcements and some catalogs mailed; oral or written appraisals offered for negotiable fee.

Flomaton Antique Auction
Herbert P. Heller, Auctioneer
Route 1, Box 196-A
207 Palafox Street
Flomaton, Alabama 36441
(205) 296-3710 or (205) 296-3059
(On Florida state line; forty miles north of Pensacola on Highway 29)

Specializing in American antiques, collectibles and fine art; sale of estates and private collections; antiques sales held approximately every three weeks; specialized sales feature Victoriana, art glass, and country pine furniture; consignments; merchandise purchased for sales.

No buyer's premium; mail and telephone bids accepted; checks accepted with proper ID; no credit cards. Full payment day of sale; pickups within 30 days.

Sale announcements and catalogs mailed; oral or written appraisals offered for variable fee.

Blount County Auction
J. L. Reno, Doug Reno, Auctioneers
PO Box 100
Locust Fork, Alabama 35097
(205) 681-0119 or (205) 798-0614
(Tallapoosa Street Exit off Interstate 59 North—then straight on Highway 79; near Birmingham)

Antiques sale held every four to six weeks on Saturday, generally at 6:30 p.m.; estate sales; some consignments; most property purchased for sales.

No buyer's premium; mail and telephone bids accepted from known customers; in-state checks accepted with proper ID; out-of-state checks with bank letter of credit; Master Charge and Visa accepted. Full payment night of sale; pickups within two weeks.

Sale announcements mailed.

Ginny's Antique and Auction Gallery
Colonel Rex McCrary, Auctioneer
2016 Airport Boulevard, Box 6086
Mobile, Alabama 36660
(205) 478-6609

Specializing in English imports and estate sales; sales held monthly or every six weeks; featuring antiques and turn-of-the-century furniture and bric-a-brac; specialized sales of art glass, oil paintings; consignments; property purchased for sales.

No buyer's premium; mail and telephone bids accepted; checks accepted with proper ID; Master Charge, Visa and American Express accepted. Full payment night of sale; pickups within one week.

Sale announcements and brochures mailed; oral or written appraisals offered for negotiable fee.

Mountaintop Flea Market   W   XXXX
Route 1
Altoona, Alabama 35952
(205) 589-2706
Contact: Melton or Janie Terrell
(Off Highway 278 West, not too far from Fort McClellan)

Indoor/outdoor market; 1,500 dealers; began in 1974; open Sunday, 5:00 a.m. to 5:00 p.m., year round; free admission; space rental; $2.00 outside, $5.00 outside shed, $7.00 inside; no reservations needed.

Variety of new and used merchandise, collectibles, antiques, crafts and produce; food; restrooms; parking; nearby motel and campgrounds.

Ta-Co-Bet Trade Days   W   XXX
Route 1
Dutton, Alabama 35744
Contact: Russell DePaul, PO Box 198, Valley Head, Alabama 35989
(Three miles southeast of Scottsboro)

Indoor/outdoor market; 175 dealers; began in 1976; open Saturday and Sunday, 6:00 a.m. till dark, year round; free admission; space rental: $2.00 per day inside, $1.00 outside for 10' x 10'; reservations needed.

Mostly secondhand merchandise and produce, few antiques or collectibles; restaurant; restrooms; parking; nearby motel and campground.

Lacon Trade Days   W   XXXX
Old Highway 31
Falkville, Alabama 35622
(205) 784-5091
Contact: Temperance McGee, PO Box 179, Falkville, Alabama 35622
(Take Lake Lacon Exit off I-65 North)

Outdoor market; 300 dealers; began about 1965; open Saturday, Sunday and holidays, 5:00 a.m. to 6:00 p.m.; free admission; space rental: $1.00 per shed; no reservations needed.

Mostly new merchandise, some secondhand items and crafts, very few antiques; food; restrooms; ample parking; nearby motels.

Gardendale Antique Mall   D   X
2455 Decatur
Gardendale, Alabama 35071
(205) 631-8869
(Highway 31 North or I-65)
Contact: Bill Stone

Indoor market; 14 dealers; began in 1965; open Tuesday through Sunday, 9:00 a.m. to 5:00 p.m., year round; free admission; space rental: $40.00 to $55.00 per month for 12' x 15'; no reservations needed.

Mostly antiques and secondhand items, some new merchandise; snack bar; restrooms; parking; nearby motels.

Evans Flea Market   W   XXXX
Route 1, Box 338
Harpersville, Alabama 35078
(205) 672-7462
Contact: Margaret Evans
(Highway 280, thirty-seven miles south of Birmingham)

Indoor/outdoor market; 250 sellers; began about 1976; open Saturday and Sunday, 6:00 a.m. until dark, year round; free admission; space rental: from $2.00 for 6' x 10' open to $8.00 for large enclosed area; no reservations needed.

Mostly antiques and collectibles, a lot of new merchandise and secondhand items, some arts and crafts; snack bar with hot breakfast; restrooms; parking; nearby motels.

Bonanza Farmers and Flea Market   W   X
Millbrook, Alabama 36054
(205) 285-5145
Contact: Mrs. Chris C. Norris, PO Box 485, Millbrook, Alabama 36054, (205) 285-5144
(I-65 North to Exit 179, Millbrook-Prattville, turn east then south to Service Road)

Note: Listings are alphabetical by town.

Indoor/outdoor market on 50 acres; 20 sellers; began in 1979; open Saturday and Sunday, 8:00 a.m. to dark, year round; free admission; space rental: $5.00 for 10' x 10' inside, $3.00 for 15' x 24' outside; no reservations needed.

Mostly secondhand and new merchandise, increasing number of antiques and collectibles; nearby restaurant; restrooms on grounds; abundant parking; motel across the street.

First Monday Flea Market   M XXXX
Courthouse Square
Scottsboro, Alabama 35768
Contact: Scottsboro City Hall, (205) 574-3100
(Center of downtown Scottsboro)

Outdoor market; 250 to 500 dealers; open first Monday (and the preceding Sunday) of each month, year round; free admission; space rental: $5.00 for car length.

Variety of collectibles, antiques and secondhand items, no new merchandise; snack bars; restrooms; on-street parking; motels nearby.

Midway Trade Day   W X
Route 1
Trinity, Alabama 35673
Contact: Flora Allred, (205) 974-8057
(Twelve miles west of Decatur on Highway 24)

Outdoor market; 15 to 20 dealers; began in 1978; open Friday through Sunday, 6:00 a.m. to 9:00 p.m., year round; free admission; space rental: $1.00 per yard space, $1.50 per booth; no reservations needed.

Mostly new and secondhand merchandise, some antiques and collectibles; barbecue stand; restrooms; parking; no nearby motels.

ARKANSAS

Antique House Auction Gallery
Paul Emerson, Manager
905 Autumn Road
Little Rock, Arkansas 72211
(501) 225-3696
(Off Interstate 430 and Interstate 630 Interchange)

Antiques and collectibles sale held second Monday of every month, featuring furniture, bric-a-brac, silver; specialized sales of coins, jewelry and watches; estate sales; consignments; property purchased for sales.

No buyer's premium; mail bids accepted with cashier's check; telephone bids not accepted; checks accepted with approved credit through bank reference or letter of credit; no credit cards. Full payment day of sale; pickups within 30 days.

Sale announcements mailed; some catalogs; oral and written appraisals offered for negotiable fee, minimum $20.00.

International Antiques, Inc.
4005 Landski Drive
North Little Rock, Arkansas 72118
(501) 758-5167 or (501) 758-8041
(Off Burns Park Exit on Interstate 40 to 176 East to MacArthur, first large building on left)

Antiques sales held approximately every two to three months; featuring American, Continental and English antique furniture, including antique desks and office accessories, mirrors, 18th and 19th century English, Austrian, French, German and American furniture, clocks, bronzes, paintings, etchings, musical instruments, cut glass, lighting fixtures, and architectural items, including stained glass, beveled glass, and painted glass; estate sales; consignments; property purchased for sales.

No buyer's premium; mail and telephone bids accepted; checks accepted with two forms of proper ID; Master Charge and Visa accepted. Full payment day of sale; pickups within five days.

Sale announcements and some catalogs mailed; written appraisals offered for minimum fee of $25.00.

Stailey's Flea Market   W   X
Route 4, Box 94
Alexander, Arkansas 72002
(501) 847-3726
Contact: John and Opal Stailey
(Exit 126, I-30, north three blocks, west one mile on Highway 5)

Indoor/outdoor market; 14 sellers; began in 1966; open Saturday and Sunday 8:00 a.m. to 6:00 p.m., year round; free admission; space rental: $3.00 for 8' x 16' area; no reservations needed.

Mostly secondhand and household items; some antiques, collectibles and new merchandise; nearby restaurant; restrooms; parking for cars, campers and motor homes.

America's Flea Market   ★ W XX
310 West Main
Batesville, Arkansas 72501
(501) 793-7508
Contact: Ronald Newberry
(Call for directions)

Indoor market; 50+ dealers; began in 1980; open Friday 1:00 p.m. to 9:00 p.m., Saturday and Sunday 8:00 a.m. to 6:00 p.m., year round; free admission; space rental: $15.00 and up for 10' x 10' to 20' x 10'; no reservations needed.

Equal variety of antiques, collectibles, new merchandise, secondhand items, crafts and produce; food; restrooms; ample free parking; nearby motels; occasional auctions.

Snow Springs Park and Flea Market ★ W XX
Highway 7
Hot Springs, Arkansas 71901
Contact: John Woodal, PO Box 1032, Hot Springs, Arkansas 71901,
(501) 623-7530
(North on Highway 7, five miles from downtown Hot Springs)

Outdoor market under shade trees; 65 dealers; open Saturday and Sunday, all
day, year round; free admission; space rental: $5.00 for table under shed with
electricity; no reservations needed.

    Lots of antiques and collectibles, new and used merchandise; country and
western music on Sundays; concession stands; restrooms; parking; monthly
auctions.

Giant Flea Market W X
8610 New Benton Highway
Little Rock, Arkansas 72209
(501) 565-9915
Contact: L.E. Sale, 17301 Elvin Road, Little Rock, Arkansas 72204,
(501) 821-3091
(Exit 130 North on I-30, cross over overpass, or exit 132 South on I-30)

Indoor/outdoor market; 50 dealers; began about 1968; open Saturday and
Sunday, 7:30 a.m. to 5:00 p.m., year round; free admission; space rental: $3.00
weekly for a table; reservations needed.

    Mostly antiques, collectibles and secondhand items, some new merchandise
and arts and crafts; food; restrooms; parking; nearby motels.

Old Theater Flea Market D X
116 South Second Street
Rogers, Arkansas 72756
(501) 636-9824 or (501) 751-1234 (evenings)
Contact: Dawn M. Alexander
(US Highway 71 into downtown Rogers, half block south of intersection with
Highway 62)

Indoor market housed in an old theater building in the Ozark mountains; 20
sellers; began in 1977; open Monday through Saturday, 9:00 a.m. to 5:00 p.m.,
year round; free admission; space rental: $60.00 monthly, $20.00 weekly, $8.00
weekend, for 12' x 12'; reservations needed.

    Mostly antiques and collectibles housed in booths named after old classic
movies; also used book, record and tape store; lobby converted to mini-
restaurant; restrooms; parking; nearby motels.

FLORIDA

Sunshine Auction Service

Colonel Al Thompson, Auctioneer
2301 San Juan Avenue
Avon Park, Florida 33825
(813) 453-5351
(Sales held at various locations—check mailings for directions)

Sales held one to three times weekly; specialized sales of dolls, cars, flywheel engines, Hummels; estate sales; consignments only.

No buyer's premium; mail and telephone bids accepted; checks approved prior to sale accepted; Visa and Master Charge accepted. Generally full payment and pickups day of sale.

Sale announcements and some catalogs mailed; oral appraisal offered free of charge.

Foxhall Antique Gallery

Dan Sexton, Auctioneer
8500 Cortez Road
Bradenton, Florida 33505
(813) 792-7508
(Fifty miles south of Tampa)

Antiques sale held second weekend of the month, year round, featuring variety of American and Continental furniture, metals, glass, porcelain, and Oriental antiques; specialized sale of antique dolls held in the fall; estate sales; consignments; property purchased for sale.

No buyer's premium; mail and telephone bids accepted; checks accepted with proper ID; Visa and Master Charge accepted; full payment generally at time of sale; pickups within one week.

Sale announcements mailed; catalogs for all sales; oral and written appraisals offered for hourly fee of $25.00.

Albritton Realty & Auction Company, Inc.

Kale Albritton, Auctioneer
314 North Kentucky Avenue
Lakeland, Florida 33801
(813) 687-3938 or (813) 687-0610
(Three blocks north of Main Street)

Complete auction service dealing in antiques and specialized collections as well as real estate and business liquidations; sales held twice a month as merchandise is available; specialized sales include jewelry, antique tools, primitive utensils, Oriental collectibles; estate sales; consignments; property purchased for sale.

No buyer's premium; telephone bids accepted; checks with proper ID accepted; no credit cards. No deposit necessary to hold purchases; full payment and pickups within one week.

Mailing list for sale announcements available; written appraisals offered for negotiable fee at minimum of $200.00.

North Davis Auction Gallery
9201 North Davis Highway
Pensacola, Florida 32504
(904) 477-8558

General antiques and collectibles sale held every Saturday at 7:00 p.m.; featuring American antiques, including furniture, glassware, bric-a-brac, and some Oriental items; estate sales; consignments; property purchased for sale.

No buyer's premium; mail and telephone bids accepted; in-state checks accepted with proper ID; out-of-state checks accepted with bank letter of credit; Master Charge and Visa accepted. Full payment day of sale; pickups within nine days.

Sale announcements mailed; oral and written appraisals offered for an hourly fee of $50.00, with minimum charge of $25.00.

Schrader Galleries
211 Third Street South
Saint Petersburg, Florida 33701
(813) 823-5657

A leading gallery in Florida, specializing in antiques; general antiques sale held approximately every six weeks; estate sales; consignments; property purchased for sales.

No buyer's premium; mail and telephone bids accepted; checks accepted with bank reference; no credit cards. Full payment and pickups at time of sale.

Mailing list available for sale announcements; mailed catalog ($5.00 or $10.00) admits two people to sale; oral or written appraisals offered for negotiable fee.

Bridges Antiques & Auction
Colonel Garry Tuttle, Auctioneer
Route 4, Box 52-A (Highway 46)
Sanford, Florida 32771
(305) 323-2801 or (305) 322-0095

(One and one-half miles east of Interstate 4)

Specializing in antiques; sales generally held the last Saturday of each month; specialized sales include Victoriana Hummels, art glass, jewelry, furniture, dolls; estate sales; consignments only.

No buyer's premium; mail bids accepted; checks accepted with bank letter of credit; Master Charge and Visa accepted. Full payment day of sale; pickups within 10 days.

Sale announcements and some catalogs mailed; oral and written appraisals offered for minimum fee of $75.00.

William James Alquist Auctions
William James Alquist, Auctioneer
PO Box 154
Sanibel Island, Florida 33957
(813) 472-2357
Highlands, North Carolina 28741
(704) 526-2701
Salem, Connecticut
(203) 859-1357
(On site or in rented halls—see mailings for directions)

Three to four sales held during winter season in Florida; two to three sales held during summer in North Carolina; and during spring and late fall, in Connecticut; general antique sales include early American, Victorian and English furniture, china, bric-a-brac, glass, paintings, silver; estate sales; consignments; merchandise purchased for sales.

No buyer's premium; mail and telephone bids accepted; traveler's checks, or personal checks with bank letter of credit, accepted; no credit cards. Full payment day of sale; pickups within two days.

Sale announcements and some catalogs mailed; oral and written appraisals offered for negotiable fee.

Trosby Auction Galleries
905 Railroad Avenue
West Palm Beach, Florida 33401
(305) 659-1775
499 Biscayne Boulevard
Bayfront Auditorium
Miami, Florida
(305) 446-3436
81 Peachtree Park Drive
Atlanta, Georgia 30309
(404) 237-1779

Fine art and antiques sales held at all three galleries; specialized sales feature Oriental art and paintings; estate sales; consignments; limited amount of property purchased for sales.

Ten percent buyer's premium; mail bids accepted; telephone bids from established customers accepted; checks with proper ID accepted; no credit cards. Purchases held with a 25% deposit; full payment and pickups within 10 days.

Sale announcements and catalogs mailed; appraisal services offered.

Three Star Flea Market   W   XX
2390 South Orange Blossom Trail
Apopka, Florida 32703
(305) 293-2722
Contact: Mary Markeson, Route 1, Box 380 C., Apopka, Florida 32703
(On Highway 441, eight miles north of Orlando)

Note: Listings are alphabetical by town.

Indoor/outdoor market; 55 dealers; began in 1969; open Saturday and Sunday, dawn to dusk, year round; free admission; space rental: $5.20 for 12' x 10' per day; reservations needed.

Wide variety of merchandise including antiques, collectibles, new merchandise, household items, arts and crafts, produce and miscellaneous items; food wagon; restrooms; parking; two motels next door.

Arcadia Drive-In   W X
Highway 17 North
Arcadia, Florida
(813) 494-2321
Contact: Tony or Ruby Diliberto, PO Box 1371, Arcadia, Florida 33821
(Four miles north of Arcadia)

Outdoor market; 20 to 35 dealers; began in 1978; open Saturday and Sunday, during winter season, 8 a.m. to 5 p.m.; free admission; space rental: $1.50 for parking space; no reservations needed.

Mostly secondhand or household items, some new merchandise and produce, few antiques and collectibles; food; restrooms; parking; nearby motels.

Economy Flea Market   W X
700-A South Brevard
Arcadia, Florida 33821
(813) 494-9991
Contact: Ralph Carbone, Route 1, Box 349, Arcadia, Florida 33821, (813) 756-8727
(Call for directions)

Indoor/outdoor market; 30 to 50 dealers; began in 1977; open every Friday, Saturday and Sunday, year round; free admission; space rental: varies; no reservations needed.

Variety of merchandise including secondhand and new merchandise, produce, antiques, collectibles and crafts; no food; restrooms; parking; nearby motels.

Roma Flea Market   W XXX
5715 Fifteenth Street East
Bradenton, Florida 33508
(813) 756-9036
Contact: Mr. and Mrs. Thomas Lewis, 4906 34th Avenue West, Bradenton, Florida 33529, (813) 792-4552
(Highway 301 South, quarter mile past Oneco traffic light)

Indoor/outdoor market; 125 dealers; began in 1975; open Saturday and Sunday 8:00 a.m. to 5:00 p.m., year round; free admission; space rental: $5.00 daily outside, $60.00 to $80.00 per month inside, various sizes; reservations needed in winter.

Mostly secondhand and household items and new merchandise, some antiques and collectibles; restaurant on premises; restrooms; parking; nearby motels.

Airport Mart ★ W XXX
11555 Spring Hill Boulevard
Brooksville, Florida 33512
(904) 796-0268
Contact: Louis Mlecka
(At Airport Industrial Park, just south of Brooksville off US Highway 41)

Indoor/outdoor market; 125 dealers; began in 1977; open Friday, Saturday and Sunday, 9:00 a.m. to 4:00 p.m., year round; free admission; space rental: $30.00 per month for 8' x 12' lockup space; reservations needed for lockup spaces.

Mostly antiques, collectibles and new merchandise, some used items and produce; food; restrooms; parking; complete hookup for R/V;auctions every Saturday at 7:30.

Colburn's Flea Market ★ W XXXX
1211 US 98 North
Brooksville, Florida 33512
(904) 796-2908
Contact: Colonel Denver Colburn
(On US 98 North, west of the city)

Indoor/outdoor market; 200+ dealers; began in 1971; open Saturday and Sunday, year round; free admission; space rental: $2.00 and up; no reservations needed.

Variety of merchandise, including new and used items, crafts, collectibles, antiques, produce; food; restrooms; parking; nearby motels; occasional auctions.

Gulf to Bay Drive-In Theater Flea Market W XX
25 North Belcher Road
Clearwater, Florida 33516
(813) 442-4729
Contact: Jesse Bearden, 1630 Illinois Road, Clearwater, Florida 33516, (813) 442-3383
(Call for directions)

Outdoor market; 100 dealers; began in 1976; open every Sunday, 8:00 a.m. to 3:00 p.m., year round; free admission; space rental: $2.00 for 20' x 10'; no reservations needed.

Mostly secondhand and household items, some antiques and new merchandise; food; restrooms; parking; nearby motels.

Tri-City Flea Market, Inc. D XXXX
14015 US Highway 19 South
Clearwater, Florida 33516
(813) 536-6979
Contact: William Wright
(Near Ulmerton Road—State Route 688)

Outdoor market; 336 dealers; began in 1978; open Thursday through Sunday, 7:30 a.m. to 6:00 p.m.; free admission; space rental: $3.00 per day for covered 10' x 10' space; reservations advisable.

Antiques, collectibles, crafts, new and used merchandise, and lots of produce; refreshment stands; restrooms; parking; nearby motels, overnight R/V parking for vendors.

Joylan Drive-In   W XX
US 301 North
Dade City, Florida 33525
(904) 567-5085
Contact: Eddie Whidden, PO Box 498, Dade City, Florida 33525
(Two miles north of Dade City)

Outdoor market; 50 to 100 dealers; began in 1976; open Sunday, 6:00 a.m. to 3:00 p.m., year round; free admission; space rental: $2.00 for 20'; no reservations needed.

Mostly new and secondhand merchandise, antiques, some produce; food; restrooms; parking; nearby motels.

Hi-Way Airport Swap Meet   W XXXX
1930 Federal Highway (US 1)
Dania, Florida 33304
(305) 524-0308
Contact: Jack Hegarty
(I-95 to Griffin Road or State Route 84 Exits, east to US 1)

Outdoor market; room for 700 dealers; began in 1979; open Saturday and Sunday, 6:00 a.m. to 2:00 p.m.; free admission; space rental: $2.00 Saturday, $3.00 Sunday; reservations recommended.

Mostly new and secondhand merchandise, some antiques, collectibles and crafts; snack bar; restrooms; parking; nearby motels.

Allandale Flea Market   W XXX
5008 Ridgewood Avenue
Daytona Beach, Florida 92019
(904) 767-7229
Contact: Tom Hall, Route 2, Box 379, Daytona Beach, Florida 32019
(On US 1, two miles from the beach)

Outdoor market; 180 dealers; began in 1974; open Saturday and Sunday, 7:00 a.m. to 5:00 p.m.; free admission; space rental: $3.00 for 4' x 8' table; reservations needed.

Antiques, collectibles, secondhand items and new merchandise; food; restrooms; parking; nearby motels.

The Antique Marketplace   W XX
2399 North Federal Highway
Delray Beach, Florida 33444
(305) 276-8539
Contact: Mary Menchel

Indoor/outdoor market; 50 to 100 dealers; open Saturday and Sunday, 8:00 a.m. to 5:00 p.m., year round; 25¢ admission; space rental: $15.00 per weekend for booth and table; reservations needed.

Mostly decorator items, antiques, collectibles, some new merchandise; no food; restrooms; parking; nearby motels.

Mostly decorator items, antiques, collectibles, some new merchandise; no food; restrooms; parking; nearby motels.

Delray Swap Shop   **W   XXXX**
1601 North Federal Highway
Delray Beach, Florida 33444
(305) 276-4012
Contact: Hayden Bivins or Robin Bradford
(I-95 or Florida Boulevard to Delray Beach Exit, east to US 1)

Outdoor market; 250 dealers; open Saturday and Sunday; free admission; space rental: $3.00 Saturday, $4.00 Sunday; no reservations needed.
Mostly new and secondhand merchandise, some antiques, collectibles and crafts; snack bar; restrooms; parking; nearby motels.

Thunderbird Swap Shop   **★   D   XXXX**
3291 West Sunrise Boulevard
Fort Lauderdale, Florida 33311
(305) 581-6281
Contact: Dempsey Birchfield
(Take I-95 to Fort Lauderdale, Sunrise Boulevard Exit West, go west one mile)

Indoor/outdoor market; 2,000 outside dealers, 175 inside; began in 1968; open Wednesday through Sunday, 6:00 a.m. to 4:00 p.m.; 75¢ admission Saturday and Sunday, 25¢ other days; space rental: $3.00 to $10.00 outside, $225.00 to $250.00 per month inside; reservations needed.
Mostly new and secondhand merchandise, some antiques, collectibles, crafts and plants; several snack bars; restrooms; parking; nearby motels; occasional auctions.

Krazy Days Traders Mart   **★   D   X**
3809 US 19 North
Holiday, Florida 33590
(813) 934-0001
Contact: Lorraine Drouin, 3999 US 19 North, Holiday, Florida 33590, (813) 934-6782

Indoor market; 40 dealers; began in 1975; open seven days a week, 8:00 a.m. to 5:00 p.m.; free admission; space rental: $5.00 per day, $20.00 per week for 10' x 10'; no reservations needed.
Mostly secondhand items and crafts, few antiques or collectibles, some new merchandise and produce; restaurant; restrooms; parking; nearby motels; occasional auctions.

Howard's Flea Market   **W   XXX**
Route 2, Box 205
Homosassa, Florida 32646
(904) 628-4656
Contact: Karen Howard, Star Route 2, Box 8626, Inverness, Florida 32650, (904) 628-4656
(On US 19 three miles south of Homosassa Springs)

Indoor/outdoor market; 200 dealers; open every Saturday and Sunday, year round; free admission; space rental: $3.50 for three tables; reservations preferred.

Variety of all types of merchandise including new and second, antiques and collectibles, produce, arts and crafts; four concessions; free parking; restrooms; motels and campground nearby.

Sunshine Flea Market   W XXXX
2815 Sunset Boulevard
Hudson, Florida 33568
(813) 863-1805
Contact: Charles Stumm, 7800 113th Street, Suite 203, Seminole, Florida 33542, (813) 393-1922
(Quarter mile east of US Highway 19, near State Road 52 intersection)

Indoor/outdoor market; 250 dealers; began in 1975; open Saturday and Sunday, 7:30 a.m. to 5:30 p.m., year round; free admission; space rental: $4.00 outside, $6.00 under cover; reservations needed.

Mostly secondhand and household items lots of antiques and collectibles, some new merchandise; three snack bars; restrooms; parking; nearby motels.

Inverness Flea Market   W XXX
Citrus County Fairgrounds
US 41
Inverness, Florida 32650
Contact: Loyd E. Pyle, 202 Trout Avenue, Inverness, Florida 32650, (904) 726-8184
(One mile south of Inverness)

Indoor/outdoor market; 180 dealers; began in 1971; open Saturday, 8:00 a.m. to 5:00 p.m., year round; free admission; space rental: $2.50 outside, $3.50 to $5.50 inside, size varies from 8' x 10' or 15' to 12' x 12'; reservations require advance payment.

.Wide variety of merchandise, mostly new and household items and produce, small percentage of antiques, collectibles and crafts, fresh baked bread, cheeses from Wisconsin, Ohio and Pennsylvania; food; restrooms; parking; nearby motels.

Bayard Antique Village   W X
US 1 South
Jacksonville, Florida 32224
(904) 268-9712
Contact: Mrs. J. Searcy, 12561 Phillips Highway, Jacksonville, Florida 32224, (904) 268-9712
(Exit US 1 South off I-95 for three miles)

Indoor market; 25 dealers; began in 1967; open Saturday and Sunday, 9:00 a.m. to 5:00 p.m.; free admission; space rental: $8.00 for 10' x 8' x 10'; no reservations needed.

Mostly antiques and collectibles, some secondhand merchandise; snack bar; restrooms; parking; nearby motel.

Farmers Market   W   XXX
1780 West Beaver Street
Jacksonville, Florida 32209
(904) 354-2821
Contact: Tom Morris

Indoor/outdoor market; 125 dealers; began in 1938; open Friday, Saturday and
Sunday year round; free admission; space rental: $5.00 per day for 10' x 10';
reservations recommended.

Mostly produce with some secondhand merchandise, antiques and collectibles; two restaurants; restrooms; parking; nearby motels.

Jacksonville Playtime Flea Market   W   XXXX
6300 Blanding Boulevard
Jacksonville, Florida 32210
(904) 771-2300
Contact: Rob Robson, 2505 Highway 50, Titusville, Florida 32780
(Four miles north of I-295 on Blanding Boulevard)

Outdoor market at drive-in theatre; 400 dealers; began in 1978; open every
Wednesday, Saturday and Sunday, year round, free admission; space rental: free
on Wednesday, $2.00 Saturday, $3.00 Sunday; no reservations needed.

Mostly secondhand and household items, some collectibles, crafts and new
merchandise; snack bar; restrooms; parking; nearby motels.

Key Largo Flea Market   W   XX
Mile Market 105.7
Key Largo, Florida 33037
Contact: Jennie Taylor, PO Box 97, Key Largo, Florida 33037, (305) 451-2186
(US 1, south of Homestead)

Outdoor market; 100 dealers; began in 1972; open Sunday, 8:00 a.m. to 5:00 p.m.,
year round; free admission; space rental: $6.00 for 12' space; reservations
needed.

Mostly secondhand items and collectibles, some antiques and new merchandise; lunch wagon; restrooms; parking; nearby motels.

Lakeland Farmers Market   W   XXXX
2701 Swindell Road
Lakeland, Florida 33801
(813) 682-4809
Contact: Ann Edwards, 659 Howard Avenue, Lakeland, Florida 33801, (813)
683-4389
(One mile east of I-4 Exit on Memorial Boulevard)

Indoor/outdoor market; 260 sellers; began in 1971; open every Thursday through
Sunday, year round; free admission; space rental: $3.00 to $5.00 a day, 10' x 10'
under shed with table, 25' x 16' open area; reservations needed for Saturday and
Sunday.

Mostly produce, secondhand and household items and new merchandise,
some antiques and collectibles; two food concessions; restrooms; parking;
nearby motels.

Note: Listings are alphabetical by town.

The Maitland Flea Market, Inc.   W XXXX

1941 Highway 17-92
Maitland, Florida 32751
(305) 339-2920
Contact: Dale Tucker
(Near Orlando, from Disney World go north on I-4 to Maitland Boulevard
East Exit; go to 17-92 then north five blocks)

Indoor/outdoor market in the town; 240 sellers outside and 100 inside shops;
began in 1970; open Saturday and Sunday, 8:00 a.m. to 5:00 p.m., year round; 50¢
per car admission; space rental: $4.00 for outside tables, $5.50 for field spaces;
reservations needed two weeks in advance.

Mostly secondhand antiques and collectibles, a large percentage of new
merchandise and crafts, produce; seven food concessions; restrooms; parking;
nearby motels.

Lakeshore Swap Meet   W XXXX

1000 North State Road 7
Margate, Florida 33063
(305) 972-3248
Contact: Warren Mason
(Turnpike Exit 24 Pompano, or I-95 to Atlantic Boulevard and go west)

Outdoor market; 300 dealers; began 1976; open Tuesday, Saturday and Sunday,
6:00 a.m. to 2:00 p.m.; free admission; space rental: Tuesday free, Saturday
$3.50, Sunday $6.00; reservations recommended.

Mostly new and secondhand merchandise, few antiques and collectibles;
snack bar; restrooms; parking; adjacent motel.

Tropicaire Flea Market   W XXXX

7751 SW Fortieth Street
Miami, Florida 33155
(305) 264-4535
(Palmetto Expressway (826) at SW Fortieth Street—Bird Road)

Outdoor market; 700 dealers; began in 1962; open every Saturday and Sunday
6:00 a.m. to 4:00 p.m., year round; 25¢ admission; space rental: for one- and two-
car spaces, $3.50 and $4.50 Saturday, $8.00 and $11.00 Sunday; reservations
needed Sunday only.

New and secondhand items, antiques and collectibles; food; restrooms;
parking; nearby motels.

Oakland Park Flea Market   W XXX

3161 Oakland Park Boulevard
Oakland Park, Florida 32760
(305) 949-7959
Contact: Ms. Terry Degoff
(Half mile off I-95)

Indoor market; 120 dealers; began in 1972; open Friday, 10:00 a.m. to 9:00 p.m., Saturday and Sunday, 10:00 a.m. to 7:00 p.m.; free admission; space rental: $400.00 + per month on yearly basis; reservations needed on lease rentals.

Mostly new clothing; few antiques, collectibles, crafts and art objects; snack bar; restrooms; parking; nearby motels.

Cypress Hut Flea Market   W   XX
647 Highway 441 South
Okeechobee, Florida 33472
(813) 763-5104
Contact: Gil Boggs
(Five miles south on 441 from Okeechobee City)

Outdoor market under large shade trees; began in 1970; 100 dealers; open Saturday and Sunday, year round; free admission; space rental: $5.00 for 4' x 8' table and car space; reservations recommended.

Mostly household, secondhand and new merchandise, some antiques and collectibles; food; restrooms; parking; nearby motels.

Big Swappers Flea Market   W   XXX
Nova Drive-In Theatre
Nova Road at Hand Avenue
Ormand Beach, Florida
(904) 672-3014

Outdoor market; 150 to 190 dealers; began in 1976; held Friday, Saturday, and Sunday, year round; 10¢ admission; space rental: $4.00 daily for 20' car or truck space; no reservations needed.

Variety of new and used merchandise, antiques, collectibles; food; restrooms; parking; nearby motels.

Bostic Big Oak Flea Market   W   X
538 Pace Road
Pace, Florida 32570
(904) 994-8985
Contact: Alton Bostic, 541 Plant Avenue, Milton, Florida 32570
(On Highway 90 between Milton and Pensacola)

Outdoor market; 20 dealers; began in 1977; open Friday, Saturday and Sunday, year round; free admission; space rental: $2.50 outside, $3.50 inside; no reservations needed.

Variety of new and used merchandise, antiques, collectibles and produce; food; restrooms; parking; nearby motels.

Country Fair, Inc.   W   XXXX
PO Box 609
Palmetto, Florida 33561
(813) 722-5633
Contact: W. W. Cartwright
(Northeast corner Highways 41 and 301)

Outdoor market; 350 dealers; open every Saturday and Sunday, 6:30 a.m., year round; free admission; space rental: $4.00 under shed; no reservations needed.

Wide variety of merchandise including new and secondhand merchandise, antiques and collectibles, produce, arts and crafts; food; restrooms; parking; nearby motels.

Quayside Thieves Market   **W   XX**
700 South Palafox Street
Pensacola, Florida 32501
(904) 476-3677 or (904) 433-9930
Contact: Marguerite Cummings
(From I-10, exit south on I-110, follow to end and exit right, continue to waterfront)

Indoor market with additional space under covered patio; 75 dealers; began in 1974; open Saturday and Sunday, 7:00 a.m. to 5:00 p.m.; free admission; space rental: $5.00 and up for various size areas with table; reservations advisable.

Mostly antiques and collectibles, some secondhand merchandise, very little new; food; restrooms; parking; nearby motels.

West-Side Flea Market and Auction Sales   **★ D XXX**
4610 Mobile Highway
Pensacola, Florida 32506
(904) 456-9811
Contact: Ron Holsen or Randy Griener
Exit 2 off I-10 to Highway 90)

Indoor/outdoor market; 160 sellers; began in 1974; open seven days a week, 8:00 a.m. to 5:00 p.m., year round; free admission; space rental: $3.00 per day for a 4' x 8' table; reservations needed.

Mostly new and secondhand items, about 20% antiques and collectibles, some arts and crafts; chuckwagon food and 24-hour pancake house; restrooms; parking; two major motels nearby; space for motor homes and trailors; auctions every Sunday at 3:00.

49'er Flea Market   **W   XXX**
10525 Forty-ninth Street North
Pinellas Park, Florida 33520
(813) 576-3367
Contact: Ned Burket or Ruth Eldridge
(Just north of the US 19 overpass)

Indoor/outdoor market; 200 dealers; began in 1976; open Saturday and Sunday, 8:00 a.m. to 4:00 p.m., year round; admission charged; space rental: $3.00 to $9.00 for 8' x 10' open shed; reservations needed.

Mostly secondhand and household items, lots of antiques, collectibles and crafts; food; restrooms; parking; nearby motels.

Country Village Flea Market W XX

Route 9, Box 400
Plant City, Florida 33566
(813) 752-4670
Contact: Ferris Waller, Route 7, Box 640, Plant City, Florida 33566, (813)
752-3645
(One mile north of I-4 on State Route 39)

Indoor/outdoor market; 50 to 100 sellers; began in 1980; open Wednesday,
Saturday and Sunday, 8:00 a.m. to 4:00 p.m., year round; free admission; space
rental: $3.00 to $4.00 per day;, some covered stalls; reservations recommended.

Mostly collectibles, secondhand merchandise and antiques, some new merchandise and produce; snack bar; parking; restrooms; two large motels nearby.

Beach Drive-In Swap Meet W XXXX

Thirteenth and Old Dixie Highway
Riviera Beach, Florida 33404
(305) 844-5836
(I-95 to Blue Herron Boulevard Exit, east to Dixie Highway)

Outdoor market, 250 dealers; began in 1973; open Wednesday, Saturday and
Sunday, 6:00 a.m. to closing; free admission; space rental: Wednesday free,
Saturday $3.00, Sunday $5.50 to $6.50; reservations recommended.

Mostly new and secondhand merchandise, some antiques, collectibles and
crafts; snack bar; beer and wine; restrooms; parking; nearby motels.

Ye Olde Flea Market W X

US Highway 1
Saint Augustine, Florida 32084
(904) 824-1228
Contact: Robert E. Cleland, Route 3, Box 14, Saint Augustine, Florida 32084
(East State Route 16 off I-95 to US 1 North)

Indoor/outdoor market; 22+ dealers; began in 1977; open Friday, Saturday and
Sunday, year round; free admission; space rental: $3.00 per 4' x 8' table;
reservations suggested.

Variety of new and used merchandise, antiques, collectibles, some produce
and crafts; food; restrooms; parking; nearby motels.

Sanford Village Super Flea Market D XXXX

1500 French Avenue (Highway 17-92)
Sanford, Florida 32771
(305) 323-5454
Contact: J.W. Jones, PO Box 2195, Sanford, Florida 32771, (305) 322-5579
(I-4 to Sanford Exit to 17-92 South, thirty-five miles from Disney World)

Indoor/outdoor market; 250 dealers; began in 1975; open every Wednesday,
Friday, Saturday, Sunday, 7:30 a.m. to dark, year round; free admission; space
rental: $4.00 to $8.00 for 4' x 8' to 4' x 16' area; reservations recommended.

Mostly secondhand and household items and produce, some antiques,
collectibles, arts, crafts and new merchandise; two snack bars; restrooms;
parking; nearby motels.

Trail Drive-In Flea Market　　　　　　　　　　W XX
6801 North Trail
Sarasota, Florida 33580
(813) 355-5336
Contact: C.D. Nester
(Across US 41 from Sarasota-Bradentown Airport)

Outdoor market; 35 to 125 dealers; began in 1979; open Saturday and Sunday,
8:00 a.m. to 4:00 p.m., year round; free admission; space rental: $2.00 Saturday,
$3.00 Sunday for 20' x 20'; no reservations needed.
　　Variety of secondhand items, new merchandise, antiques, collectibles, crafts
and produce; food; restrooms; parking; nearby motels.

B & A Flea Market　　　　　　　　　　　　W XXXX
2201 SE Indian Street
Stuart, Florida 33494
(305) 283-7015
Contact: Bobbi Bova or Bev Ettenson
(One mile south of Stuart on US Highway 1)

Indoor/outdoor market; about 250 dealers; began in 1975; open Saturday and
Sunday, year round; free admission; space rental: $2.00 to $5.00 for 8' x 10' for
outside table, waiting list for inside booth; reservations recommended.
　　Variety of antiques, collectibles, new and used merchandise, arts and crafts;
food; restrooms; parking; nearby motels.

American Legion Flea Market　　　　　　　　W XX
929 East 139th Avenue
Tampa, Florida 33612
(813) 971-3699
Contact: American Legion Post Commander
(Take I-75 Fletcher Avenue Exit. East to Nebraska Avenue, north to 139th)

Indoor/outdoor market; 100 dealers; began in 1978; open Saturday and Sunday,
year round; free admission; space rental: $1.00 (plus tax) for outdoor 15' x 25',
$4.00 (plus tax) for indoor booth; reservations recommended.
　　Mostly secondhand, household and new merchandise, some antiques and
collectibles; snack bar; restrooms; parking; nearby motels.

The Flea Market　　　　　　　　　　　　　W X
1370 Capitol Circle NW
Tallahassee, Florida 32304
(904) 576-4950
Contact: Odessa Steyerman
(Just south of US 90 West, two miles south of I-10 Exit 28)

Indoor/outdoor market; 10 dealers; began about 1972; open every Saturday and
Sunday, 11:00 a.m. to 6:00 p.m., year round; free admission; space rental: $1.50
for 4' x 6' table; no reservations needed.

Lots of collectibles and antiques, some secondhand and household merchandise; no food available; restrooms; parking; nearby motels.

Waldo Farmer's & Flea Market   W   XXXX
Highway 301
Waldo, Florida 32694
(904) 468-2255
Contact: Sally Blakewood, PO Box 1117, Hawthorne, Florida 32640, (904) 481-2311
(Nine miles south of Stark)

Indoor/outdoor market; 700 dealers; began in 1974; open Saturday and Sunday, 7:00 a.m. to 6:00 p.m., year round; free admission; space rental: $4.00 per day for 10' x 10' under covered shed; some lock-up spaces; no reservations needed.

Mostly secondhand and household items, some produce and new merchandise, fewer antiques, collectibles and crafts; food; restrooms; parking; nearby motels and camping (free to dealers).

Farmers Flea Market   D   XXXX
1200 South Congress Avenue
West Palm Beach, Florida 33406
(305) 965-1500
Contact: Jeanne R. Martin
(One mile south of the airport)

Indoor market; 250 dealers; began in 1947; open Thursday through Saturday, 10:00 a.m. to 9:00 p.m., Sunday, 12 noon to 6:00 p.m.; free admission; space rental: varies; reservations necessary.

Almost all new merchandise, some secondhand, very few antiques or collectibles; six restaurants; restrooms; parking; nearby motels.

GEORGIA

G. W. Tims Antique Auction Company
G. W. Tims, Auctioneer
Highway 41, PO Box 601
Adairsville, Georgia 30101
(404) 386-3010
(Four miles south of Adairsville)

Antiques sale held every two weeks on Thrusday evenings; featuring American furniture, some glassware; estate sales; consignments; property purchased for sales.

No buyer's premium; mail and telephone bids accepted; checks accepted with previously established credit through bank letter; no credit cards. Full payment at time of sale; pickups within two weeks.

Brochures mailed.

Note: Listings are alphabetical by town.

Kennedy Antique Auction Galleries, Inc.

David Russell, Auctioneer
1088 Huff Road
Atlanta, Georgia 30318
(404) 351-4464

Weekly sale every Monday at 7:30 p.m., exclusively a variety of English furniture and bric-a-brac, from Victorian era to 1930s, stained glass windows and doors; specialized sales, held five to six times a year, featuring period furniture, stripped pine, and finer quality items; all merchandise imported from England; primarily dealers but collectors welcome; no consignments.

No buyer's premium; mail and telephone bids not accepted; checks with proper ID accepted, Master Charge and Visa accepted. Full payment at time of sale; pickups within seven days.

Specialized sale announcements only mailed.

A B C D Auction Gallery

Fred Bate, Auctioneer
1 Clarendon Avenue
Avondale Estates, Georgia 30002
(404) 294-8264 or (404) 294-8286
(In metropolitan Atlanta area)

General auctions, of consigned merchandise only, held twice a week on Mondays and Wednesdays, or as needed; specialized sales include glass, guns, silver, porcelain, furniture, pocket knives; estate sales; no property purchased for sales.

Ten percent buyer's premium required on some merchandise; mail and telephone bids accepted; checks with proper ID accepted; no credit cards. Full payment at sale; pickups within two days.

Sale announcements mailed; catalogs for all sales on request; written appraisals offered for an hourly fee of $45.00.

D. S. Clarke Auction Gallery

2106 Cobb Parkway SE
Marietta, Georgia 30080
(404) 955-0895
(Highway 41 at Windy Hill Road)

Sales generally held every week on Fridays at 7:30 p.m., featuring furniture and bric-a-brac; specialized sales of clocks, stained glass and architectural items, porcelain, copperware; silver, primitive furniture, and Oriental rugs; estate sales; consignments; some property purchased for sales.

Ten percent buyer's premium on some merchandise; mail and telephone bids accepted; checks accepted with proper ID; no credit cards. Full payment day of sale; pickups as arranged.

Sale announcements and catalogs mailed; oral appraisals at gallery offered free of charge; written appraisals for an hourly fee of $50.00.

Pardue's Antique Auctions
Claud Pardue, Auctioneer
Route 1
Talmo, Georgia 30575
(404) 693-2500
(On Highway 129 at Exit 50, between Interstate 85 and Gainesville, Georgia)

American antiques, collectibles, and general merchandise, auctioned the first and third Friday of every month at 7:00 p.m.; estate sales; consignments; no property purchased for sales.

No buyer's premium; mail and telephone bids accepted; checks accepted with driver's license or proper ID; Master Charge and Visa accepted. Full payment at time of sale; pickups within one week.

Sale announcements mailed.

De Santis Auction Co.
Pete DeSantis, Jr., Auctioneer
Pavo Road
Thomasville, Georgia 31792
(912) 226-8849
(All sales held on site or in rented halls—check mailings)

Specializing in estate sales and antique shop liquidations; specialized sales of antique automobiles; consignments; property purchased for sales.

No buyer's premium; mail and telephone bids accepted with a 25% deposit; checks accepted from customers with previously established credit through bank letter; no credit cards. Full payment and pickups same day.

Sale announcements mailed; written appraisals offered for an hourly fee of $35.00 plus travel expenses.

Delight's Antique and Flea Market   W XXXX
4375 Cobb Parkway
Acworth, Georgia 30101
(404) 974-9218
Contact: Delight Tumlin, 4361 Dallas Road, Acworth, Georgia 30101, (404) 974-5256
(From Atlanta take I-75 to Exit 121, north on US 41 for two miles)

Indoor/outdoor market on 10 acres; 225 dealers; began in 1977; open Friday 11:30 a.m. on, Saturday, Sunday and holidays, 8:00 a.m. on; free admission; space rental: $1.00 to $3.00 per day for 12′ x 14′; reservations needed.

Mostly antiques and collectibles, some secondhand and new merchandise; food; restrooms; parking; nearby motels.

The Atlanta Flea Market   W XXXX
2424 Piedmont Road NE
Atlanta, Georgia 30324
(404) 266-2495
Contact: Jack Hodgkins
(I-85 to Piedmont Road Exit, go north one mile)

Indoor market; 375 dealers; began in 1974; open Friday and Saturday, noon to 9:30 p.m., Sunday, noon to 7:00 p.m.; free admission; space rental: $200.00 per month for 12' x 14'; reservations recommended.

Mostly antiques, collectibles and crafts, very little new merchandise; food; restrooms; parking; nearby motels.

Elco's Georgia Antique Fair and Flea Market M XXXX

Lakewood Fairgrounds
Atlanta, Georgia 30308
Contact: Ellen Peabody, PO Box 54048, Atlanta, Georgia 30308, (404) 872-1913 or 876-2129
(Lakewood Freeway Exit 88, off I-75 and I-85)

Indoor market; 838 dealers; began in 1973; open second weekend of every month; 9:00 a.m. to 6:00 p.m. on Saturday, 10:00 a.m. to 6:00 p.m. on Sunday; free admission; space rental: $35.00 per weekend for 8' x 10'; reservations needed.

Antiques, collectibles, and some new merchandise, crafts and art bojects; food; restrooms; parking; nearby motels.

New Town Flea Market W X

Route 5
Calhoun, Georgia 30701
(404) 625-1157
Contact: Earl Abernathy, Route 5, Iracille Lane, Calhoun, Georgia 30701
(From I-75 take Red Bud Exit to New Town Road)

Outdoor market; 50 dealers; began in 1977; open Friday, Saturday and Sunday, 7:00 a.m. on, year round; free admission; space rental: $1.00 for 12' x 12' covered shed with table; no reservations needed.

Mostly secondhand and household items, some collectibles and antiques, some new merchandise; food; restr-oms; parking; nearby motels.

Chamblee Flea Market and Antiques D X

2390 Carroll Avenue
Chamblee, Georgia 30341
(404) 451-3341
Contact: Betty Keith
(285 Loop to Exit 25, south on Buford Highway to Carroll Avenue)

Indoor/outdoor market; 20 dealers; began in 1979; open every Friday, Sunday and Monday, noon to 6:00 p.m., Saturday 10:00 a.m. to 6:00 p.m.; free admission; space rental: $100.00 per month for 10' x 12' inside booth; reservations needed.

Variety of new merchandise and secondhand items, a lot of produce, some collectibles and antiques; food; restrooms; parking; nearby motels.

Flea Market at Forest Square ★ W XXX

4855 Jonesboro Road
Forest Park, Georgia 30050
(404) 361-1221
Contact: Joan Browne, PO Box 1382, Forest Park, Georgia 30050
(One-and-a-half miles south of I-285)

Indoor market; 150 dealers; began in 1978; open Friday and Saturday, 10:00 a.m. to 9:00 p.m., Sunday and holidays, noon to 6:00 p.m., year round; free admission; space rental: $30.00 per week for 9' x 15'; no reservations needed.

Mostly new merchandise; some secondhand and household items, few antiques and collectibles; four restaurants; restrooms; parking; nearby motels; occasional auctions.

Auntie's Antiques and Flea Market   W   XX
7471 Highway 85
Riverdale, Georgia 30296
(404) 996-9967
Contact: Nell Benefield
(From downtown Atlanta, 15 minutes south on Highway 75)

Outdoor market; 80 dealers; began in 1969; open Saturday and Sunday, year round; free admission; space rental: $3.00 Saturday, $4.00 Sunday for 10' x 10'; no reservations needed.

Mostly secondhand and household items, some antiques, collectibles and new merchandise; nearby restaurants; restrooms; parking; nearby motels.

First Saturday Festival   ★   M   X
Rousakis Plaza, River Street
Savannah, Georgia 31401
(912) 234-0295
Contact: Debra Mock, PO Box 572, Savannah, Georgia 31402, (912) 234-0295
(I-16 to Bay Street, north on Abercorn Street to River Street)

Outdoor market on the Savannah River; 35 to 50 dealers; began in 1973; open first Saturday of each month, 9:00 a.m. to 6:00 p.m.; free admission; space rental: $15.00 for 10' x 12'; reservations needed.

Mostly antiques, collectibles, arts and crafts; restaurants nearby; restrooms; parking; nearby motels; annual auction, usually in June.

KENTUCKY

The Auction Mart
Raymond Knapp, Auctioneer
1021 Bardstown Road
Louisville, Kentucky 40204
(502) 451-2242

Sales start every Tuesday at 10:00 a.m. and last 10 to 12 hours; merchandise comprised of antiques and general household goods, including Victorian furniture, cut glass, and some silver; estate sales; predominantly consignments; some merchandise purchased for sales.

No buyer's premium; mail and telephone bids accepted; checks accepted with proper ID; no credit cards. Full payment day of sale; pickups within three days.

Sale announcements mailed; oral and written appraisals offered for negotiable fee.

Camp Nelson Flea Market   W X
Camp Nelson Recreation Area
Camp Nelson, Kentucky 40444
(606) 885-9304
Contact: Jean Goins
(Twenty miles south of Lexington on old US 27, at the Kentucky River)

Outdoor market; 30 dealers; open Saturday, Sunday and holidays, May 15 through October; free admission; space rental: $4.00 per day for 10' x 14' under pavilion with two tables; no reservations needed.
   Mostly secondhand and household items, some antiques and collectibles; food; restrooms; parking; nearby campgrounds.

E'Town Flea Market   W XXX
Highway 31W North
Elizabethtown, Kentucky 42701
(502) 737-6361
Contact: Bill Routt, Route 8, Box 120, Elizabethtown, Kentucky 42701

Indoor/outdoor market; 120 dealers; open Friday, Saturday and Sunday, year round; free admission; space rental: $3.00 to $10.00 for 10' x 20' to 12' x 30'; no reservations needed.
   Variety of collectibles, antiques, secondhand items and crafts; food; restrooms; parking; nearby motels.

Country World Flea Market   W XXXX
US 460
Georgetown, Kentucky 40324
(502) 863-9185
Contact: Glenn Juett, 111 Montgomery Avenue, Georgetown, Kentucky 40324, (502) 863-0289
(Take Georgetown Exit off I-75, one mile east to US 460)

Outdoor market; 150 to 300 dealers; began in 1970; open every weekend, April to October, 6:00 a.m. Friday until Sunday night; free admission; space rental: $4.50 Saturday, $6.50 Sunday for 14' x 30'; no reservations accepted—first come, first served.
   Variety of secondhand items, new merchandise, antiques, collectibles, crafts and produce; restaurant and food concessions; restrooms; parking; nearby motels.

Mayfield-Graves County Park Flea Market   ★ XXX
Fairgrounds
Mayfield, Kentucky 42066
(502) 247-0049
Contact: Gilliam Guthrie, Park Director, PO Box 801, Mayfield, Kentucky 42066
(West on Housman Street, turn right at Fairgrounds)

Indoor/outdoor market; 150 dealers; began in 1976; open second and third Monday of each month, 5:00 a.m. to 1:30 p.m.; free admission; space rental: $2.00 per day for 14' x 28'; no reservations needed.

Variety of collectibles, antiques, new merchandise, secondhand items and crafts; food; restrooms; parking; nearby motels; auctions three or four times a year.

Mount Sterling Court Days   A XXXX
City Hall
40 Broadway
Mount Sterling, Kentucky 40353
(606) 498-3785
Contact: City Clerk's Office, 40 Broadway, Mount Sterling, Kentucky 40353
(Off I-64, thirty-five miles east of Lexington)

Outdoor market; 500 dealers; began in 1879, if not earlier; held annually, weekend of the third Monday in October; free admission; space rental: $65.00 for three days, 9' x 19'; reservations needed.

Variety of new and secondhand merchandise, antiques, collectibles and crafts; food; restrooms; on-street parking; nearby motels.

LOUISIANA

Morton's Auction Exchange
P. B. Alford, J. Fowler, D. Goldberg, M. Goldberg, M. Russo, Auctioneers
643 Magazine Street
New Orleans, Louisiana 70130
(504) 561-1196

Bi-weekly sales all year; specialized sales feature Victoriana, English, Irish and Continental furniture, Orientalia, silver, American and European paintings, watercolors, and prints; estate sales; consignments; property purchased for sales.

Ten percent buyer's premium; telephone bids accepted; checks accepted with bank references; no credit cards. Purchases held with a 25% deposit; full payment and pickups within 30 days.

Sale announcements and catalogs mailed; written appraisals offered for 1% of total value of item or an hourly fee of $100.00.

Sanchez Antiques and Auction Galleries
F. Sanchez, T. Sanchez, Auctioneers
4730 Magazine Street
New Orleans, Louisiana 70115
(504) 524-0281 or (504) 891-3785

General antiques sale held every other week on Mondays at 10:00 a.m.; over 400 lots of American and Continental furniture, cut glass, silver, clocks; major sale

Note: Listings are alphabetical by town.

held at least once annually of fine art, art pottery and jewelry; estate sales; consignments; property purchased for sales.

No buyer's premium; mail and telephone bids accepted; checks accepted with proper ID; no credit cards. Payment generally due day of sale; pickups within one week.

Sale announcements mailed; oral and written appraisals offered for negotiable fee.

Ponchatoula Auction Company

Harry Hunt, Auctioneer
Main Street
Ponchatoula, Louisiana 70454
(504) 386-8974

Specializing in American antiques; weekly antiques sale held Saturdays at 7:00 p.m. throughout the year; specialized sales of clocks, jewelry; estate sales; consignments; property purchased for sales.

No buyer's premium; mail and telephone bids not accepted; checks accepted with proper ID; no credit cards. Full payment day of sale; pickups within two days.

Sale announcements mailed; oral or written appraisals offered for negotiable fee.

Harry Hunt & Associates Auctioneers

Harry Hunt, Auctioneer
Route 4, Box 332B
Zachary, Louisiana 70791
(504) 654-4432, (504) 654-2398
(Sales held on site or at specified locations—check mailings)

Specializing in estate sales and household liquidations; approximately six sales monthly featuring antiques and household merchandise; specialized sales of pottery, clocks, jewelry, furniture; consignments; property purchased for sales.

No buyer's premium; mail and telephone bids accepted; checks accepted with bank letter of credit; no credit cards. Full payment day of sale; pickups as arranged.

Sale announcements mailed; oral and written appraisals offered for negotiable fee.

Deep South Flea Market   W   XXXX

5350 Florida Boulevard
Baton Rouge, Louisiana 70807
(504) 923-0142
Contact: Bill Vallery
(Exit I-10 to College)

Indoor market; 275 dealers; began in 1974; open every weekend, Friday, 12:00 p.m. to 6:00 p.m., Saturday 10:00 a.m. to 7:00 p.m., Sunday 11:00 a.m. to 7:00 p.m.; free admission; space rental: $40.00 per weekend for 8' x 10'; reservations needed.

Variety of secondhand merchandise, produce, antiques, collectibles, crafts, art objects; food; restrooms; parking; nearby motels.

The Great Louisiana Flea Market   W   XXX

Airline Highway
Gonzales, Louisiana 70737
(504) 644-7545
Contact: R. D. Bozeman
(In southern Gonzales, between New Orleans and Baton Rouge)

Indoor/outdoor market; 200 dealers; began in 1979; open Friday, Saturday and Sunday, 10:00 a.m. to 6:00 p.m.; free admission; space rental: $135.00 a month for 12' x 12' indoors; reservations needed.
Variety of new and used merchandise, antiques, collectibles, crafts, art objects, produce; food; restrooms; parking; nearby motels.

Finders Keepers Trade Exchange   W   X

425 North Railroad
Jennings, Louisiana 70546
(318) 824-6275
Contact: Gary Davis
(On corner of Highway 90 [Cutting Avenue] and Railroad Avenue)

Indoor/outdoor market; 6 to 10 dealers; began in 1974; open Saturday and Sunday, year round, except holidays; free admission; space rental: reasonable for unlimited space; no reservations needed.
Mostly new merchandise, lots of antiques, collectibles and secondhand items; food; restrooms; parking; nearby motel.

190 Trading Post Flea Market   W   X

Route 2, Box 445 A
Lacombe, Louisiana 70445
(504) 882-5336
Contact: Mrs. M.C. Mooty
(Highway 190 Exit off I-10, west ten miles)

Indoor/outdoor market; 35 dealers; began in 1968; open Saturday and Sunday, 10:00 a.m. to 5:00 p.m., year round; free admission; space rental: $4.00 per weekend for 12' x 24'; reservations needed in summer for tables.
Mostly antiques and collectibles, some crafts and new and secondhand merchandise; food; restrooms; parking; nearby motels.

Pioneer Acadian Flea Market   X

Lafayette, Louisiana 70506
(318) 332-3502
Contact: Gerald Goudeau, 223 Luke Street, Lafayette, Louisiana 70506, (318) 235-2752
(Exit 109 off I-10)

Indoor market; 14 dealers; began in 1977; open second and fourth weekend of each month; free admission; space rental: $5.00 per day; no reservations needed.

Variety of collectibles, crafts, antiques, and secondhand merchandise; food; restrooms; parking; nearby motels.

MISSISSIPPI

C.S.A. Auction Company
Conny Dixon, Auctioneer
1805 Highway 15 North
Ripley, Mississippi 38663
(601) 837-8148

Approximately four to six sales held yearly featuring estate property and antiques including, furniture and bric-a-brac; no consignments; all merchandise purchased for sales.

No buyer's premium; mail and telephone bids not accepted; checks accepted with proper ID and bank letter of credit; no credit cards. Full payment at time of sale; pickups when convenient.

Sale announcements and brochures mailed; oral and written appraisals offered for negotiable fee.

Thieves Market   W X
US Highway 61
Natchez, Mississippi 39120
(601) 445-4034
Contact: R.L. Atkins, Route 4, Box 76, Natchez, Mississippi 39120
(Two miles north of city limits)

Indoor/outdoor market; 10 to 25 dealers; began in 1976; open Saturdays 9:00 a.m. to 6:00 p.m., Sundays 12 noon to 6:00 p.m.; free admission; space rental: $12.50 per day for 12' x 20'; reservations recommended.

Variety of collectibles and secondhand items, antiques, some crafts; no food available; restrooms; parking; nearby motels.

Trading Post   5D X
101 Porter Avenue
Ocean Springs, Mississippi 39564
Contact: Pat Bills, 139 Slowan, Ocean Springs, Mississippi 39564, (601) 875-2981
(Ocean Springs end of Biloxi Bay Bridge, Highway 90)

Indoor/outdoor market; 30 dealers; open seven days a week, 7:00 a.m. to 5:00 p.m.; free admission; space rental: $2.00 per day; no reservations needed.

Mostly antiques and collectibles, small amount of secondhand merchandise; food available; restrooms; parking; nearby motel; four annual antique shows.

Ripley's First Monday Trade Day   M   XXXX
Highway 15 South
Ripley, Mississippi 38663
(601) 837-7442
Contact: Wayne Windham, (601) 837-4250
(Take US 22 to Walnut, then south on US 15 to Ripley)

Outdoor market; 600 dealers; began about 1880; open the weekend preceding the first Monday of each month; free admission; space rental: $5.00 per day, $10.50 per three-day weekend for 18' x 20' space; reservations helpful.

Equal variety of antiques, collectibles, new and used merchandise, art and crafts; restaurant and snack bars; restrooms and showers; parking; nearby motels.

NORTH CAROLINA

Robert D. Bunn, Antiques
Robert D. Bunn, Auctioneer
13 Biltmore Avenue
Asheville, North Carolina 28801
(704) 254-3911

Specializing in on-site estate sales throughout North Carolina, South Carolina, Virginia and Tennessee, and retail sale of antiques at Asheville address; approximately 10 to 12 estate sales yearly, including variety of fine antiques; property purchased for store only.

No buyer's premium; mail and telephone bids not accepted; checks accepted, though merchandise may be held until check clears; no credit cards; purchase of catalog required to enter some sales. Full payment day of sale; pickups within three days.

Sale announcements mailed; oral and written appraisals offered for negotiable fee.

Russakoff Auction
Richard Russakoff, Auctioneer
M.P. 11 Beach Road, Box 608
Nags Head, North Carolina 27959
(919) 441-6201 or (919) 441-6541

Antiques and collectibles sale usually held weekly, or at least twice a month; featuring jewelry, Victorian, Art Deco, Eastlake, Mission and Hitchcock furniture, glass, china; estate sales; consignments; property purchased for sales.

No buyer's premium; mail and telephone bids accepted; checks accepted with proper ID, Master Charge, Visa and American Express accepted. Full payment and pickups within 24 hours.

Sale announcements mailed; some catalogs; specialize in jewelry appraisals; oral appraisals for fee of $10.00 per item; written appraisals at hourly rate of $35.00; $10.00 for additional research, $5.00 for clerical.

Childs Auction Company, Inc.
PO Drawer 1
Sanford, North Carolina 27330
(919) 775-7618
(Sales located north of Sanford on Highways 15 & 501)

Specializing in antiques and collectibles; two to three sales monthly, including variety of antique pine, walnut, cherry, mahogany furniture and mixed antiques; sales held on Saturdays, at 7:00 or 7:30 p.m.; specialized sales of depression glass, clocks, guns; estate sales; consignments; property purchased for sales.

No buyer's premium; mail and telephone bids accepted; checks accepted with bank letter of credit; Master Charge and Visa accepted. Full payment night of sale; pickups within two weeks.

Sale announcements mailed; catalogs for some sales; appraisals offered within 50 mile radius for fee of $25.00 plus expenses.

Asheboro Flea and Produce Market   W X
Highway 220 South Bypass
Asheboro, North Carolina 27203
(919) 625-6463
Contact: Charles Vuncannon, 1114 Shamrock Road, Asheboro, North Carolina 27203
(Take McDowell Road Exit to Lambeth Drive to Mine Road)

Outdoor market; 20 dealers; began in 1980; open Saturday, 7:00 a.m. until dark; free admission; space rental: $3.00 for 15'; no reservations needed.

Variety of merchandise including produce, secondhand items, antiques, collectibles and crafts; food concession; restrooms; parking; nearby motels.

Dreamland Drive-In Flea Market   W XXXX
South Tunnel Road
Asheville, North Carolina 28803
(704) 255-7777
Contact: Dusty Pless
(US Highway 74 to State Highway 81)

Outdoor market; 400 dealers; began in 1971; open every Friday, Saturday and Sunday, year round; free admission; space rental: $2.00 Friday, $4.00 Saturday or Sunday for 22'; reservations needed.

Wide variety of merchandise; food; restrooms; parking; nearby motels.

Metrolina Flea Market   XXXX
7100 Statesville Road North
Charlotte, North Carolina 28213
Contact: Hazel Christensen or Lou Grandmaison
(Two miles north from I-85; half mile from I-77)

Indoor market; 850 dealers; began in 1968; held first and third weekends of every month, 12:00 p.m. to 8:00 p.m. on Friday, 8:00 a.m. to 5:00 p.m. on

Saturday and Sunday; $1.00 admission; space rental: $15.00 for 8' x 10'; reservations needed.
Variety of secondhand merchandise, antiques, collectibles, crafts, art objects, and produce on first weekend; mostly antique furniture on third weekend; snackbar; restrooms; parking; nearby motels.

Super Flea Flea Market   M XXXX
Coliseum
Greensboro, North Carolina
(919) 373-8515
Contact: Smith/Tomlinson Corporation, PO Box 16122, Greensboro, North Carolina 27402
(All highways well marked to Coliseum area)

Indoor market; 350 dealers; began in 1976; open once a month, Saturday 8:00 a.m. to 6:00 p.m., Sunday 1:00 p.m. to 6:00 p.m., call ahead for exact dates; 75¢ admission; space rental: $30.00 for 8' x 12'; reservations needed.
    Mostly antiques and collectibles, some new merchandise; snack bar; restrooms; parking; nearby motels.

Greenville Collectors Club Antique Show and Flea Market   A X
Evans Mall
Evans Street
Greenville, North Carolina 27834
Contact: Mickey and Martha Elmore, 105 North Jarvis Street, Greenville, North Carolina 27834, (919) 752-3456
(In the center of town between Third and Fifth Streets)

Outdoor market; 30 to 50 dealers; began in 1971; held annually, usually one day in September; free admission; space rental: $7.50 for large area; reservations recommended.
    Mostly antiques and collectibles, some secondhand and new merchandise; food concession; nearby restrooms; parking; nearby motels.

Hickory Livestock Flea Market   W XX
Sweetwater Road
Hickory, North Carolina 28601
Contact: George Hahn, Route 6, Hickory, North Carolina 28601
(Off Highway 64-40 between Hickory and Conover)

Outdoor market; 100 dealers; open Thursday, all day, year round; free admission; space rental: $3.00 to $5.00 for 12' x 20'; no reservations needed.
    Mostly new merchandise, produce and antiques; food; restrooms; parking; nearby motels.

Farmer's and Flea Market   XXXX
Route 14, Box 13
Lexington, North Carolina 27292
(704) 246-2157 or (704) 249-6087
Contact: Harold J. Fritts
(Old 64 West, three-quarters mile west of I-85)

Note: Listings are alphabetical by town.

Indoor/outdoor market; 250 dealers; began in 1972; open every Tuesday 3:30 till Wednesday at 5:00, year round; free admission; space rental: $3.00 to $4.00 for 16' x 10' stalls; no reservations needed.

New merchandise, antiques, collectibles, secondhand and household items; food; restrooms; parking; nearby motels.

Pfafftown Jaycee Antique Flea Market   M   XX
West Central Community Center
Yadkinville Road
Pfafftown, North Carolina 27040
(919) 945-5687
Contact: Bob Lohmeyer, 700 Bellview Street, Winston-Salem, North Carolina 27103, (919) 765-8291
(From Winston-Salem take Highway 67 West, right on Yadkinville Road, five miles to Center)

Indoor/outdoor market; 50 to 60 dealers; began in 1969; open second Sunday of every month, 9:00 a.m. to 4:00 p.m., year round; free admission; space rental: $5.00 for 10' x 10' inside, with table, no limit outside; reservations needed for inside space.

Lots of collectibles and antiques, some new merchandise; food; restrooms; parking; nearby motels.

Thunderbird Drive-In Flea Market   W   XXX
3774 Konnoak Drive
Winston-Salem, North Carolina 27107
(919) 788-5183
Contact: Larry G. Rogers, 1552 Harding Street, Winston-Salem, North Carolina 27107, (919) 784-6214
(Highway 52 South out of Winston-Salem to Clemmonsville Road Exit, right at stop light, turn left quarter mile)

Outdoor market; 100 to 150 sellers; began in 1973; open every Saturday and Sunday, all day, year round; free admission; space rental: $3.00 daily 10' x 12'; no reservations needed.

Mostly secondhand and household items, some collectibles and crafts; food; restrooms; parking, nearby motels.

SOUTH CAROLINA

Charlton Hall Galleries, Inc.
Ronald D. Long, Auctioneer
930 Gervais Street
Columbia, South Carolina 29201
(803) 252-7927 or (803) 779-5678

An antique business plus auction and estate service selling 18th and 19th century English and French furniture and accessories; cabinet shop on the premises produces reproductions, custom-built furniture, and restorations; generally five sales held yearly at various dates; estate sales; consignments; no property purchased for sales.

No buyer's premium; telephone bids accepted; approved checks accepted; Master Charge and Visa accepted. Purchases held with a 10% deposit; full payment and pickups within five days.

Sale announcements mailed; written appraisals offered for an hourly fee of $75.00.

Lowcountry Flea Market   M   XX
Gaillard Auditorium
Charleston, South Carolina 29240
(803) 577-7400
Contact: The Nelson Garrett's Inc., PO Box 4031, Columbia, South Carolina 29240, (803) 788-5269
(At the east end of I-26 take Meeting Street Exit, go six blocks to Calhoun Street and turn left)

Indoor market; 60 dealers; open third weekend, May to December, 9:00 a.m. to 6:00 p.m.; 75¢ admission; space rental: $25.00 for 10' x 10' area for two days; reservations recommended.
Variety of antiques, collectibles, new merchandise, secondhand items and crafts; food; restrooms; parking; nearby motels.

The Cattle Barn Flea Market   ★ D XXXX
912 Poinsett Highway
Greenville, South Carolina 29608
(803) 242-3092
Contact: Gary F. Bruce, PO Box 3825, Park Place Branch, Greenville, South Carolina 29608
(Off Poinsett Highway behind the Goodwill Store and Bruce Plaza)

Indoor/outdoor market; 350 dealers; began in 1980; open Wednesday and Friday, noon to 9:00 p.m., Saturday, 7:00 a.m. to 9:00 p.m., Sunday, 1:00 p.m. to 6:00 p.m., year round; free admission; space rental: $3.00 per day for 12' x 12' area, $5.00 for open air booth, monthly rates indoors; reservations needed.
Variety of antiques, collectibles, secondhand items, new merchandise, produce and crafts; food; restrooms; parking; nearby motels; monthly antique auctions, weekly car auctions on Friday.

Smuggler's Cove Flea Market   ★ W&D X
Highway 17 North
Myrtle Beach, South Carolina 29577
(803) 272-8221
Contact: Susan Duke, PO Box 93, Myrtle Beach, South Carolina 29577, (803) 449-7947
(North on Highway 17 to North Myrtle Beach)

Indoor/outdoor market; 20 to 35 dealers; began in 1976; open weekends September through May, seven days a week from Memorial Day to Labor Day; free admission; space rental: $6.00 per day for 12' x 12'; reservations recommended in summer.

Mostly new merchandise, some art, antiques and secondhand items; snack bar; restrooms; parking; nearby motels and many campgrounds; occasional auctions.

TENNESSEE

Clement's Antiques of Tennessee, Inc.
Northgate Gallery
5520 Highway 153
Chattanooga, Tennessee 37343
(615) 842-4177
(615) 842-5992
Office and antique shop:
7022 Dayton Pike
Chattanooga, Tennessee 37343
(615) 877-6114
(Twelve miles north of city center, Chattanooga)

Fine art and antiques sale held first Saturday of every month includes paintings, rugs, porcelain, silver; estate sales; consignments; property purchased for sales.

No buyer's premium; mail and telephone bids accepted; checks accepted with previously established credit through bank letter of credit or reference; no credit cards. Full payment generally due day of sale; 25% deposit necessary to hold mail and phone bids; pickups within one week.

Catalogs mailed; oral appraisals at gallery offered free of charge; written appraisals, for merchandise auctioned at gallery, offered free; otherwise, for percentage dependent on value of item.

Estate Gallery
Larry Sims, Auctioneer
115 West Vine Street
PO Box 87
Murfreesboro, Tennessee 37130
(615) 890-2067
(On Interstate 24 thirty-two miles south of Nashville)

Primarily handles estate sales; sales held twice a month; antiques include American furniture, European furniture, glass; specialized sales feature drugstore and general store collectibles; consignments; merchandise purchased for sales.

No buyer's premium; mail and telephone bids accepted with 25% deposit sent by check; checks accepted with bank letter of credit; no credit cards. Purchases held with a 25% deposit; full payment within one week; pickups within two weeks.

Sale announcements and catalogs mailed; written appraisals offered for fee of $100.00 and up.

Miller's Auction Gallery

George Miller, Jr., Auctioneer
Route 7, Knoxville Highway
Newport, Tennessee 37821
(615) 623-8221

Specializing in antiques and estate sales; four mixed antique sales held yearly, generally one each season, on a Saturday; featuring Victorian and custommade furniture, glass, paintings, clocks, Oriental rugs; specialized sales of clocks, jewelry, art glass; approximately two estate sales held monthly—usually at gallery, some on site within Tennessee; consignments only.

No buyer's premium; mail and telephone bids accepted; checks accepted with previously established credit through proper ID or bank letter; no credit cards. Full payment day of sale; pickups within one week.

Sale announcements and brochures mailed; written appraisals offered for negotiable fee.

Powell Auction

Howard Phillips, Auctioneer
Emory Road
Powell, Tennessee 37921
(615) 938-8103 or (615) 947-0595
(In east Tennessee, five miles north of Knoxville; take Interstate 75 North to Emory Road Exit)

Sales held every Saturday at 7:00 p.m.; two sales per month feature antiques and collectibles exclusively, including furniture and glass; two sales of both antiques and used furniture, handmade crafts; estate sales, consignments; property purchased for sales.

No buyer's premium; mail and telephone bids not accepted; checks accepted with proper ID; no credit cards; full payment day of sale; pickups within two weeks.

TM Auction Company

Charles Changas, Auctioneer
4900 Chamliss Street
West Knoxville, Tennessee 37919
(615) 584-9641

Auctions featuring Tiffany lamps, fine jewelry, oil paintings, oak and period furniture, pottery, porcelain, art glass; approximately 30 sales held each year, at no fixed schedule; estate sales; consignments; property purchased for sales.

No buyer's premium; mail and telephone bids accepted from established customers; first-time bidders must leave a 25% deposit; checks accepted with previously established credit through bank letter; Master Charge and Visa accepted. Full payment day of sale; pickups as arranged.

Sale announcements and some catalogs mailed; written appraisals offered for negotiable fee.

Carrier's Flea Market

W XXX

11 East Highway
Bristol, Tennessee
Contact: J. W. Carrier, Route 1, Box 103A, Bluff City, Tennessee 37618, (615) 538-7177
(Between Bristol and Johnson City Highway, I-81 Exit 1; half mile south of Bristol International Raceway)

Outdoor market; 100 + dealers; open Saturdays and Sundays, year round; free admission; space rental: $2.50 for 12'; no reservations needed.

Mostly collectibles and antiques, some new and secondhand merchandise; food vendors; restrooms; ample parking; nearby motels.

Shady Lake Flea Market

W XX

Highway 70 North
Crossville, Tennessee 38555
(Between Nashville and Knoxville, take Jamestown Exit off I-40)

Outdoor market; 20 to 100 dealers; began in 1979; open Saturday, Sunday and holidays, 6:00 a.m. to 4:00 p.m., mid-March through December; free admission; space rental: $2.00 per day for 14' x 25'; no reservations needed.

Variety of secondhand and household items, new merchandise, antiques and collectibles; food; restrooms; parking; nearby motels and campgrounds.

Franklin Flea Market

W X

City of Franklin Mall
Franklin, Tennessee 37064
Contact: Art Waller
(Five miles west of I-65, twenty miles south of Nashville)

Indoor/outdoor market; 35 dealers; began in 1975; open every Wednesday, year round; free admission; space rental: $6.00 indoors, $3.00 outdoors; no reservations needed.

Mostly collectibles, secondhand items and antiques, some new merchandise and crafts; food; restrooms; parking; nearby motels.

Appalachian Trade Festival

★ A XXXX

Appalachian Fairgrounds
Gray, Tennessee
(615) 246-4500
Contact: Jim Cornell, PO Box 1406, Kingsport, Tennessee 37662, (615) 246-4500
(Gray Exit off State Route 137 between Kingsport and Johnson City)

Indoor market; 250 dealers; began in 1977; held annually, usually the last weekend (plus Monday) in May; admission $1.50 adults, $1.00 children; space rental: $20.00 to $35.00; reservations needed.

Mostly antiques and collectibles, some arts and crafts; food; restrooms; parking; nearby motels; on-site camping; auction on Monday.

Antique City Flea Market   ★ XX
Route 2, Highway 45 South
Humboldt, Tennessee 38343
(901) 784-3422
Contact: Buster Henley
(Exit 80B off I-40, go six miles north, between Humboldt and Jackson)

Indoor/outdoor market; 80 dealers; began in 1976; open first, second and third weekends of every month; free admission; space rental: $5.00 outside, $15.00 for 12' x 12' inside for weekend; no reservations needed.

Mostly antiques and collectibles, few secondhand and household items; food; restrooms; parking; nearby motels; annual auction on July 4.

Carroll County Flea Market   M X
Highway 70 East
Huntingdon, Tennessee 38344
(901) 986-9476
Contact: Buddy Carter, Route 4, Huntingdon, Tennessee 38344, (901) 986-9476
(Call for directions)

Indoor/outdoor market; 20 dealers; began in 1979; open first weekend of each month; free admission; space rental: $5.00 and up for 10' x 10' and up; no reservations needed.

Mostly new and secondhand merchandise, some antiques and arts and crafts; food; restrooms; parking; nearby motels.

Knoxville Fairgrounds Antique Flea Market   M XXXX
PO Box 9247
Knoxville, Tennessee 37920
(615) 573-7489
Contact: Ralph Green
(I-40 East to Rutledge Park Exit)

Indoor market; 250 dealers; began in 1976; open third weekend each month, 10:00 a.m. to 6:00 p.m.; 50¢ admission; space rental: $25.00 per weekend for 10' x 10'; reservations preferred.

Mostly antiques and collectibles, some new merchandise; three snack bars; restrooms; plenty of parking; 12 nearby motels.

Parkland Flea Market   ★ W XXX
Route 6
Lebanon, Tennessee 37087
(615) 444-9915
Contact: Perry Lanius, Route 4, Box 532, Lebanon, Tennessee 37087, (615) 444-0712
(Take 231 South from Lebanon, six miles from Cedars of Lebanon State Park)

Note: Listings are alphabetical by town.

Indoor/outdoor market; 100+ dealers; began in 1977; open every Saturday and Sunday 7:00 a.m. till dark; free admission; space rental: $3.50 outside, $5.00 under roof; reservations needed.

Wide variety of antiques, collectibles and secondhand items, some new merchandise and arts and crafts; restaurant; restrooms and showers; free parking; nearby motels and campgrounds; occasional auctions.

Memphis Flea Market   W XXXX
Mid-South Fairgrounds
East Parkway and Central Avenue
Memphis, Tennessee 38104
Contact: Fred or Ruth Hicks, Route 1, Fairview, Tennessee 37062, (615) 799-0084 or (615) 799-2912

Indoor/outdoor market; 250 dealers; began in 1972; open Saturdays 9:00 a.m. to 6:00 p.m., Sundays noon to 6:00 p.m.; free admission; space rental: $30.00 inside, $15.00 outside for 10' x 10'; reservations recommended.

Mostly antiques, some collectibles, secondhand items and new merchandise; food; restrooms; parking; nearby motels.

Mid-South Flea Market   XXX
Mid-South Fairgrounds
Central Avenue and East Parkway
Memphis, Tennessee 38104
Contact: Coleman-Simmons Promotions, PO Box 40776, Memphis, Tennessee 38104, (901) 725-0633

Indoor/outdoor market; 200 dealers; began in 1971; open first, second and fourth weekends of each month except May and September, 9:00 a.m. to 6:00 p.m.; 50¢ admission; space rental: $10.00 per day for 9' x 12'; reservations recommended.

Mostly antiques, collectibles, and secondhand goods, some new merchandise and crafts; foods; restrooms; parking; nearby motels.

Nashville Flea Market   M XXXX
Fairgrounds
Wedgewood Avenue
Nashville, Tennessee 38111
Contact: Fred or Ruth Hicks, Route 1, Fairview, Tennessee 37062, (615) 799-0084 or (615) 799-2912
(Wedgewood Avenue Exit, go south one mile)

Indoor/outdoor market; 350 dealers; began in 1968; open one weekend per month, Saturday 9:00 a.m. to 6:00 p.m., Sunday noon to 6:00 p.m.; free admission; space rental: $25.00 to $30.00 for 10' x 10'; reservations needed.

Mostly antiques, some collectibles, new and secondhand merchandise; food; restrooms; parking; nearby motels.

Center Hill Flea Market and Auction ★ W
Miller Road and Short Mountain
Smithville, Tennessee 37166
Contact: Dr. Melvin Blevins, 207 South Mountain, Smithville, Tennessee
37166, (615) 597-7001
(Take I-40 to Highway 70 Exit to Smithville)

Indoor market; 20 dealers; began in 1980; open every Friday, Saturday and
Sunday; free admission; space rental: $10.00 to $15.00 for 10' x 20'; no
reservations needed.

Variety of antiques, collectibles, new and secondhand merchandise; restrooms; parking; nearby motels; Friday night auctions.

Dee's Antique Flea Market W XXXX
Highway 11-E
Telford, Tennessee 37690
(615) 753-4241
Contact: D.J. Meade, Dee's Antique Barn, Highway 11-E, Telford, Tennessee
37690
(Three miles south of Jonesboro on 11-E)

Outdoor market; 300 l dealers; began in 1970; open Sundays, 7:00 a.m. to 5:00
p.m., year round: free admission; space rental: $3.00 daily for 12' x 25', $16.00
monthly; no reservations needed.

Mostly new merchandise, large number of collectibles and antiques; food;
restrooms; plenty of parking; nearby motels.

Arnold Drive-In Theatre Flea Market W X
Highway 55
Tullahoma, Tennessee 37388
(615) 455-4080
Contact: Toy Waggoner, PO Box 599, Tullahoma, Tennessee 37388, (615)
455-5749
(Nine miles off I-24, Highway 55 Exit)

Outdoor market; 40 to 50 dealers; began in 1960; open every Saturday, year
round; free admission; space rental: $2.00 for 20' x 20'; no reservations needed.

Variety of antiques, collectibles and new merchandise, some produce, arts
and crafts; food; restrooms; parking; nearby motels.

VIRGINIA

Wilson Galleries
Dean and Mark Wilson, Auctioneers
PO Box 102
Fort Defiance, Virginia 24437
Gallery: US Route 11
(US Route 11, three miles north of Staunton, beside Wilco service station in
Verona)

Antiques sale on third Saturday of every other month, starting January; featuring American and English furniture from 18th to early 19th centuries, silver, Oriental rugs, paintings; estate sales; consignments only.

No buyer's premium; telephone bids accepted; checks with proper ID accepted; no credit cards. Full payment same day; pickups within seven days.

Sale announcements and catalogs mailed.

B & W Auction
9097 Euclid Avenue
Manassas, Virginia 22110
(703) 361-1030
(Thirty miles from Washington, D.C.)

Weekly general sales of household merchandise, furniture, antiques, glassware, on Thursdays at 7:30 p.m.; consignments; property purchased for sales.

No buyer's premium; mail and telephone bids not accepted; personal checks accepted on approval; Master Charge and Visa accepted. Full payment night of sale; pickups within five days.

Sale announcements sometimes mailed.

Laws
7209 Centreville Road
Manassas, Virginia 22110
(703) 361-3148
Laws Auction #2:
8104 Centreville Road
Manassas, Virginia 22110

General sales, including a variety of oak furniture, held every Friday night at 6:00 p.m. in Laws Auction Building #2; antiques and estate sales, featuring mainly Victorian furniture and furnishings, held the first weekend of the month at the main building on Centreville Road; four catalog sales, specializing in period furniture and accessories, held in January, April, July, and October; consignments; property purchased for sales.

No buyer's premium; mail and telephone bids accepted; checks accepted; Master Charge and Visa accepted. Full payment at sale; pickups within five days.

Catalogs of four yearly sales and estate sales mailed; oral and written appraisals offered for negotiable fee.

Zedd's Auctions
Calvin Zedd, Auctioneer
795 Monticello Avenue
Norfolk, Virginia 23510
(804) 623-4999

Sales held every three weeks, on either Thursday or Saturday at 10:30 a.m.; featuring general merchandise, some antiques and collectibles; estate sales; no consignments; property purchased for sales.

No buyer's premium; mail and telephone bids not accepted; checks accepted with proper ID; no credit cards. Purchases held with a 25% deposit; full payment and pickups within three days.

Sale announcements and some catalogs mailed; oral and written appraisals offered for negotiable fee.

Harlowe Auction Ltd.
William W. Harlowe, Auctioneer
Box 111
Troy, Virginia 22974
(804) 293-2904
(Sales at Boar's Head Inn on 250, west of Charlottesville)

Annual Oriental rug sale in February and coin sale in August, held at the Boar's Head Inn; estate sales; consignments; property purchased for sales.

No buyer's premium; mail and telephone bids accepted; checks with proper ID, or established credit through bank reference, accepted; no credit cards. Full payment day of sale; pickups generally within two days.

Sale announcements mailed.

Alta Vista-Hurt Jaycees First Saturday Trade Lot　　　　　M　XXX
Highway 29
Alta Vista, Virginia 24517
(804) 369-5065
Contact: H.C. Wheeler, 1013 Seventh Street, Alta Vista, Virginia 24517
(Between Lynchburg and Danville)

Outdoor market; 200 dealers; began in 1911; open first Saturday of each month, noon Friday to midnight Saturday; free admission; space rental: $4.00 for 10' x 20'; no reservations needed.

Mostly antiques, collectibles, and secondhand merchandise, some produce; food; restrooms; parking; nearby motels.

Labor Day Gun Show and Flea Market　　　　　A　XXXX
Routes 58 and 221 West
Hillsville, Virginia 24343
(703) 728-9810
Contact: Melvin Webb, Route 2, Box 39A, Hillsville, Virginia 24343
(One mile off I-77)

Indoor/outdoor market; 400 dealers; began in 1967; held annually, Labor Day weekend; $1.00 admission; space rental: inside $15.00 to $24.00, outside $10.00; reservations needed.

Guns, coins and knives inside, variety of antiques, collectibles, secondhand and new merchandise outside; food; restrooms; parking; nearby motels.

Flea Market   W X
Antique Center of Leesburg
326 East Davis Avenue
Leesburg, Virginia 22075
(703) 777-9666
Contact: Betty Hutton, Route 4, Box 40A, Leesburg, Virginia 22075, (703) 777-5358
(Route 7 west to South King Street, near Route 7/15 Bypass)

Indoor shops (11 dealers), outdoor market; 10 to 15 dealers; began in 1976; open Saturday and Sunday, 10:00 a.m. to 5:00 p.m.; free admission; space rental: $10.00 per day; reservations needed.
  Antiques and collectibles only; no food; restrooms; parking; nearby motels.

The Hitching Post Flea Market   ★ W X
9396 Richmond Highway
Lorton, Virginia 22079
(703) 339-5678
Contact: Uta Kirchner or Donna Wilson, 207 South Fairfax Street, Alexandria, Virginia 22314, (703) 548-0314
(Route 1 South from Alexandria)

Indoor/outdoor market; 20 to 30 dealers; began in 1979; open every Saturday and Sunday, year round; free admission; space rental: $5.00 per table; reservations needed.
  Variety of antiques, collectibles, new and used merchandise, produce, arts and crafts; food; restrooms; parking; nearby motels; auctions one Thursday a month.

Luray Flea Market   ★ W X
Route 211 East
Luray, Virginia 22835
(703) 743-5895
Contact: Charles or Audrey Morris, Route 2, Box 41, Luray, Virginia 22835, (703) 743-6725
(Route 495 to Route 66 to Warrentown, Virginia, Route 211 east to Luray)

Outdoor market; 15 dealers; began in 1977; open Saturday, Sunday and holidays, June to October; free admission; space rental: $5.00 for first 3' x 7' table, $1.00 each additional table; no reservations needed.
  Mostly collectibles and antiques, some new merchandise and crafts; food; restrooms; parking; nearby motels and campgrounds; occasional auctions.

Bellwood Flea Market   W XXX
9201 Jefferson Davis Highway
Richmond, Virginia 23234
(804) 275-1187
Contact: A. T. Kline, 4501 Stanbrook Drive, Richmond, Virginia 73234, (804) 276-2731
(Exit 6-A off I-95)

Outdoor market; 200 dealers; began in 1970; open every Saturday and Sunday, 7:00 a.m. to 4:30 p.m; 40¢ admission; space rental: $4.00 per day; no reservations needed.

Variety of secondhand items, collectibles, new merchandise, produce, antiques, arts and crafts; food; restrooms; parking; nearby motels.

Trail Drive-In Flea Market   W XXX
Trail Drive-In Theatre
Route 1, Box 157
Roanoke, Virginia 24012
(703) 342-0279
Contact: Tom Davis or James Swortzel
(US 460 east of Roanoke)

Outdoor market; 200 dealers; began in 1971; open every Saturday, 6:00 a.m. to 4:00 p.m., year round; free admission; space rental: $4.00 per day for 18' x 20'; first come first served—no reservations needed.

Mostly secondhand and household items, some antiques and collectibles; food; restrooms; parking; nearby motels.

304 Flea Market   D X
Route 1, Box 155
Scottsburg, Virginia 24589
(804) 454-6766
Contact: Robert E. Davis
(Seven miles east of South Boston, Highway 304, near 360)

Outdoor market; three to six dealers; began in 1979; open seven days a week, 8:00 a.m. to 10:00 p.m.; free admission; space rental: $3.00 per day; no reservations needed.

Mostly collectibles, antiques, and produce, some new and secondhand merchandise; food; restrooms; parking; nearby motels.

Carter's Flea & Farmer's Market   W
US Route 17
South Gloucester, Virginia 23061
(804) 693-4530
Contact: Philip Carter, Route 3, Box 231, South Gloucester, Virginia 23061
(About twenty-five miles from Williamsburg)

Indoor/outdoor market; began in 1977; open Saturday, 9:00 a.m. to 5:00 p.m., and Sunday 1:00 p.m. to 6:00 p.m.; free admission; space rental: $7.00 daily, $10.00 both days for table or $18.00 for booth; reservations needed for booth only.

Mostly new merchandise, variety of secondhand merchandise, antiques, collectibles, crafts, art objects; snack bar; restrooms; parking; nearby motels.

Note: Listings are alphabetical by town.

Strasburg Flea Market   ★ W X
306 East King Street
Strasburg, Virginia 22657
(703) 465-3711
Contact: Michael Paper, 206 Sharpe Street, Strasburg, Virginia 22657
(Route 81 to Strasburg Exit, Route 11 to corner of Route 55)

Indoor/outdoor market; 20 to 30 dealers; began in 1979; open Friday, Saturday
and Sunday, 10:00 a.m. to 7:00 p.m., year round; free admission; space rental:
$8.00 per day for 8' x 12' to 20' x 12'; reservations needed indoors only.

Mostly antiques and collectibles, some secondhand and household items;
food; restrooms; parking; nearby motels; auctions every Tuesday at 6:30 p.m.

Verona Antique Market and Wharf Antique Mall   D X
PO Box 317
Verona, Virginia 24482
(703) 885-0485
Contact: Rocky Simonetti
(Exit 59 off I-81, take US 11 three miles north of Staunton)

Indoor/outdoor market; 40 dealers; began in 1970; open Thursday and Friday,
10:00 a.m. to 5:00 p.m., Saturday and Sunday, 9:00 a.m. to 6:00 p.m., year round;
free admission; space rental; $60.00 per month for 18' x 30'; reservations
needed.

Mostly antiques, some collectibles; no food; restrooms; parking; nearby
motels.

Skyline Flea Market   W X
Route 250 West
Waynesboro, Virginia 22980
(703) 942-5541
Contact: Joe Berry, 101 King Avenue, Waynesboro, Virginia 22980

Outdoor market; 40 dealers; began in 1975; open Sunday, 8:00 a.m. to 4:00 p.m.,
April to October; 25¢ admission; space rental: $4.00 per day, $2.00 for a table; no
reservations needed.

Variety of secondhand items, collectibles, antiques and new merchandise;
food; restrooms; parking; nearby motels.

MIDWEST

Traditionally, the Midwest is not supposed to possess the glamor of some other regions of the country. It is neither coastal, mountainous nor sub-tropical. But it has been traversed, heavily settled, successfully farmed and industrialized for well over 100 years, and the nine states in the region are now sources for a good proportion of the antiques and collectibles of today. Nearly a quarter of the 100 biggest cities in the United States are in the Midwest, and with all those people, auctions and flea markets are well-stocked.

Major Midwestern auction houses include Chicago Art Galleries and Hanzel Galleries in Chicago; Garth's Auctions in Delaware, Ohio; the Milwaukee Auction Galleries in Wisconsin; the C. B. Charles and DuMouchelle galleries in Detroit; Gene Harris in Marshalltown, Iowa; Schmidt's Antiques in Ypsilanti, Michigan; and the Rose Galleries in Roseville, Minnesota, near St. Paul and Minneapolis.

Ohio, Illinois and Indiana have the most flea markets, and that is not counting the markets just a few miles over a state line. A particularly good area for collectors is that which surrounds Detroit—the city itself and within an hour's drive south, north or west. The New Giant flea is in Burton-Flint; the Week End market in Charlotte is west of Detroit; there's a market on Eight Mile Road right in the city itself; there's a biannual flea held at Flat Rock, just west of the city; New Boston, Pontiac, Wayne and Ypsilanti all have markets and are within a few minutes of the city limits, and the Mason Antique Flea Market is also close.

A broad range of antiques and collectibles are offered at Midwestern sales and fleas. I feel that collectors in the Midwest form a real democracy—although the reasons are unknown, the scope of the objects they collect and the wide range in age of the items seems to be greater than anywhere else. Merchandise at auctions and flea markets includes every kind of glassware, old farm equipment and tools, stoneware and some 20th-century potteries, 1930s radios, coin-operated machines and old kitchen gadgets. You might expect them to be headquartered in Detroit, but the largest auctioneer of old cars in the country is Kruse International in Auburn, Indiana. Every two weeks people from all over the world come to bid on brass-and-gas automobiles, classy convertibles and coupes, and one-of-a-kind cars made for sheiks and movie stars.

Ohio auctions, like sales in neighboring Pennsylvania, are often focused on Americana and folk art, particularly Amish crafts. It is still a good bet that many items are found close to their origins. Therefore, a good place to look for Amish crafts would be in the east-central part of the state, in Tuscarowas County. Early rubber products might be found around Akron; Rookwood pottery around Cincinnati; glasswares of all ages around Toledo, Cambridge, Tiffin and Bellaire.

People who live in the Midwest get accustomed to the many interesting museums and sights, but for those who plan to travel to the region on an antiquing tour, some of the places might be a pleasant surprise. A mind-boggling display of industrialism, for example, with everything from the tools of steel-working to a real coal mine, are to be seen at Chicago's Museum of Science and Industry. Especially intriguing is the building itself, which is a reconstruction of the Fine Arts Building at the 1893 Columbian Exposition. At the Deere & Company Center in Moline, Illinois, farm machinery and agricultural tools are on display. Of particular interest to travelers/collectors is Conner Prairie, a pioneer settlement restored to its 19th-century appearance, in Indianapolis. An extraordinary collection of Americana—from Thomas Alva Edison's phonograph to a blacksmith's shop, from blown glass to antique automobiles—can be seen at Greenfield Village, Henry Ford Museum in Dearborn, Michigan, part of metropolitan Detroit. In Holland, Michigan, where tulips bloom so profusely that you will believe you *are* in Holland, is the Baker Museum for Furniture Research. I may be prejudiced in favor of childhood thrills, but surely the Circus World Museum in Baraboo, Wisconsin, should be irresistible even to those who don't collect circus memorabilia. In Cleveland, Ohio, the Western Reserve Historical Society operates displays of Indian relics, turn-of-the-century trade shops, and the Frederick C. Crawford Auto-

Aviation Museum. Also good for collectors of Indian relics is the Piqua Historical Area at Piqua, Ohio. Finally, Toledo has in its art museum one of the finest and most complete glass collections in the world.

There are several big antique shows in the Midwest. Every month about 300 dealers convene in Ann Arbor, near Detroit; the University-Liggett Antiques Show is held annually in Gross Pointe, Michigan, also close to the city. The Lake Forest Academy-Forest Hall Antiques Show is held every year in Lake Forest, Illinois.

For listings and reviews of Midwestern auctions, flea markets and for the dates of shows, check *Ohio Antique Review, Tri-State Trader, Antique Trader, Antique Monthly, Collectors News, Spinning Wheel, The Magazine ANTIQUES* and local newspapers.

ILLINOIS

Antique Exchange Auctions
Mike Jeremiah, Bill Mortell, Auctioneers
417 East Broadway
Alton, Illinois 62002
(618) 462-4881

Office located in St. Louis area and sales held at various rented halls (check mailings); general antiques and collectibles sale held every three months, featuring oak, Victorian and Federal period furniture, clocks, lamps, and glassware; estate sales; consignments; property purchased for sales.

No buyer's premium; mail and telephone bids accepted; cashier's checks accepted, or personal checks with bank letter of credit; no credit cards. Full payment day of sale; pickups within seven days.

Sale announcements mailed; written appraisals offered for minimum fee of $200.00.

Direct Auctioneers/Galleries
Michael Modica, Auctioneer
7232 North Western Avenue
Chicago, Illinois 60645
(312) 465-3300

General antique and estate sales held weekly; specialized sales of bronzes, coins, and Oriental art; consignments; property purchased for sales.

No buyer's premium; mail and telephone bids accepted with cash deposit; checks accepted from established customers; Visa accepted. Twenty-five percent deposit necessary to hold purchase; full payment and pickups within three days.

Sale announcements mailed; oral and written appraisals offered for fee dependent on value of item.

Hanzel Galleries, Inc.

William E. Hanzel, John Hanzel, Auctioneers
1120 South Michigan Avenue
Chicago, Illinois 60605
(312) 922-6234

Specializing in the dispersal of private collections and estates, auctions held when sufficient property is accumulated; specialized sales include fine art, American, English and Continental furniture, silver, china, glass, bronzes, clocks, Oriental art and rugs, music boxes, jewelry, manuscripts, autographs and books; predominantly consignments; limited amount of property purchased for sales.

No buyer's premium; telephone bids accepted; checks from established customers, or certified checks, accepted; no credit cards. Purchases held with a 25% deposit; full payment and pickups within five days.

Sale announcements mailed; catalogs of all sales; written appraisals offered for variable fee.

Boomgarden-King Auctions

Doug and Randy Boomgarden, Auctioneers
Box 4989, Route 51 North
Davis Junction, Illinois 61020
(815) 393-4417, (815) 393-4735, (815) 393-4986
(On Route 51, nine miles south of Rockford)

General auction held every three months; specialized sales include dolls, guns, antique farm equipment; estate sales; consignments; property purchased for sales.

No buyer's premium; mail bids accepted; traveler's checks, certified checks, or personal checks with two forms of ID accepted; no credit cards. Full payment day of sale; pickups generally same day.

Sale announcements and some catalogs mailed; written insurance appraisals offered for an hourly fee of $70.00.

Pace Auctions

Gordon Pace, Auctioneer
Office: 1591 Ellinwood Street
Des Plaines, Illinois 60016
(312) 296-0773
Auctions: American Legion Hall
Golf and East River Roads,
Des Plaines, Illinois 60016

General antiques and collectibles sale held every Monday night at 7:00 p.m. at the American Legion Hall; specialized sales include Hummels, coins, windows, coin-operated machines, and are held at the Chevy Chase Country Club in nearby Wheeling; estate sales; consignments; property purchased for sales.

No buyer's premium; mail and telephone bids accepted; checks accepted; Master Charge and Visa accepted. Full payment and pickups day of sale.

Sale announcements and some catalogs mailed; oral and written appraisals offered for negotiable fee.

Dunning's Auction Service
C. P. Terry Dunning, Auctioneer
755 Church Road, PO Box 866
Elgin, Illinois 60120
(312) 741-3483
(Northwest corner of Interstate 90 and Route 31)

Approximately two general antiques, fine art, and collectibles sales held per month; estate sales; consignments; no property purchased for sales.

No buyer's premium; mail and telephone bids accepted; checks accepted with in letter of credit and proper ID; Master Charge and Visa accepted. Prefer payment in full day of sale, but will hold with 25% deposit; pickups within seven days.

Sale announcements mailed; written appraisals offered for hourly fee.

Chicago Art Galleries, Inc.
Richard Friedman, Auctioneer
1633 Chicago Avenue
Evanston, Illinois 60201
(312) 475-6960
(First suburb north of Chicago)

Holds fine art and personal property auctions eight to ten times yearly; specializing in the sale of antiques, furniture, decorative objects, Oriental art, jewelry, porcelains, bronzes, coins, stamps, Art Nouveau, Art Deco, literary property; specialized sales of rugs, oil paintings, silver; estate sales; consignments; property purchased for sales.

No buyer's premium; mail bids accepted; checks accepted, but must clear before merchandise is released; no credit cards. Purchases held with a 25% deposit; full payment and pickups within 72 hours.

Sale announcements and catalogs mailed; written appraisals offered, for estate and insurance purposes only, for minimum fee of $30.00.

Stumpf Auction Company
Ted Stumpf, Wendell Short, Auctioneers
102 South Market
Mascoutah, Illinois 62258
(618) 566-7664 or (618) 566-2899
(Most sales on site—check mailings for directions)

Twelve to 15 general auctions, including one or two antique auctions, held monthly; estate sales; consignments; no property purchased for sales.

Note: Listings are alphabetical by town.

No buyer's premium; mail and telephone bids accepted; checks accepted with proper ID; no credit cards. Payment in full day of sale; pickups as arranged.

Sale announcements mailed; written appraisals offered for negotiable fee.

Col. Chuck's Auction Gallery

Col. Chuck Housh, Auctioneer
Box 265, Manhattan-Monee Road
Monee, Illinois 60449
(312) 534-0284
(Half mile east of Interstate 57)

Antiques sale held the second Wednesday of every month at 6:30 p.m.; specialized sales include collectors plates in May and November, antique clocks in April and October, and tool auctions two or three times a year; estate sales; general consignments every Saturday at 12:30 p.m.; no property purchased for sales.

No buyer's premium; mail and telephone bids not accepted; checks accepted with driver's license and two additional forms of ID; Master Charge and Visa accepted. Purchases held with a 15% deposit; full payment and pickups within four days.

Sale announcements mailed; written appraisals offered for fee dependent on value of item.

Wapella Auction House

Marvin Haycraft & Sons, Auctioneers
Route 51
Wapella, Illinois 61777
(217) 935-6286 or (309) 473-2415

Family-run business specializing in estate sales, antiques, household goods, liquidations and real estate; general auction Wednesday nights; specialized sales on Saturdays and Sundays; larger two to three day sales feature antiques; estate sales; consignments; property purchased for sales.

No buyer's premium; mail and telephone bids accepted; checks accepted from established customers who have registered and received buyer number; no credit cards. Full payment day of sale; pickups as soon as possible.

Sale announcements and some catalogs mailed; written appraisals offered for variable fee.

Addison Friends of the Library Flea Market   A   XX

235 North Kennedy Drive
Addison, Illinois 60101
(312) 543-3617
Contact: President, Friends of the Library
(Route 83 north to Lake Route 20, west to corner of Kennedy and Lake)

Outdoor market; 75 dealers; began in 1977; held third Saturday every September, 9:00 a.m. to 4:00 p.m.; free admission; space rental: $5.00 for space 10' wide; reservations needed.

Mostly secondhand and household items, books, some crafts, no antiques, few collectibles; food; restrooms; parking; nearby motels.

Tri-State Swap-O-Rama ★ W XXXX
4350 West 129th Street
Alsip, Illinois 60658
Contact: James Pierski, 5630 North Elston Avenue, Chicago, Illinois 60646,
(312) 774-3900
(Tri-State Expressway to Cicero Exit, get off at 131st Street)

Indoor market; 200 dealers indoors, 200 to 600 outdoors; began in 1979; open
every Saturday, Sunday and Wednesday, 7:00 a.m. to 4:00 p.m., year round,
Thursday evenings in summer, 3:00 p.m. to 9:00 p.m.; 50¢ admission; space
rental: $3.00 to $10.00 for 8' x 10' area indoors, 13' x 26' outdoors; reservation
needed.
Mostly new merchandise, some secondhand items, antiques and collectibles;
three snack bars; indoor restrooms; parking; R/V; auctions twice a year;
expositions, garage sales, homemade craft days.

Antique Show & Flea Market M X
4-H Fairground Center, Route 30
Amboy, Illinois 61310
Contact: Robert Mitchell, 211 East Main, Amboy, (815) 857-2253
(Three miles outside Amboy; ninety miles west of Chicago)

Indoor/outdoor market; 42 dealers; began in 1977; held third Sunday of every
month, 9:00 a.m. to 5:00 p.m.; 50¢ admission; space rental: $20.00 inside, $10.00
outside, with table; reservations needed inside.
Mostly antiques, collectibles, secondhand merchandise, few crafts and art
objects; food; restroom; parking; nearby motels.

Skylark Swap-O-Rama W XXX
Skylark Drive-In Theater
Aurora, Illinois 60505
Contact: James L. Pierski, Swap Shop Inc., 5630 North Elston Avenue,
Chicago, Illinois 60646, (312) 774-3900
(Just west of Route 59)

Outdoor market; 160 dealers; began in 1977; open Sundays, 7:00 a.m. to 4:00
p.m., April through October; 50¢ admission; space rental: $5.00 for 13' x 26';
reservations needed.
Mostly new merchandise, a lot of secondhand and household items, some
collectibles, few antiques; food; restrooms; parking; no nearby motels.

Barrington Annual Flea Market A X
Langendorf Park
Barrington, Illinois 60010
Contact: Mrs. Alfred Munson, 803 Dundee Avenue, Barrington, Illinois
60010, (312) 381-4224
(Route 14 to Route 59)

Indoor/outdoor market; 50 dealers; began in 1967; held annually, usually in
September; 50¢ admission; space rental: $14.00 with table; reservations needed.

Mostly antiques and collectibles, very little new or secondhand merchandise; food; home baked goods; restrooms; parking; nearby motel.

Beardstown Fall & Fun Festival   A   X
City Square
Beardstown, Illinois 62618
Contact: L. Milton McClure, PO Box 170, Beardstown, Illinois, (217) 323-2211
(Forty-five miles west of Springfield, on Route 125)

Outdoor market; 15 dealers; held one weekend in September, Saturday, 10:00 a.m. to 8:00 p.m., Sunday 11:30 a.m. to 8:00 p.m.; free admission; space rental: $15.00 for 10' x 8'; reservations helpful.

Mostly crafts; some antiques, collectibles, produce; food stands; restrooms; parking; nearby motels.

Belleville Flea Market   M   XXXX
Belle Claire Exposition Center
Belleville, Illinois 62220
(618) 235-2231 or (618) 235-0660
Contact: Mary Santucci, 2114 East A Street, Box 371, Belleville, Illinois
(Routes 13 and 159, I-64 and I-70)

Indoor market; 439 dealers; began in 1974; held third weekend of every month, Saturday and Sunday, 10:00 a.m. to 5:00 p.m.; free admission; space rental: $9.00 per table; reservations needed.

Mostly coins, secondhand merchandise, antiques, collectibles, some produce and art objects; food; restrooms; parking; motels.

Reach Out Flea Fair   A   X
2334 New Street
Blue Island, Illinois 60406
(312) 389-4029
Contact: Connie Motyll
(130th Street between Western and Gregory Streets)

Outdoor market; 35 dealers; began in 1973; open third Saturday in June, 9:00 a.m. to 3:00 p.m.; free admission; space rental: $6.00 for picnic table; reservations needed.

Mostly secondhand and household items, lots of new merchandise, some antiques and collectibles; food; restrooms; parking; nearby motels.

Double Drive-In Flea Market   W   XXXX
2800 West Columbus
Chicago, Illinois 60652
(312) 925-9602
Contact: Clarence J. Brooks

Outdoor market; 700 dealers; began in 1970; open Saturday and Sunday, year round; 50¢ admission; space rental: $6.00 Saturday, $12.00 Sunday for 16' x 12'; no reservations needed.

Variety of secondhand items, new merchandise, antiques, collectibles, crafts and art; food; restrooms; parking.

Midway Swap-O-Rama ★ W XXX
6333 South Cicero Avenue
Chicago, Illinois 60638
Contact: James L. Pierski, Swap Shop Inc., 5630 North Elston Avenue, Chicago, Illinois 60646, (312) 774-3900
(Cicero Avenue to Sixty-third Street, to former Toys-R-Us Building)

Indoor market; 150 dealers; began in 1975; open Saturday and Sunday, 7:00 a.m. to 4:00 p.m., October to April; 50¢ admission; space rental: $8.00 to $10.00 for 8' x 10'; reservations recommended.

Mostly new merchandise, some secondhand and household items, few collectibles, no antiques; snack bars; restrooms; parking; no nearby motels; annual Christmas auction.

Roaring Drunk Antique and Collectible Show M X
Butterfield Road at Spring Road
Elmhurst, Illinois 60126
(312) 834-5400
Contact: Peter and Emily Larson, 35537 Elizabeth Street, Warrenville, Illinois 60555, (312) 393-1796
(On Butterfield Road, Route 56)

Indoor/outdoor market; 35 inside dealers, outside number varies; began in 1970; open second Sunday of each month, 9:00 a.m. to 4:00 p.m., year round; admission $1.00; space rental: $20.00 to $25.00 indoors, $12.00 outdoors; reservations needed for inside.

Only antiques and collectibles; food; restrooms; parking; nearby motels.

Glen Bard South Booster Flea Market A XXX
Glen Bard High School and Butterfield Park Boulevard
Glenn Ellyn, Illinois 60137
(312) 858-5186
Contact: Laura Borsodi, 23 West 226 McCrely, Glenn Ellyn, Illinois 60137
(East West Tollway going west off Route 53 to Route 56 North, then west to Park Boulevard)

Indoor market; 120 dealers; began in 1971; open one weekend in March, on Saturday, 9:00 a.m. to 5:00 p.m., and Sunday 1:00 p.m. to 5:00 p.m.; 75¢ admission; inquire about space rental.

Variety of secondhand merchandise, antiques, collectibles, crafts, art objects; food; restrooms; parking; motels.

Grayslake Swap-O-Rama W XX
Routes 120 and 83
Grayslake, Illinois 60030
Contact: Swap Shop Inc., 5630 North Elston Avenue, Chicago, Illinois 60646, (312) 774-3900
(Just north of Chicago)

Outdoor market; 100 dealers; began in 1972; open Sundays and holidays, April to November; 50¢ admission; space rental: $5.00 for 8' x 19'; no reservations needed.

Mostly new merchandise and secondhand and household items, some antiques and collectibles; food; restrooms; parking; no nearby motels.

Helvetia Flea Market   M XX
Lindendale Park
Highland, Illinois 62249
(618) 654-6656
Contact: D.R. Seifried, Sr., 18 Valentine Lane, Highland, Illinois 62249, (618) 654-2581
(Thirty miles east of St. Louis, Missouri, three miles off I-70)

Indoor market; 100 dealers; began in 1968; open second Sunday of each month, 9:00 a.m. to 4:00 p.m.; free admission; space rental: $7.00 per 8' table; reservations needed.

Mostly antiques and collectibles, some secondhand and household items, some new merchandise; food; restrooms; parking; nearby motels.

Montana Charlie's Little America   W XXXX
I-55 and Joliet Road
LeMont, Illinois 60439
(312) 448-4739
Contact: Margaret Bowman, 10301 West 125th Street, Palos Park, Illinois 60464, (312) 448-4739
(Exit 269 off I-55)

Outdoor market; 200 to 300 dealers; began in 1970; open Saturday, Sunday and holidays, dawn to dusk, April through November; admission $1.00 per car; space rental: $5.00 Saturday, $10.00 Sunday for 16' x car length paved space; no reservations needed.

Variety of collectibles, secondhand items and antiques; hot dog stand; outdoor restrooms; overnight parking; nearby motels.

Northlake Swap-O-Rama   W XXX
401 Lake Street
Northlake, Illinois 60164
Contact: James Pierski, 5630 North Elston Avenue, Chicago, Illinois 60646, (312) 774-3900
(Lake Street or North Avenue to the Northlake Hotel, one mile west of Manheim Road)

Outdoor market; 125 sellers; began in 1979; open Sundays, 7:00 a.m. to 4:00 p.m., April through October; 50¢ admission; space rental: $7.00 for 13' x 26' area; no reservations needed.

Mostly new merchandise, some secondhand, few antiques and collectibles; snack bar; restrooms; parking; nearby motels.

"53" Swap-O-Rama   W   XX
Rand and Hicks Road (Routes 12 and 53)
Palatine, Illinois 60067
Contact: Swap Shop Inc., 5630 North Elston Avenue, Chicago, Illinois 60646, (312) 774-3900
Outdoor market; 100 dealers; began in 1976; open Sundays, 7:00 a.m. to 4:00 p.m., April through October; 35¢ admission, space rental: $5.00 for 19' x 10' plus car; no reservations needed.

Mostly new merchandise, lots of secondhand and household items, some antiques and collectibles; food; restrooms; no nearby motels.

Central States Threshermen's Reunion Flea Market   A   XXX
4-H Park Fairground on 4-H Road
Pontiac, Illinois 61764
Contact: Robert Snow, 703 South Main Street, Pontiac, Illinois 61764, (815) 844-5294
(Exit 23 North)

Indoor/outdoor market; 150 dealers; began in 1975; held annually for five days ending Labor Day; $2.00 admission; space rental: $5.00 for 8'; no reservations needed.

Mostly antiques and collectibles, some crafts and secondhand merchandise; food; restrooms; parking; nearby motels.

Princeton Antique Flea Market   M   XX
Princeton Fairgrounds
Princeton, Illinois 61356
(815) 872-1601
Contact: Toni Martin, Route 44, Princeton, Illinois 61356

Indoor market; 60 dealers; began in 1965; open second Sunday of every month; 50¢ admission; space rental: $10.00 for 9½'x 11'; reservations needed.

Mostly antiques and collectibles, very little new and secondhand merchandise; food; restrooms; ample parking; nearby motels.

Greater Rockford Antiques and Flea Market   W   XXX
Highway 51 and Sandy Hollow Road
Rockford, Illinois 61109
(815) 397-6683
Contact: Jerry and Carol Shorkey, 6350 Canyon Wood, Rockford, Illinois 61109, (815) 397-6687
(Tollway 90 to Bypass 20, Highway 51, Eleventh Street North Exit)

Indoor/outdoor market; 170 dealers; began in 1976; open every Saturday and Sunday, 8:00 a.m. to 5:00 p.m., year round; free admission; space rental: $18.00 per weekend inside, $14.00 outside; reservations needed inside.

Variety of collectibles, antiques, new merchandise and household items, also arts and crafts; food; restrooms; parking; six motels within one block.

Note: Listings are alphabetical by town.

Kane County Fairgrounds Flea Market   M   XXXX
Randall Road
St. Charles, Illinois 60174
(312) 377-9859
Contact: Mrs. J.L. Robinson, 307 Sandholm Street, Geneva, Illinois 60134,
(312) 232-6264
(Go through St. Charles on Route 64)

Indoor/outdoor market; 250 to 400 dealers; began in 1966; held first Sunday of
each month; 7:00 a.m. to 4:00 p.m., year round; $1.00 admission; space rental:
$25.00 outside, $30.00 to $35.00 inside for 14' x 14'; reservations recommended.
    Antiques, collectibles and secondhand merchandise; food; restrooms; park-
ing; nearby motels.

Springfield Drive-In Flea Market   W   XXX
3135 Singer Avenue
Springfield, Illinois 62703
(217) 528-4111
Contact: Richard Goyne
(Bypass 66 and Cook Street)

Outdoor market; 150 to 200 dealers; began in 1976; open every Sunday 9:00 a.m.
to 3:00 p.m., April to November; admission 50¢ per person, $1.00 per carload;
space rental: same as admission price for unlimited space; no reservations
needed.
    Variety of secondhand and household items, antiques and collectibles, new
merchandise, some crafts and produce; food; restrooms; parking; nearby motels.

Towanda July 4th Flea Market   A   XX
Towanda Park
Towanda, Illinois 61776
Contact: Lyle and Mary Merritt, Box 97, Towanda, Illinois 61776, (309)
728-2810
(Exit 171 off I-55, northeast of Normal, Illinois)

Outdoors amid parades, flower shows and fireworks; 100 dealers; annual Fourth
of July; free admission; space rental: $8.00 for 12' x 10'; no reservations
accepted—first come, first served.
    Mostly antiques and collectibles, some secondhand and household items, arts
and crafts; food; restrooms; parking; nearby motels.

Waukegan Flea Market   W   XXX
1700 North Lewis Avenue
Waukegan, Illinois 60085
(312) 662-9665
Contact: Sophie Zelnia, 6954 North Sheridan Road, Chicago, Illinois 60626,
(312) 465-2615
(I-94 West to Belvidere Exit, East to Lewis Avenue)

Indoor market; 100 to 200 dealers; began in 1978; open every Friday, Saturday and Sunday, year round; 25¢ admission; space rental: $18.00 per weekend for 9' x 18'; no reservations needed.

Mostly new merchandise and secondhand and household items; some antiques and collectibles; food; restrooms; parking; nearby motels.

Twin Flea Market   W   XXXX
1010 South Milwaukee Avenue
Wheeling, Illinois 60090
(312) 537-8223
Contact: William Carey, 1713 Myrtle Drive, Mount Prospect, Illinois 60056, (312) 439-6142
Outdoor market; 150 to 500 dealers; began in 1973; open Saturday and Sunday, April through October; admission 25¢ Saturday, 50¢ Sunday; space rental: $4.00 Saturday, $10.00 Sunday, for 17'; no reservations needed.

Mostly new merchandise and secondhand and household items, few antiques or collectibles; food; restrooms; parking; nearby motels.

INDIANA

Kruse International
Dean V. Kruse, Auctioneer
Kruse Building
Auburn, Indiana 46706
(219) 925-4004 or (800) 328-5633
(Auburn Exit, Interstate 69)

Specializing in collector car sales; auctions held every two weeks; estate sales; consignments; no property purchased for sales.

No buyer's premium; mail bids accepted; telephone bids from established customers accepted; purchase of catalog required to enter most sales; checks accepted with bank letter of credit; establish credit by calling toll free number; Visa and Master Charge accepted. Full payment same day or by agreement; pickups within five days.

Sale announcements and catalogs mailed; written appraisals offered for minimum fee of $25.00.

Doug Davies
Doug Davies, Auctioneer
Office: R 2, Springboro Road
Brookston, Indiana 47923
(317) 563-3600
Auctions: Delphi Armory
Highway 18
Delphi, Indiana 46923
(One hundred miles north of Indianapolis)

Sales at the Armory approximately every one to two months; featuring 18th and 19th century country furniture, accessories and Americana; estate sales; consignments; property purchased for sales.

No buyer's premium; mail and telephone bids accepted; certified checks, traveler's checks, or personal checks—with two forms of proper ID—accepted; no credit cards; full payment day of sale; pickups generally same day.

Sale announcements mailed; oral and written appraisals offered for an hourly fee of $15.00.

Verlon Webb Auctions
Verlon Webb and Tony Theders, Auctioneers
311 North Spruce Street
Centerville, Indiana 47330
(317) 855-5542
(Two blocks from Route 40)

General auctions, featuring predominantly Victorian antiques, held once a month; specialized sales include cut glass, Hummels, art glass, dolls, coins, oak furniture, early furniture and accessories; estate sales; consignments; property not purchased for sales.

No buyer's premium; mail and telephone bids accepted; checks accepted; checks over $500.00 require letter of reference from bank; no credit cards; 10% deposit necessary to hold purchase; full payment and pickups within 10 days.

Sale announcements mailed; some catalogs available; written appraisals offered for a fee dependent on value of item.

Canaan Fall Festival Antique Flea Market   A XX
Route 1
Canaan, Indiana 47224
(812) 839-4770
Contact: Gary Handlon
(Twelve miles northeast of Madison, on State Route 62)

Outdoor market; 100 dealers; began in 1964; open second weekend in September, Friday, 5:00 p.m. to 10:00 p.m., Saturday, 9:00 a.m. to 10:00 p.m., Sunday, noon to 6:00 p.m.; free admission; space rental: $6.00 per day, $10.00 per weekend for 15' x 20'; reservations recommended.

Mostly antiques and secondhand merchandise, some collectibles, art, crafts and produce; food; restrooms; parking; nearby motels.

Barn and Field Flea   D XXXX
9600 West 151st Parrish
Cedar Lake, Indiana 46303
(219) 696-7368
Contact: D. Corey, PO Box 411, Cedar Lake, Indiana, 46303
(Route 41 to Cedar Lake stop light, east to Parrish Avenue, then two miles south)

Country market with rustic atmosphere; 450 dealers; began in 1968; open every Thursday through Sunday, year round; free admission; space rental: $1.00 Thursday, Friday, and Saturday, $2.00 Sunday; reservations suggested.

Mostly antiques and collectibles, little new merchandise and crafts; food concessions; restrooms with showers; parking; nearby motels; overnight facilities at market.

Uncle John's Flea Market W X
15205 Wicker Avenue
Cedar Lake, Indiana 46303
(219) 696-7070
Contact: John A. Lail, (219) 696-7946
(On Route 41, nine miles south of US Route 30)

Indoor/outdoor market; 50 permanent dealers; began in 1975; open every Saturday and Sunday, 9:00 a.m. to 5:00 p.m., year round; free admission; space rental: $40.00 per month, 12' x 16' indoors; no reservations needed.

Mostly secondhand and household items, some new merchandise, few antiques or collectibles; food; restrooms; parking.

Webb's Antique Shop and Flea Market D X
311 East Main
Centerville, Indiana 47330
(317) 855-2282
Contact: Ellis Webb
(Three miles south of I-70, or five miles west of Richmond on US 40)

Indoor/outdoor market; 15 dealers; began in 1978; open seven days a week, 9:00 a.m. to 6:00 p.m., year round; free admission; space rental: $15.00 per week for 12' x 12'; reservations needed.

Lots of antiques and collectibles, some secondhand items; no food available; restrooms; parking; nearby motels and campgrounds.

Friendship Flea Market A XXXX
Highway 62
Friendship, Indiana 47021
(812) 667-5645
Contact: Tom Kerr, 464 Madison Pike, Covington, Kentucky 41017, (606) 341-1400
(275 West to Lawrenceboro Exit, 50 West to Dillsboro, then six miles west on 62)

Indoor/outdoor market; 500 dealers; began in 1968; open two weekends per year, usually May and August; free admission; space rental: $10.00 for 10' x 10' inside, 20' x 30' outside; reservations needed.

Only antiques and collectibles; food; restrooms; parking; nearby motels; live music.

Putnam County Flea Market A X
National Guard Armory
Green Castle, Indiana 46135
(317) 653-4897, or (317) 653-8220
Contact: William Calhoun, Route 4, Green Castle, Indiana 46135. (Take Highway 231 or 43 North)

Indoor market; 30 dealers; began in 1976; held twice a year in spring and fall on a Saturday, 8:30 a.m. to 5:00 p.m.; free admission; space rental: $10.00 to $15.00 for 10' x 10'; reservations needed.

Variety of used merchandise, antiques, collectibles, crafts, art objects, and produce; food; restrooms; parking; nearby motels.

"41" Swap-O-Rama   W   XXX
"41" Drive-In Theatre
2500 South Calumet Avenue
Hammond, Indiana 46320
(312) 774-3900
Contact: Swap Shop Inc., 5630 North Elston, Chicago, Illinois 60646, (312) 774-3900

Outdoor market; 150 dealers; began in 1975; open Sundays and holidays, 7:00 a.m. to 4:00 p.m., April through mid-November; 50¢ admission; space rental: $5.00 for 6' x 15' plus car; no reservations needed.

Mostly new and secondhand merchandise, very few antiques or collectibles; food; restrooms; parking; no nearby motels.

The Community Expo Center   ★   W   XXXX
8341 Indianapolis Boulevard
Highland, Indiana 46322
(219) 838-3500
Contact: Ira Saunders
(One mile south of I-80 and 94 on US 41)

Indoor market; 400 dealers; began in 1980; open Saturday and Sunday, 8:00 a.m. to 5:00 p.m., year round; 50¢ admission; space rental: $10.00 daily for 10' x 10'; no reservations needed.

Variety of new and used merchandise, antiques, collectibles, produce, crafts, and art objects; restaurant; restrooms; parking; nearby motels; dealer's auction held Monday, 2:00 p.m.; public auction held Friday and Saturday, 6:30 p.m.

Antique Flea Market   W   XX
Indiana State Fairgrounds
Agriculture Building
Indianapolis, Indiana 46201
(317) 674-6450
Contact: L-W Promoters, PO Box 69, Gas City, Indiana

Indoor market; 80 dealers; began in 1979; held Saturday, 10:00 a.m. to 7:00 p.m., and Sunday, 10:00 a.m. to 5:00 p.m.; space rental: $60.00 for four tables, $45.00 for three tables; reservations needed.

Variety of antiques, collectibles, art objects and secondhand merchandise; snack bar; restrooms; parking; nearby motels.

Big Red Flea Market & Auction ★ W XXX

Indianapolis, Indiana
Contact: John Mason, PO Box 415, Zionville, Indiana 46077
(I-65 at Route 334, Exit 130, next to 76 Truck Stop)

Indoor/outdoor market; 180 dealers; began in 1980; held Friday, 6:00 p.m. to 9:00 p.m., Saturday, 10:00 a.m. to 10:00 p.m. and Sunday, 10:00 a.m. to 5:00 p.m.; free admission; space rental: $25.00 a week for 12' x 12'; reservations needed.

Variety of used merchandise, antiques, collectibles, crafts and art objects; food; restrooms; parking; nearby motels; antiques auction held every Saturday at 7:00 p.m.

Traylor's Antique Flea Market W XXX

7159 East Forty-sixth Street
Indianapolis, Indiana 46226
(317) 545-0339
Contact: Leo or Laura Traylor, 4512 Callahan Street, Wanamaker, Indiana 46239, (317) 862-5192
(One block east of Shadeland Avenue Exit off I-465)

Indoor/outdoor market; 53 inside, 50 outside dealers; began in 1970; open every Saturday and Sunday, 9:00 a.m. to 5:00 p.m., year round; free admission; space rental: $20.00 to $26.00 per week for 8' x 10' booth; reservations needed inside.

Only collectibles and antiques; food; restrooms; parking; nearby motels.

Kokomo Emporium W X

111 East Sycamore Street
Kokomo, Indiana 42800
Contact: Tommy Tomlinson, PO Box 1, Kokomo, Indiana, (317) 689-8585
(Fifty miles north of Indianapolis)

Indoor market; 15 to 25 dealers; began in 1979; open Saturday and Sunday, 10:00 a.m. to 6:00 p.m.; free admission; space rental: $10.00 daily for 10' x 10'; reservations needed.

Variety of new and used merchandise, antiques, collectibles, crafts, a few art objects; restrooms; parking; nearby restaurants and motels.

Halfway Flea Market W X

Corner of State Road 36 and Carlos Road
Modac, Indiana 47358
(317) 853-5029

Indoor/outdoor market; 25 dealers; began in 1971; open Sunday, 7:00 a.m. to 4:00 p.m., year round; free admission; space rental: $2.00 outside, without table; $3.00 inside, with table; reservations needed inside.

Mostly used merchandise, antiques, collectibles and produce, little new merchandise, crafts and art objects; snack bar; restrooms; parking; nearby motels.

Note: Listings are alphabetical by town.

Bill DeWert Antique and Collectibles Show　　　M　XX
38th Street Indiana State Fairground
Route 3
Monroeville, Indiana 46773
(467) 623-3511
Contact: Bill DeWert

Indoor market; 100 dealers; began in 1977; held on one weekend a month, 12:00 p.m. to 9:00 p.m. Friday, 10:00 a.m. to 7:00 p.m. on Saturday and Sunday; 50¢ admission; space rental: $30.00 for 10' x 13' booth space with tables; reservations needed.

All antiques, collectibles and art objects; food; restrooms; parking; nearby motels.

White County Old Settler's Day Flea Market　　　A　X
Broadway and Railroad Streets
Monticello, Indiana 47960
(219) 583-8554
Contact: Jody Headdy, RR 3, Box 609, Monticello, Indiana 47960

Outdoor market; 20 to 25 dealers; began in 1972; held on "Old Settler's Day," usually fourth Saturday in August, 9:00 a.m. to 5:00 p.m.; free admission; space rental: $5.00 for two parking places; reservations needed.

Mostly antiques, collectibles and crafts, some secondhand and new merchandise; local restaurants and snack bar; restrooms; parking; nearby motels and campgrounds.

Thieves Market　　　W　X
2309 East Edison
South Bend, Indiana 46615
(219) 233-9820
Contact: Francis Harris
(Off Ironwood Drive)

Indoor/outdoor market; 40 dealers; began in 1968; open Saturday and Sunday, 10:00 a.m. to 6:00 p.m., year round except Christmas and Easter; free admission; space rental: $4.00 for 12' x 25' outside; no reservations needed.

Mostly antiques and collectibles, contemporary arts and crafts; snack bar; restrooms; parking; nearby motels.

Vigo County Historical Antique Flea Market　　　A　X
Historical Museum of the Wabash Valley
1411 South Sixth Street
Terre Haute, Indiana 47802
(812) 235-9717
Contact: Dorothy W. Jerse
(Three blocks east of US Highway 41, take Washington Street to South Sixth)

Outdoor market; 39 dealers; began in 1969; held annually, usually in June, 9:00 a.m. to 5:00 p.m.; free admission; space rental: $10.00; reservations needed.

Mostly antiques and collectibles, some crafts, herbs and plants; food; parking; restrooms; nearby motels.

Vigo County Historical Society Antique Flea Market   A X
Markle House
4900 Mill Dam Road
Terre Haute, Indiana 47805
Contact: Dorothy Jerse, Vigo County Historical Society, 1411 South Sixth Street, Terre Haute, Indiana 47802, (812) 235-9717
(Northeast on Lafayette Avenue from US 41 to Park Avenue, east to Otter Creek)

Outdoor market; 20 to 25 dealers; began in 1976; held annually on a Sunday in September; free admission; space rental: $10.00; reservations recommended.

Mostly antiques and collectibles, some crafts, herbs and plants; food; restrooms; parking; nearby motels.

Big Red Flea Market   ★ W XXX
11777 Lafayette Road, PO Box 415
Zionsville, Indiana 46077
(317) 769-3266
Contact: John C. Mason, 11777 Lafayette Road, RR 1, Whitestown, Indiana 46075
(North of Indianapolis on I-65, Zionsville Exit 130)

Indoor/outdoor market; 40 to 125 dealers; began in 1980; open every Friday, Saturday and Sunday, year round; except Christmas; free admission; space rental: inside 12' x 12' for three-day weekend is $25.00, outside 20' x 30'; no reservations needed.

Variety of new merchandise, antiques, collectibles, secondhand and household items, crafts; snack bar; restrooms; parking; nearby motels; auctions every Saturday night at 7:00 p.m.

IOWA

Thurn Auction Service
L. J. Thurn, Brian Thurn, Auctioneers
920 36 Street SE
Cedar Rapids, Iowa 52403
(319) 362-4168
(Most sales held at Holiday Inn, Junction of 218 and Interstate 80, Iowa City, Iowa)

Antiques and collectibles sale generally held on the first and third Sundays of every month at the Holiday Inn; estate sales; consignments only; no property purchased for sales.

No buyer's premium; mail and telephone bids not accepted; checks with proper ID accepted; no credit cards. Full payment and pickups same day.

Richard's Auction Gallery
Richard Ness, Auctioneer
527 East Locust Street
Des Moines, Iowa 50309
(515) 282-8293 or (515) 266-1043
(Off Interstate 80, East Sixth Street Exit, four blocks south of 235 Freeway)

Monthly, and larger quarterly, sales of antiques and collectibles held on Saturdays and Sundays; specialized sales of dolls, art glass, toys, furniture, and clocks; estate sales; consignments; property purchased for sales.

No buyer's premium; mail and telephone bids accepted if accompanied by 50% payment in cashier's check; checks with letter of credit and proper ID accepted; no credit cards. Purchases held with a 50% deposit; full payment in 10 days; pickups within 30 days.

Sale announcements and catalogs available; oral and written appraisals offered for fee of 20% of items valued under $1,000.00, 10% of items valued over $1,000.00.

Ken Gooch Sales & Auction Service
Perry Cook, Auctioneer
Dexter, Iowa 50070
(515) 789-4406
(Exit 100 on Interstate 80)

Approximately two sales (at gallery and other sites) held per month, featuring antiques and collectibles, as well as farm and household merchandise; specialized sales of coins, clocks and watches, furniture, glassware, dolls and toys; estate sales; consignments; property purchased for sales; retail store on premises.

No buyer's premium; mail and telephone bids accepted with certified check; checks accepted with bank letter of credit; no credit cards. Generally, full payment day of sale; pickups same day unless otherwise arranged.

Sale announcements mailed; oral or written appraisals offered for negotiable fee; no charge if auctioned by Ken Gooch Sales.

Renaissance
Mike Hammes, Auctioneer
Box 4
Guernsey, Iowa 50172
(319) 685-4251
(Exit 201—three miles south of Interstate 80)

Antique auctions, featuring American furniture, held once a month; estate and private collection sales; specialized sales include art glass, furniture, clocks, coins, rugs, toys; consignments; property purchased for sales.

No buyer's premium; mail and telephone bids accepted with 25% deposit; checks accepted with previously established credit through bank reference; full payment same day; pickups when convenient.

Sale announcements mailed; printed catalogs for most sales; written or oral appraisals offered for hourly fee of $25.00.

Hartford Palace Antiques
Park Bingley, Auctioneer
135 Elm
Hartford, Iowa 50118
(515) 989-0428
Gallery: Highway 5
Hartford, Iowa 50118
(Thirteen miles southeast of Des Moines, Iowa)

Specializing in Victorian antiques and collectibles; monthly sales; major annual sale in January; estate sales; consignments; property purchased for sales.

Ten percent buyer's premium on some sales; telephone bids accepted; cash preferred; checks accepted with bank letter of credit; no credit cards; full payment and pickups within one week.

Sale announcements and catalogs mailed; written appraisals offered for variable fee.

Bryant Auction Service
Richard Bryant, Auctioneer
R 3, Box 245
Keokuk, Iowa 52632
(319) 463-7727
(Highway 61-218, six miles north of Keokuk)

Antiques auction and flea market held third Sunday of each month at 12:30 p.m.; general household goods and some antiques every Thursday; specialized sales include coins, guns, dolls, glass, American period furniture; estate sales; consignments; merchandise purchased for sales.

No buyer's premium; mail and telephone bids accepted; checks accepted from established customers through bank reference; no credit cards.

Payment schedule and pickups by arrangement. Sale announcements mailed; oral or written appraisals offered for variable fee.

Gene Harris Antique Auction Center, Inc.
Gene Harris, Auctioneer
203 South Eighteenth Avenue
Marshalltown, Iowa 50158
(515) 752-0600 or (515) 752-3974

Located in a multi-building complex; weekly auctions of antiques and collectibles; monthly auctions of furniture, early furnishings, and art glass; bi-annual clock sale in April and October; annual toy auction first Saturday of July; two annual stoneware auctions; specialized sales of dolls, radios, musical instruments, custard glass, or particular collections; estate sales; consignments; some property purchased for sales.

Ten percent buyer's premium; telephone bids accepted; checks accepted with proper ID and letter of credit from bank; no credit cards. Full payment day of sale; pickups within 30 days.

Sale announcements and some catalogs mailed; oral appraisals offered for minimum fee of $35.00.

Tom's Country Market   W   X
Highways 9 and 65
Manly, Iowa 50456
(515) 454-2207
Contact: Patty Walker, Box 532, Manly, Iowa 50456, (515) 454-2997
(Halfway between Minneapolis and Des Moines)

Outdoor market; 12 dealers; began in 1970; open weekends during summer season; free admission; space rental: $7.00 for 6' x 8' for two days; no reservations needed.

Mostly collectibles, antiques and new merchandise, some crafts; food; restrooms nearby; parking; nearby motels.

Central Iowa Fair Flea Market   X
Fairgrounds
Route 2
Marshalltown, Iowa 50158
(515) 753-3671
Contact: Carole Storjohann, Route 5, Marshalltown, Iowa 50158, (515) 474-2452
(One mile north of Highway 30 on Governor Road to Olive Street, half block east)

Indoor/outdoor market; 45 dealers; began in 1975; open two Sundays per month in winter, one Sunday a month in summer, call ahead for dates; free admission; space rental: $5.00 for 8' x 10' table; reservations needed inside.

Mostly antiques, collectibles and crafts, some secondhand items; food; restrooms; parking; nearby motels.

Collector's Fair   X
Ottumwa Coliseum
Highways 34 and 63
Ottumwa, Iowa 52501
Contact: Dolores Jones, 602 Morris Street, Ottumwa, Iowa 52501, (515) 682-0071

Indoor market; 50 dealers; began in 1970; open third weekend in January, March, May, September, and November, 9:00 a.m. to 5:00 p.m.; 50¢ admission; space rental: $12.50 for 2½' x 8' table; reservations needed.

Mostly collectibles and antiques, some new merchandise and crafts; food; restrooms; parking; nearby motels.

Town & Country Jubilee   A   X
Shenandoah, Iowa 51601
Contact: Dwaine E. Miller, Route 2, Box 16, Northboro, Iowa, (712) 534-2267
(Highway 59 and Route 2)

Outdoor market; 50 dealers; began in 1975; held annually on one Saturday in September, 8:00 a.m. to 9:00 p.m.; free admission; space rental: $10.00 for 22' x 16'; no reservations needed.

Variety of used or secondhand merchandise, glassware, antiques, collectibles, crafts and art objects; food; restrooms; parking; nearby motels.

Dubuque Flea Market   A   XX
Dubuque County Fairgrounds
Dubuque, Iowa
(319) 556-9849 (market), (319) 588-1406 (Monday through Friday)
Contact: Norma Koppen, 1887 Carter Road, Dubuque, Iowa 52001, (319) 583-7940
(Five miles west of town on Highway 20)

Indoor/outdoor market; 100 dealers; began in 1970; held on Sunday, 8:00 a.m. to 4:00 p.m., four times a year; 50¢ admission for adults; space rental: $8.00 for 8' space with table, $9.00 for wall space, $6.00 for outside space with no table; reservations needed.

Variety of secondhand merchandise, antiques, collectibles, and art objects, some crafts and produce; food; restrooms; parking; nearby motels.

KANSAS

Woody Auction & Real Estate Company
John M. Woody, Auctioneer
212 East Fourth, PO Box 618
Douglass, Kansas 67039
(316) 746-2694
(Held at different locations—check announcements)

Specializing in sale of estates and antique collections; specialized sales feature R.S. Prussia china, carnival glass, dolls, cut glass, and art glass; schedule of sales varies; no consignments; no property purchased for sales.

No buyer's premium; mail bids accepted with a 25% deposit; checks accepted with previously established credit; no credit cards. Full payment at sale; pickups at sale, or as arranged.

Sale announcements and catalogs mailed; appraisals offered occasionally.

Mid-America Auction Company
Ralph Thummel, Auctioneer
214 East Walnut
Salina, Kansas 67401
(913) 825-2900, (913) 825-8418
(Sales held at different locations in Salina—one hundred miles southwest of Topeka, capital of Kansas—check mailings)

Antiques and collectibles sale held every two months on Sunday at noon; consignments; property purchased for sales.

No buyer's premium; mail and telephone bids accepted; local checks from established customers accepted; out-of-state checks accepted with previously

Note: Listings are alphabetical by town.

established credit; no credit cards. Full payment at time of sale; pickups following day.

Sale announcements mailed.

Theurer Auction & Realty Service
2117 North "A"
Wellington, Kansas 67152
(316) 326-7315
(Thirty miles south of Wichita)

Caters to local clientele; specializes in farm machinery and real estate sales; 30% to 50% of merchandise antiques and collectibles, including furniture, glassware, and collectibles; most sales held on site within 50-mile radius; sales occasionally held at above office address; approximately three to four sales per year; consignments only; no property purchased for sales.

No buyer's premium; mail and telephone bids accepted with a deposit of 20% to 25%; checks accepted from established customers, or with bank letter of reference; no credit cards. Full payment and most pickups day of sale.

Sale announcements mailed; written appraisals offered for negotiable fee.

Lowell Dalton Auction
Cecil M. Dalton, Fred Spencer, Auctioneers
1360 South Broadway
Wichita, Kansas 67211
(316) 263-9501
2130 North Market
Wichita, Kansas 67214

Antiques and fine art featured at sale held middle of each month; retail shop at same location; sales on North Market usually twice a month; specialized sales feature bronzes, art glass, clocks, carvings, paintings; consignments; no property purchased for sales.

No buyer's premium; mail and telephone bids not accepted; checks accepted with proper ID and bank letter of credit; no credit cards. No deposit necessary to hold purchases; full payment within two weeks; pickups within 30 days.

Sale announcements mailed; oral and written appraisals offered free of charge.

Quantrill's Flea Market   W   X
811 New Hampshire Street
Lawrence, Kansas 66044
(913) 842-6616
Contact: Randolph S. Davis, PO Box 971, Lawrence, Kansas 66044, (913) 841-1325
(East Lawrence Exit off I-70, thirty miles west of Kansas City)

Indoor market; 40 dealers; began in 1971; open Saturday and Sunday, 10:00 a.m. to 5:00 p.m., year round; free admission; space rental: $13.00 and up for 100 to 500 square feet; reservations needed.

Antiques and collectibles, some crafts and art; snack bar; restrooms; parking; nearby motels.

Opolis Flea Market   W   X
Highways 171 and 57
Opolis, Kansas 66760
Contact: Norma Kukovich, Box 42, Opolis, Kansas, (316) 231-2543

Indoor/outdoor market; 10 dealers; began in 1977; open Saturday, Sunday and holidays year round; free admission; space rental: $4.00 for 6' x 8' inside, $2.00 outside; reservations needed inside.

Mostly collectibles and antiques, some secondhand merchandise; snack bar; restrooms; parking; nearby motels.

Topeka Flea Market   W   X
1935 North Topeka
Topeka, Kansas 66601
(913) 233-5207
Contact: Kenneth Byler
(Near Kansas City)

Indoor market; 50 dealers; began in 1979; open Friday and Saturday, 9:00 a.m. to 5:00 p.m.; free admission; $10.00 daily for 8' x 10½'; no reservations needed.

Variety of new and secondhand merchandise, antiques, collectibles, crafts, produce, art objects; food; restrooms; parking; nearby motels.

Village Flea Market   ★   W   XXX
2301 South Meridian
Wichita, Kansas 67213
(316) 942-8263
(At corner of Pawnee)

Indoor/outdoor market; 150 dealers; began in 1974; open Friday, Saturday and Sunday, 9:00 a.m. to 6:00 p.m., year round; free admission; space rental: 18¢ per square foot; reservations needed.

Mostly new merchandise, some antiques, collectibles and secondhand items and crafts; food; restrooms; parking; nearby motels; auctions in winter.

MICHIGAN

Stalker & Boos, Inc.
David Stalker and Frank H. Boos III, Auctioneers
280 North Woodward
Birmingham, Michigan 48011
(313) 646-4560
(Located in Great American Insurance building)

General sales of consigned antique and general merchandise—including Oriental art, silver, porcelain, period furniture—usually held four times a year; estate sales; no property purchased for sales.

Ten percent buyer's premium; mail and telephone bids accepted; checks accepted with proper ID; no credit cards. No deposit necessary to hold purchases; full payment and pickups within three days.

Sale announcements mailed; catalogs for all sales; oral appraisals offered for fee of $20.00; written appraisals for $60.00.

Dumouchelle Art Galleries Company
Lawrence and Ernest Dumouchelle, Auctioneers
409 East Jefferson Avenue
Detroit, Michigan 48226
(313) 963-6255
(Across from the Renaissance Center)

General auctions, featuring fine arts, furnishings, and collectibles, usually held on the third weekend of the month; specialized sales include Oriental rugs and furniture; some mail auctions; retail floor at same location open Monday through Saturday from 9:30 a.m. to 5:30 p.m.; estate sales; consignments; merchandise purchased for sales.

No buyer's premium; mail and telephone bids accepted; checks and major credit cards accepted. Deposits necessary to hold purchases; full payment and pickups within six days.

Sale announcements, brochure highlighting upcoming events and catalogs available; oral and written appraisals offered for hourly fee of $75.00, at $150.00 minimum.

C. B. Charles Galleries, Inc.
C. B. Charles, Auctioneer
825 Woodward Avenue
Pontiac, Michigan 48053
(313) 338-9203
(Interstate 75 north of Detroit, Square Lake Road Exit; west one mile to Woodward Avenue, north one mile)

Specializing in selling estates and private collections; general antiques sales and specialized sales—of art glass, paintings, Orientalia, rugs—held at least once a month; consignments; merchandise purchased for sales.

No buyer's premium; mail and telephone bids accepted; personal or business checks accepted with ID; American Express, Visa, Master Charge accepted. Full payment day of sale; pickups within three days.

Sale announcements mailed; catalogs for all sales; written appraisals offered for fee based on time and value.

Schmidt's Antiques, Inc.
N. Iver Schmidt, Auctioneer
5138 West Michigan Avenue (US Highway 12)
Ypsilanti, Michigan 48197
(313) 434-2660
(Three miles west of Ypsilanti)

Importing and selling antiques since 1939; monthly auctions held first Saturday of each month and the Friday evening preceding; specialized sales include Chinese art and artifacts; clocks, Wedgwood, and sales of large private collections; estate sales; no property purchased for sales.

No buyer's premium; telephone bids accepted; checks accepted with driver's license and credit card; Visa and Master Charge accepted; purchases held with 25% deposit; full payment and pickup within 30 days.

Sale announcements mailed; some catalogs; written appraisals offered for 1% of total value of item, minimum charge of $50.00.

Delfre's Flea—Farmer's Market ★ W X
South Old Highway 51
Applegate, Michigan 48401
Contact: Deloris or Fred Cummings, 3314 Old 51, Croswell, Michigan 48422, (313) 679-2380
(Six miles north of Croswell, on Old 51)

Outdoor market, 25 dealers; began in 1979; open Wednesdays and Sundays, Memorial Day through October, 10:00 a.m. on; free admission; space rental: $2.00 for large area; no reservations needed.

Variety of new and secondhand merchandise, a few collectibles, arts and crafts; lunch wagon; restrooms; parking; nearby motels and Lake Huron campground; auctions on Saturday evenings.

New Giant Flea Market ★ W XXX
5350 Davison Road
Burton-Flint, Michigan 48509
(313) 742-5371
Contact: Jerry Keely, 8175 North Seymour Road, Flushing, Michigan 48433, (313) 639-2810
(From I-75 go east of M2-1 Freeway, exit Belsay Road, north to Davison)

Indoor market; 180 dealers; began in 1980; open Friday noon to 9:00 p.m., Saturday and Sunday 9:00 a.m. to 6:00 p.m.; free admission; space rental: $33.00 for three days, 10' x 12'; no reservations needed.

Variety of antiques, collectibles, new merchandise and crafts; food; restrooms; parking; nearby motels; occasional auctions.

Caravan Antiques Market A XXXX
St. Joseph County Fairgrounds
State Route 86
Centreville, Michigan 49023
Contact: J. Jordan Humberstone, 2995 Iroquois, Detroit, Michigan 48214, (313) 571-0452

Indoor/outdoor market; 450 sellers; began in 1973; held first Sunday in June, second Sunday in July and August, 8:30 a.m. to 4:30 p.m.; $1.00 admission; space rental: $25.00 for 25' x 25' outside, $30.00 for 10' x 10' inside, tables extra; reservations needed.

Antiques and collectibles only; food; restrooms with showers; free parking; nearby motels.

Week End Flea Market   W   X
Pearl Street at Lovett Street
Charlotte, Michigan 48813
(517) 543-2230
Contact: Frank Palmer, 202 Pearl Street, Charlotte, Michigan 48813
(I-69 midway between Lansing and Battle Creek)

Indoor/outdoor market; 50 sellers; began in 1976; open every Saturday and
Sunday, 10:00 a.m. to 5:00 p.m., year round except Christmas and Easter; free
admission; space rental: $3.50 for table, $5.00 for 9' x 16' booth; no reservations
needed.
    Lots of collectibles, crafts, secondhand and new merchandise, no antiques;
food; restrooms; parking, nearby motels.

Open Air Flea Market   W   XXXX
Belair Drive-In Theater
8600 Eight Mile Road
Detroit, Michigan 48234
(313) 366-7200
Contact: Fred Pellerito, 3000 Town Center, Suite 1780, Southfield, Michigan
48075, (313) 358-1928
(East of Van Dyke Avenue, near I-94)

Outdoor market; 250 to 300 dealers; began in 1973; open Wednesday, Saturday
and Sunday, May to November; free admission; space rental: $15.00 for 15' x 18';
no reservations needed.
    Mostly secondhand, household items and produce, few antiques and collecti-
bles; food; restrooms; parking; nearby motels.

Flat Rock Historical Society   A   XX
City Park
Telegraph Road
Flat Rock, Michigan 48134
Contact: Jim Bobcean, 25877 East Huron River Drive, Flat Rock, Michigan
(313) 782-4143
(Off US 24)

Outdoor market; 75 dealers; began in 1974; held twice a year, first Sunday in
May and first Sunday in October; free admission; space rental: $15.00 for 16' x
24'; reservations needed.
    Variety of used merchandise, antiques, collectibles, crafts, art objects; food;
restrooms; parking; nearby motels.

Saugatuck Antique and Flea Market   ★   W   X
3604 Sixty-fourth Street
Hamilton, Michigan 49419
(616) 857-2726
Contact: Everett or Suzanne Slentz
(Highway 40 off I-196, just south of Holland)

Indoor/outdoor market; 50 dealers; began in 1970; open Saturday, Sunday and holidays, March through November; free admission; space rental: $4.00 for 20' frontage; no reservations needed.

Mostly collectibles and antiques, very little new merchandise; food; restrooms; parking; nearby motels; monthly auctions.

Mason Antique Flea Market   **W   X**
208 North Mason Street
Mason, Michigan 48854
(517) 676-9753
Contact: George Parish, 3329 West Miller Road, Lansing, Michigan 48910, (517) 882-2826
(US 127 between I-96 and I-94, take Mason Holt Exit to Mason Street)

Indoor market; 45 dealers; began in 1971; open every Sunday and Wednesday, 10:00 a.m. to 6:00 p.m., year round; free admission; space rental: $12.00 and up weekly for 10' x 12'; no reservations needed.

Mostly collectibles and antiques with a variety of secondhand, new merchandise, arts and crafts; food nearby; restrooms; parking; nearby motels.

Hump-T-Dump Flea Market   **D   X**
9510 Old US 31
RR
Montague, Michigan 49437
(616) 894-8559
Contact: Sharon Briggs, 9500 Old US 31, RR Montague, Michigan 49437, (616) 894-8753
(Two and one-half miles south of Rothbury, three miles north of Montague)

Indoor market; four to five dealers; began in 1979; open Tuesday through Sunday, 10:30 a.m. to 6:00 p.m.; free admission; space rental: $3.00; no reservations needed.

Mostly secondhand and household items, some new merchandise, few antiques or collectibles; food; restrooms; parking; nearby motels.

Mana Civic Center Flea Market   **W   X**
3521 Hoyt Street
Muskegon Heights, Michigan 49444
(616) 733-4064
Contact: Ralph and Leona Sharp, 3527 Hoyt, Lot 107, Muskegon Heights, Michigan 49444, (616) 739-5546
(On the corner of Seaway Drive and Hoyt Street)

Indoor/outdoor market; 30 to 40 sellers; began in 1972; open every Saturday, 6:00 a.m. to 3:00 p.m., outside June to September only, inside October through May; free admission; $4.00 for inside table; reservations needed.

Mostly secondhand and household items, some new merchandise, few antiques and collectibles; food; restrooms; parking; nearby motels.

Note: Listings are alphabetical by town.

Penn-Huron Flea Market   W XXX

17076 Huron River Drive
New Boston, Michigan 48164
(313) 753-4133
Contact: Arnold and Richard Slater, 8100 Longworth, Detroit, Michigan
48209, (313) 841-2196
(Just west of I-275)

Outdoor market; 40 to 150 dealers; began in 1963; open Saturday and Sunday,
9:00 a.m. to 5:00 p.m., year round; free admission; space rental: $5.00 for 15'; no
reservations needed.

Mostly secondhand and new merchandise, very few antiques or collectibles;
food; restrooms; parking; nearby motels.

Reits Flea Market   W XXXX

Red Arrow Highway, Route 1
Paw Paw, Michigan 49079
(616) 657-3428
Contact: Bill or Cathy Reits, Route 1, Box 222, Paw Paw, Michigan 49079,
(616) 657-3428
(Five miles west of Paw Paw on Red Arrow Highway, twelve miles west of
Kalamazoo)

Indoor/outdoor market; 300 to 500 sellers; began in 1967; open every Saturday,
Sunday and holiday, May through October; free admission; space rental: $3.50
for 21'; no reservations needed.

Mostly antiques and collectibles; some secondhand and new merchandise,
few arts, crafts or produce; restaurant and snack bar; 9 restrooms; 10 acres of
parking; nearby motels and on-site campgrounds.

Country Fair Flea Market   ★ W XXXX

2045 Dixie Highway
Pontiac, Michigan 48055
(313) 338-7880
Contact: Chuck Holland
(At end of Telegraph Road; take I-75 or Route 59)

Indoor/outdoor market; 600 to 700 dealers; began in 1976; open Friday, 4:00 p.m.
to 9:00 p.m., Saturday, and Sunday 10:00 a.m. to 6:00 p.m., year round; free
admission; inquire about space rental; reservations needed.

Mostly furniture, variety of secondhand merchandise, antiques, collectibles,
crafts, art objects; snack bar; restrooms; parking; nearby motels; annual
antiques auction held in summer.

Ward's Flea Market   W X

Route 3 Blue Star Highway
South Haven, Michigan 49090
(616) 637-2745
Contact: Byron Paul Ward
(Three and one-half miles south on US 31 from State Highway 140, thirty
miles west of Kalamazoo)

Outdoor market; 10 sellers; began in 1975; open Saturdays and Sundays from end of May to Labor Day; free admission; space rental: $2.00 for 10' x 15'; no reservations needed.

Mostly secondhand and household merchandise, some new merchandise and crafts, no antiques or collectibles; food stands; restrooms; parking; nearby motels.

Trufant Livestock Sale and Flea Market ★ W XXXX
303 North "C" Street
Trufant, Michigan 49347
(616) 984-2168
Contact: Maurice Petersen, 13670 22 Mile Road, Trufant, Michigan 49347,
(616) 984-2160
(About thirty-five miles north and east of Grand Rapids)

Outdoor market; 250 to 300 dealers; began in 1960; open Thursdays, May through October; free admission; space rental: $3.00 for 15' frontage; no reservations needed.

Lots of antiques, collectibles and secondhand items, some new merchandise and produce; food; restrooms; parking; motel within 15 miles; used merchandise auction every Thursday at noon.

Wayne Farmer's and Flea Market W XX
38000 Michigan Avenue
Wayne, Michigan 48184
(313) 336-7540
Contact: Robert Skolnik, 37630 Michigan Avenue, Wayne, Michigan 48184,
(313) 729-4506
(US 12 Exit—Michigan Avenue—off I-275)

Indoor market; 45 to 70 dealers; began in 1974; open Saturday and Sunday, 8:00 a.m. to 5:00 p.m., May to October; free admission; space rental: $7.00 to $10.00 per day; reservations recommended.

Mostly secondhand and household items, some collectibles, antiques and new merchandise; food concession; restrooms; parking; nearby motels.

Giant Flea Market W XXX
214 East Michigan
Ypsilanti, Michigan 48197
(313) 971-7676 or (313) 487-5890
Contact: Carol Hanna
(I-94 to Huron Street Exit, north to Michigan Avenue, right three blocks to downtown Ypsilanti)

Indoor market year round, outdoor dealers in summer; 200 dealers; began in 1976; open Fridays 6:00 p.m. to 10:00 p.m., Saturday and Sundays 10:00 a.m. to 6:00 p.m., year round; free admission; space rental: $18.00 per weekend for 5' x 10' area; reservations helpful.

Variety of antiques, collectibles, secondhand and new merchandise, crafts, plus a consignment area; food stand; restrooms; parking; nearby motels.

MINNESOTA

Central Auction Co.

Charles W. Weinberger, Auctioneer
4020 Central Avenue
Minneapolis, Minnesota 55421
(612) 781-0300

Sales held each week on Mondays and Thursdays at 7:00 p.m.; include surplus, salvage and general merchandise; roughly 25% antiques and collectibles (1820-1930), such as clocks, dishes, and oak, walnut, mahogany furniture; estate sales; mostly consignments; some property purchased for sales.

No buyer's premium; mail and telephone bids not accepted; checks accepted with proper ID; no credit cards. Full payment night of sale; pickups within two days.

Sale announcements mailed.

Rose Galleries, Inc.

Gerald H. Kaufhold, Auctioneer
1123 West County Road "B"
Roseville, Minnesota 55113
(612) 484-1415
(Midway from downtown St. Paul and Minneapolis)

General antique auctions held Wednesdays at 7:00 p.m.; inspection day of auction from 11:00 a.m. to 7:00 p.m.; items include fine art, furniture and furnishings, art glass, china, pottery, metals, Orientalia, early weapons, watches, clocks, books; specialized sales of similar merchandise every other Monday at 6:00 p.m.; inspection on Sunday at 2:00 to 8:00 p.m. and Monday 11:00 a.m. to 6:00 p.m.; estate sales; consignments; property purchased for sales.

Five percent buyer's premium; telephone bids accepted; checks generally held until day after auction, or accepted with good references; Visa and Master Charge accepted. Full payment day of sale; pickups within one week.

Catalogs for all sales available during inspection period; written appraisals offered for fee of $50.00 per half hour.

Alexandria Flea Market   W X

Douglas County Fairgrounds
Alexandria, Minnesota 56308
(612) 763-6355
Contact: Ray Lund, PO Box 266, Alexandria, Minnesota 56308, (612) 763-6355
(North off I-94, through city to north gate of Fairgrounds)

Outdoor market with shade trees; 25 dealers; began in 1975; open Saturday, Sunday and holidays, 9:00 a.m. to 5:00 p.m., last weekend in May through Labor Day; free admission; space rental: $6.00 for up to 30' of grass; no reservations needed.

Lots of antiques and collectibles, some secondhand merchandise and produce; local restaurants; restrooms; parking; nearby motels.

Rainbow Bait Flea Market   W X
Box 302
Highway 78N
Battle Lake, Minnesota 56515
(218) 864-5569
Contact: Lori Edlund, Box 447, Battle Lake, Minnesota 56515, (218) 864-5513

Outdoor market; 20 to 40 dealers; began in 1965; open Saturday and Sunday, May to September; free admission; space rental: $5.00 per day for 16'; reservations taken.

Mostly collectibles and antiques, very little secondhand merchandise or crafts; food; restrooms; parking; nearby motels.

Annual Swap Meet and Flea Market   A XXXX
South St. Louis County Fairgrounds
Boundary Avenue
Duluth, Minnesota 55810
Contact: Shirley Van Dell, Studebaker Drivers Club, PO Box 1004, Duluth, Minnesota 55810, (218) 624-5932
(Take Boundary Avenue Exit off I-35, north to the end, about one and one-half miles)

Indoor/outdoor market; 275 to 300 dealers; began in 1971; held second Saturday and Sunday in August; $1.00 admission; space rental: $5.00 for 8' x 10' indoors, 10' x 20' outdoors; reservations preferred.

Variety of collectibles and antiques, new and used merchandise, arts and crafts, antique automobile parts; food; restrooms; parking; nearby motels; antique car show on Sundays.

Farmers Market   W XX
312 Lakeside Avenue
Minneapolis, Minnesota 55405
(612) 333-1718
Contact: Alvin Bren, 12535 Beach Circle, Eden Prairie, Minnesota 55344, (612) 941-2156
(Lyndale to Highway 55, turn right on Border Avenue and go two blocks)

Indoor/outdoor market; 60 dealers; began in 1970; open Saturdays, 5:30 a.m. to 1:00 p.m.; free admission; space rental: $6.00 for 10' plus car space; no reservations needed.

Mostly produce and new merchandise, some antiques and collectibles; food; restrooms; parking; nearby motels.

Orchard Fun Market   ★ W XXX
Route 1, Box 250
Monticello, Minnesota 55362
(612) 295-2121
Contact: Joseph Osowski
(Three miles west of stop light in Monticello, quarter mile on Orchard Road)

Indoor/outdoor market in apple orchard; 120 dealers; began in 1972; open Saturday and Sunday, April to November; free admission; space rental: $5.00 to $6.00 for 10' x 11' with 4' x 8' table; no reservations needed.

Variety of secondhand and new merchandise, antiques, collectibles, crafts and produce; restaurant, snack bar and beer garden; restrooms; unlimited parking; Friday auction in June and October.

Wadena Flea Market   W   XX
Highway 71 North
Wadena, Minnesota 56482
(218) 631-3320
Contact: Pamida Discount Center, Highway 71 North, Wadena, Minnesota 56482
(Three-quarters of a mile north of intersection of Highway 71 and US 10)

Outdoor market; 50 to 75 dealers; began in 1971; open Sundays, 7:00 a.m. to 4:00 p.m.; free admission; space rental: free; no reservations needed.

Mostly secondhand and household items, some produce, very few antiques; no food; no restrooms; parking; nearby motels.

MISSOURI

Robert Merry Auction Company
Robert Merry, Auctioneer
5501 Milburn Road
Hehlville, Missouri 63129
(314) 487-3992

Specializing in antique and estate sales; sales held on site or in rental halls, on occasional weekends during the year; specialized sales of R.S. Prussia china, cut glass, carnival glass; no consignments; property purchased for sales.

No buyer's premium; mail and telephone bids accepted with a 25% deposit; cash preferred; cashier's or traveler's checks accepted; no personal checks or credit cards. Full payment and pickups at time of sale.

Sale announcements mailed; some brochures.

Sleeper Bros Auction Service
Bob Sleeper, Auctioneer
920 Elm
Higginsville, Missouri 64037
(816) 584-7019

Handling farm, real estate, household liquidations, as well as antiques; sales held at no fixed schedule; sales held on site or various locations—check mailings for directions; specialized sales of coins, glassware, general antiques; estate sales; consignments only; no property purchased for sales.

No buyer's premium; mail and telephone bids accepted; certified checks accepted or checks with proper ID; no credit cards. Purchases held with a 25% deposit; full payment and pickups as arranged.

Sale announcements and flyers mailed; oral or written appraisals offered for fee of 3% of value of item; no fee if property auctioned by Sleeper.

Pavillion Galleries
Richard McCarty, Auctioneer
Route 2, Box 147K
Joplin, Missouri 64801
(417) 781-1661

Antiques sale held last Friday of every month; featuring period furniture, oil paintings, art glass, Oriental rugs; estate sales; consignments only; no property purchased for sales.

No buyer's premium; mail and telephone bids not accepted; checks accepted with bank letter of credit; no credit cards. Full payment time of sale; pickups within two weeks.

Sale announcements mailed; catalogs for all sales; oral or written appraisals offered for negotiable fee.

Johnston Auction
James Lee Johnston, Auctioneer
Highway 24
Madison, Missouri 65263
(816) 291-5921
(At the stop light)

General auction every second and fourth Thursday at 6:00 p.m.; antiques sale on major holidays—New Year's Day, Memorial Day, July Fourth and Labor Day—at 1:00 p.m.; estate sales; consignments; merchandise also purchased for sales.

No buyer's premium; mail bids accepted; checks from established customers accepted; no credit cards. Deposits necessary to hold purchases; pickups within two days.

Sale announcements mailed; oral and written appraisals available for fee dependent on item.

Hogeye Antiques
Phillipsburg Schoolhouse
Phillipsburg, Missouri 65722
(417) 589-8493
(Exit 118, off Interstate 44)

Sales generally held at the beginning of each month, featuring Victorian and oak furniture; specialized sales of R.S. Prussia china; no consignments; all property purchased outright for sales.

No buyer's premium; mail and telephone bids accepted; checks accepted with proper ID; Master Charge accepted; full payment day of sale; pickups within 30 days.

Sale announcements mailed.

Note: Listings are alphabetical by town.

The Auction Barn
Bud Jones, Preston Hensley, Auctioneers
3418 West Division
Springfield, Missouri 65804
(417) 831-2734
(One mile off Interstate 44)

Antiques sale held first Sunday of every month at 1:00 p.m., featuring American oak and walnut Victorian furniture; general sales of both modern furniture and antiques held every Monday at 7:00 p.m.; specialized sales include art glass and cut glass, Hummels, watches; estate sales; consignments; property purchased for sales.

No buyer's premium; mail and telephone bids accepted; checks accepted with proper ID and bank letter of credit; no credit cards. Full payment day of sale; pickups within 30 days.

Sale announcements and brochures mailed; appraisals offered for an hourly fee of $50.00.

Joplin Flea Market   W   XXX
1200 Block Virginia Avenue
Joplin, Missouri 64801
(417) 623-3743
Contact: LaVerne Miller or Ed Frazier, (417) 623-6328
(Take Main Street Exit off I-44 and go north)

Indoor/outdoor market; 120 to 170 dealers; began in 1977; open Saturday and Sunday, 8:00 a.m. to 5:00 p.m., year round; free admission; space rental: $7.00 per day for 9' x 20', $12.00 a weekend; reservations needed in the winter.

Variety of antiques, collectibles and new merchandise, some crafts and secondhand merchandise; food concession; restrooms; parking; nearby motels.

Heart Bazaar   ★   D   XX
6401 East 40 Highway
Kansas City, Missouri 64129
(816) 924-7885
Contact: Michael Maturo
(I-70 east to Manchester or west to Thirty-first Exit)

Indoor market; 64 booths; began in 1980; open weekdays 1:00 p.m. to 10:00 p.m., weekends, 9:00 a.m. to 6:00 p.m.; free admission; space rental: $35.00 per week for 8' x 12'; no reservations needed.

Mostly antiques and collectibles, some new merchandise; restaurant and bar; restrooms; parking; nearby motels; auction every Tuesday at 7:00 p.m.

Nate's 63rd Street Swap Shop   W   XXXX
63rd Street near I-435
Kansas City, Missouri 64133
(816) 353-1627
Contact: Nate Shurin, PO Box 5374, Kansas City, Missouri 64131, (816) 523-0965
(Call for directions)

Outdoor market; 400 to 500 dealers; open Saturday and Sunday, 7:00 a.m. to 4:00 p.m., year round; 50¢ admission; space rental: $2.50 to $8.00; no reservations needed.

Variety of merchandise including new and secondhand items, antiques, collectibles, crafts and produce; food; restrooms; parking; tram for market patrons; nearby motels.

Old Westport Flea Market—Things Unlimited   W   X

817 Westport Road
Kansas City, Missouri 64111
(816) 753-9789
Contact: Mel Kleb II, Plaza Properties, 5028 Main, Kansas City, Missouri 64112, (816) 561-3331
(Center of town, one block east of South-West Trafficway)

Indoor market; 40 dealers; began in 1968; open every Saturday and Sunday, 10:00 a.m. to 5:00 p.m., year round; free admission; space rental: $15.00 to $40.00 for 8' x 10'; no reservations needed.

Mostly antiques and collectibles, some new merchandise; food; restrooms; parking; nearby motels.

The Country Corner Flea Market   D   XX

585 North Jefferson Street
Lebanon, Missouri 65536
(417) 588-1430
Contact: Byron Eastburn, PO Box 1140, Lebanon, Missouri 65536
(One and one-half miles north of I-44 on State Highway 5/Jefferson)

Indoor/outdoor market; 55 dealers; began in 1974; open daily 9:00 a.m. to 5:00 p.m., year round except Thanksgiving, Christmas and New Year's Day, Sunday, 1:00 p.m. to 5:00 p.m.; free admission; space rental: $6.00 per week and up for about 9' x 10' inside, $3.00 daily outside; reservations needed.

Mostly antiques and collectibles, some new merchandise; food nearby; restrooms; parking; nearby motels.

Hogeye Antique Mall and Hog Hollow Craft Center   ★ D X

Phillipsburg, Missouri 65722
(417) 589-2088
Contact: Bob or Reta Taylor, 551 South Washington, Lebanon
(Exit 118 off I-44)

Indoor market; 30 dealers; began in 1980; open seven days a week, 9:30 a.m. to 5:00 p.m.; free admission; space rental: $25.00 for school room; $15.00 for booth in auditorium; no reservations needed.

Mostly depression glass, antique furniture, secondhand merchandise, crafts and art objects; food; restrooms; parking; nearby motels; antique furniture auction held once a month.

Calamity Jane Flea Markets   A   XX
Junction US 136 & 65
Princeton, Missouri 64673
Contact: Edward Evans, Route 1, Princeton, Missouri, (816) 748-3714

Outdoor market; 65 dealers; began in 1980; held third Saturday of September, 8:00 a.m. to 5:00 p.m.; free admission; space rental: $10.00 for 22' x 14'; reservations needed.
   Mostly antiques and collectibles; food; restrooms; parking; nearby motels.

Captain Ed's Flea Market   D   X
Beach Boulevard
Rockaway Beach, Missouri 65740
(417) 561-4389
Contact: Jo Ann Pimentel
(Off Highway 176, eighteen miles east of Silver Dollar City)

Indoor market; 33 dealers; began in 1977; open April 15 until October 30; free admission; space rental: $1.50 per day for 64 square feet; reservations needed.
   Mostly antiques and collectibles, some new and used merchandise; food; restrooms; parking; nearby motels.

The Tradewinds   ★   W   XXX
875 West Malone (old 60 Highway)
Sikeston, Missouri 63801
(314) 471-3965
Contact: Daniel Byrd, 210 Miller Drive, Sikeston, Missouri 63801, (314) 471-8419
(On I-55 halfway between St. Louis and Memphis)

Outdoor market under roof; 135 dealers; began in 1972; open Thursday, Friday and Saturday, 6:00 a.m. to 6:00 p.m., year round; free admission; space rental: $5.00 for 12' x 14'; reservations recommended.
   Variety of new merchandise, antiques, collectibles, crafts and produce; restaurant; restrooms; parking; nearby motels; occasional auctions.

Olde Town Antique Mall and Flea Market   D   XX
600 Booneville
Springfield, Missouri 65806
(417) 831-6665
Contact: Thelma Wright
(One block south of Business Loop 144)

Indoor market; 90+ dealers, with individual shops on ground floor; began in 1974; open every day except Thursday, 9:30 a.m. to 5:00 p.m., year round; free admission; space rental: $6.00 and up per week; no reservations needed.
   Mostly quality antiques and collectibles, few crafts or secondhand items; cafe and cafeteria nearby; restrooms; free parking; nearby motels.

Park Central Flea Market   **D X**
429 Boonville
Springfield, Missouri 65806
(417) 866-9629
Contact: Helen Smith, Route 1, Box 21, Rogersville, Missouri 65742, (417) 753-2969
(Three blocks south of Chestnut Expressway)

Indoor market; 19 dealers; began in 1972; open Monday to Friday, 10:00 a.m. to 4:00 p.m., Saturday, 10:00 a.m. to 5:00 p.m., Sunday noon to 5:00 p.m.; free admission; space rental: $42.00 per month for 10' x 10'; no reservations needed.

Mostly collectibles and antiques, some secondhand and new merchandise; snack bar; restroom; on street parking; nearby motels.

Viking Flea Market   ★ **D X**
North Grant and Chase
Springfield, Missouri 65803
(417) 869-4237
Contact: Robert Teel, 846 Sylvania, Springfield, Missouri 65807, (417) 881-8516

Indoor market; 35 dealers; began in 1978; open weekdays 10:00 a.m. to 5:00 p.m., Sundays, 9:00 a.m. to 6:00 p.m., closed Wednesday; free admission; space rental: $9.00 per week for 4' x 8' table; reservations needed.

Mostly antiques and collectibles, very little new merchandise; no food concession; restrooms; adequate parking; nearby motels; auctions every Sunday at 4:00 p.m.

OHIO

Columbia Auction Gallery, Inc.
Judy Stevens, Auctioneer
3500 Columbia Parkway
Cincinnati, Ohio 45226
(513) 321-8210

Antiques and collectibles sale held twice a month, usually on Saturday at 10:00 a.m., Sunday at 1:00 p.m., or Monday at 6:30 p.m.; sales feature antique furniture, paintings, cut glass, china, jewelry, Oriental carpets, and Rookwood pottery; estate sales; consignments; property purchased for sales.

No buyer's premium; mail and telephone bids accepted; checks accepted with proper ID; no credit cards. Full payment day of sale; pickups within two days.

Sale announcements mailed; catalogs for some sales; oral or written appraisals offered for negotiable fee.

Main Auction Galleries, Inc.
J. Louis Karp, Auctioneer
137 West Fourth Street
Cincinnati, Ohio 45202
(513) 621-1280

Weekly general sales with some antiques on Tuesdays at 10:30 a.m.; three-day antiques and collectibles sales held at the start of each season; specialized sales include Oriental rugs, jewelry, and furniture; estate sales; consignments; property purchased for sales.

No buyer's premium; mail and telephone bids accepted with credit established prior to sale; checks accepted with previously established credit through bank reference; no credit cards. Purchases held with a 50% deposit; full payment and pickups within 48 hours.

Sale announcements mailed; catalogs for all major antiques sales; oral or written appraisals offered for negotiable fee.

Garth's Auctions, Inc. and Stratford Auction Center
Tom Porter, Tom King, Dick Bemiller, Auctioneers
2690 Stratford Road, Box 315
Delaware, Ohio 43015
(614) 362-4771, (614) 369-5085
(State Route 23, two miles south of Delaware)

Two auctions held at one location: Garth's Auctions, the parent company, handling predominantly pre-1850 furniture and accessories, with three sales a month, on Saturday at 10:00 a.m. for one-day sales, and Friday at 5:00 p.m. and Saturday at 10:00 a.m. for two-day sales; Stratford Auction Center featuring post-1850 Victorian-era antiques, art glass and modern collectibles, holding sales first and third Fridays of the month at 5:00 p.m.; specialized sales include Early American furniture, Early American glass, Victoriana, art glass and art pottery, Indian relics, guns, political items, English and French furniture and decorative ware; estate sales; consignments only; no property purchased for sales.

No buyer's premium; telephone bids accepted; checks accepted with proper ID and photograph of customer and check; no credit cards. Full payment immediately after sale; pickups as soon as possible.

Sale announcements mailed; fully-illustrated catalogs for all sales at Garth's; written appraisals offered.

Early Auction Company
Roger Early and Son, Auctioneers
123 Main Street
Milford, Ohio 45150
(513) 831-4855
(Major sales held at Drawbridge Motor Inn, on I-71 and 75, five minutes from Cincinnati Airport; other sales held at Montgomery Business Mens Club in Montgomery, Ohio, off I-71, on US 22 & 3, fifteen miles from downtown Cincinnati)

Approximately 20 antiques sales a year; major specialized sales include three Victorian art glass sales a year in spring, mid-summer and fall. Early American furniture each Labor Day, antique doll sales each spring and late fall; also six general antique sales; estate sales; consignments; property purchased for sales.

Ten percent buyer's premium on fine art sales only; mail and telephone bids accepted; checks accepted with proper ID; no credit cards. Purchases held with 20% deposit; full payment within 30 days; pickups as arranged.

Sale announcements mailed; catalogs for all major sales; oral or written appraisals offered for hourly fee of $50.00 plus travel expenses.

Fort Steuben Auction Company

Emmanuel Fellouzis, Auctioneer
Box 2250 Fernwood Road
Steubenville, Ohio 43952
(614) 264-6229, (614) 264-7146
Sales held at following four locations:
Holiday Inn, Airport, Stelzer Road, Columbus, Ohio
Ramada Inn, Airport, 1412 Beers School Road, Coraopolis, Pennsylvania
Ramada Inn, 2340 South Reynolds Street, Toledo, Ohio
Sheraton Inn, Harrisburg, Pennsylvania—Exit 18A, quarter mile north of Exit 18 off Pennsylvania Turnpike

General antiques sales held approximately once a month at all four locations; specialized sales include jewelry, Oriental art and antiques; estate sales; consignments; property purchased for sales.

No buyer's premium; mail and telephone bids accepted; checks accepted with proper ID and bank letter. Full payment and pickups day of sale.

Catalogs and sale announcements mailed; oral appraisals offered for hourly fee of $35.00; written appraisals for hourly fee of $50.00.

Clum & Noyes Auctions

Mike Clum, S. Manager, Don Noyes, Auctioneers
Box 305
Thornville, Ohio 43076
(614) 246-6851 or (614) 659-2206
(Auction barn one-quarter mile north of Thornville, on Route 188, Zion Road; thirty miles east of Columbus off I-70, Route 13 Exit four miles south)

Auctions held in heavy-timbered barn dating to 1835; approximately 20 antiques sales held a year, as needed; estate sales; consignments; property purchased for sale.

No buyer's premium; telephone bids accepted; checks accepted with proper ID, though photographs taken of all registered bidders; no credit cards. Full payment day of sale; pickups as arranged.

Catalogs and sale announcements mailed; oral or written appraisals offered for negotiable fee.

Note: Listings are alphabetical by town.

Jamie's Flea Market

W XXXX

Route 113
Amherst, Ohio 44001
(216) 986-4402
Contact: Stanley Ingersoll, 48590 Telegraph Road, Amherst, Ohio 44001, (216) 986-6071
(Half mile west of Route 58 on Route 113)

Indoor/outdoor market; 300 to 400 dealers; began in 1974; open Wednesdays and Saturdays, 8:00 a.m. to 4:00 p.m.; free admission; space rental: $5.00 for 10' x 30' outside; reservations recommended.

Variety of new and secondhand merchandise, antiques, collectibles, crafts and produce; food; restrooms; parking; nearby motels.

Shady Rest Flea Market

W XX

State Routes 250 and 93
Beach City, Ohio 44608
(216) 343-9508
Contact: Mike Unkich, Route 3, Dover, Ohio 44622
(Northwest from State Route 250)

Outdoor market; 100 dealers; began in 1972; open Sundays, April through October; free admission; space rental: $5.00 for 15' x 33'; no reservations needed.

Variety of new merchandise, secondhand items, antiques, collectibles and produce; food stand; restrooms; parking; nearby motels.

Belle Fontaine Flea Market

W X

Logan County Fairgrounds
Belle Fontaine, Ohio 43311
(513) 592-1626
Contact: William Meyer, 616 Hilltop Drive, Belle Fontaine, Ohio 43311, (513) 599-4304
(Fairground entrance off Lake Avenue, two blocks from US 68)

Indoor/outdoor market; 20 to 35 dealers; began in 1975; open Saturdays and Sundays, 9:00 a.m. to 5:00 p.m., year round; free admission; space rental: $12.00 per week for 12' x 12'; reservations needed.

Mostly antiques and collectibles, some new and used merchandise; restaurants nearby; restrooms; parking; two local motels.

Yankee Lake on-the-Green

A XXX

Route 7
Brookfield, Ohio 44430
Contact: Harold Reichard, PO Box 9, Hartford, Ohio, (216) 772-6875
(Three miles north of Brookfield, ten miles north of I-80)

Outdoor market; 150 dealers; began in 1978; held annually in June, 9:00 a.m. to 5:00 p.m.; free admission; space rental: $20.00 for 25' x 20'; reservations needed.

Mostly antiques, few crafts and art objects; restrooms; parking; nearby restaurants and motels; antique shows.

Memphis Triple Drive-In Flea Market W XXXX
10543 Memphis Avenue
Brooklyn, Ohio 44144
(216) 941-2892
Contact: Dolores Applegarth, 13822 Park Drive, Brook Park, Ohio 44142,
(216) 676-8570
(Just off I-71 near Tiedeman Road)

Outdoor market; 500 dealers; began in 1974; open Wednesdays and Saturdays,
8:00 a.m. to 4:00 p.m., early spring to late fall; 75¢ admission; space rental: $3.00
for 20' x 20'; no reservations needed.
　　Mostly secondhand and household items, some new merchandise, antiques
and collectibles; food; restrooms; parking; nearby motels.

Quaint Corner Flea Market M X
Rural Route 4, US Highway 6 and County Road 10
Bryan, Ohio 43506
(419) 636-7745
Contact: Philip and Cecilia Gonzalez, Rural Route 4, Bryan, Ohio 43506
(Between Bryan and Edgerton)

Outdoor market; 20 to 35 dealers; began in 1973; held first Sunday of each
month, May through October; free admission; space rental: $3.50 per day for 25'
space, no table; no reservations needed.
　　Mostly antiques and collectibles, some crafts and produce; lunch stand;
restrooms; parking; nearby motels.

The Great Geauga Antique Market A XXXX
Claridon-Troy Road
Burton, Ohio 44021
(216) 636-5405
Contact: Ted and Jean Taylor, 12285 Madison Road, Huntsburg, Ohio 44046
(Route 322 east of Cleveland to Claridon-Troy Road)

Outdoor market; 450 dealers; began in 1974; held first Saturday in June and first
Saturday after Labor Day, 9:30 a.m. to 5:30 p.m.; $1.00 admission; space rental:
$25.00 for 22'; reservations recommended.
　　Only antiques and collectibles; food concession; restrooms; free parking;
nearby motels.

Paris Flea Market W XXXX
2310 Ferguson Road
Cincinnati, Ohio 45238
(513) 451-1271
(I-75 to Harrison Road Exit, left on Queen City, left on Ferguson)

Outdoor market; 200 to 400 dealers; began in 1970; open Saturday and Sunday,
7:00 a.m. to 4:00 p.m.; admission 75¢ Sundays, 35¢ Saturdays; space rental:
$6.00 on Sunday, $3.50 on Saturday; no reservations needed.
　　Mostly secondhand and household items, some antiques, collectibles and
crafts; food; restrooms; parking; nearby motels.

Theron's County   W   XX
1641 Route 164
Columbiana, Ohio 44408
(216) 482-4327
Contact: Theron Lamoncha
(Half mile off Route 11)

Indoor/outdoor market; 100 dealers; began in 1965; open Wednesday and
Saturday, 9:00 a.m. to 5:00 p.m.; free admission; space rental: $3.00; no
reservations needed.

Variety of secondhand merchandise, antiques, collectibles, and crafts, some
art objects and produce; food; restrooms; parking; nearby motels and camping
facilities.

CCC Flea Market and Swap Shop   W   XXX
CCC Twin Drive-In
1375 Harrisburg Pike
Columbus, Ohio 43223
(614) 444-2313
Contact: Doug Hott, 865 King Avenue, Columbus, Ohio 43212, (614) 291-3133
(Two and one-half miles north of I-270 on Route 62 South)

Outdoor market; 200 dealers; began in 1978; open Sundays, 8:00 a.m. to 4:00
p.m., April through October; free admission; space rental: $2.00 for 20' x 20'; no
reservations needed.

Mostly secondhand and new merchandise, some antiques, collectibles and
crafts; food; restrooms; parking; nearby motels.

South Flea Market and Swap Meet   W   XXXX
South Twin Drive-In
3050 South High Street
Columbus, Ohio 43207
(614) 444-2313
Contact: Doug Hott, 865 King Avenue, Columbus, Ohio 43212, (614) 291-3133
(One and one-half miles north of I-270 on Route 23 South)

Outdoor market; 400 dealers; began in 1974; open Saturdays, 8:00 a.m. to 4:00
p.m., April through October; 50¢ admission; space rental: $2.00 for 20' x 20'; no
reservations needed.

Mostly secondhand and new merchandise, few antiques, collectibles or
crafts; food; restrooms; parking; nearby motels.

Dublin Drive-In Flea Market   W   XXXX
4148 West Dublin Granville
Dublin, Ohio 43017
(614) 889-2664
Contact: Greg Holloway
(On Highway 161, east of 33)

Outdoor market; 300 dealers; began in 1972; open Saturday and Sunday, March to November; admission 50¢ per car; space rental: $2.00 for 20' x 20'; no reservations needed.

Mostly new and secondhand merchandise, few antiques, collectibles or crafts; food concession; restrooms; parking; several nearby motels.

Gahanna Country Flea Market   A XXXX
Mill Street
Gahanna, Ohio 43230
Contact: Mrs. LaRoux Mentz, 377 Granville Street, Gahanna, Ohio 43230,
(614) 471-1657
(Route 62 Exit off I-270)

Outdoor market; 300 to 500 dealers; began in 1962; held the third Sunday of September; free admission; space rental: $20.00 to $40.00 for 10'; reservations recommended.

Mostly antiques and secondhand merchandise, some collectibles and crafts; homemade food; no restrooms; limited parking; no nearby motels.

Hilliard Antique Show & Flea Market   M XXX
Franklin County Fair
Hilliard, Ohio
Contact: Steve Stockwell, 4214 North High Street, Columbus, Ohio 43214,
(614) 263-6830 or (614) 267-8163
(Four miles northwest of Columbus, Ohio)

Indoor/outdoor market; 140 dealers; began in 1980; held one Sunday a month, 6:00 a.m. to 6:00 p.m.; 75¢ admission per car; space rental: $15.00 for 10' x 20' outside, $8.00 outside; reservations needed inside.

Mostly antiques and collectibles, some crafts and art objects; food; restrooms; parking; nearby motels.

Jefferson Flea Market   A XXX
Ashtabula County Fairgrounds
Jefferson, Ohio 44047
Contact: Mabel Bigley and Carol Curran, Cascade Valley Farms, RD3,
Painesville, Ohio 44077, (216) 354-8849
(I-90 and Route 45 South)

Outdoor market; 150 dealers; began in 1960; held twice a year, second Saturday in June and Saturday after Labor Day, 10:00 a.m. to 5:00 p.m.; $1.00 admission; space rental: $20.00 for 25'; reservations needed.

All antiques and collectibles; snack bar; restrooms; parking; nearby motels.

Johnstown Lions Club Annual Flea Market   A XX
Public Square
Johnstown, Ohio 43031
(614) 967-6016
Contact: Dick Scovell, 6066 Johnstown-Alexandria Road, Johnstown, Ohio
43031, (614) 967-1279
(Intersection of US Highway 62 and State Route 37)

Outdoor market; 60 dealers; began in 1972; held every Memorial Day; free admission; space rental: $5.00 for 12' x 12' paved area; reservations needed.

Mostly new merchandise, secondhand and household items; some antiques and collectibles; food; restrooms; parking; nearby motels.

Lima Westside Lion's Club & Antique Flea Market   A   X
Allen County Fairgrounds
Lima, Ohio 45801
Contact: Harold Crawford, 746 North Elizabeth, Lima, Ohio, (419) 228-6469
(At intersection of Routes 75 and 309)

Indoor/outdoor market; 46 dealers; began in 1972; held twice a year, in February and September, on Saturday, 9:00 a.m. to 6:00 p.m., and Sunday, 10:00 a.m. to 5:00 p.m.; admission 50¢; space rental: $20.00 for 8' x 12'; reservations needed.

Variety of antiques, collectibles, secondhand merchandise, crafts, art objects; food; restrooms; parking; nearby motels.

Land of Legends Festival Flea Market   A   XXX
Box 779, Downtown Square
Newark, Ohio 43055
Contact: Rod Wolverton, 63 Wallace Street, Newark, Ohio 43055, (614) 345-2454
(Take I-70 East from Columbus to Route 79 North to Downtown Square)

Outdoor market under large shade trees; 150 to 200 dealers; held second and third weekend in June; free admission; space rental: $15.00 for 10' x 20'; reservations recommended.

Mostly antiques, collectibles, arts and crafts, some new merchandise; restaurants; restrooms; several parking areas; nearby motels.

Bloomfield Auction and Flea Market   ★   W   XX
Route 87
North Bloomfield, Ohio
(216) 876-4993
Contact: Charles and Mary Roscoe, 8183 Route 193, Farmdale, Ohio 44417
(On Route 87, half mile west of Route 46)

Indoor/outdoor market; 75 to 100 dealers; began in 1942; open Thursdays, 8:00 a.m. to 4:00 p.m., year round; free admission; space rental: $5.00 for 10' x 12'; reservations needed.

Variety of merchandise, including produce, meats, cheeses, crafts, secondhand items, antiques and collectibles; food; restrooms; parking; nearby motels; auctions every Thursday.

Southwest Licking Music Boosters Antique Show and Flea Market

A XX

Watkins Memorial High School
Watkins Road
Pataskala, Ohio 43062
(614) 927-3846
Contact: Ida Bowers, 1027 Pike Street SW, Box 61, Etna, Ohio 43018, (614) 927-8878
(Close to Columbus, I-70 to Exit 118, north to Route 40, east at red light to County Road 42)

Indoor market; 95 to 100 dealers; began in 1970; held once a year, last Sunday in March or first in April, 9:00 a.m. to 5:00 p.m.; 50¢ admission; space rental: $10.00 for 5' x 10'; reservations needed.

    Mostly antiques and collectibles, some crafts and new and secondhand merchandise; food; restrooms; parking; nearby motels.

Piqua Flea Market

A XX

Piqua Mall
I-75 and US 36
Piqua, Ohio 45356
(513) 779-9933
Contact: R.M. Coble, 1215 Forrest Avenue, Piqua, Ohio 45356, (513) 773-3780

Indoor market; 60 dealers; began in 1975; open second weekend in February, May and September; free admission; space rental: $50.00 for 10' x 12'; reservations needed.

    Mostly antiques, collectibles and crafts; snack bars; restrooms; parking; nearby motels.

The Springfield Antique Show and Flea Market

M XXXX

Clark County Fairgrounds
Springfield, Ohio 45503
Contact: Knight-Magill, 5140 Morris Road, Springfield, Ohio 45502, (513) 399-2261
(Exit 59 off I-70)

Indoor/outdoor market; 400 to 600 dealers; began in 1970; open first weekend per month, year round, set-up on Friday evenings; 50¢ admission; space rental: $18.00 for wall, $15.00 for aisle, 10' x 10' inside, 10' x 20' outside; reservations recommended.

    Mostly antiques and collectibles, with crafts and produce; food; restrooms; free parking; many nearby motels.

Warren Flea Market Inc.

W XX

428 Main Street SW
Warren, Ohio 44481
(216) 399-8298
Contact: Elizabeth Stein, 370 Colonial Drive, Youngstown, Ohio 44505, (216) 759-2638
(Near Route 422, the Youngstown-Warren Road)

Note: Listings are alphabetical by town.

Indoor/outdoor market; 60 to 100 dealers; began in 1975; open Tuesdays and Saturdays, 8:00 a.m. to 5:00 p.m., year round; free admission; space rental: $3.50 indoors, $5.00 outdoors, tables furnished; reservations advised.

Variety of collectibles, produce, antiques, household goods and new merchandise; snack bar; restrooms; parking; nearby motels.

Central Ohio Gun and Indian Relic Collectors Association Flea Market   M   XXXX
Fairgrounds
134 East Ohio Avenue
Washington Court House, Ohio 43160
(614) 335-1854
Contact: Coyt Stookey, 134 East Ohio Avenue, Washington Court House, Ohio 43160
(Between Routes 62 and 22)

Indoor/outdoor market; 200 to 1,000 dealers; began in 1955; open one weekend per month, Friday noon to 6:00 p.m., Saturday and Sunday 7:30 a.m. to 6:00 p.m.; free admission; space rental: $3.00 to $5.00 per day; reservations needed for indoor space.

Mostly antiques and collectibles, some new and used merchandise; food; restrooms; parking; nearby motels usually booked early.

Farm and Flea Market   ★   W   XXXX
1270 Route 22 West
Washington Court House, Ohio 43160
(614) 335-9780
Contact: Tom Hixson
(On Route 22 across from the Fairgrounds)

Indoor/outdoor market; 200 to 350 dealers; began in 1980; open Saturdays and Sundays, 9:00 a.m. to 6:00 p.m., year round; free admission; space rental: $10.00 per day for 10' x 10'; reservations needed.

Lots of antiques, collectibles and secondhand merchandise, some new merchandise and crafts; food; restrooms; parking; nearby motels; auctions every Saturday, 6:00 p.m. to 9:00 p.m.

Montrose Drive-In Theatre Flea Market   W   XXXX
4030 West Market Street
West Akron, Ohio 44313
(216) 666-3000
Contact: Lou Ratener, PO Box 5346, Akron, Ohio 44313
(I-77 and State Highway 18 to West Akron)

Outdoor market; 150 to 350 dealers; began in 1974; open Saturdays and Sundays, 7:00 a.m. to 4:00 p.m., April through November; 50¢ admission; space rental: $3.00 Saturday, $4.00 Sunday for 22'; no reservations needed.

Variety of secondhand items, new merchandise, collectibles and antiques; refreshment stand; restrooms; parking; several motels.

Hartville Flea Market

XXXX

State Route 619
Hartville, Ohio 44632
(216) 699-3952
Contact: Howard Miller, 788 Edison Street, Hartville, Ohio 44632, (216) 877-2949
(From Route 80 take Route 43 South 13 miles to Route 619, one mile west of Hartville)

Indoor/outdoor market; 500 dealers; began in 1939; open Mondays and Thursdays, year round; free admission; space rental: $5.00 Monday, $3.00 Thursday for 12' x 31' outside; no reservations needed.

Mostly antiques and collectibles, some new merchandise, secondhand items and crafts; local restaurant; restrooms; acres of parking; nearby motels.

WISCONSIN

Milwaukee Auction Galleries

Gary Hollander, Molly Salisbury, Auctioneers
4747 West Bradley Road
Milwaukee, Wisconsin 53223
(414) 355-5054
(Actually in the village of Brown Deer, north of Milwaukee; from Chicago, take Interstate 94 to Interstate 43 North, exit on Good Hope Road, to Green Bay Road to West Bradley)

Offers eight yearly scheduled sales featuring fine art and antiques—including oil paintings and engravings, Oriental art and rugs, period furniture, estate furnishings, porcelains, silver, jewelry, collectibles, household goods; specialized sales periodically of original posters, artwork; estate sales; consignments only.

Ten percent buyer's premium; mail and telephone bids accepted; checks accepted with established credit through bank reference; Master Charge and Visa accepted for purchases over $180.00. Full payment and pickups within three days.

Sale announcements and catalogs mailed; oral appraisals offered free of charge for consigned items; written appraisals for minimum of $50.00 hourly fee.

Bob Vogel Auction Service

Bob Vogel, Auctioneer
Idle Hour Mansion
1421 Mansion Drive
Monroe, Wisconsin 53566
(608) 897-2508 or (608) 325-5165

Handling antiques at the Mansion at least once each month, generally on Sundays; including specialized sales of coins, dolls, cars; household and estate sales held weekends on location; consignments; no property purchased outright.

No buyer's premium; mail and telephone bids accepted; checks accepted with proper ID or bank letter of credit; no credit cards. Full payment at time of sale; pickups within one week.

Sale announcements mailed; written appraisals offered for negotiable fee.

Travis Auction Galleries, Inc.

Dean Travis, Auctioneer
1442 Underwood Avenue
Wauwatosa, Wisconsin 53213
(414) 453-0342
(Near Milwaukee)

A family-run business; holds five-night sales generally at the end of each month at 6:30 p.m.; featuring antiques and collectibles, such as Victorian through early 1920s furniture, paintings, china, art glass, jewelry; two nights are specialized sales of railroad items, 20th century war collectibles, primitive and pine furniture and furnishings, etc.; bi-annual Christmas Tree ornament sale held every October and November; estate sales; consignments; no property purchased for sales.

No buyer's premium; mail and telephone bids accepted; approved checks accepted; Master Charge accepted. Full payment night of sale; pickups within seven days.

Sale announcements mailed; oral and written appraisals offered for an hourly fee of $35.00.

Barretts Auction Service, Ltd.

Jack A. and Michael J. Barrett, Auctioneers
4120 Eighth Street South, PO Box 692
Wisconsin Rapids, Wisconsin 54494
(715) 423-2252
(Highway 13 South—two blocks south of Wisconsin Rapids)

Year-round general sales every Thursday evening include household and business goods, estate merchandise, antiques and collections; specialized sales—of guns, coins, antiques and collectibles—at least three times yearly; consignments; property purchased for sales.

No buyer's premium; mail and telephone bids accepted; certified, traveler's and local checks accepted, or merchandise held until check clears; no credit cards. Purchases held with a 25% deposit; full payment within 48 hours; pickups within five days.

Sale announcements and some catalogs mailed; written appraisals offered for variable fee.

Riverside Ballroom Flea Market   M XXX

Main and Newall
Green Bay, Wisconsin 54302
Contact: Bob Zurko, RR 4, Box 358-B, Shawano, Wisconsin 54166, (715) 526-9472

Indoor market; 100 + dealers; open third Sunday of every month from November to March, 10:00 a.m. to 4:00 p.m.; $50CT admission; space rental: $15.00 for 14' x 6' with table; reservations needed.

Mostly antiques and collectibles; lunch available; restrooms; parking; nearby motels.

The Barn   W X
Highway 53
Haugen, Wisconsin 54841
(715) 234-2615
Contact: Vern or Louise Gabriel, Route 1, Box 82, Sarona, Wisconsin 54870
(Two miles from end of Highway 53)

Indoor/outdoor market; 10 dealers; began in 1976; open Saturday and Sunday, April through October (or first weekend in November); free admission; space rental: $3.00 outside, $4.00 inside, 4' x 8' tables; reservations needed.

Mostly collectibles, some antiques, secondhand merchandise and new items; food; restrooms outside; free parking; nearby motel and campgrounds.

Community Auction and Flea Market   ★ XXX
Route 2, Highway 8 West
Ladysmith, Wisconsin 54848
(715) 532-7853
Contact: Cecil and Betty Van Wey, (715) 532-3661
(Four miles west of Junction of Highways 8 and 27, sixty miles north of Eau Claire)

Outdoor market on 16 acres; 130 dealers; began in 1927; open fifth and twentieth of each month, April through October plus some other days; admission 50¢ per car; space rental: $5.00 for 14' x 20', many with 30" x 12' tables; no reservations needed.

Variety of merchandise including secondhand, household items, farm machinery, new merchandise, crafts, collectibles and a few antiques; food; restrooms; parking; nearby motels; auctions held.

Highway 51 Flea Market   W X
Route 3, Box 212
Merrill, Wisconsin 54452
(715) 536-3002
Contact: Dale Kienz
(Three miles north of Merrill)

Outdoor market; 50 dealers; began in 1972; open Saturday and Sunday, May to September; free admission; space rental: $2.50 per day; no reservations needed.

Variety of new and used merchandise, crafts, collectibles, produce, antiques; restaurant; restrooms; parking; nearby motels.

Old Rock School Arts and Crafts Center Flea Market   A   X
1400 South Marquette Road
Prairie du Chien, Wisconsin 53821
(608) 326-8122
Contact: Eva Poladna, 527 North Michigan, Prairie du Chien, Wisconsin 53821
(Wisconsin Highways 60, 35 and Iowa 18)

Outdoor market; 13 dealers; began in 1967; held annually—call ahead for dates; free admission; space rental: $6.00 per day for 20' x 20'; reservations recommended.

    Variety of merchandise including antiques, collectibles, secondhand and new merchandise, produce, art and crafts; food; restrooms; parking; nearby motels.

Pea Pickin' Flea Market   W   XXX
Route 2, Box 145
St. Croix Falls, Wisconsin 54024
(715) 483-9460
Contact: Mr. & Mrs. Leonard Sommers
(Highway 8 and 35, five miles east of St. Croix Falls)

Indoor/outdoor market; 150 dealers; began in 1970; open Saturday, Sunday and holidays, year round; free admission; space rental: $5.00 per day; no reservations needed.

    Wide variety of new merchandise, secondhand items, crafts, collectibles, antiques and produce; food; restrooms; parking; nearby motels.

Summer Flea Market   ★   W   XXXX
Shawano County Fairgrounds
Highway 29
Shawano, Wisconsin 54166
(715) 526-9285
Contact: Bob Zurko, RR 4, Box 358-B, Shawano, Wisconsin 54166, (715) 526-9472
(Thirty minutes west of Green Bay)

Outdoor market; 200 to 250 dealers; began in 1971; open Sundays, May through October, Saturdays, June, July and August; 50¢ admission; space rental: $6.50 for 20' frontage; no reservations needed.

    Mostly antiques and collectibles, some new and used merchandise; food; restrooms; parking; nearby motels and campgrounds; country auctions on alternating Saturdays.

SOUTHWEST

Arizona, California, Colorado, Nevada, New Mexico, Oklahoma, Texas, Utah

Families moving west 100 years ago did not transport heavy furniture or pianos. They took instead small keepsakes, their jewelry and picture albums. It is perhaps for this reason that a Southwestern collector is often more thrilled by a late 19th-century calling card tray than his New England counterpart; for him, it is a valued antique. In fact, some of the most avid Victoriana collectors live in California.

While big-city auctions in this eight-state region feature fine period furniture, silver and crystal, some of the more common specialties in the Southwest are American oak furniture (particularly from the turn-of-the-century up to the 1930s), old cooking and farming implements, country store and advertising collectibles, dolls and toys, and Oriental art objects, the latter because of the trade with the Orient which was based in California.

Several houses specialize in American Indian and Western art and artifacts. Specifics include Navajo weavings, pottery, silver and turquoise jewelry—especially the not-made-for-tourist pieces known as "pawn" jewelry, after the fact that it was often pawned at reservation trading posts to pay for supplies. While fads for Indian jewelry may come and go and come again back east, in the Southwest these native treasures never lose status. One of the best known of the Indian/Western galleries is the Scottsdale Gallery in Van Nuys, California. Another, Rawhide, is in Scottsdale, Arizona. Its setting is an 1880s Western town—and offers stage coach rides, gun fights and even a rodeo.

California and Texas have the greatest concentration of auctions and flea markets. The oldest auction firm in the West is Butterfield and Butterfield, established in 1865 in San Francisco. Other major houses include Sotheby Parke Bernet in Los Angeles, California Book Auction Galleries in San Francisco and Hollywood, Clement's Antiques of Texas, near Dallas, and Ledbetter's Auction Gallery in Phoenix.

The Rose Bowl in Pasadena, California, is the site of the

biggest flea in the Southwest, by far. The market is divided into areas for antiques, secondhand goods, produce and new items, and certainly the excitement level during the monthly markets is as high as at any New Year's Rose Bowl Game. Other well-known fleas are the Spring Valley Swap Meet; Lancaster Flea Market; Vermont Swap Meet, in Gardena; and Cherry Valley Swap Meet in Fresno. Many California "swap meets" (a Western term for flea markets) are strung along the coast, close to major cities like San Francisco, San Diego and Los Angeles. In Texas, flea markets are most commonly found near Houston, Fort Worth, Dallas, El Paso and San Antonio. A good hunting ground for antiques in Oklahoma is the Tulsa Flea Market, held at the city's Fairgrounds.

For travelers and collectors, all the eight states offer sights and sites of interest. Pioneer Arizona is a reconstruction not far north of Phoenix. Western history is epitomized at the Tombstone National Historic Site, and for collectors of Indian artifacts, the Arizona State Museum in Tucson offers interesting displays. Many many museums are found in California, among them: the San Joaquin County Historical Museum, with a large collection of old tools; the Museum of Dentistry at Orange; the Will Rogers State Historic Park at Pacific Palisades; the Orange Empire Railway Museum in Perris; the Fine Arts Gallery of San Diego, with many exhibits of Oriental art; and restored houses at Old Town San Diego State Historic Park. There is a huge maritime collection at the San Francisco Maritime Museum Association. Of special interest in Colorado are the Kachina dolls of the Hopis at the University of Colorado Art Museum in Boulder and the Oriental and textile collections at the Denver Art Museum . There's an enormous transportation museum at Harrah's Automobile Collection in Reno, Nevada, and in Santa Fe, New Mexico, is an outstanding collection of Navaho artifacts at the Museum of Navaho Ceremonial Art, Inc. Also in Santa Fe is the amazing Museum of International Folk Art. The history of the American cowboy can be traced at the Museum of the American Vaquero in Las Cruces, New Mexico. There's a very extensive gun display (more than 20,000) plus musical instruments and steins at the J. M. Davis Gun

Collection in Claremore, Oklahoma. In Ft. Worth, Texas, is found Log Cabin Village, a restoration of several cabins, all furnished in 19th-century style. An outstanding collection of decorative arts is found at The Bayou Bend Collection in Houston; a large collection of logging tools is housed at the Texas Forestry Museum in Lufkin; and the San Antonio Museum Association operates a number of interesting historic homes and collections. A well-named museum in Utah is the Man and Bread Museum at Utah State University in Logan. Nineteenth-century farming is the subject of displays and demonstrations.

The major antique shows in the Southwest are the Santa Monica Antiques Show and Sale in California; the Tri-Delta Charity Show in Dallas, Texas; the Newport Harbor Art Museum Antiques Show in Newport Beach, California; and the Theta Charity Show in Houston.

For listings and reviews of Southwestern auctions and flea markets, as well as dates for the large antique shows, check *Antique Trader, Antique Monthly, West Coast Peddler, Native Arts/West, Bay Area Collector, The Magazine ANTIQUES* and local newspapers.

ARIZONA

Arizona Auction Gallery
Scott Rhodes, Auctioneer
839 East Camelback Road
Phoenix, Arizona 85013
(602) 266-1665

Antiques sale generally held third Sunday of every month, year round; specialized sales of clocks, R.S. Prussia china, period furniture from Louis XV to early 20th century; estate sales; consignments; property purchased for sales.

No buyer's premium; mail and telephone bids accepted; checks accepted with proper ID; Master Charge and Visa accepted. Purchases held with 33% deposit; full payment and pickups within three days.

Sale announcements mailed; catalogs for all sales; oral or written appraisals offered for minimum hourly fee of $100.00.

Ledbetter's Auction Gallery
915 North Central Avenue
Phoenix, Arizona 85004
(602) 257-1455

General antique auctions every two or three weeks, usually on Sundays; specialized annual auctions include Oriental art and antiques, toys, dolls and banks; country store and advertising collectibles, and clocks; estate sales; consignments; merchandise purchased for sales.

Ten percent buyer's premium; mail and telephone bids accepted at discretion of gallery; local checks accepted with Arizona driver's license and bank card; out-of-state checks accepted with bank letter of credit or previously established credit; no credit cards accepted. Full payment same day; most pickups within one day.

Sale announcements mailed; oral appraisals at gallery usually free, written appraisals, $35.00 and up.

Rawhide
R. G. Warner, Auctioneer
23023 North Scottsdale Road
Scottsdale, Arizona 85255
(602) 992-6111
(Four miles north of Bell Road)

Situated in an 1880s Western town; bi-monthly antique sales held Friday evenings at 7:00 p.m. from September to mid-July; monthly sales held Sunday afternoons from October to May; sales feature Western artifacts, Indian art, paintings, and horse-drawn vehicles; some European artifacts; estate sales; consignments; property purchased for sales.

No buyer's premium; mail and telephone bids accepted with 25% deposit; checks accepted with proper ID and bank guarantee; no credit cards. Purchases held with a 25% deposit; full payment in three days; pickups within one week.

Sale announcements mailed; written appraisals offered for an hourly fee of $25.00.

Claypool's
310 Main Street   W   X
Bullhead City, Arizona 86430
Contact: Claypool's, 725 Broadway, Needles, California 92363, (714) 326-2109

Outdoor market; 10 to 15 dealers; open Sunday, 8:00 a.m. to dark, year round; free admission; free space rental; no reservations needed.

Mostly secondhand and household items, some new merchandise and antiques; baked goods and coffee available; no restrooms; parking; nearby motels.

Claypool's Flea Market   X
Twelfth and Kofa
Parker, Arizona 85344
Contact: Claypool's, 725 Broadway, Needles, California, 92363 (714) 326-2109

Outdoor market; 25 dealers; open first and third Saturdays of every month, 8:00 a.m. to dark, year round; free admission; free space rental: no reservations needed.

Mostly secondhand and household items, some antiques and new merchandise; baked goods and coffee available; no restrooms; parking; nearby motels.

Phoenix Park 'N Swap   W XXXX
3801 East Washington
Phoenix, Arizona 85034
(602) 273-1258
Contact: Greyhound Dog Track, 3801 East Washington, Phoenix, Arizona 85034
(I-10 to Fortieth Street Exit, north to corner of Washington)

Indoor/outdoor market; 1,500 dealers; began about 1959; open Friday 7:00 a.m. to 1:00 p.m., Saturday and Sunday 5:30 a.m. to 4:00 p.m.; 50¢ admission; space rental: $5.00 Saturday, $7.00 Sunday, for 9' x 18'; reservations recommended.

Mostly new and secondhand merchandise, some antiques, collectibles, arts and crafts; food; restrooms; parking; nearby motels.

Phoenix Trade Fair   W XX
3839 West Indian School Road
Phoenix, Arizona 85019
(602) 278-6221
Contact: Kathy Cline
(Entrance on Thirty-eighth Avenue and Indian School Road)

Indoor/outdoor market; 100 sellers; began about 1973; open Friday, 12:00 to 9:00 p.m., Saturday and Sunday, 8:00 a.m. to 5:00 p.m., year round; free admission; space rental: $6.00 outdoors, indoor rates vary; no reservations needed.

Variety of merchandise distributed among antiques, collectibles, household items, new merchandise, arts and crafts; home-cooked daily specials, beer on tap; restrooms; parking; nearby motel; Bingo Thursday through Sunday at 7:00 p.m.

Swap-O-Rama   W XXXX
3636 South Forty-eighth Street
Phoenix, Arizona 85040
(602) 968-8609
Contact: William Stevens, Sr.
(Forty-eighth Street and I-10)

Outdoor market (covered spaces with lighting); 500 sellers; began about 1974; open Wednesday, 1:00 p.m. to 10:30 p.m., Saturday and Sunday, 6:00 a.m. to 5:00 p.m.; 50¢ admission; space rental: $4.00 for 10' x 15'; reservations advisable.

Wide variety of merchandise; food; restrooms; parking; nearby motels; occasional specialty auctions.

Park 'N Swap   W   XXXX

2601 South Third Avenue
Tucson, Arizona 85713
(602) 623-4012
Contact: Bob Pendrase
(From I-10 west on Twenty-second Street to Fourth Avenue, south on Fourth
Avenue to Thirty-sixth Street)

Outdoor market; 200 to 400 sellers; began about 1965; open Saturday and
Sunday, 6:00 a.m. to 4:00 p.m.; no admission charge; space rental: $3.00 for 10' x
20' paved area; no reservations needed.

No antique dealers, variety of secondhand items, collectibles, new merchandise, crafts, produce; food; restrooms; parking; nearby motels.

CALIFORNIA

West Coast Auction Company
J. Chapanar, Auctioneer
1630 North State College Boulevard
Anaheim, California 92806
(714) 773-9818

Sales held every two weeks on Fridays at 7:00 p.m. featuring antiques and
collectibles only; consignments; property purchased for sales.

No buyer's premium; mail and telephone bids not accepted; checks accepted
with proper ID; Master Charge and Visa accepted. Full payment day of sale;
pickups within four days.

Sale announcements mailed.

The All-American Collector's Auction
3817 Riverside Drive
Burbank, California 91505
(213) 846-5775

Specializing in antique and collectible toys and advertising items; two major
sales a year, at no fixed schedule; consignments; property purchased for sales.

No buyer's premium; mail and telephone bids accepted; checks accepted with
proper ID; no credit cards. Full payment and pickups day of sale.

Sale announcements mailed; purchase of catalog required to enter sale; oral
or written appraisals offered for fee of 1% of value of item.

Chico Auction Gallery
Jack Harbour, Auctioneer
926 West Eighth Street
Chico, California 95926
(916) 345-0431

Antiques and collectibles sale held first Friday of every month; featuring American oak furniture, glass; estate sales; consignments; property purchased for sales.

No buyer's premium; mail and telephone bids accepted; checks accepted with two forms of ID; for purchases over $1,000.00 letter of credit required; Visa and Master Charge accepted. Full payment day of sale; pickups within one week.

Sale announcements mailed; oral and written appraisals $35.00 for first hour, $20.00 each additional hour.

Joel L. Malter & Company, Inc.
PO Box 77
Encino, California 91316
(213) 784-7772
(Sales held at local hotels—check mailings)

Specializing in coins and ancient art; six to eight sales held a year, usually on weekends; estate sales; consignments; property purchased for sales; some mail-bid sales.

No buyer's premium; mail and telephone bids accepted; checks accepted with proper ID or previously established credit; no credit cards. Payment in full and pickups must be made within 30 days.

Purchase of catalog required to enter all sales; mailing list available for sale announcements; written appraisals offered for 1.5% of estimated value of property.

Folsom Auction Gallery
Lucky Jenkinson, Auctioneer
314 East Bidwell
Folsom, California 95630
(916) 985-2902
(Sixteen miles from Sacramento)

Antiques and collectibles sale held first and third Thursday of every month; featuring oak, walnut and mahogany furniture, Victoriana; specialized sales of private collections such as toys; estate sales; consignments; property purchased for sales.

No buyer's premium; mail and telephone bids accepted; checks accepted with ID; no credit cards. Full payment night of sale; pickups within one week.

Sale announcements mailed.

Cobb's Midstate Auctions
Cecil G. Cobb, Auctioneer
2223 North Weber Avenue
Fresno, California 93705
(209) 264-3868 or (209) 787-3253
(Just off Highway 99 at the Clinton off-ramp)

Approximately three general sales held each month, primarily antiques and collectibles, with some used furniture included; occasional specialized sales of toys and dolls; estate sales; consignments; merchandise purchased for sales.

Note: Listings are alphabetical by town.

No buyer's premium; mail and telephone bids accepted; checks accepted with proper ID; no credit cards. No deposit necessary to hold purchase. Full payment and pickup by noon of day following sale.

Sale announcements mailed; written appraisals offered for fee (usually $50.00 per hour).

Fresno Auction Service
Rex Irwin, Auctioneer
1516 H Street
Fresno, California 93721
(209) 486-8402

Sales predominantly of antiques and collectibles held on the first and third Saturdays of each month; sales include American oak furniture up to the 1930s; some estate sales; consignments; property purchased for sales.

No buyer's premium; mail and telephone bids not accepted; checks accepted; Master Charge and Visa accepted. Full payment at sale; pickups when convenient.

Sale announcements mailed; oral and written appraisals offered for negotiable fee.

Midstate Galleries
Cecil Cobb, Auctioneer
2223 North Weber
Fresno, California 93705
(209) 264-3868

Antiques, collectibles, and fine art sale twice a month; featuring oak and walnut furniture, bronzes, art glass; specialized sales of fine art prints and paintings, Western art; estate sales; consignments; property purchased for sales.

No buyer's premium; mail and telephone bids accepted; checks accepted with ID; no credit cards. Full payment within one day; pickups within two days.

Sale announcements mailed; catalogs available for estate sales; oral and written appraisals offered for hourly fee of $65.00.

Warner & Company Auction
Bob Warner, Auctioneer
1420 East Arrow Highway
Irwindale, California 91706
(714) 620-1497 or (213) 359-1181
(One mile south of junction of Interstate 210 and Interstate 605)

Antiques, including variety of Victorian and oak furniture and collectibles featured at sales held every two weeks on Monday at 7:00 p.m.; estate sales; consignments; some property purchased for sales.

No buyer's premium; mail and telephone bids accepted after in-person inspection of merchandise; checks accepted with proper ID; Visa and Master Charge accepted. Full payment night of sale; pickups as arranged.

Sale announcements mailed.

Sotheby Parke Bernet, Inc.

Peter McCoy, Marvin Newman, Reupert Fennell, Joan Hartley, Alexander Rose, Auctioneers
7660 Beverly Boulevard
Los Angeles, California 90036
(213) 937-5130

Antiques sale generally held once a month, featuring furniture, decorations, Oriental works, jewelry, paintings and prints; three or four specialized sales held yearly (one or two in fall, one in spring, one in summer), with furniture, decorative arts, Orientalia and high quality jewelry, American and European prints and paintings, and arms and armour; estate sales; consignments; no property purchased for sales.

Ten percent buyer's premium. Consult New York Sotheby Parke Bernet listing for more particulars.

J. J. J. Auction Gallery

Joe Maestro
3210-C Production Avenue
Oceanside, California 92054
(714) 757-9118

American furniture, particularly oak and Victorian walnut, and American collectibles featured in general auction held every other Friday at 6:30 p.m.; specialized sales—of dolls, Hummels, and glass, among others—take place on Sundays at 1:30 p.m.; estate sales; consignments; property purchased for sales.

No buyer's premium; certified checks, or California checks with two forms of ID accepted; Visa and Master Charge accepted. Purchases must be paid for in full on day of sale; pickups within five days.

Sale announcements mailed.

Baker's Auction

Dean Baker, Auctioneer
14100 Paramount Boulevard
Paramount, California 90723
(213) 531-1524
(Twenty minutes south of Los Angeles)

General antiques sale, including wide selection of American oak furniture, lasts from eight to twelve hours on the first Sunday of every month; estate sales; consignments; property purchased for sales.

No buyer's premium; mail and telephone bids accepted with 30% deposit; checks accepted with two local IDs; Visa and Master Charge accepted. Unless prior arrangements made, full payment same day and pickups within two days.

Partial listing of merchandise available by mail.

Butterfield & Butterfield

Bernard Osher, John Gallo, Auctioneers
1244 Sutter Street
San Francisco, California 94109
(415) 673-1362

Founded in 1865; approximately eight auctions held each month, with specialized sales in art, furniture, jewelry, and Oriental rugs; estate sales; consignments; property purchased for sales.

Ten percent buyer's premium; mail and telephone bids accepted; checks accepted with established credit through bank reference; no credit cards. No deposit necessary to hold purchase; full payment and pickups within five days.

Catalogs and sale announcements mailed. Large staff offers written appraisals for percentage of value of item.

California Book Auction Galleries
Maurice F. Powers, Auctioneer
358 Golden Gate Avenue
San Francisco, California 94102
(415) 775-0424
1749 North La Brea Avenue
Hollywood, California 90046
(213) 658-6888

Monthly sales held in both San Francisco and Hollywood, featuring fine and rare books, maps and manuscripts; specialized sales include books and materials related to California and the American West, modern first editions, fine pr ess books, prints, graphics, and photographica estate libraries; Consignments or merchandise purchased outright for sales. Fifty percent of auctions conducted by mail.

Ten percent buyer's premium; mail and telephone bids accepted; checks with proper ID accepted; Visa and Master Charge accepted. No deposit necessary to hold purchase; payment due when invoiced; pickups within a week, unless shipped.

Sale announcements mailed; catalogs available; written appraisal services offered for fee of $40.00 per hour, minimum: $25.00.

Golden Movement Emporium
Don Kennedy, Auctioneer
2821 Main Street
Santa Monica, California 90405
(213) 396-3193
(Sales held in Los Angeles area—check mailings for directions)

Annual sale held in early summer, featuring architectural antiques such as stained glass windows, doors, room interiors, bars, building facades; consignments; property purchased for sales.

No buyer's premium; mail and telephone bids not accepted; checks accepted with previously established credit; American Express, Master Charge, and Visa accepted. Full payment due day of sale; pickups as arranged.

Sale announcements and catalogs mailed; written appraisals offered for variable fee.

International Antique Center and Auction Gallery
Don Holcomb, John Boudier, Auctioneers
3576 Santa Rosa Avenue
Santa Rosa, California 95401
(707) 584-0438
(Half block north of Todd Road Exit off Interstate 101)

At least one sale monthly, featuring antiques and general merchandise, held on Sundays at 11:00 a.m.; specialized sales feature early American antiques, including cooking and farming implements; books and paper collectibles; dolls; estate sales; consignments; merchandise purchased for sales.

No buyer's premium; mail and telephone bids accepted; checks with proper ID accepted; no credit cards. Purchases must be paid for in full day of sale; one-third deposit necessary to hold absentee bid; pickups within five days.

Sale announcements mailed; oral and written appraisals offered for variable fee.

Scottsdale Auction Gallery
Michael Kalman, Auctioneer
6518 Van Nuys Boulevard
Van Nuys, California 91401
(213) 780-1558

Specializing in sales of American Indian and Western art; frequent sales every month; estate sales; consignments; merchandise purchased for sales.

No buyer's premium; mail and telephone bids accepted; checks with proper ID accepted; Visa and Master Charge accepted; credit established with bank letter. Purchases held with a 10% deposit: full payment and pickups within 10 days.

Sale announcements mailed; some catalogs; written appraisals offered for variable fee.

Edward's Drive-In Swap Meet   W   XXXX
4469 Live Oak Avenue
Arcadia, California 91006
(213) 447-9266
Contact: Mr. Cisneros
(Three miles west of the 605 Freeway)

Indoor market; 1,000 dealers; began in 1970; open Saturday and Sunday, 6:00 a.m. to 3:30 p.m.; admission 25¢ Saturday, 35¢ Sunday; space rental: $2.50 Saturday, $4.50 Sunday for 4' x 10'; no reservations needed.

Variety of antiques, collectibles, new merchandise, secondhand items, produce and crafts; food; restrooms; parking; nearby motels.

Stagecoach Territory: Big Red Barn Flea Market   W   XXXX
1000 Highway 101
Aromas, California 95004
(408) 422-1271
(Fifteen miles north of Salinas, forty miles south of San Jose)

Outdoor market; 325 dealers; began in 1970; open Saturday and Sunday, 7:00 a.m. to 5:00 p.m., year round; shops inside Barn, 10:00 a.m. to 5:00 p.m., all week; $1.00 admission per car; space rental: $7.00 Saturday, $8.00 Sunday for 11' x 27'; reservations advisable.

Quality antiques and collectibles, some produce; food; wine and cheese room; restrooms; parking; nearby motels.

Campbell Center Flea Market ★ M XX
1775 Winchester Boulevard
Campbell, California 95008
(408) 378-9191
Contact: M.C. "Ollie" Olszewski
(Highway 17 to Hamilton, left on Winchester to Campbell Center)

Outdoor market; 60 dealers; began in 1972; open second Saturday and Sunday of every month; free admission; space rental: $5.00 per day for 20' x 20'; no reservations needed.

Mostly antiques and collectibles, some crafts and secondhand items; food; restrooms; parking; nearby motels; auctions in spring and fall.

A C Flea Market W XXXX
20820 Oak Street
Castro Valley, California 94546
(415) 582-0346
Contact: Tom Laber

Indoor/outdoor market; 300 dealers; began in 1968; open every Friday, Saturday, Sunday, 6:00 a.m. to 5:00 p.m.; free admission; space rental: $9.00 for 12' x 25'; reservations needed.

Wide variety of merchandise including antiques, collectibles, new and used items, and produce; food; restrooms; parking; nearby motels.

Ceres Penny Market W XXXX
Whitmore and Blaker Streets
PO Box 35
Ceres, California 95307
(209) 537-3323
Contact: George B. Enck, 2730 Reeding Avenue, Ceres, California 95307, (209) 538-1252
(On Highway 99, three miles south of Modesto or seventy-two miles south of Sacramento)

Outdoor market; 300 sellers; began in 1957; open every Sunday, 5:00 a.m. to 3:00 p.m., year round; 25¢ to 50¢ per car admission; space rental: $7.00 for 20' x 40'; reservations needed.

Mostly secondhand and household items, a lot of new merchandise; few antiques and collectibles; food; parking; restrooms; nearby motels.

Maclin Open-Air Market and Auctions ★ W XXXX
1902 Valley Boulevard
Colton, California
(714) 877-0790
Contact: Bradley D. Larsen, 7407 Riverside Drive, Ontario, California 91761,
(714) 984-5131
(Take Pepper Street Turnoff—off Highway 10—to Valley)

Outdoor market; 550 sellers; began in 1949; open Thursday and Saturday, 7:30
a.m. to dusk, year round; free admission; space rental: $15.00 for covered booth;
reservations recommended.

Mostly new merchandise; few antiques, collectibles and crafts; food; restrooms; parking; nearby motels; furniture and general merchandise auctions on
Thursdays.

De Anza College Flea Market M XXXX
21250 Stevens Creek Boulevard
Cupertino, California 95014
(408) 996-4946
Contact: Sharon J. Kemp, Associated Students of De Anza College, 21250
Stevens Creek Boulevard, Cupertino, California 95014
(Highway 280 North, S'Vale/Saratoga Exit to Stevens Creek)

Outdoor market on college campus; 500 sellers; began in 1970; open first
Saturday of every month, 8:00 a.m. to 4:00 p.m.; free admission; space rental:
$8.00 for 26' x 13' booth; reservations needed prior to the 15th of each month.

Mostly secondhand items, a lot of new merchandise and antiques, some
collectibles and crafts; student-run food concessions; restrooms; parking; nearby
motels.

Escondido Swap Meet
635 West Mission Avenue
Escondido, California 92025
(714) 745-3100
Contact: Mike Daniels
(I-15 Freeway to Escondido, then Valley Parkway off Ramp East, and go
north on Quince to Mission Avenue)

Indoor/outdoor market; several hundred dealers; open every Friday, Saturday,
and Sunday, year round except Christmas Day; 35¢ admission; space rental:
$5.50 per 500 square foot booth; no reservations needed.

Variety of new and used merchandise, antiques and collectibles, crafts and
produce; food; restrooms; parking; nearby motels.

Redwood Flea Market XX
Redwood Acres Fairgrounds
3750 Harris Street
Eureka, California
Contact: Paul Krebs, 2235 Broadway, Eureka, California 95501, (707) 442-2667

Note: Listings are alphabetical by town.

Indoor market; 100 dealers; began in 1971; inquire about dates; 25 admission; space rental: $6.00 for 3' x 8'; reservations needed.

Mostly collectibles and antiques, some new and used merchandise, crafts and produce; food; restrooms; parking; nearby motels.

Historic Folsom Annual Flea Market
Historic Folsom Annual Peddlar's Faire   A   XXXX
Sutter Street
Folsom, California 95630
(916) 351-0824
Contact: Bonnie McAdams, Sutter Street Merchants' Association, PO Box 515, Folsom, California 95630
(From I-80, turn at Greenback Lane or Madison Avenue; from Highway 50 [Freeway] turn at Folsom or Scott Road)

Outdoor market; 325 dealers; began in 1966; Flea Market usually third Sunday in April; Faire usually third Sunday in September; $1.00 admission; space rental: $30.00 for 7' x 10'; reservations needed.

Mostly antiques and collectibles; food; restrooms; parking; nearby motels.

Cherry Swap Meet and Auction   ★   W   XXXX
4640 South Cherry Avenue
Fresno, California 93706
(209) 266-9856
Contact: M. Frank Meyer
(Two miles south of Jensen Avenue Off Ramp from Highway 99)

Outdoor market under shade trees; 500 dealers; began in 1935; open every Tuesday, Saturday and Sunday, 6:30 a.m. to 4:00 p.m., year round; 50 admission; space rental: $6.00 large area, many with table; no reservations needed.

Mostly secondhand and household items, some new merchandise, few antiques and collectibles; four food concessions; parking; restrooms; nearby motels; miscellaneous auction Tuesday and Saturday.

Galt Flea Market   ★   XXXX
1050 "C" Street
Galt, California 95632
(209) 745-2437
Contact: Gladys Martinez, 820 Lincoln Way, Galt, California 95632, (209) 745-2437, or City of Galt, City Hall, (209) 745-4535
(Highway 99 to Central Galt Exit, go to top of overpass, turn right going south to market, at old Sacramento County Fairgrounds, can walk from town)

Outdoor market; began about 1935; 250 sellers; open Tuesday 1:00 p.m. to 5:00 p.m., Wednesday 5:30 a.m. to 4:00 p.m., year round; free admission; space rental: $6.00 for 8' x 4' table or space; no reservations needed.

Mostly new and secondhand merchandise, some good antiques and collectibles; eight lunch wagons; portable toilets; parking; motel seven miles away; miscellaneous auction every Wednesday at 9:00.

Vermont Swap Meet   W XXXX
17737 South Vermont Avenue
Gardena, California 90247
(213) 324-0923
Contact: David Underwood
(Harbor Exit to Artesic Exit, or 91 Freeway to Vermont Avenue)

Outdoor market; 650 dealers; began in 1970; open every Saturday and Sunday, 6:00 a.m. to 3:00 p.m.; 50 admission; space rental: $8.00 to $9.00 for 10' x 20'; reservations needed.

Mostly secondhand and household items, some new merchandise; food; restrooms; parking; nearby motels.

Rotary Flea Market   A XXX
Fairgrounds
King City, California 93930
Contact: Moylen Peterson, King City Rotary, PO Box 611, King City, California 93930, (408) 385-3889
(Take Canal Street Exit from Highway 101 to Division Street)

Indoor/outdoor market; 200 sellers; began in 1969; held first Sunday in April every year; 75 admission; space rental: $10.00 for first space ($7.50 additional spaces), 10' x 15' outdoor, 10' x 10' indoor; reservations needed.

Mostly new and secondhand merchandise, alot of antiques and collectibles, arts and crafts; food; restrooms; parking; nearby motels.

Peddlers Village U.S.A.   W XXXX
Highway 74 at I-15
Lake Elsinore, California 92330
(714) 674-9974
Contact: Jerry Harmatz, 106 South Main Street, Lake Elsinore, California 92330, (714) 674-2817

Outdoor market on 24 acres; 300 sellers; began in 1970; open every Saturday and Sunday, year round; free admission; space rental: $45.00 monthly for 10' x 20' sheds, $3.00 daily for open spaces with 4' x 8' tables; reservations needed for sheds.

Variety of merchandise, mostly new, some antiques and collectibles; snack bar, potluck dinner last Sunday every month; restrooms; parking; hookups for travel trailers; live country music; nearby motels.

Lancaster Flea Market   A XXXX
155 East Avenue I
Lancaster, California 93534
Contact: Betty Smith, Lancaster Chamber of Commerce, 44943 Tenth Street West, Lancaster, California 93534, (805) 948-4518
(Highway 14 to Avenue I Off Ramp; east on Avenue I to State Fairgrounds)

Indoor/outdoor market; 800 dealers; began about 1960; held first Sunday in October, third Sunday in May, 9:00 a.m. to 5:00 p.m., 25 to 50 admission; space rental: $10.00 outside, $15.00 inside; reservations advisable, one month in advance, remaining spaces rented early morning of sale.

Mostly new merchandise, some antiques, fewer collectibles and secondhand items; food; restrooms; parking; nearby motels.

Lodi District Chamber of Commerce Flea Market   A   XXXX
Lodi Wine and Grape Festival Grounds
413 East Lockeford Street
Lodi, California 95240
(209) 334-4773
Contact: Lodi District Chamber of Commerce, 215 West Oak Street, PO Box 386, Lodi, California 95240
(Two blocks off Highway 99, at the central Lodi exit)

Indoor/outdoor market; 500 sellers; began in 1973; held first Sunday in May and October; admission 50; space rental: $10.00 for 12' x 12' outdoors, $20.00 for 10' x 10' indoors; reservations needed.

Mostly secondhand household items and new merchandise, some antiques and collectibles; food; restrooms; parking; nearby motels.

Morgan Hill Flea Market   W   XXX
140 East Main Street
Morgan Hill, California 95037
(408) 779-3809
Contact: James Ahlin
(Route 101 to Morgan Hill, left at the bank to Main Street)

Outdoor market under shade trees; 125 sellers; began in 1963; open every Saturday and Sunday, 7:00 a.m. to 7:00 p.m., year round; free admission; space rental: $6.00 for 3' x 12' table; reservations needed.

Mostly secondhand and household items, some new merchandise, antiques and crafts; food; restrooms; parking; nearby motels.

Claypool's Flea Market   X
725 Broadway
Needles, California 92363
(714) 326-2109

Outdoor market; 15 to 20 dealers; open second and fourth Saturday of each month, 8:00 a.m. to dark, year round; free admission; free space rental; no reservations needed.

Mostly secondhand and household items, some new merchandise and antiques; baked goods and coffee available; no restrooms; parking; nearby motels.

Oceanside Swap Meet   W   XXXX
3480 Mission Avenue
Oceanside, California 92054
(714) 757-5286
Contact: Howard Morgan, 635 West Mission Avenue, Escondido, California 92025, (714) 745-3100
(I-5 Freeway to Oceanside, take Mission Avenue Exit off Ramp East)

Outdoor market; several hundred dealers; began in 1973; open Saturday, Sunday and Monday, 6:30 a.m. to 3:00 p.m., year round except Christmas Day; 35¢ admission; space rental: $5.50 for 500 square foot booth; no reservations needed.

Variety of new and used merchandise, antiques, collectibles, crafts, art objects; food; restrooms; parking; nearby motels.

Maclin Open-Aire Market and Auctions ★ W XXXX
7407 Riverside Drive
Ontario, California 91761
Contact: Bradley D. Larsen, (714) 984-5131
(One mile east of Euclid Avenue, Highway 83)

Outdoor market; originally a livestock market; 550 sellers; began as auction in 1936, flea market began in 1957; open Tuesday and Sunday 7:00 a.m. to dusk, year round; free admission; space rental: $15.00 for covered booth; reservations needed.

Mostly new merchandise, some crafts and produce; few antiques and collectibles; food; restrooms; parking; nearby motels; livestock, furniture and general merchandise auctions on Tuesdays.

Rose Bowl Antique Flea Market M XXXX
Rose Bowl at Brookside Park
Pasadena, California
(213) 588-4411
Contact: R.G. Canning Enterprises, PO Box 400, Maywood, California 90270, (213) 587-5100
(210 Freeway to Rose Bowl Drive)

Outdoor market; 1,500 dealers; began in 1968; open second Sunday of every month, year round; $2.50 admission; space rental: $40.00 for 10' x 20' plus space for car; reservations needed.

Mostly antiques and collectibles, some new merchandise and crafts; food; restrooms; parking; nearby motels.

Beach School Flea Market A XXX
100 Lake Avenue
Piedmont, California 94611
Contact: Flea Market Chairperson, c/o Beach School
(Exit off Route 580 at Grand Avenue turn left four-fifths mile to Linda, up hill to school)

Outdoor market; 135 dealers; began in 1971; held first Sunday in October, 10:00 a.m. to 4:00 p.m.; admission charge; space rental: $10.00 for 10' x 10'; reservations needed by August.

All secondhand and household items; food; restrooms; parking; nearby motels.

Mission Drive-In Swap Meet W XXXX
Mission and Ramone
Pomona, California 91766
(714) 628-7943
Contact: Ron Bacon, 12353 Napa Drive, Chino, California 91710

Indoor/outdoor market; 500 dealers; began in 1955; open Saturday and Sunday, 6:00 a.m. to 3:00 p.m., year round; 35¢ admission; space rental: $4.00 Saturday, $5.00 Sunday for 18' x 20'; no reservations needed.

Mostly new and secondhand merchandise, some antiques and collectibles, very few crafts; food; restrooms; parking; nearby motels.

Epperson Brothers Auction and Flea Market ★ W XXX

5091 Fig Tree Lane
Redding, California 96002
(916) 365-7242
Contact: Jack Epperson, (916) 365-4612
(From Highway 44, take Airport Road south one and one-half miles to Fig Tree Lane, one mile east to market)

Outdoor market with large shade trees; 50 to 150 dealers; began in 1962; open every Saturday 9:00 a.m. to 5:00 p.m., Sunday 6:00 a.m. to 5:00 p.m., year round; admission 50¢ on Sunday; space rental: tables $3.00 Saturday, $5.00 Sunday, sheds $55.00 per month; no reservations needed.

Lots of secondhand and household items, some new merchandise, crafts, antiques, and collectibles; four food concessions, one bar; restrooms; parking; nearby motels; auctions first and third Wednesdays at 6:30 p.m.

Auction City and Flea Market ★ W XXXX

8521 Folsom Boulevard
Sacramento, California 95826
(916) 383-0880 or (916) 383-0950
Contact: Harold Hennessey
(Highway 50 to Watt Avenue South, right on Folsom Boulevard)

Indoor/outdoor market; 300 dealers; began in 1965; open Saturday and Sunday, 9:00 a.m. to 5:00 p.m.; free admission; space rental: $8.80 for first 4' x 8' table, additional tables $4.40; reservations recommended.

Mostly antiques and collectibles, with new and used merchandise; food; restrooms; parking; nearby motels and trailer park; auctions of new merchandise, 11:00 a.m. both days.

Swap-N-Save W XXXX

689 South "E" Street
San Bernardino, California 42408
(714) 885-0201
Contact: Tom or Ted Scharf, 7014 Conejo, San Bernardino, California 92404, (714) 888-9076
(I-15 to San Bernardino; Mill Street Off Ramp, east to "E" Street)

Market on paved lot; 500 sellers; began about 1970; open every Sunday 6:00 a.m. to 2:00 p.m., year round; 25¢ admission; space rental: $5.00 for 10' x 18' area plus room for vehicle; reservations needed.

Mostly secondhand and used merchandise, some antiques and collectibles; food; restrooms; parking; nearby motels.

San Fernando Swap Meet and Flea Market   W   XXXX
585 Glenoaks Boulevard
San Fernando, California 91340
(213) 361-9956
Contact: Harold G. Solie, 503 Huntington Street, San Fernando, California
91340
(Freeway 118 to Glenoaks Boulevard)

Outdoor market; 500 sellers; began in 1972; open every Saturday, Sunday, and
Tuesday; $1.00 admission; space rental: $6.00, $7.00 and $10.00 for 16' x 36' area;
no reservations needed.

Mostly new merchandise, some secondhand items, very few antiques and
collectibles; food; restrooms; parking; nearby motels.

San Juan Bautista Flea Market   A   XXXX
Route 156
San Juan Bautista, California 95045
(408) 623-4666
Contact: Rebecca McGovern
(Off Route 156, from US 101; forty-five miles south of San Jose)

Outdoor market; 500 dealers; began in 1968; held annually, on first Sunday of
August; free admission; space rental: $30.00 for 7' x 10' booth; reservations
needed.

Mostly antiques and collectibles; some miscellaneous merchandise; food;
restrooms; parking; nearby motels.

Flea-Esta   A   XXXX
Downtown Parking Lot
San Rafael, California
Contact: San Rafael Chamber of Commerce, 633 Fifth Avenue, San Rafael,
California 94901, (415) 454-4163
(Near Highway 101, twenty miles north of San Francisco)

Outdoor market; 220 dealers; began in 1978; held first Sunday in May, 9:00 a.m.
to 4:00 p.m.; free admission; space rental: $20.00 for one parking space;
reservations needed.

Mostly secondhand items, new merchandise and crafts, some antiques and
collectibles; food; portable toilets; parking; nearby motels.

Skyview Flea Market   W   XXXX
2240 Soquel Drive
Santa Cruz, California 95060
(408) 429-8775
Contact: Joe Costanza, 101 Alamo Avenue, Santa Cruz, California 95060, (408)
429-8775
(Off Highway 1 at Soquel Drive, across from Dominican Hospital)

Outdoor market on grounds of drive-in theater; 150 to 300 sellers; began in 1972;
open every Saturday and Sunday, year round; admission 25¢ Saturday, $1.00

Note: Listings are alphabetical by town.

Sunday; space rental: $3.00 Saturday, $10.00 Sunday, for 20' x 20' area; no reservations needed, first come—first served.

Mostly antiques and collectibles, some secondhand and new merchandise; snack bar; drive-in's restrooms; parking; nearby motels.

40-8 Flea Market   XXXX
State Route 12
Santa Rosa, California 95405
Contact: Flea Market Chairman, PO Box 9191, Santa Rosa, California 95405
(Directly opposite Sonoma County Fairgrounds)

Outdoor market; 306 sellers; began in 1968; held one Sunday in May, June, August, September and October; free admission; space rental: $6.00 for 18' x 18' paved surface; reservations needed.

Mostly antiques and secondhand merchandise, some new merchandise and collectibles; snack bar; restrooms; parking; several nearby motels.

Santa Rosa Indoor Flea Market   W   XXXX
Sonoma County Fairgrounds
Santa Rosa, California 95405
(707) 539-7307
Contact: Mr. or Mrs. Mark
(Call for directions)

Indoor market; 250 dealers; began in 1970; open Sundays, mid-October through April; 25 admission; space rental: $7.00 for 8' x 10'; reservations needed.

Mostly secondhand items, antiques and collectibles; food; restrooms; parking; nearby motels.

Saugus Swap Meet   W   XXXX
Saugus Speedway Grounds
25000 Soledad Canyon Road
Saugus, California 91350
(805) 259-3886
Contact: Marshall Wilkings, PO Box S, 22500 Soledad Canyon Road, Saugus, California 91350
(I-5 to Valencia Boulevard, east three miles)

Outdoor market; 1,000 dealers; began in 1963; open Sunday, 6:00 a.m. (sellers), 7:00 a.m. (buyers) to 3:00 p.m., year round; $1.00 admission; space rental: $12.00 to $22.00 for 20' x 16'; no reservations needed.

Mostly new merchandise with the remainder a variety of antiques, collectibles, secondhand items, produce, crafts; food; restrooms; parking; one nearby motel.

Midgley's Country Flea Market   W XXXX
2200 Gravenstein Highway South
Sebastopol, California 95472
(707) 823-7874
Contact: C.H. Midgley
(North on Highway 101 to Sebastopol, take Cotati Turn-off; west on 116 or
south on Gravenstein Highway five miles)

Outdoor market; 450 dealers; began in 1971; open Friday, Saturday and Sunday,
6:30 a.m. to 5:00 p.m., year round; free admission; space rental: $5.00 for 4' x 8'
table ($1.00 on Friday); no reservations needed.
    Mostly secondhand and new merchandise, some antiques, collectibles, crafts
and produce; home-cooked food; restrooms; parking; two nearby motels.

Spring Valley Swap Meet   W XXXX
6377 Quarry Road
Spring Valley, California 92077
(714) 463-1194
(Highway 5 South to 805 South to South Bay Freeway East, seven and one-
half miles to Quarry Road)

Outdoor market; 1,000 dealers; began in 1972; open every Saturday and Sunday
7:00 a.m. to 4:30 p.m., year round; 50¢ admission; space rental: $5.00 Saturday,
$7.00 Sunday, for a paved 10' x 23' surface; no reservations needed.
    Mostly household items, secondhand and new merchandise, very few an-
tiques or collectibles; snack bar and vendors; restrooms; parking; six motels and
campgrounds nearby.

Stockton Flea Market   ★ W XXX
2542 South Eldorado Street
Stockton, California 95206
(209) 465-9933
Contact: Roy Harwell, 1776 Morefield Avenue, Stockton, California 95206,
(209) 462-5066
(From I-5 take Eighth Street Off Ramp to Eldorado South to flea market;
from Highway 99 take Charter Way Off Ramp south to Eldorado South)

Indoor market; 200 sellers; began in 1965; open every Saturday and Sunday, 8:00
a.m. to 5:00 p.m., year round; free admission; space rental: $25.00 per weekend
for 100 square feet, reservations needed.
    Mostly household items, secondhand and new merchandise, scattered an-
tiques, collectibles and crafts; one restaurant, two snack bars; restrooms;
parking; nearby motels; new merchandise auctions every weekend.

Cherry Chase Center Antique Trade Faire   M XXX
El Camino and Bernardo
Sunnyvale, California
Contact: Betty Rowland, 835 Mary Avenue, Sunnyvale, California 94087,
(408) 736-7222
(Forty miles south of San Francisco on Highway 82)

Outdoor market; 200 dealers; began in 1971; held first Sunday of every month, 10:00 a.m. to 5:00 p.m., year round; free admission; space rental: $14.00 for 12' x 14'; reservations needed.

Only quality antiques and collectibles including toys, furniture, jewelry, Indian artifacts and silver; food available nearby; restrooms; parking; nearby motels.

Star Lite Drive-In Swap Meet   W   X
Gorgonio Drive
29 Palms, California 92277
Contact: Ray Kinsman, 6937 Elm Avenue, 29 Palms, California 92277, (714) 367-7893
(Three blocks east of stop light on Highway 62 and Adobe Road, turn left, go two blocks)

Outdoor swap market; 30 to 40 dealers; began in 1978; open Sundays, 6:00 a.m. to dark, September to June only, closed for heat in July and August; free admission; space rental: $3.00 for 20' x 20'; no reservations needed.

Mostly garage-sale merchandise, some antiques and collectibles; food; restrooms; parking; nearby motels.

Spring of Fall Chamber of Commerce Flea Market   A   XX
Andrew's Park
East Monte Vista Avenue
Vacaville, California 95688
(707) 448-6424
Contact: Thomas McNunn, 400 East Monte Vista Avenue, Vacaville, California 95688, (707) 448-6424
(On I-80 between Sacramento and San Francisco)

Outdoor market; 100 sellers; began in 1974; held two days a year; in April and October; 9:00 a.m. to 5:00 p.m.; free admission; space rental: $8.00, $13.00 and $22.00 for 10' x 10', 10' x 15', 20' x 20'; reservations needed.

Mostly secondhand and household items, small percentage of antiques, collectibles, crafts and new merchandise; food concession; restrooms; parking; nearby motels.

Napa-Vallejo Flea Market   ★   W   XXXX
303 Kelly Road
Vallejo, California 94590
(707) 226-8862
Contact: Nelson Harding
(Halfway between Napa and Vallejo on Highway 29)

Indoor/outdoor market; 500 sellers; began in 1949; open every Sunday, 6:00 a.m. to 5:00 p.m., year round; free admission; space rental: starts at $7.00 per space, with table; reservations needed for three-table spaces.

Mostly new merchandise, some secondhand, fewer antiques and collectibles; two snack bars; restrooms; parking; nearby motels; auctions usually held every other month.

Visalia Sales Yard ★ W XXX
29660 Road 152
Visalia, California 93277
(209) 734-9092
Contact: Paul W. Furnas, 1216 South Central Avenue, Visalia, California
93277, (209) 733-5270
(From Highway 99 take Freeway 198 East through town to Lover's Lane and
go north)

Outdoor market; 150 dealers; began in 1950; open Thursday, year round; free
admission; space rental: $4.00 per 10' of space; no reservations needed.

Mostly secondhand items and new merchandise, some antiques, collectibles
and produce; restaurant on premises; restrooms; parking; nearby motels;
antique and used furniture auctions every Thursday at 2:00 p.m.

The Flea Market Inc. ★ W XXXX
12000 Berryessa Road
San Jose, California 95133
(408) 289-1550
Contact: John Linhart
(Between Highway 101 and Freeway 680)

Outdoor market; 1,200 to 1,800 dealers; began in 1960; open Saturday, Sunday
and holidays, 7:30 a.m. to dusk, year round; free admission; space rental: $12.50
per day for 14' x 20'; no reservations needed.

Mostly secondhand and new merchandise, few antiques, collectibles or
produce; American and Mexican food; entertainment; restrooms; parking;
nearby motels; auctions every Saturday and Sunday.

COLORADO

Connell Auctions
Bob Connell, Auctioneer
200 First Street, PO Box 1027
Ault, Colorado 80610
(303) 834-1113 or (303) 834-1148
(Sixty-five miles north of Denver)

Specializing in oak furniture, from 1900 to 1910; approximately eight sales a year
as merchandise becomes available; estate sales; consignments; property purchased for sales.

No buyer's premium; mail and telephone bids accepted from established
customers; checks accepted with proper ID; Master Charge and VISA accepted.
Full payment day of sale; pickups within three days.

Sale announcements and some catalogs mailed; oral and written appraisals
offered for negotiable fee.

Pacific Auction, Inc.
Gus Pacific, Auctioneer
9138 North Ninety-fifth Street
Longmont, Colorado 80501
(303) 772-9401
(Thirty-five miles north of Denver)

Antiques and collectibles sales held the first Saturday of each month; general merchandise sold each week; estate sales; consignments; property purchased for sales.

No buyer's premium; mail and telephone bids accepted; checks accepted with proper ID; no credit cards. Full payment day of sale; pickups within 24 hours.

Sale announcements mailed; oral and written appraisals offered for 3% of value of item.

Antique and Collectables Sale   M   XX
City Auditorium
Colorado Springs, Colorado 80903
(303) 475-7324
Contact: Harvey Black, 225 East Brookside, Colorado Springs, Colorado 80906
(Turn off I-25 at Business Exit, four blocks on right)

Indoor market; 80 dealers; began in 1963; held first weekend of each month; 50¢ admission; space rental: $15.00 for 8' x 30'; reservations needed.

Antiques, collectibles, new merchandise, arts and crafts; food; restrooms; parking; nearby motels.

Mile High Flea Market, Inc.   W   XXXX
5200 East Sixty-fourth Avenue
Commerce City, Colorado 80022
(302) 289-4656
Contact: Andrew L. Hermes
(Call for directions)

Outdoor market; 500 to 800 dealers; began in 1976; open every Saturday and Sunday, 6:00 a.m. to 5:00 p.m., year round; admission 25¢; space rental: $7.00 for 12' x 25' paved area; no reservations needed.

Variety of merchandise including secondhand and household goods, new merchandise, antiques and collectibles; food; restrooms; parking; nearby motels.

Denver Antique Market   W   XX
2727 West Twenty-seventh Avenue
Denver, Colorado 80211
(303) 455-9175 or (303) 455-9948
Contact: Andy or Sally Burnett, 11306 East Seventh Avenue, Aurora, Colorado 80010, (303) 364-9469
(Two blocks east of North Federal Boulevard)

Indoor market; 65 dealers; began in 1971; open every Saturday and Sunday, 10:00

a.m. to 6:00 p.m., year round; 50¢ admission; space rental: from $27.50 for 8' x 10' booth to $38.50 for 8' x 20'; two-day set-ups only; reservations needed.

Antiques with some collectibles and art; snack bar; restrooms; private parking; nearby motels.

NEVADA

Fernley Fun Fair Flea Market ★ W X
Exit 46 off I-80 East
Fernley, Nevada 89408
(702) 575-4774
Contact: Vern Heater, PO Box 481, Fernley, Nevada 89408, (702) 575-2720
(Thirty miles east of Reno)

Indoor/outdoor market; 30 dealers; began in 1977; open Friday, Saturday and Sunday, year round; free admission; space rental: $4.00 to $10.00 per day for spaces 10' x 24' and larger; no reservations needed.

Mostly new and secondhand merchandise; some antiques, collectibles and crafts; food; restrooms; parking; nearby motels; auctions Sundays at 1:00 p.m.

I-15 Swap Meet W X
3328 Losee Road
North Las Vegas, Nevada 89030
(702) 642-8923
Contact: Wayne and Perley Terry, 6349 Parsifal Place, Las Vegas, Nevada 89107, (702) 878-1914
(Take the Cheyenne Ramp off I-15, go left over Freeway, then right)

Indoor/outdoor market; 50 dealers; began in 1979; open Saturday and Sunday, 8:30 a.m. to 4:00 p.m.; 50¢ admission; space rental:indoors $10.00 per day for 10' x 10', outdoors $6.00; no reservations needed.

Equal variety of second items, new merchandise, antiques, collectibles, crafts and produce; snack bar and deli; restrooms; parking; several nearby motels.

El Rancho Flea Market W XX
555 El Rancho Drive
Sparks, Nevada 89431
(702) 329-7109
Contact: Michael Pontrelli, 2695 West Plumbstone, Reno, Nevada 89509
(Take Highway 80 to B-4th Street)

Outdoor market; 40 to 70 dealers; began in 1977; open Saturday and Sunday, 8:00 a.m. to 4:00 p.m., March through November; 25¢ admission or 50¢ per car; space rental: $6.00 first time, $4.00 each time thereafter for 18'; no reservations needed.

Mostly secondhand or household items, Western ranch "junk," some new merchandise and collectibles; food; restrooms; parking; nearby motels.

Note: Listings are alphabetical by town.

NEW MEXICO

Pattin Auction Company
Ronald Pattin, Auctioneer
411 Marble Northeast
Albuquerque, New Mexico 87102
Auctions: 6403 Coor Southwest
Albuquerque, New Mexico 87105
(505) 242-6329

Antiques and collectibles sale twice a month; featuring Victorian, early American and English furniture, ruby glass, carnival glass; estate sales; consignments only; no property purchased for sales.

Ten percent buyer's premium; mail and telephone bids accepted; checks accepted with proper ID; certified checks preferred from out-of-state purchasers; no credit cards. Full payment night of sale; pickups within one day.

Sale announcements mailed; written appraisals offered for negotiable fee.

Show and Sell   W XXXX
State Fairgrounds
Albuquerque, New Mexico 87108
(505) 255-8255
Contact: Robert Fulton, PO Box 3384, Albuquerque, New Mexico 87190
(Exit I-40 at Louisiana Street, go south four blocks)

Outdoor market; 700 dealers; began in 1969; open every Saturday and Sunday, weather permitting, except September; free admission; space rental: $5.00 for 12' x 16'; no reservations needed.

Mostly secondhand and new merchandise, few antiques and collectibles; food; restrooms; parking; nearby motels.

Trader Jack's Flea Market   W XXXX
2850 Cerrillos Road
Santa Fe, New Mexico 87501
(505) 455-7874
Contact: Jack or Caggie Daniels, PO Box O, Pajoaque Station, Santa Fe, New Mexico 87501
(One block north of Holiday Inn)

Outdoor market; 400 dealers; began in 1975; open Friday, Saturday and Sunday, year round; free admission; space rental: $4.00 per day for 12'; no reservations except by the month.

Mostly secondhand and household items and produce/livestock, some antiques, very little new merchandise; food; restrooms; parking; nearby motels.

OKLAHOMA

Sam's
Sam Driggers, Auctioneer
1930 East Highway 66
El Reno, Oklahoma 73036
(405) 262-5471 or (405) 262-5600
(Thirty miles west of Oklahoma City)

Antique furniture sale held first Saturday of every month from 6:00 p.m. to midnight, 600 to 700 lots of predominantly Victorian and turn-of-the-century pieces; antique glass, clocks, lamps, and small items sold on preceding Friday at 6:00 p.m.; estate sales; consignments only; no property purchased for sales.

No buyer's premium; mail and telephone bids accepted with a 50% deposit; checks with proper ID accepted; Master Charge and Visa accepted. Purchases held with a 25% deposit; full payment in five days; pickups within ten days.

Sale announcements mailed.

Antiques Inc.
Dean Kruse, Auctioneer
PO Box 1887
Muskogee, Oklahoma 74401
(918) 683-3281
(Auctions held at International Petroleum Exposition Building at Fairgrounds in Tulsa, Oklahoma)

Annual sale of antique automobiles held in June at the IPE Building; also featuring wheels, English antiques, silver, maps and documents; estate sales; consignments; property purchased for sales.

No buyer's premium; telephone bids accepted; checks accepted with bank reference; Visa and Master Charge accepted. Full payment within three days; pickups within three days.

Sale announcements and catalogs mailed; oral or written appraisals offered for negotiable fee.

Williams Auction Company
Bill Williams, Auctioneer
5528 Forty-ninth West Avenue, South
Tulsa, Oklahoma 74107
(918) 446-4307

Two-day sales held approximately every six weeks on Saturday and Sunday at 11:00 a.m.; featuring primarily antiques and collectibles, including much antique furniture; estate sales; consignments; property purchased for sales.

No buyer's premium; mail and telephone bids not accepted; in-state checks accepted with proper ID; out-of-state checks accepted with bank letter of credit; Master Charge and Visa accepted. Full payment at time of sale; pickups within one week.

Sale announcements mailed.

Lawton Flea Market Inc. ★ XXX

1130 East Gore Boulevard
Lawton, Oklahoma 73501
Contact: Joseph Reynolds, 910 B Avenue, Lawton, Oklahoma 73501,
(405) 355-1292
(Near Pioneer Expressway and Montego Bay Motel)

Outdoor market under shade trees; 150 dealers; began in 1974; open Friday,
Saturday and Sunday, first and third weekend of every month; free admission;
space rental: $4.00 for 15' x 20'; reservations helpful.

Lots of antiques, secondhand items and new merchandise, some collectibles;
food; restrooms; parking; nearby motel; campground; occasional auctions.

Flea Market M XX

Oklahoma City State Fairground
Oklahoma City, Oklahoma 74104
Contact: Ted Lefler, 2019 East Twelfth, Winfield, Kansas
(I-40 and May Avenue)

Indoor market; 100 dealers; began in 1980; held once a month, on Saturday and
Sunday, 10:00 a.m. to 6:00 p.m.; 50¢ admission; space rental: $20.00 to $25.00 per
weekendfor 10' x 10'; reservations needed.

Mostly antiques, collectibles, secondhand merchandise, and art objects,
some crafts; food; restrooms; parking; nearby motels.

Perry Flea Market M XX

Downtown Square
Perry, Oklahoma 73077
Contact: Emma Lou Hasenfratz, Box 724, Perry, Oklahoma 73077,
(405) 336-4676

Outdoor market; 60 dealers; began in 1973; open first Saturday of each month;
free admission; space rental: $3.00 for two parking spaces; reservations needed.

Mostly antiques, collectibles and secondhand merchandise, some crafts;
food; restrooms; parking; nearby motels.

Flea Market M X

Cimarron Country Ballroom
Stillwater, Oklahoma 74074
(405) 624-8538
Contact: Gene and Gail Pendleton, Route 4, Box 59, Stillwater, Oklahoma
74074
(Six and one-half miles south of Stillwater on Highway 177)

Indoor/outdoor market; 30 to 40 dealers; began about 1976; open third Saturday
of each month, 7:00 a.m. to 4:00 p.m., year round; free admission; space rental:
$4.00 for a 2' x 8' table, $6.00 for two tables; reservations needed unless you
bring your own table.

Mostly collectibles and used merchandise, some new merchandise, crafts, a
few antiques; food; restrooms; parking; nearby motels.

Persimmon Hollow Antique Village & Flea Market   **W X**
Seventy-first Street and Garnett Road
Tulsa, Oklahoma 74107
(918) 252-7113
Contact: Roy L. Baker, 1215 South Onasso, Tulsa, Oklahoma 74107
(One block east of intersection)

Indoor/outdoor market; 25 dealers; began in 1979; open Saturday and Sunday,
9:00 a.m. to 5:00 p.m.; free admission; space rental: waiting list, no reservations
needed.

    Mostly oak furniture, variety of secondhand merchandise, produce, an-
tiques, collectibles; food, restrooms; parking; nearby motels.

Tulsa Flea Market   **W XXX**
Fairgrounds, Youth Building
Tulsa, Oklahoma 74107
(918) 932-9371
Contact: P. Larry, PO Box 4511, Tulsa, Oklahoma 74104, (918) 936-1386
(I-44 to Yale Avenue Exit, north to Twenty-first Street, west two and one-
half miles to Fairgrounds)

Indoor market; 120 dealers; began in 1971; open Saturday, 8:00 a.m. to 5:00 p.m.,
year round; free admission; space rental: $10.00 to $15.00 for 10' x 12';
reservations needed.

    Mostly collectibles and antiques; food; restrooms; parking; nearby motels.

TEXAS

Bogan's Auction Barn
Harold E. Bogan, Auctioneer
Route 3, Box 707
Alvin, Texas 77011
(713) 482-6983, (713) 482-9811, or (713) 649-3002
(Highway 35, four miles south of Pearland; seventeen miles from downtown
Houston)

Weekly sales of American antiques held Thursdays at 7:30 p.m.; estate sales;
consignments only; no property purchased for sales.

    No buyer's premium; mail and telephone bids accepted; checks accepted with
three proper forms of ID; Master Charge and Visa accepted. Full payment day of
sale; pickups within two days.

    Sale announcements mailed; written appraisals offered for minimum fee of
$50.00.

Lufkins

Larry Thompson, Auctioneer
PO Box 9194
Austin, Texas 78766
(512) 345-9729
(Mail bid auctions at this address; other auctions held on site—check mailings for directions)

Antique sales held three or four times a year; specialized sales of Hummel figurines, plates, bells; estate sales; consignments; property purchased for sales.

No buyer's premium; mail and telephone bids accepted; in-state checks or checks from established customers accepted; Visa and Master Charge accepted. Full payment due day of sale, or ten days after invoiced for mail bids; pickups as arranged.

Sale announcements mailed; catalogs for all sales; written appraisals offered for hourly fee of $25.00, at minimum charge of $20.00.

Clements Antiques of Texas, Inc.

Chas W. Clements, Norman Garrett, Jeff Garrett, J.D. Lewis, Sandra C. Garrett, Auctioneers
PO 727
Interstate 20 East at FM Road, 740 Exit
Forney, Texas 75126
(214) 226-1520 or (214) 226-3044
(Twenty minutes east of Dallas)

Specializing in fine arts and antiques; sales generally held second Saturday of each month at noon; specialized sales of paintings, rugs, novelties; estate sales; consignments; merchandise purchased for sales.

Mail and telephone bids accepted; checks with proper ID accepted; American Express, Master Charge and Visa accepted. Purchases must be paid for in full at time of sale; pickups within 14 days.

Mailing list for catalogs and sale announcements available; oral appraisals offered free of charge; written appraisals for an hourly fee of $35.00.

North Texas Auction

Billy Ray McGee, Auctioneer
3623 Decatur
Fort Worth, Texas 76106
(817) 624-3511 and (817) 626-8858

General antiques and collectibles sale held at least twice monthly at 7:00 p.m., generally on Friday nights; estate sales; consignments; property purchased for sales.

No buyer's premium; telephone bids accepted; checks with proper ID accepted; no credit cards. Full payment day of sale; pickups within seven days.

Sale announcements mailed; oral or written appraisals offered for an hourly fee of $25.00.

Harvey's and Sons Auction

Harvey Braswell, Auctioneer
1402-6 West Main Street
Grand Prairie, Texas 75050
(214) 262-5715 or (914) 528-9331
(Highway 80, three miles east of 6 Flags Mall and various locations in Texas, Arkansas and New York)

American antiques and collectibles, some Oriental art, guns, music boxes, clocks, Hummels, featured at sales the third Saturday of every month and preceding Friday at 6:00 p.m.; estate sales; consignments only; no property purchased for sales.

No buyer's premium; mail and telephone bids not accepted; checks accepted with proper ID; Visa and Master Charge accepted. Full payment at time of sale or as arranged; pickups generally within two days.

Sale announcements mailed.

E. & M. Alexander, Auctioneers

Isidor Taylor, Auctioneer
1285 North Post Oak Road
Houston, Texas 77055
(713) 688-5900
(Between Old Katy Road and Hempstead Highway; off Interstate 10)

Weekly auctions held, including specialized sales of clocks and jewelry; all merchandise on consignment basis, none purchased outright; estate sales.

No buyer's premium; mail and telephone bids accepted; checks accepted with proper ID; Visa, American Express and Master Charge accepted. Full payment following sale; pickups within two days.

Sale announcements mailed; some catalogs; written appraisals offered for variable fee.

James Fletcher Galleries

James Fletcher, Auctioneer
2119 Westheimer
Houston, Texas 77098
(713) 527-0822

Specializing in French antiques, particularly country and period furniture from 1700s to early 1900s and cut glass; approximately six yearly sales, no fixed schedule; estate sales; no consignments; property purchased for sales.

No buyer's premium; mail and telephone bids accepted; cashier's checks or local checks with proper ID accepted; out-of-state checks require bank letter of credit; no credit cards. Full payment at time of sale; pickups within one day.

Sale announcements and catalogs mailed.

Note: Listings are alphabetical by town.

Webster's Auction Palace

William I. Webster, Auctioneer
14463 Luthe Road
Houston, Texas 77039
(713) 442-2351 or (713) 442-7131
(South of International Airport)

Weekly antiques sale held every Friday at 7:00 p.m., year-round except holidays; specialized sales feature antique silver and jewelry, McCoy pottery, guns, coins, dolls and doll furniture, glassware, including crystal, Depression glass and art glass; estate sales; consignments only; no property purchased for sales.

No buyer's premium; mail and telephone bids accepted; checks accepted with proper ID; no credit cards. Full payment night of sale; pickups within two days.

Sale announcements mailed.

Kingsville-Edlin Auctions

Bob, Rocky, Pat and Sam Edlin, Auctioneers
1202 North Sixth Street
Kingsville, Texas 78363
(512) 592-1007
334 South Chaparral Street
Corpus Christi, Texas 78401
(512) 882-7253

Features American and English antiques; Kingsville sale held every Friday at 7:00 p.m.; Corpus Christi sale every Saturday at 7:00 p.m.; specialized sales include antique plates, glass, and coins; estate sales; consignments; property purchased for sales.

No buyer's premium; telephone bids sometimes accepted; checks with proper ID accepted; Master Charge and Visa accepted. Purchases held with a 30% deposit; lay-a-way plan available; full payment within 60 days; pickups when convenient.

Sale announcements mailed; written appraisals offered for fee of $25.00 per hour.

A-I Auction House

Ross Lucas, Auctioneer
1905 South Shaver
Pasadena, Texas 77502
(713) 472-3777 or (713) 473-0373

Sales held twice a month on Saturdays at 7:00 p.m.; featuring American antiques with a variety of oak and pine furniture; estate sales; consignments; property purchased for sales.

No buyer's premium; mail and telephone bids not accepted; checks accepted with proper ID; no credit cards. Full payment night of sale; pickups within two weeks.

Sale announcements mailed; appraisals offered for negotiable fee.

Bill Sayre's Auction Service

Bill Sayre, Auctioneer
211 East Pasadena Freeway
Pasadena, Texas 77503
(713) 477-9453

Antiques sales held every Friday night at 7:30 p.m.; alternating English and American antiques every other week, including furniture and furnishings, bric-a-brac, coins, advertising posters; estate sales; consignments only; no property purchased for sales.

No buyer's premium; mail and telephone bids not accepted; traveler's checks, certified checks, or local checks with proper ID accepted; no out-of-state checks or credit cards. Full payment at time of sale; pickups by 5:30 p.m. Monday.

Paul Gaston & Associates, Inc.

Paul Gaston, Auctioneer
104 Ash Bend Drive
Rockwall, Texas 75087
(214) 475-2460
(On-site sales at various locations—check mailings)

Antiques and fine art auction held once a month; machinery and business liquidations held six times a month; estate sales; consignments only; no property purchased for sales.

No buyer's premium; mail and telephone bids not accepted; checks accepted with bank letter of credit; no credit cards. Full payment and most pickups day of sale.

Sale announcements and catalogs mailed; oral and written appraisals offered free for items sold by firm.

Flea Market of Aransas Pass   W XX

Highway 35
Aransas Pass, Texas 78336
(512) 758-2663
Contact: Jim Walkins, PO Box 363, Aransas Pass, Texas 78336, (512) 758-2749
(Twenty-four miles north of Corpus Christi)

Indoor/outdoor market; 60 dealers; began in 1977; open every Saturday and Sunday; free admission; space rental: $6.00 daily for 10' x 12'; reservations needed.

Mostly secondhand and household items, some antiques, collectibles and new merchandise; food; restrooms; parking; nearby motels.

Oak Hill Flea Market   W X

5526 Highway 290 West
Austin, Texas 78735
(512) 892-3403
Contact: Carleton or Evelyn Kelley, 900 Redd Street, Austin, Texas 78745, (512) 442-7051
(From I-35 take Ben White Boulevard Exit, Exit Loop 360)

Indoor/outdoor market; 20 to 30 dealers; began in 1977; open every Saturday and Sunday, 9:00 a.m. to 5:30 p.m., year round; free admission; space rental: $5.00 Saturday, $6.00 Sunday for 12' x 12' stall; reservations needed.

Variety of antiques, collectibles and secondhand items, some new merchandise; food; restrooms; parking; nearby motels.

Pirate's Den Flea Market   D   X
11704 North Lamar
Austin, Texas 78753
(512) 836-4966
Contact: Bob Barron
(North on I-35 to Braker Lane, west to North Lamar)

Indoor/outdoor market; 20 dealers; began in 1969; open every day except Monday, 9:00 a.m. to 6:00 p.m.; free admission; space rental: $5.00 per weekend for 3' x 8' covered spaces; reservations recommended in spring and fall.

Mostly antiques and collectibles, some secondhand and household items; food; restrooms; parking; nearby motels.

Ballinger Antiquearama   XX
Ballinger, Texas 76821
(915) 365-3262
Contact: Buddy McQueen, 1000 Tenth Street, Ballinger, Texas 76821
(Held variously at Community Center, Courthouse Lawn or City Park)

Indoor/outdoor market; 60 dealers; began in 1969; held every third weekend, year round; free admission; space rental: $10.00 per weekend; reservations needed.

Mostly antiques and collectibles; food; restrooms; parking; nearby motels.

Larry's Antique Mall and Flea Market   XX   W
7150 Eastex Freeway
Beaumont, Texas 77708
(713) 892-4000
Contact: Larry or Justine Tinkle
(Highways 69-96-287 north or Eastex Freeway at Highway 105 Exit)

Indoor/outdoor market; 75 dealers inside, unlimited outside; open Saturday 10:00 a.m. to 6:00 p.m., Sunday 1:00 p.m. to 6:00 p.m., year round; free admission; space rental: $75.00 per month; reservations needed.

Mostly antiques and collectibles, some new merchandise, art and crafts; food; restrooms; parking; nearby motels.

Original Flea Market   X
1617 East Third Street
Big Spring, Texas 79720
(915) 263-4252
Contact: Mabel Kountz, Box 1828, Big Spring, Texas 79720, (915) 263-7162
(Off I-20 at Holiday Inn)

Outdoor market under trees; 30 dealers; began in 1966; open three days a week, 8:00 a.m. to 6:00 p.m.; free admission; space rental: $4.00 daily for grassy plot; no reservations needed.

Variety of antiques, collectibles, new merchandise, secondhand items; food sometimes sold; restrooms; parking.

Bonham Trade Days
Armory Pavilion
Bonham, Texas 75418
(214) 583-3500
Contact: Bryce McIntyre, 605 Hunter, Bonham, Texas 75418
(West side of Bonham)

Outdoor market; 30 dealers; began in 1975; open second weekend of each month; free admission; space rental: $1.00 per day for 12′ x 12′ under pavilion or unlimited outside space; reservations needed for pavilion space.

Mostly secondhand and household items, a lot of antiques, collectibles and crafts; food; restrooms; parking; nearby motels.

Buffalo Gap Flea Market ★ M XXX
Old Settlers Grounds
Buffalo Gap, Texas 79508
(817) 442-1500
Contact: Gene Ingram, Box 144, Cisco, Texas 76437, (817) 442-1500
(FM 89 south of Abilene, eleven miles off Ballinger-Winters Freeway)

Outdoor market under shade trees; 175 dealers; began in 1975; open third Saturday (plus Friday and Sunday), March through November; free admission; space rental: $10.00 per weekend for 12′ x 24′; no reservations needed.

Variety of secondhand and household items, new merchandise, produce, antiques and collectibles; food; restrooms; parking; nearby motels; occasional auctions on Sunday afternoons.

Canton First Monday Trade Days M XXXX
Highway 19
Canton, Texas 75103
(214) 567-4300
Contact: Gerald Turner, Box 245, Canton, Texas 75103
(Sixty miles east of Dallas on I-20, then one mile south on 19)

Outdoor market; 2,000+ dealers; began in 1875; held first Monday of each month and the weekend preceding it, beginning 7:00 a.m. on Friday; free admission; space rental: $11.00 to $26.00 for 12′ x 20′; reservations needed.

Wide variety of merchandise including antiques, collectibles, secondhand and new merchandise, produce, arts and crafts; food; restrooms; parking; nearby motels.

White Elephant   **W   XXXX**
15662 East Freeway
Channelview, Texas 77530
(713) 452-9022
Contact: Earlene Johnson, (713) 452-0922
(Take Sheldon Exit off I-10 East)

Indoor/outdoor market; 300 dealers; began in 1971; open every Saturday and
Sunday, 8:00 a.m. to 6:00 p.m.; free admission; space rental: 12' x 14' booth, 3' x
6' outdoor table; no reservations needed.
  Mostly secondhand and household items, some antiques, collectibles, crafts,
new merchandise; food; restrooms; parking; nearby motels.

Christoval Park Trade Days   **M   X**
Christoval Park
Christoval, Texas 76935
(915) 365-3262
Contact: Buddy McQueen, 1000 Tenth Street, Ballinger, Texas 76821,
(915) 365-3262
(Nineteen miles from San Angelo Highway 277)

Outdoor market; 50 dealers; began in 1973; open fourth weekend of each month,
April through October; free admission; space rental: $9.00 per weekend for 12' x
24'; reservations needed.
  Mostly antiques and collectibles, some new merchandise; food; restrooms;
parking; nearby motels.

Burd's Flea Market   **XXX**
929 East Henderson and Highway 67
Cleburne, Texas 76031
(817) 645-4468
Contact: Mrs. Ted Burd or Mrs. Sid Ellis, PO Box 64, Cleburne, Texas 76031,
(817) 641-8057
(Twenty-eight miles south of Fort Worth via Highway 174)

Outdoor market; 100 to 150 dealers; began in 1970; open every Wednesday and
Thursday, year round; free admission; space rental: $3.00 for 12' area; no
reservations needed except for multiple adjacent spaces.
  Mostly antiques and collectibles, some new merchandise and arts and crafts;
food; restrooms; parking; nearby motels.

Big D Bazaar   **W   XXXX**
3636 North Buckner Boulevard
Dallas, Texas 75228
(214) 328-6117
Contact: Margaret Tallman
(Five miles east of downtown Dallas, just north of I-30 on Loop 12)

Indoor market; 250 dealers; began in 1976; open every Friday, Saturday and
Sunday, 10:00 a.m. to 7:00 p.m.; free admission; space rental: $105.00 to $185.00
per month for 8' x 12' or 10' x 14' booth; reservations needed.

Mostly antiques and collectibles, some new merchandise, arts and crafts; food; restrooms; parking; nearby hotel.

Turney's Trading Post   W   XX
310 South Carroll
Dallas, Texas 75226
(214) 823-4689
Contact: Jim or Becca Turney
(Haskel Peak Exit off I-30, go to Carroll and turn left)

Indoor/outdoor market; 75 dealers; began in 1962; open Saturday and Sunday, 9:00 a.m. to 5:00 p.m., year round; free admission; space rental: $2.50 to $7.50 per day for 12' x 16' lockups; reservations needed.

Mostly secondhand and household items, few antiques, some new merchandise; no food available; restrooms; parking; nearby motels.

Indoor Flea Market   ★   D   XX
8150 Dyer Street
El Paso, Texas 79904
(915) 755-9825
Contact: Pardon D. Jameson
(Route 54 at Hercules Street and Titanio Street)

Indoor/outdoor market; 75 dealers; began in 1976; open seven days a week, 7:00 a.m. to 10:00 p.m.; free admission; rental space: $5.00 per day inside for 5' x 10', free outside; no reservations needed.

Mostly secondhand and household items, fair amount of antiques and collectibles, some new merchandise; restaurants nearby; restrooms; parking; nearby motels; occasional auctions.

Vikon Village Flea Market   D   XXXX
2918 Jupitor Road
Garland, Texas 75041
(214) 271-0565
Contact: Max Alford
(Two blocks north of I-635)

Indoor market; 225 dealers; began in 1974; open for dealers only Monday, Thursday, Friday, 10:00 a.m. to 5:00 p.m., for public, Saturday and Sunday, 10:00 a.m. to 7:00 p.m.; free admission; space rental: $1.00 and up per foot (10' x 10' smallest space); reservations needed.

Mostly antiques and collectibles, some new merchandise; food; restrooms; parking; nearby motels.

Traders Village, Inc.   W   XXXX
2602 Mayfield Road
Grand Prairie, Texas 75051
(214) 647-2331
Contact: Irving L. Taggart
(Five miles south of Six Flags Over Texas, Theme park, off State Highway 360)

Note: Listings are alphabetical by town.

Outdoor market; 1,100 dealers; began in 1974; open every Saturday and Sunday, 8:00 a.m. to dusk, year round; admission $1.00 per car; space rental: $7.00 daily for open space, $11.00 for covered area, $115.00 to $145.00 per month for enclosed building; reservations recommended for covered areas.

Wide variety of antiques, collectibles, arts, crafts, new and secondhand merchandise; food; restrooms; parking; nearby motel and RV park; rodeo arena and a variety of special events.

Country Weekend Common Market   W XX
5115 South Shaver
Houston, Texas 77034
(713) 947-8522
Contact: Haskell Brewer or Jim Hines

Indoor/outdoor market on 10 acres; 100 dealers; began in 1979; open Saturday and Sunday, 7:00 a.m. to 7:00 p.m.; free admission; space rental: $15.00 for 100 square feet; reservations needed.

Variety of merchandise including antiques, collectibles, crafts, secondhand items and new merchandise; food; restrooms; parking; nearby motels.

Four Seasons Common Market, Inc.   D XXXXX
4412 North Shepherd
Houston, Texas 77018
(713) 697-4765
Contact: Shirley Jackson
(One mile north off 610 N Loop, on Shepherd at West Crosstimbers)

Indoor market; 300 dealers; began in 1973; open Monday, Thursday and Friday, 10:00 a.m. to 6:00 p.m., Saturday and Sunday 9:00 a.m. to 6:00 p.m.; free admission; space rental: 8' x 10' booth $70.00 per month, inside table $24.00 per weekend, outside table $15.00; reservations needed.

Lots of collectibles and new merchandise, few antiques; food; restrooms; parking; nearby motels.

Houston Flea Market   W XXXX
6116 Southwest Freeway
Houston, Texas 77057
(713) 782-0391
Contact: Gladys Harlow
(West Park Exit off Freeway 59)

Indoor/outdoor market; 500+ dealers; began in 1969; set-up and reserve Friday, 8:00 a.m. to 5:00 p.m., Saturday and Sunday, 8:00 a.m. to 6:00 p.m., year round; free admission; space rental: $2.00 Friday, $17.00 Saturday, $28.00 Sunday for 10' x 25'; reservations needed.

Variety of collectibles, antiques, new and secondhand merchandise, some crafts and produce; seven food concessions; restrooms; $1.00 parking; nearby motels.

Flea Market   W XX
2323 Avenue K
Lubbock, Texas 79505
(806) 747-8281
Contact: Pauline Gibbs, 3420 Twenty-eighth Street, Lubbock, Texas 79509,
(806) 795-2432
(Between Twenty-third and Twenty-fourth Streets)

Indoor/outdoor market; 100 dealers; began in 1974; open every Saturday and
Sunday, 9:00 a.m. to 6:00 p.m., year round; free admission; space rental: varies
according to size; reservations accepted.
　　Mostly antiques, collectibles and new merchandise, some secondhand and
household items; food; restrooms; parking; nearby motels.

3rd Monday Trade Day   M XXXX
Highway US 380 West
McKinney, Texas 75069
(214) 542-7174
Contact: Billy Loftice, PO Box 614, McKinney, Texas 75069
(Two miles west of Highway 75)

Indoor/outdoor market; 1,500 dealers; began in 1964; open third Saturday,
Sunday and Monday of each month; free admission; space rental: $8.00 per
weekend for 12' x 28'; no reservations needed.
　　Wide variety of antiques, collectibles, new merchandise, secondhand and
household items; food; restrooms; parking; nearby motels.

Cole's Antique Village and Flea Market   W XXXX
1014 North Main
Pearland, Texas 77581
(713) 485-2277
Contact: E. J. Cole or Glenda Bridgman
(South on I-35 out of Houston to Pearland, on the right just past Clear Creek
Bridge)

Indoor/outdoor market; 500 dealers; began in 1967; open every Friday, Saturday
and Sunday, 8:00 a.m. to 6:00 p.m., year round; free admission; space rental:
inside tables and 10' x 10' space $17.50 and $22.00 per weekend, outside covered
tables $20.00; reservations needed inside.
　　Mostly antiques, collectibles and secondhand merchandise; three restaurants; restrooms; parking; nearby motels.

Eisenhauer Road Flea Market   ★ D XXX
3903 Eisenhauer Road
San Antonio, Texas 78218
(512) 653-7592
Contact: Harry Weiss
(Between Austin and I-35)

Indoor market; over 100 dealers; began in 1978; open every Wednesday,
Thursday, and Friday, 12:00 a.m. to 7:00 p.m., and Saturday and Sunday,

9:00 a.m. to 7:00 p.m.; free admission; space rental: 90¢ per square foot; reservations needed one week in advance.

Mostly antiques, some new and used merchandise, collectibles, crafts, produce, art, and jewelry; snack bar; restrooms; parking; nearby motels; monthly auctions held.

San Antonio Flea Market

D XXXX

1428 Austin Highway
San Antonio, Texas 78209
(512) 828-1488
Contact: Harold J. Smith
(On Austin Highway near Sheraton Motor Inn)

Outdoor market; 240 dealers; began in 1976; open Wednesday, Thursday and Friday, noon to dusk, Saturday and Sunday, 8:00 a.m. till dusk; free admission; space rental: $20.00 for 10' x 25' with table; reservations needed.

Mostly antiques and collectibles, lots of new merchandise, some secondhand items; food; restrooms; parking; nearby motels.

Swappers Park

W XXXX

9906 Moursund Boulevard at 410 Loop
San Antonio, Texas 78215
Contact: H. R. Tharp, 610 East Josephine Street, San Antonio, (512) 222-9985

Outdoor market; 400 dealers; began in 1974; open Saturday and Sunday, year round; free admission; space rental: $3.00 daily for 12' x 16' or 12' x 20' car space; no reservations needed.

Variety of new and used merchandise, antiques, collectibles, crafts, produce, art objects, even sailboats, livestock and farm equipment; Mexican and American food; restrooms; parking; nearby motels.

Cactus Jack Festival

★ A X

Fairgrounds
Uvalde, Texas 78801
(512) 278-3361
Contact: Bill Dillard, PO Box 706, Uvalde, Texas 78801
(Highway 90 West)

Indoor/outdoor market under shade trees; 50 dealers; began in 1971; held first weekend in June; free admission; space rental: $10.00 for 10' x 15', $20.00 for 10' x 30'; reservations needed.

Mostly crafts, collectibles, antiques and art; food; restrooms; parking; nearby motels; Lions Club auction.

Victoria Flea Market

W X

Foster Field
Victoria, Texas 77901
Contact: Lewis C. Vanorman, Route 5, Box 143A, Victoria, Texas 77901, (512) 578-8021
(From Highway 59 turn and follow signs at Victoria Regional Airport)

Indoor/outdoor market; 20 dealers; began in 1975; open every Sunday 10:00 a.m. to 4:00 p.m.; free admission; space rental: 12' x 12' area is $3.00 outside, $5.00 inside; reservations needed five days in advance.

Mostly secondhand and household items, antiques and collectibles, some new merchandise; food; restrooms; parking; nearby motels.

The Flea Market and Trade Center   W   XXX
2820 Holliday
Wichita Falls, Texas 76301
(817) 767-9038
Contact: Roy or Joan Parish, 4428 Sisk, Wichita Falls, Texas 76310,
(817) 692-0305
(Top end of Holliday Creek)

Indoor/outdoor market; 140 dealers; began in 1965; open every Saturday and Sunday year round; free admission; space rental: $4.00 for open 12' x 16' area, $6.00 under shed; reservations needed for inside or sheds.

Variety of antiques, collectibles, crafts, secondhand and new items; snack bar; restrooms; parking; nearby motels.

Wimberley Lion's Market   M   XXX
Intersection of Ranch Roads 12 and 2325
Wimberley, Texas 78676
(512) 847-2391
Contact: James McCrocklin, PO Box 575, Wimberley, Texas 78676,
(512) 847-2315
(One mile out of Wimberley)

Outdoor market; 150 dealers; began in 1970; open first Saturday of each month from May to October, 8:00 a.m. to 5:00 p.m.; free admission; space rental: $55.00 per season for 12 ' by 14'; reservations needed.

Variety of antiques, collectibles, secondhand items, new merchandise, produce and crafts; food; restrooms; parking; nearby motels.

UTAH

Olson's Auction & Antiques
Tom Olson, Auctioneer
4303 South Main
Murray, Utah 84107
(801) 261-4258
(Close to Salt Lake City)

Weekly antiques and collectibles sale held Saturday and Sunday at 2:00 p.m.; including furniture and Tiffany and Handel glass; estate sales; consignments; property purchased for sales.

No buyer's premium; mail and telephone bids accepted; checks accepted with two forms of ID; Master Charge and Visa accepted. Full payment within three days; pickups within 24 hours after payment.

Sale announcements mailed; oral and written appraisals offered for hourly fee of $25.00.

Redwood Drive-In Swap Meet   W   XXXX
3688 South Redwood Road
Salt Lake City, Utah 84119
(801) 973-7089
Contact: Harold or Douglas Cowley
(I-15 to Thirty-third South Exit, go west nine blocks, south three blocks)

Outdoor market; 500 dealers; began in 1968; open Saturdays from May to October, Sundays from February to December, 8:00 a.m. to 5:00 p.m.; 25¢ admission; space rental: $7.00 for 18' x 18'; reservations accepted for Sundays, not available for Saturdays.

Mostly secondhand and household items, some new merchandise, antiques and collectibles; large snack bar; restrooms; parking; nearby motels.

NORTHWEST

Idaho, Montana, Nebraska, North Dakota, Oregon, South Dakota, Washington, Wyoming

The relatively sparse settlement in the Northwest accounts for the scarcity of auctions and flea markets in comparison with other regions of the country. Greater concentration of both can be found in the more heavily-populated coastal areas of Washington and Oregon, in Nebraska, and near major cities and towns.

Despite the small number of auctions in the Northwest, it is the prime source for three collecting specialties: American Indian art, Eskimo art, and artifacts of the Old West. Antique guns and firearms are also well represented and, along the Pacific Coast, Oriental art objects are commonly found at sales.

Much of the merchandise at Northwestern sales is not truly antique (that is, over 100 years old). A great portion of the region was, in fact, frontier wilderness a century ago. Montana, Washington, and the Dakotas became states in 1889; Wyoming joined the Union in 1890—it is not surprising that an 80-year-old item, whether an old telephone or an oak highboy, is considered "antique." Collectibles, reminiscent of frontier days, often include old coffee tins and grinders, mining and lumbering tools, lamps, barbed wire, and trading-post items.

There is also something for traveling collectors in the Northwest. A large American Political Items Collection is housed at the Blaine County Historical Museum in Hailey, Idaho and, not surprisingly, there are mining museums in Wallace, Idaho, and Butte, Montana. Also in Montana is the Museum of the Plains Indian in Browning; frontier displays and Western paintings and sculpture are featured at the Montana Historical Society in Helena; and a number of pioneer buildings have been preserved and restored in Virginia City. Along with some of the most spectacular scenery in the country, Oregon has several museums and sites of interest to collectors: Pioneer Village and the Jacksonville Museum in Jacksonville; the Butler Museum of American Indian Art at Eugene; the Collier State Park Logging Museum at Llamath Falls; the Douglas County Museum in Roseburg; and the Tillamook County Pioneer Museum in

Tillamook. North Dakota has the Buffalo Trails Museum of Indian artifacts and historic buildings which have been restored in Epping, and an interesting collection of coin-operated phonographs and other musical machines are on exhibit at the Schlafmann Museum in Turtle Lake. South Dakota has a doll museum at Mitchell. Also in Mitchell are a Museum of Pioneer Life, and other pioneer museums are found in Aberdeen and Rapid City. The "Shrine to Music" Museum with thousands of musical instruments is at the University of South Dakota in Vermillion. In Seattle there are a number of museums— including the Costume and Textile Study Center at the University of Washington; the Museum of Flight; the Museum of History and Industry, with many examples of the applied and decorative arts; and the Seattle Art Museum with many fine Oriental collections. In Walla Walla, Washington, is a museum complex with a pioneer village and many agricultural tool displays. Finally, in Wyoming are many pioneer museums, scattered throughout the state in Casper, Douglas, Evansville, Green River, Lander, and Thermopolis. Also of interest to some collectors is the Warren Military Museum in Cheyenne. Most museums in the state have American Indian collections, reflecting the intense interest in that subject in the whole of the Northwest.

For listings and reviews of auctions and flea markets, check *The Antique Trader, West Coast Peddler, Collectors News, Native Arts/West* and local newspapers.

IDAHO

Antique Peddlar's Fair   A   X
Trail Creek Village
Ketchum/Sun Valley, Idaho 83340
Contact: Jan Perkins, Fort Boise Collector's Club, 2902 Brenemaw, Boise, Idaho 83703, (208) 345-0755
(Take Route 93 off I-84)

Indoor/outdoor market; 50 dealers; began in 1974; held Fourth of July and Labor Day weekends; 50¢ admission; space rental: $10.00 to $15.00 per booth; reservations needed.
    Only antiques and collectibles; food; restrooms; parking; nearby motels.

MONTANA

Mandeville Auction Service

John Mandeville, Auctioneer
1121 Mandeville Lane
Bozeman, Montana 59715
(406) 587-7832
(Sales held at various locations—check mailings for directions)

Handle sales of estates, farms, household merchandise and antiques; approximately five antiques sales yearly; two annual antiques and collectibles sales, in August and April, at Gallatin County Fairgrounds at North Black, Bozeman; consignments only; no property purchased for sales.

No buyer's premium; mail bids accepted with check for full amount; checks accepted with proper ID; no credit cards. Full payment and pickups day of sale.

Sale announcements and brochures mailed; written appraisals offered for an hourly fee of $25.00.

Doug Allard

Doug Allard, Auctioneer
PO Box 460
Saint Ignatius, Montana 59865
(406) 745-2951
Regularly scheduled sales at following locations:
Sunburst Hotel
4925 North Scottsdale Road
Scottsdale, Arizona 85251
Brook Lake Community Center, South 356 & Highway 99
Federal Way, Washington 98002 (near Seattle)
Kelly's Restaurant, Northeast Seventy-eighth and Seattle Freeway
Vancouver, Washington 98662 (near Portland)

Specializing in the sale of American Indian and Eskimo art, artifacts and collectibles, including rugs, baskets, pottery, beaded items, jewelry; major annual sale in Scottsdale, each spring; sales held every one or two months in both Washington locations, other locations periodically; entrance to some sales by catalog only; estate sales; consignments; property purchased for sales.

No buyer's premium; mail and telephone bids accepted; checks under $1,000.00 accepted with proper ID; checks over $1,000.00 accepted with bank letter of credit; Visa, Master Charge, American Express, accepted. Full payment and pickups day of sale.

Sale announcements and catalogs mailed; written appraisals offered for negotiable fee.

NEBRASKA

Kaufman & Dolezal

842 Summer
Lincoln, Nebraska 68502
(402)477-7565
(All auctions held on site—check mailings)

Specializing in estate and personal property sales; half of merchandise usually comprised of antiques and collectibles, including furniture from late 19th and early 20th centuries, glassware, china, pottery, primitives, toys, marbles; usually two sales a week; all sales within Nebraska, Iowa, and South Dakota on commission basis; no consignments; no property purchased for sales.

No buyer's premium; mail and telephone bids not accepted; checks accepted with proper ID; no credit cards. Full payment and pickups day of sale.

Sale announcements mailed; oral appraisals offered for a negotiable fee.

Omaha Auction Center Ltd.
7531 Dodge Street
Omaha, Nebraska 68114
(402) 397-9575

Mixed sales of general merchandise and antiques held three times a month, usually on Sundays at 1:00 p.m.; antiques and collectibles sales held approximately six times a year, including oak and walnut furniture and Depression glass; specialized sales of old radios and parts, dolls; estate sales; consignments; property purchased for sales.

No buyer's premium; mail and telephone bids accepted with a 25% deposit; checks accepted with proper ID; Master Charge and Visa accepted. Full payment due within 24 hours; pickups within three weeks.

Sale announcements mailed; catalogs available for specialized sales; written appraisals offered for $35.00 hourly fee; oral appraisals free of charge.

All American Auction Gallery
Gary A. Crosby, Auctioneer
Ong, Nebraska 68254
(402) 284-2231
(Forty-five miles from York, Nebraska, on Interstate 80)

Specializing in antiques and estate sales; most sales held the second Sunday of each month; featuring oak and Victorian furniture, collectibles; estate sales; consignments; some property purchased for sales.

No buyer's premium; mail and telephone bids accepted with a 10% deposit; checks accepted with proper ID; no credit cards. Full payment day of sale; pickups as arranged.

Sale announcements mailed; oral or written appraisals offered for negotiable fee.

Pershing Auditorium Flea Market   M   XX
226 Centennial Mall South
Lincoln, Nebraska 68501
(402) 477-3762
Contact: Tom Schleicher
(I-80 to "M" Street, to Fifteenth Street)

Indoor market; 100 dealers; began in 1978; open Saturday and Sunday, 10:00 a.m. to 6:00 p.m., usually third weekend of each month; 50¢ admission; space rental: $1.25 per front foot, 13', 21', 29'; reservations needed.

Mostly antiques and collectibles; food concession; restrooms; parking; nearby motels.

Omaha Swap and Flea Mart ★ W XX
5610 Redick
Omaha, Nebraska 68152
(402) 571-5712
Contact: V. R. Mullin, 6826 North Fifty-sixth, Omaha, Nebraska 68152
(Two miles south of I-680, Forty-eighth Street Exit)

Indoor/outdoor market; 100 dealers; began in 1979; open Saturday and Sunday, April through December; free admission; space rental: $5.00 for 10' x 10'; no reservations needed.

Mostly secondhand and new items, some antiques, collectibles and produce; no food concession; restrooms; parking; nearby motels; occasional auctions.

NORTH DAKOTA

Penfield Auction Realty
Bob Penfield, Auctioneer
Box 111
Bowman, North Dakota 58623
(701) 523-3652
(On-site estate sales—check mailings for directions)

Specializing in estate sales, real estate and antiques, within North Dakota, South Dakota, Montana, Idaho and Washington; approximately 20 sales a month, featuring antiques and collectibles, household goods, farm machinery; consignments only; no property purchased for sales.

No buyer's premium; mail and telephone bids accepted; checks accepted with proper ID; no credit cards. Full payment and pickups at time of sale.

Sale announcements mailed; some catalogs; appraisals offered for fee of 10% of value of item.

Magic City Flea Market M XXX
North Dakota State Fairgrounds
Business Highway 2
Minot, North Dakota 58701
(701) 352-1289
Contact: R.W. Timboe, Box 1672, Minot, North Dakota 58701

Indoor/outdoor market; 100 to 150 dealers; began in 1975; open second Saturday of each month except January; 25¢ admission; space rental: $6.00 for 10' x 10' stall inside, unlimited space outside; no reservations needed.

Variety of antiques, collectibles, new and secondhand merchandise, crafts and produce; food; restrooms; parking; nearby motels.

OREGON

O'Gallery
Dale O'Grady, Tom O'Grady, Auctioneers
537 Southeast Ash Street
Portland, Oregon 97214
(503) 238-0202

A family-run gallery; three-day sales held every five weeks on Monday, Tuesday, and Wednesday at 7:00 p.m., featuring antiques—including Oriental rugs and art objects such as 19th century porcelain and carvings, English Edwardian furniture, some period furniture, Tiffany lamps, art glass, cut glass, and antique cars; also, antique and used furnishings, jewelry, firearms; estate sales; consignments; property purchased for sales.

Ten percent buyer's premium; mail and telephone bids accepted; checks accepted with proper ID; American Express, Master Charge and Visa accepted. Full payment and pickups within two days.

Sale announcements mailed; catalogs for all sales, $2.00; written appraisals offered for 1.5% of value of item, minimum charge $50.00.

Lang Sales Company Auctioneers
PO Box 255
Silverton, Oregon 97381
(503) 653-1160 or (503) 873-5289
(On-site estate sales—check mailings)

Specializing in estate sales and business liquidations within Oregon, Washington and Idaho; over 50 sales per year; some consignments; no property purchased for sales.

No buyer's premium; mail and telephone bids accepted; checks accepted with proper ID; in some cases, merchandise held until check clears; no credit cards. Full payment at sale; pickups within 48 hours.

Sale announcements and some catalogs mailed; oral or written appraisals offered for negotiable fee.

Heart of the Valley Flea Market   M X
Benton County Fairgrounds
Corvalis, Oregon 97330
(503) 757-1521
Contact: Larry Bell, Route 1, Box 436, Philomath, Oregon 97370,
(503) 929-3825

Indoor market; 50 dealers; began in 1973; open usually first Sunday of the month, September to June; 25¢ admission; space rental: $5.00 for 3' x 8' table; reservations needed.

Mostly antiques, collectibles and secondhand merchandise; food; restrooms; parking; no motels.

Picc-A-Dilly Flea Market XXXX
Lane County Fairgrounds
796 West Thirteenth
Eugene, Oregon 97402
(503) 683-5589
Contact: Clyde or Rosemary Major, PO Box 2364, Eugene, Oregon 97402
(Freeway to Eugene, follow signs to Fairgrounds)

Indoor market; 250 to 500 dealers; began in 1970; open various weekends, June through December, call ahead for dates; 25¢ and 50¢ admission; space rental: $6.50 to $7.50 for 8' x 2½' table; reservations recommended.

Mostly collectibles and secondhand items, some antiques; food; restrooms; parking; nearby motels.

Banner Flea Market W X
4871 SE Tualalin Valley Highway
Hillsboro, Oregon 97123
(503) 640-6755
Contact: Lynn Selfridge, 450 SE Twenty-sixth Avenue, Hillsboro, Oregon 97123, (503) 648-1533
(Two miles east of downtown Hillsboro)

Indoor/outdoor market; 50 dealers; began in 1967; open Friday, Saturday and Sunday, noon till 5:30 p.m., year round; free admission; space rental: $8.00 for 4' x 8' area for three-day weekend; reservations preferred.

Variety of collectibles, antiques, new merchandise, secondhand items, art and crafts; no food available; restrooms; parking; nearby motels.

Linkville Flea Market M XX
3531 South Sixth Street
Klamath Falls, Oregon 97601
(503) 884-4352
Contact: Elizabeth Boorman, 5420 Cottage, Klamath Falls, Oregon 97601
(Two and one-half miles south of Klamath Falls)

Indoor/outdoor market; 50 to 60 dealers; began in 1974; open one weekend per month, call ahead for dates; 25¢ admission; space rental: $5.00 for 3' x 6' table; reservations needed.

Mostly secondhand and household items, few antiques, collectibles, and crafts; food; restrooms; parking; nearby motels.

Lebanon Flea Market A XX
Lebanon Armory
Maple Street
Lebanon, Oregon 97355
(503) 362-1063
Contact: Vaughn Hayden, Capitol Promotions, 5724 Aetna Street SE Salem, Oregon 97301, (503) 585-1263

Note: Listings are alphabetical by town.

Indoor market; 100 dealers; began in 1974; held twice a year, usually in November and March; 35¢ admission; space rental: $6.00 for 3' x 8' table; reservations recommended.

Mostly collectibles, antiques and secondhand merchandise, some new merchandise and crafts; food; restrooms; parking; nearby motels.

Newport Flea Market   M   XX
Newport Armory
Highway 101
Newport, Oregon 97365
(503) 585-1263
Contact: Vaughn Hayden, Capitol Promotions, 5724 Aetna Street, SE, Salem, Oregon 97301, (503) 362-1063
(Near center of city)

Indoor/outdoor market; 100 dealers; began in 1969; open usually second weekend of each month, 9:30 a.m. to 5:00 p.m., special shows on Memorial Day and Labor Day; 50¢ admission; space rental: $6.00 daily for 3' x 8' table; reservations needed inside.

Mostly antiques, collectibles and secondhand merchandise; food; restrooms; parking; nearby motels.

Valley Flea Market   W   X
917 West Main
Philomath, Oregon 97370
(503) 929-4144
Contact: Franklyn Miller, PO Box 254, Tangent, Oregon 97389, (503) 928-3603
(From I-5 go west sixteen miles on 34)

Indoor market; 50 dealers; began in 1977; open Saturday and Sunday 9:00 a.m. to 6:00 p.m., year round; free admission; space rental: $5.00 per 3' x 8' table; reservations needed.

Variety of new merchandise, antiques, collectibles, secondhand items and crafts; restaurant; restrooms; parking; nearby motels.

Holgate Flea Market   W   XXX
10350 SE Holgate
Portland, Oregon 97266
(503) 760-8346
Contact: Rick McDonald, (503) 761-1929
(I-80 to Eighty-second Avenue South to Holgate, than east twenty-one blocks)

Indoor market; 130 dealers; began in 1977; open Saturday and Sunday, 8:00 a.m. to 5:00 p.m., year round; 25¢ admission; space rental: $6.00 per day for 3' x 7' table; reservations needed.

Mostly collectibles and antiques, lots of secondhand and new merchandise, some art, crafts and produce; food available; restrooms; parking; nearby motels.

Springers Flea Market
W   X

18300 SE Richey Road
Portland, Oregon 97236
(503) 665-3568
Contact: Jack or Diane Fox
(Turn south at 190 and Powell, go twelve miles to Richey Road)

Indoor/outdoor market; 85 dealers; began in 1972; open Saturday and Sunday, 9:30 a.m. to 5:00 p.m., year round; 25¢ admission; space rental: $15.00 per weekend; reservations needed.

Variety of collectibles, antiques, new merchandise, secondhand items and crafts; food; restrooms; parking; nearby motels.

Sunday Flea Market
W XX

Memorial Coliseum
Portland, Oregon 97212
(503) 246-9996
Contact: Don Wires, 7128 SW Capitol Hill Road, Portland, Oregon 97219
(I-5 North or South to Coliseum Exit)

Indoor market; 50 to 75 dealers; began in 1977; open Sundays; 50¢ admission; space rental: $7.50 for 8' x 2½'; reservations recommended.

Mostly antiques and collectibles, some new and secondhand merchandise; food; restrooms; $1.00 parking; nearby motels.

Salem Flea Market
XXXX

Oregon State Fairgrounds
Silverton Road and Seventeenth Street
Salem, Oregon
Contact: Frank E. Haley, 4795 North Rivercrest Drive, Salem, Oregon 97303, (503) 393-2897
(Market Street Exit off I-55 Freeway, west to Seventeenth Street, north to Silverton Road)

Indoor market; 450 dealers; began in 1966; open usually second and fourth Sunday of January through May and September through December, second Sunday only in June, and the Fourth of July weekend; six of weekends are special: pottery, paper, dolls, etc.; 50¢ admission; space rental: $6.00 per table; reservations needed.

Mostly antiques and collectibles, some new merchandise; food; restrooms; parking; nearby motel and trailer park.

Winter, Spring, Summer Flea Market
A XX

451 Avenue A
Seaside, Oregon 97138
(503) 738-8585
Contact: Joy Macy, PO Box 25, Seaside, Oregon 97138
(Off Route 101, seventy-nine miles northwest of Portland)

Indoor market; 100 dealers; began in 1975; open three times a year, usually February, May and August; 35¢ admission; space rental: $10.00 for 8' x 30" table for two days; reservations needed.

Mostly secondhand items and crafts, no antiques; concession stand; restrooms; parking; nearby motels.

Outdoor Thieves Market   W   X
Highway 220
Sumpter, Oregon 97877
Contact: Kelly Olson, Box 546, Sumpter, Oregon 97877, (503) 894-2235
(84 North to Baker, Oregon, nine miles south on 7, then twenty miles west on Highway 220)

Outdoor market; began in 1970; 10 to 20 dealers every weekend; 90 to 140 dealers at three-day holiday markets; held Memorial Day weekend, Fourth of July and Labor Day weekends; free admission; space rental: $5.00 per table, $4.50 per 12' space; reservations with $10.00 deposit required for three-day weekends.

Mostly collectibles and antiques, some new and secondhand merchandise; food; restrooms; parking; nearby motels and campgrounds.

SOUTH DAKOTA

Wild Bill's Trading Post and Auction House
Wild Bill Hickok, Auctioneer
Box 361
Hot Springs, South Dakota 57747
(605) 745-3475

Sales held weekly on Fridays at 7:00 p.m., featuring general merchandise ranging from tools to furniture; antiques and collectibles sales held six to seven times yearly, on Saturdays from 10:30 a.m. to 7:30 p.m., featuring American oak, walnut and cherry furniture, Western frontier items, Indian artifacts; estate sales; consignments; property purchased for sales.

No buyer's premium; mail and telephone bids accepted; checks accepted with proper ID; no credit cards. Full payment at time of sale; pickups as arranged.

Sale announcements mailed; oral or written appraisals offered for negotiable fee.

Black Hills Flea Market   W   XX
Keystone Route, Box 100
Rapid City, South Dakota 57701
(605) 343-6477
Contact: Paul and Maybelle Ashland, 909 St. Francis, Rapid City, South Dakota 57701, (605) 348-1981
(South City Limits, on US 16 West—Rushmore Road)

Indoor/outdoor market; 70 dealers; began in 1976; open weekends, May through September; free admission; space rental: $4.00 per day for 12' x 20' outside; $7.50 for 9' x 12' inside; tailgate set-up $3.00; reservations needed inside.

Mostly secondhand and household items, some antiques, collectibles and new merchandise; snack bar; restrooms; free parking; adjacent motel.

Rapid City Original Flea Market & Antique Sale   M   XXX
444 Mount Rushmore Road North
Rapid City, South Dakota 57701
(605) 394-4115
Contact: Mrs. Robert Orelup, 2631 Lawndale Drive, Rapid City, South Dakota 57701, (605) 342-2524 or (605) 343-2597
(Off I-90, on route to Mt. Rushmore, Civic Center Exit)

Indoor market; 150 to 200 dealers; began in 1964; held monthly on weekends, call for dates; 50¢ admission; space rental: $12.00 per table; reservations advised.

Mostly antiques, collectibles and crafts; food; restrooms; parking; nearby motels.

WASHINGTON

Trade Winds West
Rod Sauvageau, W. L. Phillips, Auctioneers
PO Box 4306
Vancouver, Washington 98662
518 Main Street
Vancouver, Washington 98660
(206) 696-1380

Specializing in American Indian art and antique guns; four to six sales, held annually, feature American Indian art, Eskimo art, all tribal art, Western art, antique guns and weaponry; estate sales; consignments; merchandise purchased for sales.

No buyer's premium; mail bids accepted; checks from established customers or with bank letter, accepted; Visa and Master Charge accepted. Purchases held with 20% deposit; full payment as arranged; most pickups at time of sale.

Sale announcements mailed; catalogs for all sales; oral or written appraisals offered for negotiable fee.

Country Estate Auctions
William A. Ehli & Sons, Auctioneers
Highway 507, PO Box 722
Yelm, Washington 98597
(206) 458-7111
(East City limits of Yelm on Highway 507)

Run by the third generation of Ehli family auctioneers; specializing in estate sales; sales held at auction center every three weeks; consignments; property purchased for sales.

No buyer's premium; mail and telephone bids accepted; checks accepted with proper ID; Master Charge and Visa accepted. Purchases held with a 20% deposit; full payment and most pickups within seven days.

Sale announcements mailed; printed catalog for all sales.

Seaway Flea Market   W X
Benner Road
Copalis Beach, Washington 98535
(206) 289-3423
Contact: Harold McLaughlin, 111 Chenault, Hoquiam, Washington 98550, (206) 532-3931
(Through Aberdeen-Hoquiam to the coast, then five miles north of Ocean Shores)

Indoor market; 10 to 18 dealers; began in 1975; open Saturday and Sunday, 9:00 a.m. to 5:00 p.m., year round; free admission; space rental: $7.50 per day for 4' x 8' table; reservations needed.

Mostly secondhand and household items, with mixture of antiques, collectibles, new merchandise and crafts; no food available; restrooms; parking; nearby motels.

Sea-Tac Flea Market   W X
34300 Pacific Highway South
Federal Way, Washington 98003
(206) 838-0797
Contact: Dean Jay Grefthen
(Exit 142B off I-5, west to Highway 99 and turn north)

Indoor market; 50 dealers; began in 1968; open Saturday and Sunday, 10:00 a.m. to 6:00 p.m., year round; free admission; space rental: $7.00 per day; reservations needed in winter.

Variety of new and used merchandise, antiques, collectibles, arts and crafts; food; restrooms; parking; nearby motels.

Overniter Swap Meet   W X
6611 296th East
Graham, Washington 98338
(206) 847-9675
Contact: Forest Dick Haag
(South from Tacoma on Highway 7 to 296th Street, turn left)

Indoor/outdoor market; 20+ dealers; began in 1980; open Saturdays and Sundays, year round; free admission; space rental: $3.50 per day for 12' x 16'; no reservations needed.

Variety of household and secondhand merchandise; snack bar; restrooms; parking; nearby motels.

Pasco Armory Flea Market   A XX
127 West Clark Street
Pasco, Washington 99301
(509) 545-2409
Contact: SFC Earle I. Scott, Pasco Armory
(At corner of First Street)

Indoor market; 55 dealers; began in 1973; held semi-annually in February or March and September or October, Saturday 10:00 a.m. to 6:30 p.m., Sunday 10:00 a.m. to 4:30 p.m.; 50¢ admission; space rental: $15.00 for 3' x 8' table for weekend; reservations needed.

Variety of antiques, collectibles, new and secondhand merchandise; food; restrooms; ample parking for cars and R/Vs; nearby motels.

Annual Prosser Flea Market   A XX
611 Sixth Street
Prosser, Washington 99350
(509) 786-2626
Contact: Phil Blakney, Sixth and Meade, Prosser, Washington 99350,
(509) 786-2330
(Off State Highway 12)

Outdoor market; 60 dealers; began in 1971; held last weekend in September; free admission; space rental: $10.00 for weekend; reservations needed.

Variety of collectibles, new and secondhand merchandise, antiques, crafts and produce; food; restrooms; parking; nearby motels.

Angle Lake Flea Market   D X
19832 Pacific Highway South
Seattle, Washington 98182
(206) 878-8161
Contact: John Brewer, 13710 139th Avenue SE, Renton, Washington 98055,
(206) 255-2039
(Exit off I-5 at 200th Street, go one-half mile to Pacific Highway South, turn right to market)

Indoor market; 35 dealers; began in 1970; open Thursday through Sunday, 10:00 a.m. to 6:00 p.m., year round; free admission; space rental: $9.00 for 10' x 8' booth for four days; reservations preferred.

Mostly antiques and collectibles, very little secondhand merchandise; no food available; restrooms; parking; nearby motels.

WYOMING

Art's Auction House
Arthur Mahnke, Auctioneer
216 South Main
Lusk, Wyoming 82225
(307) 334-3779

Note: Listings are alphabetical by town.

Approximately 30 to 40 sales held yearly, featuring furniture, farm machinery, livestock, or antiques; estate sales; consignments only; no property purchased for sales.

No buyer's premium; mail and telephone bids accepted; checks accepted with proper ID; no credit cards. Full payment in 10 days; pickups within 30 days.

Sale announcements mailed; appraisals offered free of charge.

Central Wyoming Antique Flea Market   X

306 North Durbin
Casper, Wyoming 82601
Contact: Bruce Smith, 1625 South Kenwood, Casper, Wyoming 82601,
(307) 234-6663
(Center Street Exit off I-25, south to "A" Street, east two blocks to Durbin)

Indoor market; 25 dealers; began in 1976; usually open the third weekend of every other month, beginning in February; free admission; space rental: $6.00 per table; reservations needed.

Mostly antiques and collectibles, very little new and secondhand merchandise; food; restrooms; parking; nearby motels.

ADDENDUM: PERIODICALS OF INTEREST TO COLLECTORS

ACQUIRE
170 Fifth Avenue
New York, New York 10010

AMERICANA
381 West Center Street
Marion, Ohio 43302

AMERICAN COLLECTOR
Drawer C
Kermit, Texas 79745

ANTIQUE COLLECTING
American Antique Collector
Box 327
Ephrata, Pennsylvania 17522

ANTIQUE & COLLECTORS MART
15100 West Kellogg
Wichita, Kansas 67235

ANTIQUE MONTHLY
PO Drawer 2
Tuscaloosa, Alabama 35402

ANTIQUES AND THE ARTS WEEKLY
The Newtown Bee
Newtown, Connecticut 06470

ANTIQUES AND AUCTION NEWS
Box B
Marietta, Pennsylvania 17547

THE ANTIQUES JOURNAL
Box 1046
Dubuque, Iowa 52001

THE ANTIQUES PRESS:
Florida's Newspaper of Antiques & Collectibles
PO Box 12047
St. Petersburg, Florida 33733

ANTIQUES WORLD
122 East Forty-Second Street
New York, New York 10017

ANTIQUE TOY WORLD:
The Magazine for Toy Collectors Around the World
3941 Belle Plaine
Chicago, Illinois 60618

THE ANTIQUE TRADER WEEKLY
PO Box 1050
Dubuque, Iowa 52001

ART & ANTIQUE AUCTION REVIEW
University Arts, Inc.
IFM Building
Old Saybrook, Connecticut 06475

ART & ANTIQUES:
The American Magazine for Connoisseurs and Collectors
1515 Broadway
New York, New York 10036

ART & AUCTION
Auction Guild
250 West Fifty-Seventh Street
New York, New York 10019

BAY AREA COLLECTOR
PO Box 1210
Fremont, California 94538

BOTTLE NEWS
Box 1000
Kermit, Texas 79745

CALIFORNIA COLLECTOR ANTIQUES INVESTMENT JOURNAL
PO Box 812
Carmichael, California 95608

THE COLLECTOR/INVESTOR
740 Rush Street
Chicago, Illinois 60611

COLLECTOR'S ITEMS
Box 1275
San Luis Obispo, California 93406

COLLECTORS NEWS
Box 156
Grundy Center, Iowa 50638

COUNTRY AMERICANA
R D 1
Washington, New Jersey 07882

EARLY AMERICAN LIFE
Box 1831
Harrisburg, Pennsylvania 17105

THE GLAZE
PO Box 4929 G.S.
Springfield, Missouri 65804

GUN WEEK
Box 150
Sidney, Ohio 45365

HOBBIES:
The Magazine for Collectors
1006 South Michigan Avenue
Chicago, Illinois 60605

THE JERSEY DEVIL
New Egypt Auction & Farmers Market
Route 537
New Egypt, New Jersey 08533

KOVELS ON ANTIQUES AND COLLECTIBLES:
The Confidential Newsletter for Dealers and Collectors
Antiques, Inc.
PO Box 22200
Beachwood, California 44122

The Magazine ANTIQUES
551 Fifth Avenue
New York, New York 10017

MAINE ANTIQUE DIGEST
Jefferson Street
Box 358
Waldoboro, Maine 04572

MILITARY COLLECTORS NEWS
Box 7582
Tulsa, Oklahoma 74105

NATIONAL ANTIQUES REVIEW
Box 619
Portland, Maine 04104

NATIVE ARTS/WEST
Box 31196
Billings, Montana 59107

THE NEW YORK ANTIQUE ALMANAC
of Art, Antiques, Investments, & Yesteryear
PO Box 335
Lawrence, Long Island, New York 11559

THE NEW YORK-PENNSYLVANIA COLLECTOR
Wolfe Publications, Inc.
4 South Main Street
Pittsford, New York 14534

OHIO ANTIQUE REVIEW
PO Box 538
Worthington, Ohio 43085

OLD BOTTLE REVIEW
Box 243
Bend, Oregon 97701

OLD CARS
Krause Publications
Iola, Wisconsin 54945

THE PLATE COLLECTOR
Box 1041
Kermit, Texas 79745

POTTERY COLLECTORS NEWSLETTER
Box 446
Asheville, North Carolina 28802

RARITIES:
The Magazine of Collectibles
Behn-Miller Publishers, Inc.
17337 Ventura Boulevard
Encino, California 91316

RELICS
Box 3338
Austin, Texas 78764

SPINNING WHEEL
Antiques & Early Crafts
American Antiques and Crafts Society
Fame Avenue
Hanover, Pennsylvania 17331

TRI-STATE TRADER
PO Box 90
Knightstown, Indiana 46148

WEST COAST PEDDLER
P O Box 4489
Downey, California 90241

SPECIALIZED AUCTIONS/SUBJECT INDEX

AUCTION INDEX

FLEA MARKET INDEX